Community Living for
People with Developmental and
Psychiatric Disabilities

# Community Living for People with Developmental and Psychiatric Disabilities

Edited by
John W. Jacobson, Ph.D.,
Sara N. Burchard, Ph.D., and
Paul J. Carling, Ph.D.

The Johns Hopkins University Press
Baltimore and London

© 1992 The Johns Hopkins University Press
All rights reserved
Printed in the United States of America on acid-free paper

The Johns Hopkins University Press
701 West 40th Street
Baltimore, Maryland 21211-2190
The Johns Hopkins Press Ltd., London

Library of Congress Cataloging-in-Publication Data

Community living for people with developmental and psychiatric disabilities / edited by John W. Jacobson, Sara N. Burchard, and Paul J.
Carling.
       p.    cm.
  Includes bibliographical references and index.
  ISBN 0-8018-4282-4 (alk. paper)
  1. Mentally ill—Rehabilitation—United States.  2. Developmentally disabled—Rehabilitation—United States.  3. Mentally handicapped—Rehabilitation—United States.  4. Group homes for the
mentally handicapped—United States.  5. Community mental health
services—United States.  I. Jacobson, John W.  II. Burchard, Sara N.
III. Carling, Paul J.
  [DNLM: 1. Community Mental Health Services.  2. Deinstitutionalization.  3. Mental Disorders—rehabilitation.  4. Mental Retardation—rehabilitation.    WM 30 C7314]
RC439.5.C655  1992
616.89′03—dc20
DNLM/DLC
for Library of Congress                    91-20849

# Contents

# List of Contributors

*Lee J. Ackerman, M.S.,* Assistant Planner, Planning Unit, New York State Office of Mental Retardation and Developmental Disabilities, Albany, New York

*Mary Ann A. Allard, Ph.D.,* Co-director, Social Sciences Research, Shriver Center, Waltham, Massachusetts

*Deborah Allness, M.S.S.W.,* Director, Wisconsin Office of Mental Health, Madison, Wisconsin

*Maureen M. Black, Ph.D.,* Assistant Professor, Department of Pediatrics, Western Health Center, University of Maryland at Baltimore, Baltimore, Maryland

*Valerie J. Bradley, M.A.,* President, Human Services Research Institute, Cambridge, Massachusetts

*Sara N. Burchard, Ph.D.,* Associate Professor, Department of Psychology, University of Vermont, Burlington, Vermont

*Paul J. Carling, Ph.D.,* Director, Center for Community Change through Housing and Support, University of Vermont, Burlington, Vermont

*Elaine R. Carpenter, M.S.N.,* Director, State Adult Mental Health and Community Support Program Services, Office of Mental Health, Department of Health and Social Services, Madison, Wisconsin

*Laurie C. Dietzel, M.A.,* Research Assistant, Department of Psychology, University of Maryland, College Park, Maryland

*Rosemary Duran, M.S.W.,* Director of Services, Transitional Services, Inc., Buffalo, New York

*Mary E. Evans, Ph.D.,* Principal Research Scientist, Bureau of Evaluation and Services Research, New York State Office of Mental Health, Albany, New York

*Betsy J. Galligan, Ph.D.,* Director of Program Evaluation, J. N. Adam Developmental Services Office, Perrysburg, New York

*Heather M. Gates, M.B.A.,* Program Manager, Holyoke/Chicopee Area

Office, Massachusetts Department of Mental Health, Holyoke, Massachusetts

*Lawrence R. Gordon, Ph.D.*, Associate Professor, Department of Psychology, University of Vermont, Burlington, Vermont

*John R. Guastaferro, M.S.*, Executive Director, Restoration Society, Buffalo, New York

*Joseph E. Hasazi, Ph.D.*, Associate Professor, Department of Psychology, University of Vermont, Burlington, Vermont

*John W. Jacobson, Ph.D.*, Associate Planner, Planning Unit, New York State Office of Mental Retardation and Developmental Disabilities, Albany, New York

*F. James Kearney, J.D., Ph.D.*, Staff Attorney, Office of the Attorney General, Maryland Department of Health and Mental Hygiene, Springfield Hospital Center, Sykesville, Maryland

*William Knoedler, M.D.*, Director, Program in Assertive Community Treatment, Madison, Wisconsin

*K. Charlie Lakin, Ph.D.*, Research Director, Institute on Community Integration, University of Minnesota, Minneapolis, Minnesota

*Sheryl A. Larson, M.A.*, Research Assistant, Institute on Community Integration, University of Minnesota, Minneapolis, Minnesota

*S. Sinikka McCabe, M.S.*, Director of Technical Assistance, The Center for Community Change through Housing and Support, University of Vermont, Burlington, Vermont

*Sutherland Miller, Ph.D.*, Associate Clinical Professor, Albert Einstein College of Medicine, Bronx, New York

*Michael P. Nagy, Ph.D.*, Director of Quality Assurance, Holyoke/Chicopee Area Office, Massachusetts Department of Mental Health, Holyoke, Massachusetts

*Julie W. Rosen, Ph.D.*, Developmental Disabilities Consultant, Associates in Psychology, Burlington, Vermont

*Patricia Rutkowski, M.S.S.W.*, Clinical Consultant, Wisconsin Office of Mental Health, Madison, Wisconsin

*Michael L. Sachs, Ph.D.*, Associate Professor, Department of Physical Education, Temple University, Philadelphia, Pennsylvania

*David L. Shern, Ph.D.*, Director, Bureau of Evaluation and Services Research, New York State Office of Mental Health, Albany, New York

*Ellen Johnson Silver, M.S.*, Statistical Analyst, Preventive Intervention Research, Center for Child Health, Albert Einstein College of Medicine, Bronx, New York

*Wayne P. Silverman, Ph.D.*, Chief, Department of Psychology, New York State Institute for Basic Research in Developmental Disabilities, Staten Island, New York

*Diane Simoneau, B.A.*, Therapist, Waldorf Institute, Spring Valley, New York

*Michael W. Smull, B.A.*, Director, Applied Research and Evaluation Unit, Department of Pediatrics, University of Maryland at Baltimore, Baltimore, Maryland

*Beth H. Tanzman, M.S.W.*, Director, Community Preference Studies, The Center for Community Change through Housing and Support, University of Vermont, Burlington, Vermont

*Elia Vecchione, M.A.*, Executive Director, Resources for Community Living, Inc., Waterbury, Vermont

*Bonita M. Veysey, M.S.*, Research Scientist, Bureau of Evaluation and Services Research, New York State Office of Mental Health, Albany, New York

*Barry S. Willer, Ph.D.*, Associate Professor and Director, Rehabilitation Research and Training Center on Traumatic Brain Injury, State University of New York at Buffalo, Buffalo, New York

*Susan F. Wilson, Ph.D.*, Associate Director, The Center for Community Change through Housing and Support, University of Vermont, Burlington, Vermont

*James T. Yoe, Ph.D.*, Research Associate, Department of Psychology, University of Vermont, Burlington, Vermont

*Ihor Zankiw, M.B.A., M.S.*, Executive Director, Transitional Services, Inc., Buffalo, New York

*Warren B. Zigman, Ph.D.*, Research Scientist, New York State Institute for Basic Research in Developmental Disabilities, Staten Island, New York

# Foreword

In the 1990s, researchers, service providers, consumer groups, policymakers, and others have undertaken a reconsideration of policy priorities, specific service initiatives, and actual service delivery practices which will have a profound effect on who receives services, which services they receive, and even which fundamental outcomes the service systems should pursue in the early part of the twenty-first century. The issue of where and how to help people is a critical one, perhaps the most fundamental issue in any human services system. This book confronts many such issues directly by identifying both the beneficial effects and the limitations of some current practices; by demonstrating ways to make research and evaluation findings more relevant to program management, policy development, and the aspirations of the people served; and by dispelling erroneous assumptions about human services and the people they are intended to assist. The authors of this volume are committed to a community-based approach to supporting people with disabilities. They work from the assumption that community living will significantly improve the quality of life of people with psychiatric disabilities and people with mental retardation or other forms of developmental disability. The authors are also keenly aware that we have not been entirely successful in implementing all the community programs which are needed or in moving beyond professional responses to achieve full community membership for people.

Major federal policy initiatives continue to emerge. Three broad-based initiatives with potential for massive impact on the services to special populations are the Americans with Disabilities Act, the Fair Housing Amendments, and Healthy People 2000. The Americans with Disabilities Act and the Fair Housing Amendments reaffirm and elaborate the rights of persons with disabilities to participate fully, and with reasonable accommodations for access, in all aspects of community life, including self-determination, choice in the selection of a living situation, and productive vocational activity. Although this legislation was developed with individuals who have physical disabilities as a major constituency, it articulates strongly the extension of these rights and protections to people with psychiatric and developmental disabilities. This legislation brings these groups as partners into the disability rights movement; it will undoubtedly have profound implications for people with psychiatric or developmental disabilities.

Healthy People 2000, an initiative undertaken by the U.S. Public Health Service, relates to the establishment of health objectives for the nation for the year 2000. As these objectives are established there will be an attempt to set funding priorities as well as to guide policy considerations based on them. A number of the objectives are aimed at improving the health status of groups of people who are affected by major diseases and disabilities. Thus, people with psychiatric disabilities, mental retardation and other disabilities, or infirmities as a result of aging are included among the groups whose physical and social well-being will be affected by the health priorities of the nation.

This book addresses the state of community services in the fields of mental health and developmental disabilities in a number of important ways which are consistent with the aspirations inherent in both the Americans with Disabilities Act and Healthy People 2000, by focusing on governmental needs for accountability with regard to what services are delivered to persons in need; by focusing not only on the clinical benefits of services but also on the personal and social perspectives of consumers as valid measures of service outcome; and by recognizing that the human services work force represents a crucial resource that must be both sustained and strengthened. The perspectives and findings presented in this book will be valuable as a resource for managers of services and agencies, policy analysts, evaluators, state and national program administrators, advocates, and people preparing for roles that require a recognition that change and pressures to innovate will characterize human services for much of the near future.

Introducing innovation into existing human services will, indeed, be a very challenging enterprise. Factors such as staffing shortages, lack of well-trained community workers, shortages of adequate independent living situations, and the lack of a diversity or shortage of appropriate vocational opportunities have affected our ability to achieve the goals of service and support which are guided by our philosophies of care. Structural features of community services also present severe hindrances to innovation, efficiencies, and improved responsiveness. Although national policy tends to combine plans for different disability groups, the structure of the community services system separates services for different categorical disability groups. There is a lack of coordination in the development of new service models and of the integration of new models into existing services among disability groups despite some common needs and expectations. The preponderance of services is still not designed with substantial involvement and participation of the people who will receive the services or of their families. Moreover, unlike the physical disabilities field, few services are offered directly by people with disabilities, and self-help efforts are still at an evolutionary stage. There is a great need to communicate the best practices across different disability group services, as the authors of this book seek to do.

Another important consideration that is addressed by a number of the contributing authors relates to the application and use of research findings and evaluation studies for the development of service models and interventions as well as for the use of scientific information in developing policy. The chapters in this book show an appreciation of the complexity of factors which may mediate the identification of the effects of human services, such as the mobility of individuals in the service system, individual utilization of differing composites of services and supports, the necessity to objectify better the elusive construct of the quality of life, and the requirement to distinguish between the quality of life and the quality of care. The authors are also aware that because of the unique characteristics of each new service program, the generalizability of research results must be addressed constantly. Several contributions show a special sensitivity to the fact that the validation of a program's effects and benefits may require a longitudinal approach despite government's need for immediate feedback on social action programs. Most social action programs, once begun, remain in operation, and the long-term effects of specific or ongoing interventions, which may not be evident from initial evaluations, must be determined.

Most important, these chapters, taken together, suggest that service systems are engaged in a process of profound change, a process that represents a significant opportunity for these systems to shift their approaches to those that support full community membership for citizens with disabilities. This shift toward community integration holds great promise for people with psychiatric and developmental disabilities.

This book is an important breakthrough in that it demonstrates that researchers can work together with service providers, consumers, and policy analysts to improve the lives of people with psychiatric or developmental disabilities. The authors have taken on a complex series of tasks and done an excellent job in addressing the critical issues in mental health and developmental disabilities services. Solutions are presented which will lead to im-

portant future discussions in the human services field and to some important
modifications of existing public policies.

Louis Rowitz, Ph.D.
Professor and Associate Dean for Academic Affairs
School of Public Health
University of Illinois at Chicago

# I
# INTRODUCTION

The latter half of the twentieth century has witnessed in the United States and Canada a continuing interplay of changing public policy, practice, and research focus in the fields of developmental services and mental health services greater than that of any other period in the human services systems. In 1950, developmental and mental health services were provided almost exclusively in segregated, custodial institutions, and disability was commonly equated with an incapacity for participation and productivity in typical community settings. In the 1990s, developmental and mental health services continue to be provided, to a lesser degree, in isolated congregate settings but are increasingly available in the heart of communities and increasingly emphasize for people with disabilities the goals of participation and productivity.

Yet, considerable gaps persist between policy implementation and philosophic perspectives. Contemporary perspectives emphasize core values of self-determination, empowerment, choice, satisfaction, and participation as bench marks against which the outcomes of social reforms should be judged. These values did not emerge spontaneously within disability services but rather are an outgrowth of more fundamental social reforms embodied within legislation. More specifically, they are founded in progressive mandates such as federal civil rights acts and amendments and enabling legislation supporting the establishment and enhancement of community developmental and mental health services (e.g., Community Mental Health Centers Act, P.L. 88-164; Developmental Disabilities Assistance and Bill of Rights Act, P.L. 95-602).

1

Although the categorical legislation has provided a mechanism through which adult protective services can be supported and desirable practices described and encouraged, developmental or mental health services legislation at the federal level has not been the robust foundation for the establishment of community services or supports which it could have been. Most major challenges to institutional practices with adults have been founded in civil rights. Furthermore, in general, health planning in the United States has been "an ad hoc system based on occasional initiative and, more routinely, political compromise" (Frank, Gluck, and Buckelew 1990). Researchers note an "unwillingness of policymakers and professionals to apply what is known scientifically and technically to both primary prevention and intervention" (Baumeister 1988).

The purpose of this book is to bring together research-based information on the current best practices and models for supporting people with psychiatric or developmental disabilities in living as independently and productively as possible in their communities. Ways of providing residential support, promoting personal development and adjustment, and developing an able work force to assist with community living are examined. Barriers to the development and implementation of such practices by policymakers and service providers are also considered. The book examines the public policy processes and research that address the character and success of models for residential and personal support services for people with disabilities as well as aspects of the work life of the people who are becoming the new service providers within community environments. Needs for further research to clarify policy and program decisions are identified.

To understand best the issues addressed in this book it is important for the reader to consider the relationships among public policy formulation and implementation, applied research, and program evaluation. Policy formulation encompasses posing an issue, identifying strategies to address the issue, anticipating the consequences of adopting each strategy, assessing the desirability of each consequence, and choosing the most desirable strategy with respect to these consequences. This process is clearly paralleled at the level of service delivery by management decision-making processes. At each point in the process evaluators or applied researchers typically have the opportunity for input: to define the issue, to suggest strategies that have succeeded in the past, to identify probable consequences, and to construct criteria for desirability. The selection of the most desirable strategy remains an administrative prerogative; the evaluator or researcher has the role of assessing the processes and outcomes of policy implementation to identify the benefit.

Although the distinction may be blurred in some instances, it may be useful to consider program evaluation as an adjunct to management (i.e., guiding the operation of a program) and applied research as an adjunct to administration (i.e., guiding the operation of a system). Program evaluation involves processes and activities that are undertaken to ensure that management has the information required to render knowledgeable and accurate decisions about the operation and improvement of a program. Similarly, applied research informs administrators of dimensions of the system (through monitoring) and potential strengths, weaknesses, or opportunities.

Within this context several important points need to be stressed. First, policy formulation does not take place in a vacuum; it is constrained by available resources, by the extent to which researchers address the key issues, and by the imperfect viewpoints of the researchers and policymakers alike. Second, policy formulation is responsive to its social context. For example, in a society that values productive work as a gauge of personal worth or quality of life it may be more feasible to achieve political consensus for initiatives that encourage people to make the transition from work preparation to assisted employment rather than to expand work-preparation services. Third, at least in developmental and mental health services, policy formulation increasingly involves active participation in defining issues and desirable solutions on the part of consumers, families, and advocates.

This book includes efforts by researchers to delineate some of these issues with regard to how residence settings support, or fail to support, individuals more effectively to meet the goals of community participation and personal satisfaction; how community services contribute to social adjustment and satisfaction; and how issues related to staff roles and satisfactions affect the staff members themselves. The research and policy issues are no longer "Can these people remain in the community?" or "Who will stay in the community?", but are "What are life experiences going to be like?" and "What is the quality of life in community-supported services?" Such issues must be resolved before we can determine the means to fund supports and accommodate the numbers of people who are now demanding assistance.

# 1

# Overview of Clinical Services, Social Adjustment, and Work Life in Community Living

John W. Jacobson, Ph.D., and Sara N. Burchard, Ph.D.

There have been enormous changes in public policy and in service delivery systems for individuals with developmental disabilities and mental retardation as well as for people with psychiatric disabilities (Bruininks et al. 1987; Farkas, Anthony, and Cohen 1989). Deinstitutionalization and the development of community services have been ongoing for several decades for persons with psychiatric disabilities and for at least 15 years for persons with developmental disabilities. The types of residential, clinical, vocational, and supportive services which are available or being developed to serve persons who have been, or formerly would have been, institutionalized are diverse and ever changing, as are conceptions of what constitute best practices in service delivery.

Many commonalities are evident in policy and practice with respect to psychiatric rehabilitation and developmental disabilities services. These two service fields share many goals: consumer access to services; consumer involvement and control; involvement of family members; use of normal environments and roles in rehabilitation; development of skills related to activities of daily living, housing, and work; availability and responsiveness of advice, support, and assistance; flexibility and acknowledgment of the possible need for indefinite-term support; and the need for advocacy to support independence (Carling and Ridgway 1989). Both the developmental habilitative and psychiatric rehabilitative models adopt the guiding perspective that increases in functional (i.e., adaptive) and social skills are crucial to expanded control of the environment for persons with developmental disabilities or persistent mental disorders (Anthony 1977; Anthony and Jansen

1984; Health Care Financing Administration 1988) in combination with the development of social networks and relationships that provide supports for independent functioning (Anthony, Cohen, and Danley 1988; Anthony and Farcas 1989; Farkas, Anthony, and Cohen 1989; Felce 1988). In this chapter we will focus on developmental services, indicating as appropriate the commonalities with the field of mental health services.

## CONTEMPORARY POLICY

With the dramatic shift to service development and delivery in community settings, court-ordered closings of institutions, and public policy efforts aimed at reducing reliance on institutional settings, there has been an active, continuing, and diverse applied research effort on the part of academicians, research institutes, and state planning and policy groups. Academic research activities have involved model development (e.g., supported and competitive employment; Bellamy, Rhodes, and Albin 1986; Wehman et al. 1985), demonstration projects and identification of best practices (e.g., community residential rehabilitation, functionial assessment; Anthony 1977; Minks and Graham 1989), comparisons of the efficacy of institutional and community group home living (Conroy and Bradley 1985); follow-up evaluations of deinstitutionalization and community services (Schalock, Harper, and Genung 1981; Seltzer 1981), and program evaluation studies (Burchard et al. 1987, in press; Halpern, Close, and Nelson 1986).

Notwithstanding the identification of desirable community services and supports by advocates, consumers, model programs, evaluation research, and generally accepted public policy, there is a significant gap between generally accepted best practices and actual practices and public policy implementation. Funding mechanisms remain principally facility- or program-based and founded in the health care sector (Lakin et al. 1989). They provide limited funds to support persons in an individualized manner and to enhance their independent functioning, integration, and personal satisfaction in living, working, and leisure environments.

In both the developmental and mental health service sectors the primary sources of funding are Medicaid for services and Supplemental Security Income for housing and food (Braddock 1986a, 1986b). A large proportion of Medicaid funds is earmarked for services that are institutional in character by virtue of regulatory content (Braddock 1986a; Kiesler 1982a, 1982b). In contrast, changing philosophies in both fields have stressed increasingly individualized care models that encompass community-integrated living and working (Governor's Planning Council on Developmental Disabilities 1983, 1984).

There are growing pressures from consumers, advocates, researchers, and service providers to realign the funding of services with the nationally accepted philosophy and focus of services, the community and the individual, as evidenced by recurring proposed amendments to federal Medicaid statutes. However, there is a continued need to bring evaluation-based research data to bear on the practices that are considered exemplary and to make that information available and comprehensible to policymakers so that policy, funding, and service provision practices result in services that are rational, supportive, and productive. In addition, academic researchers, policy and planning analysts, and providers need to test and develop methods of converting older service systems, facilities, and work forces into an infrastructure that promotes viable, responsive, and accountable new services that foster the independent functioning of persons with disabilities.

## IMPEDIMENTS TO CHANGE

Despite the widespread, long-standing philosophy behind community services there are many impediments to thoroughgoing effective development and implementation of those services. Although many of these impediments could be addressed by revised funding incentives, there are other persisting issues. In developmental services the character of what constitutes best practices in residential services is continually changing, the extent of actual community integration of service recipients is not well understood, and concerns are developing with respect to the quality of care community programs are affording individuals. The need for more staff and more staff training, the reality of less money to pay for services and more needs, and the greater expectations to satisfy are also issues (Rowitz 1989). The implementation of guarantees of free and appropriate special education services has stimulated students with disabilities and their families to expect that, as adults, they will be able to participate more fully and independently in the life of the community. Opportunities and supports in the community, however, have not fulfilled these expectations (Hasazi, Gordon, and Roe 1985).

Similarly, Kiesler (1982a) characterized the key issues in the field of mental health as encompassing lack of treatment facilities and personnel for noninstitutional care; lack of coordination among responsible public agencies; lack of funding for community care; lack of attention to the long-term and cyclic nature of some mental disorders; public resistance to community programs; and community and personal resistance to closing large congregate facilities. Kiesler also noted a particularly thorny problem from the perspective of policy analysis which confronts both fields: the question of how many persons have developmental disabilities or chronic psychiatric conditions and would demand or require comprehensive community services. Estimation of demand and need is critical to the development of budget projections, work force requirements, and legislative support for reforms.

Although the results of the deinstitutionalization process in the developmental services field appear to have been beneficial (Baker, Seltzer, and Seltzer 1974; Conroy and Bradley 1985; Schalock and Harper 1985), community living facilities were generally established to provide housing, supervision, and care for persons who left large public mental retardation facilities. In fact, much of what has been accomplished in the deinstitutionalization of these facilities reflects the relocation of individuals to other forms of care rather than expanded access to services for persons who have never been served (Bruininks et al. 1987). In many instances the same regulations apply to institutional and community facilities and undoubtedly contribute to the increased cost of many community-based residential care settings (for applicable regulations see Health Care Financing Administration 1988). For example, many of the annual evaluations required for health-related disciplines in institutional contexts may be irrelevant for people without physical disabilities or chronic illnesses who are living in community facilities. Many of the developmental services community care systems have developed in parallel with other community services for dependent populations, rendering access to other forms of services difficult and encouraging total, semi-isolated, care (Castellani 1986). Fundamental resources such as adult basic education are seldom available in a way that is conducive to access by persons with chronic disabilities (McAfee and Sheeler 1987).

In the process of deinstitutionalization of mental health facilities, the establishment of community residential alternatives or support for semiindependent or independent living was not a priority (Carling and Ridgway 1989; Farkas, Anthony, and Cohen 1989; Zigler and Muenchow 1979). Similarly, the need for continuing assistance in promoting vocational productivity was seldom recognized. The potential demand for continuing and episodic community services is large: several million people in the United States probably have some form of developmental disability (Chapter 5), and it is estimated that between 1.7 and 2.4 million citizens have severe chronic psychiatric disabilities (Farkas, Anthony, and Cohen, 1989).

Policy analysts are aware of the values that characterize modern human services theory and the benefits of improved coordination of services within and across systems, increased employment and community living opportunities, enhanced social integration, expanded family support services, and improved services to persons with diagnoses of both developmental disability and mental disorder (Dumars et al. 1987; Gray and Conley 1988). With respect to residential alternatives there is also an awareness that the diversity of consumers and the available program alternatives (including nontherapeutic housing options) must correspond, that consumers of residential services require access to a full range of day activities and supports, and that appropriate managerial and administrative mechanisms must exist to maintain and bolster the provision of services (Janicki et al. 1987). Most compellingly, analysts are aware of the need to develop strategies to resolve conflicts that many believe have developed among individual needs, regulatory requirements, and funding streams (Janicki, Krauss, and Seltzer 1988a, 1988b).

As community services have developed, community service organizations have frequently evolved into large, public subsidized vendors, with inherent conflicts of interest when they advocate expansion of services. Consequently, nonprofit agencies have experienced increased control over how services are delivered in existing program environments but less control in some ways over the introduction of innovative practices and services. Parents, long the most staunch and effective advocates, have joined with consumers and academics in championing expanded services and increasingly individualized living and working circumstances for persons with developmental disabilities and mental disorders (Smull 1989; Trent 1989; Turnbull 1988). Government, recognizing that demand for residential and supportive services far outstrips supply and that only a small proportion of the potential population eligible for services is in fact served (at substantial cost), nonetheless has not yet responded fully to the challenge of developing comprehensive supportive services in the community which are adequate to address expressed demand, let alone latent demand.

### WHY POLICY LAGS BEHIND

There are many reasons why changes in public policy and funding have not kept pace with the evolution of philosophies of care. Policy analysts may share stereotypes with general society which emphasize the need for protection of persons with disabilities (Caruso and Hodapp 1988; St. Claire 1989). Certainly, one dynamic tension in human services is embodied by a shifting balance between assisting persons with disabilities in ways that involve both opportunity and risk and issues of consumer protection from harm and legal liability (real or perceived) for service providers.

Rapid change may be beyond the control of policymakers (Ruback and Innes 1988). Factors in the external environment inhibit transformation of small-scale successful demonstrations of progressive practices into an alternative available on a systems basis. In the absence of federal intervention, gradual change is typical of government programs (Shadish 1984). Finally,

policy analysts may not find existing research (i.e., that which supports progressive practice) to be applicable to the decisions that must be made (see
also Wilcox 1987; Woodhead 1988). Problems in translating research into
policy include inconsistent findings across studies; statements of problems
which are not accompanied by benefits and costs of remedial actions; and
failure to monitor the implementation as well as the outcomes of programs
and services (Maccoby, Kahn, and Everett 1983). The characteristics of research which make it useful to decision makers are focus on a high-priority
issue and practical recommendations supported by data (Weiss and Weiss
1981).

The impetus Nearly all major efforts to evaluate the quality of developmental disabilities and mental health programs have involved examination of service
development and delivery practices (Davidson and Adams 1989; Hawkins,
Fremouw, and Reitz 1981) rather than the conditions that foster careprovider
practices and setting characteristics that promote the goals of social policy,
for example client independence, physical access to and participation in the
community, and personal adjustment. Such studies provide public agencies
with the information they require to verify the extent to which programmatic
expectations are fulfilled or that problems are present which require re-
mediation. Outcomes such as consumer perceptions of independence, productivity, and integration, however, are seldom assessed (Davidson and
Adams 1989).

## Research on Community Residential Alternatives in Developmental Services

The reason for the development of community services for persons with
mental retardation and developmental disabilities was to provide opportunities to live, work, and receive habilitation in settings in the same manner as,
and to the extent possible, alongside similar aged, nonhandicapped peers.
The impetus behind community services was the adoption of the philosophy
of normalization by many advocates and professionals, court actions against
restrictive policies that denied individual rights, and national and state
legislative initiatives (Turnbull 1988). It was expected that community living would promote increased independence and opportunities for self-
determination, community integration, and productivity (Lakin et al. 1989;
Strauss et al. 1988).

Research designed to examine the success of these policy initiatives
originally addressed whether deinstitutionalization "worked" by simply determining if persons who moved into community settings remained there

or were sent to more restrictive placements (e.g., Sutter et al. 1980). It also focused on whether individuals who were placed into the community "improved" with respect to persons "matched" for adaptive and maladaptive behaviors but who had remained in institutional settings (Conroy, Efthimiou, and Lemanowicz 1982). Emphasis was on evaluating changes in the performance of independent daily living and community living skills over time (Eyman, Silverstein, and McLain 1975; Kleinberg and Galligan 1983). Some investigators even examined whether the new community placements provided more normalized life-styles for service recipients, clearly one of the major goals of the new social policy (Eyman, Demaine, and Lei 1979; Hull and Thompson 1981a, 1981b).

It became evident, however, that the evaluation of community services required examination of a much broader range of variables than skill performance or recidivism. Evaluation of residential models required examination of variables that would represent the well-articulated goals of community programs: (1) increased independence by acquisition of skills through habilitation and opportunity; and (2) life-style normalization through community integration, development of social contacts and friendships among peers without disabilities, access to normative leisure activities, increased personal autonomy, responsibility, and choice, and opportunities to work for wages in nonsegregated settings (Burchard et al., in press; Emerson 1985; Heal 1988; Hill et al. 1989).

Although there have been a few studies that have attempted to evaluate this range of variables (Halpern, Close, and Nelson 1986; Burchard et al., in press), evaluations of life-style outcomes in community programs are often confounded with residence setting differences and very likely with individual differences in the capabilities of the persons whom programs are willing to serve (Landesman and Butterfield 1987). Nonetheless, studies of life-style outcomes may assist policymakers in gauging whether, for example, social integration is a demonstrable result of various types of service settings.

Some research has indicated that the residence staff and support personnel are critical to resident quality of life (see Burchard and Thousand 1988; Landesman 1988). Nevertheless, there is also ample research demonstrating that characteristics of service settings have significant ramifications for outcomes experienced by clients with respect to performance of independent living skills, autonomy, responsibility (Campbell and Bailey 1984; Seltzer 1981), community integration, and life-style normalization (Burchard et al., in press); and for staff or personnel associated with those programs with respect to the organization and responsibility of their work roles and involvement with the people they serve (MacEachron, Zober, and Fein 1985; Felce 1988).

Programs and settings have inherent organizational and control features that affect both client and staff autonomy, choice, responsibility, and life-style (Burchard et al., in press; Campbell and Bailey 1984; Rotegard, Hill, and Bruininks 1983). Because many studies have been confounded by client and program characteristics, more research is needed to address which models of service are in fact approximating or promoting the goals of social policy for consumers.

## Community Settings and Quality of Life

More recent policy and research have become concerned with issues re-lated to the quality of life for persons receiving community services (Heal 1988; Landesman 1986), but only a small number of studies have really at-tempted to obtain information from the service recipients themselves with respect to their satisfaction with their life-style, quality of life, social sup-port, or work life (Burchard, Pine, and Gordon 1990; Halpern, Close, and Nelson 1986; Heal and Daniels 1986; Seltzer 1981; Seltzer 1984). Obtain-ing reliable information from persons with mental retardation has been an issue (Sigelman et al. 1981a, 1981b). However, investigators have de-veloped interviewing techniques that detect validity problems (Burchard, Pine, and Gordon 1990; Heal and Chadsey-Rusch 1985) and use a com-bination of structured interview and recording techniques with informants as surrogates (Kennedy, Horner, and Newton 1989; Schalock et al. 1989). Efforts to incorporate the perspectives of service consumers into research that can be used as a basis for further planning and service provision are essential.

Quality of life is a difficult concept to make operational in research (Robinson 1987). The principal difficulty is that quality of life can be viewed as a multidimensional construct (Emerson 1985; Schalock et al. 1989) that reflects the extent to which an array of wants and needs that may vary across the span of one's lifetime are satisfied (Flanagan 1978; see Table 1.1). In addition to the elements listed in Table 1.1, supports for self-direction and skill development to achieve environmental control and enrich social rela-tionships are important aspects of the quality of life for persons with chronic disabilities (Jacobson and Janicki 1987).

Quality of life considerations closely parallel components of social role valorization (Wolfensberger 1983) in which valued social roles for persons with developmental disabilities are fostered through design or use of physi-

**Table 1.1. Considerations Germane to the Quality of Life**

| Domain | Content |
|---|---|
| Physical and material well-being | Material comforts<br>Health and personal safety |
| Relationships with other people | Parents, brothers, sisters, and<br>other relatives<br>Having and raising children<br>Spouse/partner<br>Close friends |
| Social, community, and civic activities | Helping and encouraging others<br>Civic activities |
| Personal development and fulfillment | Learning<br>Understanding oneself<br>Work<br>Expressing oneself |
| Recreation | Socializing<br>Reading<br>Listening to music<br>Relaxing<br>Participating in active recreation |

*Source:* Adapted from Flanagan (1978).

cal settings, relationships and groupings, and activities. Similarly, in their analysis of the concept of quality of life, Schalock and co-workers (1989) underscored environmental control (e.g., autonomy and choice), community involvement, and social relations as the key dimensions.

AUTONOMY

Although earlier studies indicated that persons in semiindependent or supervised living situations had relatively poor access to community resources and events (Gothelf 1985; Seltzer 1981), other recent studies provide a different picture. Burchard, Pine, and Gordon (1990) found that persons living in semiindependent settings experienced greater independence and autonomy and were more actively involved in the community than their (functionally similar) counterparts who were in supervised group homes (see also Halpern, Close, and Nelson 1986). In fact, persons in semiindependent apartments had rates of community access and activities similar to those of a normative comparison group (Rosen and Burchard 1990).

Only a small number of skills may be critical to semiindependent living—skills such as distinguishing workdays from nonworkdays, which appear well within the capabilities of many persons with mild or moderate mental retardation (Rudrud and Vaudt 1986). Nevertheless, the lack of certain skills to live independently and the issues of safety and integration continue to be concerns. Halpern, Close, and Nelson (1986), for example, found that more than 20% of persons with mental retardation who moved to semiindependent settings reported difficult social and personal circumstances and experiences. Nonetheless, they also found that self-esteem and the motivation to maintain independence were generally high, and 87% reported that they liked living in their present homes.

Concerns also exist about the functional capacity of many individuals to make a direct contribution to social network formation and thus to integration through the exercise of social skills. Such skills, including the ability to make one's problems or needs known, are potentially important for the formation of support networks for more independent living and also for supportive or competitive employment (Kratchowill 1985; Mueser and Liberman 1988). Although such skills may not be prerequisites for semiindependent or independent living, they contribute to a more thorough realization of the benefits of independence and merit attention as a focus of supportive services.

Low expectations for independence may limit opportunities for increased autonomy among persons with chronic disabilities who are living in community settings, and they also probably encourage an inappropriate reliance by such persons on staff for problem solving and social support (Kaswan 1981). Substantial numbers of individuals now living in supervised settings may be capable of much greater residential independence in semiindependent or assisted settings (Edgerton 1988).

### CHOICE

Shevin and Klein define choice making as "the act of an individual's selection of a preferred alternative from among several familiar options" (1984, 160). Guess, Benson, and Siegel-Causey (1985) view choice making as an expression of autonomy and dignity, and they suggest both structuring daily routines to maximize opportunities for choice making and also systematically teaching how to make choices. Budde and Bachelder (1986) stressed further that the key elements of more autonomous living include independence and control. Opportunities for daily decision making in supervised living situations appear to be relatively circumscribed in a number of life activity areas (Dhooper, Royse, and Rihm 1989; Kishi et al. 1988) although

**Table 1.2. Findings from Observations of Community Residential Staff**

Rates of interactions between clients and staff are very low.
The majority of interactions occur with a minority of residents.
Structured settings (in which management provides staff with incentives to interact with residents) promote interactions.
Small teaching groups promote interactions.
Staff involvement in relevant decisions promotes interactions.
Practicum-based training improves staff's teaching skills.
Some trained skills generalize, and others do not for reasons that are not apparent in the context.
Training methods in which supervisors provide training to staff appear valuable.
Systems of public or private feedback can increase staff fulfillment of their duties.

*Source:* Adapted from Repp, Felce, and deKock (1987).

ing in human services. Further transfer of services to the community and expansion of supportive services will probably require greater numbers of personnel than do existing service systems and also increased accountability in the delivery of those services (Panel on the Future of the Work Force 1987). The increased accountability will require, in turn, that the work force be skilled in the delivery of services. As a consequence, there has been an increasing focus on the development of improved training opportunities for paraprofessionals and professionals prior to and during their employment in developmental and mental health services (Davidson et al. 1987; Knight et al. 1986).

The processes through which the goals of increased resident independence and integration are pursued take place in a context that is structured through management activity. Repp, Felce, and deKock (1987), in a review of the literature of group home management, identified findings that were consistent with effective promotion of resident development and social integration (see Table 1.2). Identified as especially critical activities in the facilitation of resident development were management attention to promoting rates and equitable distribution of staff-resident social interactions, use of small teaching groups, provision of practicum training by supervisors, staff participation in goal and activity selection, and feedback to the staff on the extent to which program goals were being addressed.

Recent research has focused on the identification of practices, skills, and knowledge that will assist direct care staff and managers to perform their jobs most effectively (Thousand, Burchard, and Hasazi 1986). It is critical

**Table 1.3. Staff and Manager Competencies**

| | | |
|---|---|---|
| *Direct care staff* | | |
| Competencies | 1. | Participates on team |
| | 2. | Provides safe and clean environment |
| | 3. | Manages activities of daily living |
| | 4. | Maintains client health |
| | 5. | Organizes leisure and recreational activities |
| | 6. | Maintains operations |
| Related knowledge areas | 1. | Interpersonal communication |
| | 2. | Developmental disabilities |
| | 3. | Consent decree or class action requirements |
| | 4. | Normalization |
| | 5. | Community support systems |
| | 6. | General legal issues |
| | 7. | Team process |
| | 8. | Observation and documentation |
| | 9. | Teaching techniques |
| | 10. | Organization of agency |
| | 11. | Safety |
| | 12. | Problem solving and decision making |
| | 13. | Normal growth and development |
| | 14. | Diet and nutrition |
| *Management competencies* | 1. | Normalization competencies |
| | 2. | Values-based interpersonal skills |
| | 3. | Interpersonal work skills |
| | 4. | Developmental programing and teaching competencies |

*Source:* For direct care, adapted from Bureau of Staff Development and Training (1987); for management, adapted from Burchard and Thousand (1988).

that these identified competencies are meaningfully associated with the personal development, integration, and adjustment of the persons with disabilities who are receiving supportive services from these staff persons (Burchard et al. 1987; Felce 1988; Seys and Duker 1988).

Table 1.3 displays a series of direct care staff competencies and related knowledge areas and also management competencies for developmental services residential settings. The direct care competencies were developed from a review and analysis of the role dimensions of direct care staff during the actual performance of their duties (Bureau of Staff Development and Training 1987). The staff and manager prerequisite competencies were developed through the convergence of several work function and competence methodologies (Burchard and Thousand 1988). It can be assumed that an analysis of requisite competencies in mental health settings would produce a similar composite. These activities appear to be highly compatible with the effective management strategies indicated in Table 1.2, and they underscore the importance of the ongoing involvement of management in implementing individualized objectives. Both sets of competencies involve a combination of specialized skills, practical skills in maintaining a household, and interpersonal skills that may be very important (or in fact, absolutely essential) to effective participation as a member of a small work group environment that provides therapeutic support or rehabilitation to other individuals.

## Conclusion

The need for supportive services can only grow with the greater longevity of persons with disabilities and with the greater expectations of opportunities for independence and participation engendered by reforms in special education services. However, because dramatic increases in funding for services cannot be anticipated it is essential that research provide policymakers with information about which type of supports can most effectively and efficiently provide for persons with disabilities the supports that *they want* and can promote the goals of participation, inclusion, and quality of life which *they* aspire to. It is also imperative to study ways of assisting service personnel to shift into roles that provide those needed community supports and then to study and delineate organizational or work life structures that can efficiently maintain and support them in providing those supportive services by maximizing the quality and benefits of their service.

# 2

# Community Integration of People with Psychiatric Disabilities
## Emerging Trends

Paul J. Carling, Ph.D.

This chapter presents an overview of emerging trends in the effort to provide citizens with psychiatric disabilities with decent affordable housing along with the supports needed to lead full and satisfying lives in our communities. On the one hand, the press, researchers, and advocates all debate such issues as the "failure of deinstitutionalization" and the need for "asylum" (e.g., Wasow 1986; Zipple, Carling, and McDonald 1988), the crisis of homelessness among people with mental disorders (Bachrach 1984; Baxter and Hopper 1984), the generally low quality of both community and hospital programs for these individuals (Torrey and Wolfe 1986), and the continuing orientation of these programs toward "maintenance" rather than rehabilitation (Anthony and Blanch 1989).

Although state mental health policies stress the need for comprehensive community support systems (National Association of State Mental Health Program Directors 1986), most mental health resources are still used predominantly for outdated institutional programs (Carling et al. 1987), and "model" community support programs appear to be relatively rare (Bachrach 1980). We also hear of a pervasive lack of attention to mental health consumers' rights (Chamberlin 1978; Leete 1989). On the other hand, we also read and hear about the development of more responsive and effective community support services (Stein and Test 1985), increased attention to consumer empowerment (Leete 1989), more effective and respectful clinical interventions (Anthony and Blanch 1989; Strauss 1989), and a clearer emphasis on meeting the basic needs of homes, jobs, and friends for people with disabilities (Taylor et al. 1987; Wilson, in press).

Considering these dramatically conflicting views, it has been suggested that the field of mental health is in the midst of a "paradigm shift" with regard to people who have the most severe disabilities (Blanch, Carling, and Ridgway 1988; Carling 1989), from an era of institutional and facility-based thinking to a "transitional" period in which people were seen principally as service recipients who needed a comprehensive community support system (Turner and TenHoor 1979), to a world view in which people are most commonly viewed as citizens with a potential for, and a right to, full community participation and integration (Carling 1987; Wilson, in press).

## The Background and Scope of the Problem

Since the late 1950s, we have significantly reduced public hospital use and expanded community services (Kiesler 1982a, 1982b). The critical need for stable housing linked to supports, however, has only emerged in the last 10 years as a major policy dilemma (Carling and Ridgway 1989). A majority of the 1.7 to 2.4 million Americans considered "long-term mentally ill" based on diagnosis, disability, and duration of disorder (Goldman, Gatozzi, and Taube 1981) live in inadequate housing, lack needed supports, or are homeless (Department of Health and Human Services 1983; Department of Health and Human Services Steering Committee 1980).

The problem is a complex one: without active rehabilitation, many individuals lack the skills and supports needed for successful community living. In addition, the recurring nature of long-term psychiatric disabilities may result in people losing housing as they experience repeated hospitalizations (Budson 1981; Chatetz and Goldfinger 1984). Housing discrimination based on stigma is a day-to-day reality: landlords refuse to rent to these individuals, cutting off access to normal housing (Aviram and Segal 1973; Hogan 1985a, 1985b; Segal, Baumohl, and Moyles 1980). Moreover, many people with psychiatric disabilities are poor, with average reported annual incomes from $3,000 to $7,000 and unemployment rates as high as 85% (Dion and Anthony 1987).

Failure to focus on people's permanent housing needs has had multiple effects. Many individuals remain in psychiatric hospitals because of the lack of housing (Department of Health and Human Services Steering Committee 1980). Others cycle through emergency rooms and general hospitals in costly and often inappropriate stays (Chatetz and Goldfinger 1984; Geller 1982). Many others have been moved to "custodial" nursing and boarding homes. Most of these settings lack active rehabilitation or treatment, contribute to declines in functioning, and are often exploitative (Carling 1981;

Kohen and Paul 1976; Segal and Aviram 1978; United States Senate Special Committee on Aging 1976). The lack of permanent housing and support options also results in a substantial burden on families (Hatfield, Fierstein, and Johnson 1982; Wasow 1982) who are often forced to serve as case managers and landlords with little or no support.

Of the persons who do find independent living in the community, many do so in very low-income neighborhoods in which substandard housing and high crime rates are typical. "Oversaturation" of these neighborhoods by people with disabilities often leads to community backlash (Coulton, Holland, and Fitch 1984; Ridgway 1987). Increasing numbers are homeless. Studies have reported that as few as 10% and as many of 75% of people who are homeless have severe psychiatric disabilities (General Accounting Office 1988) although they have not necessarily used mental hospitals (Baxter and Hopper 1984). Finally, people with psychiatric disabilities compete for housing with other low-income groups, most of whom are generally viewed as more suitable tenants.

## The Crisis of Affordable Housing

These housing problems are compounded by dramatic changes in the current generic housing scene. Two factors reduce access to housing for *all* people with limited incomes: a decade-long decline in affordable housing stock, and the rising cost of housing in relation to income. This combination has put home ownership out of the reach of many middle-income Americans and decent housing out of the reach of most of those at or below the poverty level. These trends have been accompanied by a cut of nearly 80% in federally assisted housing for low-income and special needs groups since 1981 and a dramatic increase in homelessness in all parts of the country (Low-income Housing Information Service 1988). Because disabilities can be economically catastrophic, people with disabilities are disproportionately represented in the group that is "very poor" or well below the poverty level.

Paradoxically, because access to affordable housing has become in effect a national crisis, the awareness of this issue by the general public and their support for increased federal and state spending and taxation for this purpose are at an all-time high (National Housing Institute 1988). Thus, even as federal housing programs were being cut in 1988 Congress was drafting sweeping new affordable housing legislation to reverse these trends (Carling 1988). These developments represent an important opportunity to introduce innovative strategies for more successful community integration to the public agenda through a focus on housing.

## Mental Health's Response

Historically, mental health agencies have viewed housing as a social welfare problem and have defined their role as "treatment." Public housing agencies, reflecting societal stigma, contend that mental health consumers need specialized residential programs and see their housing needs as a mental health responsibility (Carling and Ridgway 1989). Thus, housing needs are often ignored: residential services in mental health are typically therapeutic facilities, not housing. Transitional halfway houses proliferated in the 1960s. In the 1970s the concept of a residential continuum emerged and included a variety of models, such as quarterway houses and halfway houses (Budson 1981); three-quarterway houses (Campbell 1981); family foster care (Carling 1984); crisis alternative models (Stein and Test 1985; Test 1981); Fairweather Lodges (Fairweather 1980); apartment programs (Carling 1978; Goldmeier, Shore, and Mannino 1977; boarding homes (Kohen and Paul 1976); nursing homes (Carling 1981); and shelters for homeless persons (Bachrach 1984). These programs have typically been segregated, professionally staffed and congregate in nature (Carling and Ridgway 1989).

## The Current State of Practice

A recent national survey of more than 2,500 community residential programs in all states serving adults with psychiatric disabilities (Randolph et al. 1988) found that despite broad-scale development of residential programs in the last decade a relatively small number of agencies is involved in providing these services in most states. In spite of the continuum model, few agencies offered more than one residential option. Most programs were large congregate facilities that accounted for less than a quarter of the residences but housed the majority of residents. The newer supervised apartment programs and supportive housing approaches, which involve standard-size housing arrangements, use larger numbers of households, each of which serves a small number of people, an approach that is more consistent with normalization principles (Taylor et al. 1987; Turner and TenHoor 1979). Intermediate care facilities, nursing homes, and shelters had few formal ties with mental health services.

Transitional housing, which imposes time limits on clients, also was not as common as expected from the literature. In fact, most programs provided services on a long-term basis. Residential services, although assumed to be intensive, are staffed primarily by paraprofessionals who have not been trained in the traditional mental health core disciplines. Follow-up services were essentially informal, suggesting that efforts to assist clients to maintain stable housing may be relatively weak. Sixty thousand individuals received services from these residential programs. If we extrapolate that figure to the survey universe, it represents less than 5% of people in the United States with long-term psychiatric disabilities (Goldman, Gatozzi, and Taube 1981). This is consistent with state estimates that between 2 and 5% of people with psychiatric disabilities are served in residential programs (Ridgway 1986). Individuals served were primarily young adults with diagnoses of major mental disorders. Using a functional rating scale (ranging from functional to moderately to severely to gravely disabled), more than half of the programs reported serving persons who were moderately to severely disabled. The remaining programs served people who were either gravely disabled or functional, but surprisingly these programs served *twice* as many persons who were functional as they did those who were gravely disabled. This finding contradicts the popular notion that residential programs are serving the persons who are most gravely disabled, and it raises serious concerns over whether such scare and expensive resources should be serving so many persons who are functioning relatively well.

## The Evaluation of Current Approaches to Residential Programs

Our knowledge about what works in residential programs is hampered by both methodologic and conceptual problems. Few evaluations of community residential services have been rigorous enough for conclusions to be drawn (Braun et al. 1981; Kiesler 1982a, 1982b; Test and Stein 1978). Moreover, because the goals of community residential programs have rarely been well defined, most outcome evaluations have been conceptually flawed. The most frequently asked evaluation question has been whether or not community programs are more successful than institutional treatment in helping persons to meet basic goals of independent living. In six major reviews covering several hundred alternatives to hospitalization, only a handful of studies met basic criteria of experimental design (Braun et al. 1981; Carpenter 1978; Dellario and Anthony 1981; Kiesler 1982a, 1982b; Test and Stein 1978). Taken as a whole, these studies indicate that community-based treatment is virtually always as effective or more effective than hospital-based treatment in helping people with psychiatric disabilities to achieve employment outcomes, to gain reentry into the community, and to reduce the use of medication and outpatient services. Apparently any of a wide range of community services can assist in achieving some measure of community integration.

With regard to residential programs, Cometa, Morrison, and Ziskoven (1979, 25), reviewing a total of 109 studies, concluded that evidence of the effectiveness of transitional halfway houses in reducing recidivism, improving economic self-sufficiency and improving community adjustment was "highly suspect." Transitional residential programs may in fact be preferable to institutional care, but according to this review they fall considerably short of helping people to achieve lasting community integration.

Perhaps the most intriguing findings in this area came from an extensive study conducted by Segal and Aviram (1978) of sheltered care environments and from an analysis by Tabor (1980) of the deinstitutionalization literature. The work of Segal and Aviram indicated that characteristics of the *community* are more important than characteristics of *residents* in predicting the degree to which people actually participate in community life; specific characteristics of the facility were the least important factor. These studies suggest that outcome research should be reframed to include a focus on where people live and how they spend their time rather than focusing solely on the interventions that professionals provide.

In summary, there have been relatively few rigorous evaluations of specific residential programs and virtually no attempts to examine the success of professionals in helping people to get and keep normal housing. The lack of information on program effectiveness is a critical deficit that can result in a grossly inefficient use of resources and, most importantly, seriously curtailed opportunities for people with psychiatric disabilities.

## Problems with Traditional Approaches

Despite the growth of residential services and the emergence of new models, residential programs do not, per se, meet housing needs. In fact, serious questions have been raised about the failure to distinguish between residential treatment and housing and about the assumption that people need to participate in such programs prior to independent living (Taylor et al. 1987). The growing acceptance of a rehabilitation approach (Anthony and Jansen 1984; Blanch, Carling, and Ridgway 1988) demystifies acquiring stable housing by defining it as a process of building critical skills and supports to choose, get, and keep the housing one desires.

A range of research and training activities undertaken by the Center for Community Change (CCC) at the University of Vermont, partly in collaboration with the Center for Psychiatric Rehabilitation at Boston University, has revealed significant dissatisfaction among consumers, their families, and service providers with the concept of a residential continuum and with the transitional services model. In a summary, Carling and Ridgway (1989) point out that the notion of transitional help through a series of time-limited stays in specialized residential settings in order to achieve independent living is simplistic. The system creates major difficulties for the individual including: (1) having to learn skills that are mostly relevant to group living; (2) chronic dislocation through successive moves, because often improvement in functioning requires a physical move to another setting; and (3) an ultimate return to family, boarding home, hospital, or homelessness because of the inattention of many treatment-oriented systems to securing permanent community housing. Similarly, a residential continuum usually entails allocating resources to separate residential facilities rather than focusing on the services and supports people need to function successfully in normal housing. The transition and the continuum concepts often confuse the need for housing with the need for specific supports and, in effect, require participation in a service program in order to receive housing.

Based on these findings, Randolph et al. (1988) recommended several directions for the field: (1) moving away from the concept of a continuum of residential programs, and promoting instead the use of supports to all individuals with psychiatric disabilities regardless of where they live; (2) moving away from the use of transitional residences and congregate programming as its primary response to consumers' housing and support needs; (3) adopting and implementing a rehabilitation approach to meeting housing and support needs; (4) having consumer's preferences and choices become the single most important determinant of the options available to them; and (5) establishing as priorities those service approaches that meet the needs, in normal housing settings, of the largest number of individuals with the most severe disabilities.

## Recent Literature on Community Support and Rehabilitation

Two recent reviews of the outcome research literature on psychiatric disabilities (Anthony and Blanch 1989; Wilson, in press) summarized findings on ways to provide people with decent housing and to provide ongoing support. These reviews concluded that: (1) a psychiatric disability is not necessarily a lifelong degenerative process; (2) most people with psychiatric disabilities can maintain home, jobs, friends, and families; (3) mental health services must be highly flexible to be responsive to individual needs; correspondingly, people with the highest level of disability seem to have the most individual needs; (4) people *can* make positive choices about the kind and intensity of supports they receive; (5) given choice, most people do not define themselves principally as chronic mental patients; instead, they value independence and productivity more than any other treatment outcomes.

## Learnings from Other Fields

The field of mental health also has a great deal to learn from other groups who require special supports in their housing: people with low incomes, who are elderly, homeless, and those with developmental disabilities, including mental retardation. A recent comprehensive review of the research related to housing and community integration for all disability groups (Carling et al. 1987) summarized some applicable findings. This review concluded that: (1) housing needs are similar for each of these groups, although support needs are more varied; (2) supports appear to be the critical factor in whether people can remain in a housing situation of their own choice; (3) housing problems are less closely related to disability than they are to economic and social factors such as poverty, affordable housing trends, and discrimination; (4) strong differences of opinion often exist between professionals and consumers about specific needs for housing and supports, regardless of which disability group is involved; (5) choices and control over one's environment are critical necessities regardless of special need, and consumers wish to be centrally involved in planning their own housing and supports and to have the opportunity to manage their own services; (6) because of the lack of in-home supports and services, elderly person and people with disabilities are plagued by transience, dislocation, and the risk of institutionalization; and (7) the model of a residential continuum is increasingly beset by conceptual and practical problems. This review concluded that the broader disability community is increasingly emphasizing normal housing and the need to avoid transforming housing into service settings. Thus community integration approaches avoid congregation and segregation and instead focus on building relationships between disabled and nondisabled individuals.

## Consumer Preferences

A final area of controversy concerns the role of consumers in determining the need for housing and supports. In a countywide needs assessment in the state of Washington Daniels and Carling (1986) gathered data from both providers and their clients about their perceptions of the need for housing and supports. The results indicated almost opposite views from professionals and consumers, with the former favoring transitional, highly staffed residential programs for the great majority of consumers, and the latter expressing their preference for normal housing with flexible supports. Most consumers wanted to live with one other person rather than alone or in a larger group. Recently in Vermont the first statewide study of consumer preferences for housing and supports was undertaken (Chapter 11). The study involved a random sample of individuals who, were homeless, in the state hospital, or receiving community services for people with psychiatric disabilities. The results of this study have direct implications for the manner in which housing and support services should be delivered. Most persons preferred to live in their own apartment or house rather than in a mental health-operated facility or program, single-room occupancy hotels (SROs), with their family, or in a community care (boarding) home. The major barrier consumers saw to realizing this preference was a lack of adequate income. Most respondents wanted to move in order to live in a better location, have more space that was in better repair, and have more freedom and autonomy. People in SROs reported the least amount of satisfaction of all respondents, including those in the state hospital or who were homeless. The most preferred characteristics of living situations were freedom and autonomy, permanence, security, and privacy.

Traditionally, mental health systems have assumed that many people with psychiatric disabilities need live-in staff to assist them during crisis situations or to teach them daily living skills. However, only one tenth of the respondents reported needing live-in staff. Instead, most people preferred that the staff be available by telephone, or in person if necessary, on a 24-hour basis. As contrasted with the traditional placement approach into congregate settings, most respondents preferred not to live with other mental health consumers because they felt that it was difficult to live with other people's problems as well as their own. Instead, they wanted to live with a friend or romantic partner. This study shows that consumers of mental health services, whether homeless, in a state hospital, or in community programs, generally can articulate their needs for both housing and supports.

Finally, the perspectives of a broad range of consumers and former consumers on housing and supports were solicited in a national housing policy forum (Ridgway 1988a) attended by a group of nationally recognized consumer leaders. Individuals recounted their own experiences with homelessness and residential programs and concluded with the following recommendations. The group felt that systems should develop the housing options that most people prefer: independent or shared apartments with support services and that housing should be decent and permanent and should be developed in neighborhoods that were safe, near shopping, services, and transportation. The participants urged that support services become voluntary and focus on helping people develop skills such as how to handle stress, deal with landlords, manage money, and seek support.

With regard to income, the group urged that disability benefit levels be improved and that special funds be made available to help people move into and keep housing; such assistance would include loan funds for security deposits, rent subsidies, and the creation of employment opportunities. Participants called for improved case management through lower caseloads and higher pay and urged the creation of new staff roles similar to the personal care attendant model. They further urged that the staff be trained specifically to help people choose, acquire, and keep housing and to listen to consumers. Finally, they urged that consumers be hired and trained as service providers, including roles in outreach, case management, skills teaching, and program management.

The participants called for the development of self-help options, including user-run housing. They also pressed for greater consumer input into decision making by conducting housing forums, using former patients to collect information, and always involving consumers in planning and developing housing. Finally, the group urged that public education efforts to reduce stigma be undertaken and that public officials be educated on consumers' concerns. They urged tighter regulation of board and care homes and stressed the need for further legislation for affordable housing. Finally, they emphasized the importance of working in coalitions and keeping the public's awareness of this issue at a high level.

## The Emergence of a Supported Housing Approach

In summary then, the learnings from the community support and rehabilitation literature in mental health, from other fields, and from consumers themselves suggest that the key ingredients of community integration are a focus on consumer goals and preferences; an individualized and flexible rehabilitation process; and a strong emphasis on normal housing, work, and social networks (Blanch, Carling, and Ridgway 1988; Carling et al. 1987). In the field of mental health, this approach has been termed *supported housing* (National Institute of Mental Health 1987).

As planners and advocates focus beyond residential programs to providing broad support in all housing settings, mental health policies are being reformulated. The National Association of State Mental Health Program Directors (1987b) recently approved a policy statement that sharpens their focus even more clearly and endorses the concept of supported housing. It reads:

> All people with long-term mental illness should be given the option to live in decent, stable, affordable and safe housing, in settings that maximize their integration into community activities and their ability to function independently. Housing options should not require time limits for moving to another housing option. People should not be required to change living situations or lose housing options when their service needs change, and should not lose their place of residence if they are hospitalized. People should be given the opportunity to actively participate in the selection of their housing arrangements from among those living environments available to the general public. . . . Necessary supports, including case management, on-site crisis intervention, and rehabilitation services should be available at appropriate levels and for as long as needed by persons with psychiatric disabilities, regardless of their choices of living arrangements. Services should be flexible, individualized and provided with attention to personal dignity. Advocacy, community education and resource development should be continuous. (1–2)

Supported housing is organized around three central principles: (1) consumers choose their own living situations; (2) consumers live in normal, stable housing, not in mental health programs; and (3) consumers have the services and supports required to maximize their opportunities for success over time. Two recent reviews of the characteristics of local supported housing programs (Blanch, Carling, and Ridgway 1988) and of related state level innovations (Carling and Wilson 1989) provide information on the specifics of this approach.

## Implications for Public Policy

Systems that are moving toward a supported housing approach face significant challenges. Traditional funding streams, program requirements, administrative approaches to resource allocation and management, and even staff skills are not oriented toward intensive support for consumers in normal housing and work settings (Carling and Wilson 1989). Such systems, rather than developing more residential programs, often emphasize developing better community services; increasing consumers' income through employment and subsidies; building relationships with the public and private housing sectors to access and develop housing; focusing on tangible outcomes from their service providers; and restructuring their policies, funding, and regulations to be consistent with these outcomes. Key to success is a clear mission that articulates the role of consumers in this process, the types of housing options, and the types of services that will actually be available.

## The Need for Further Research

As public policy appears to be shifting away from an expectation that residential facilities will meet any significant proportion of the need for stable housing and community support services, additional research into questions of where and how consumers prefer to live, successful strategies for facilitating meaningful client choices and for developing housing and supports, documentation of the costs and benefits of housing and support initiatives, identification of clinical interventions best suited to normal housing, and an elaboration of the role of peer support in community success will all be vital.

Research on supported housing, to date, has consisted largely of descriptive studies of current programs (Hall, Nelson, and Fowler 1987). This is appropriate given the early state of evolution of the supported housing approach. To demonstrate the effectiveness of this approach, further studies that assist the field in operationalizing this set of concepts as well as studies that assess its impact on consumers and their families are essential.

A recent review of the research on the community integration of people with psychiatric disabilities (Carling et al. 1987) concluded that further research is *not* needed on hospital versus community alternatives or on the efficacy of residential treatment settings (e.g., group homes), particularly since these settings are so rarely defined operationally. The key unresearched questions, according to that review, are: "Where do people with mental illness live?" "Where do they want to live?" and "How can we help them succeed there?" (23). Finally, the authors note that these questions require a shift from professionally defined to consumer-defined research. This is consistent with recent calls for research on psychiatric disability to focus more on the commonalities between people with and without disabilities and to begin defining *success* in terms of quality of life variables such as physical and material well-being; relations with other people; social, community, and civic activities; personal development and fulfillment; and recreation (Wilson, in press).

The supported housing approach itself suggests a broad research agenda (Carling 1990). In promoting active consumer choice of their housing and supports, for example, we need to understand better the process of choice and how to assist people with making choices. We need to comprehend more fully the power of control and autonomy in promoting success. Further, we need consumers' perspectives and those of their families about what kinds of housing people prefer, what services and supports are helpful, and how they might best be provided. We need to understand better the capacity of consumers to manage their symptoms and their own lives and to assist each other, both individually and through consumer-operated services.

With regard to supports, we need to discover effective ways to organize services that assist people with the most severe disabilities to succeed in housing of their choice. Key issues to be explored include flexibility and individualization of services and the continuity of relationships involved. In effect, we need to uncover the ways in which services can eliminate the perceived need for specialized living arrangements (Test 1981).

Finally, with regard to housing, we need to understand the impact on success of choice versus placement and the contribution to success of particular types of neighborhoods. Broad dispersion of housing, for example, versus physical proximity clearly may have an impact on the capacity of consumers to support each other and for staff to be available and readily accessible to provide requested assistance. We must comprehend the positive value of a consumer or former patient community at the same time as we assist people to become part of the larger community. To understand better how to facilitate integration it would be helpful to study the impact of different types of living arrangements, including size, number of residents, location, and makeup of the housing, its appearance, and its stability, on relevant integration outcomes such as the number and type of relationships and activities involving people without disabilities. Through expanded research on consumer choice, housing, and supports we can build the critical knowledge base necessary to achieve community integration for people with psychiatric disabilities.

# II
# CLINICAL SERVICES

The identification of needed and effective clinical services to support people with severe psychiatric or developmental disabilities is an issue that has been drawing considerable empirical, policy, and advocacy attention. The clinical services available, the services that professionals are prepared to deliver, the venue in which they have been prepared to deliver them, and the services that consumers need and want are often disparate. Information about which clinical services are actually provided, to whom, and with what results, is often not available. Empirical demonstrations of which services are most successful in supporting individuals in community living are often lacking.

The following five chapters address a number of relevant issues with respect to the provision of clinical services in community settings to persons with severe psychiatric and developmental disabilities. Over the past two decades the efforts throughout the nation to develop effective means of meeting the needs of individuals with disabilities in their own communities have been a major impetus to evaluation research, including the development of new research tools with which to measure and evaluate effectively community integration, consumer needs and satisfaction, as well as the outcomes of specific clinical or program procedures. Four of the next five chapters present the results of current field research that exemplifies that range of objectives. The fifth chapter describes and summarizes the consumer outcomes of the application of an individualized, field-based, clinical service program for persons with severe psychiatric disabilities.

In Chapter 3 Barry Willer and his colleagues describe the development, validation, and application of a functional assessment instrument to assist in planning for individualized rehabilitation training goals. They present the application of the rehabilitation model to the field of mental health and present the results of an original research study using a self-report version of their functional assessment instrument. Their findings suggest that there are differential and higher performance expectations for persons with disabilities than for persons without them.

In Chapter 4 William Knoedler and his co-workers describe a clinical service program that was developed to provide individualized and locally administered treatment, rehabilitation, and basic services in their home communities to persons with severe and persistent mental disorders. Based upon the principle of comprehensive care in natural environments, the authors describe the development, effectiveness, and dissemination of this consumer-driven, field-based rather than center- or office-based program of individualized support service, which has been implemented successfully in Wisconsin. A case study of the program operating in a large, rural county is presented.

In Chapter 5 Michael Smull, Michael Sachs, and Maureen Black describe the development, validation, and research application of a survey instrument designed to obtain information on consumer needs, wants, and current service utilization. The Community Needs Survey, the result of a collaborative effort between university researchers and state policy planners in Maryland, can be utilized on a statewide basis to provide information in a proactive manner for planning needed clinical services for individuals with developmental disabilities. A statewide study in which the instrument was used to determine the fiscal impact of the adoption of a disability definition is presented.

Chapter 6 is also about program evaluation. Wayne Silverman, Warren Zigman, and Ellen Johnson Silver present the results of a five-year follow-up of a two-year longitudinal study in New York on the effect of extending the benefits of community living to young adults with the most severe and profound developmental disabilities, including serious medical conditions. Their empirical evidence addresses the issue of whether the medical and developmental needs of individuals with the most serious impairments require residence in specialized medical settings or whether their needs can be met in small community residences. This chapter is a good example of the vicissitudes, challenges, and compromises inherent in conducting applied clinical program research.

In the final chapter in this section, John Jacobson and Lee Ackerman present the results of a statewide, original research study that examines the prevalence and conditions under which restrictive and nonrestrictive behavioral procedures are used as clinical interventions. This chapter is important in light of the controversy surrounding the use and abuse of restrictive procedures in the clinical treatment of individuals with severe disabilities. It provides much-needed empirical information upon actual current practice to provide a realistic context for policy discussions and decisions with regard to safeguards and oversight for the use of applied behavior-analytic clinical services.

The information in these chapters is germane to people concerned with important public policy issues related to the provision of clinical services to persons with disabilities. It is also relevant to people interested in a range of applied research models and their applications to the arena of human services. These chapters represent the results of recent and ongoing research efforts designed to examine and inform providers and policymakers responsible for furthering the community integration and support of persons with severe disabilities.

# 3

# Applying a Rehabilitation Model to Residential Programs for People with Severe and Persistent Mental Disorders

Barry S. Willer, Ph.D.,
John R. Guastaferro, M.S.,
Ihor Zankiw, M.B.A., M.S.,
and Rosemary Duran, M.S.W.

This chapter concerns residential alternatives to institutions for individuals with severe and persistent mental disorders. The principles of the rehabilitation model, described below, however, include the fact that the rehabilitation process is not limited to specific impairment groups and, in fact, transcends categorical distinctions based on impairment. In other words, the rehabilitation model and more specifically, functional assessment, are relevant to all impairment groups. This chapter mentions individuals with mental disorders and brain injury because of our experience with functional assessment with these populations.

Chapter 2, on the emerging trends in psychiatric rehabilitation, provides the necessary overview of recent changes in the nature, type, and philosophic basis for rehabilitation programs for individuals with mental disorders. Carling characterized the postdeinstitutionalized period in psychiatry as a paradigm shift from a transitional period in which people are viewed as recipients of service to a world view in which people with disabilities are viewed as capable and deserving of full community integration The chapter describes the problems that resulted from deinstitutionalization including homelessness and the lack of adequate housing and supports. It recommends the rehabilitation model for residential programs for individuals with mental disorders.

One of the system's responses to the deinstitutionalization movement was the development of a variety of residential alternatives to institutions. Surveys of residential alternatives, particularly those of individuals with mental retardation, indicate that most alternatives are highly custodial in

37

nature (Lakin and Bruininks 1985) and may even promote dependence through labeling and controlling individuals' lives (Biklen and Knoll 1987). Chapter 2 argues that the system has failed to recognize the true need of individuals with disabilities, namely, available affordable decent housing. Others might argue that many individuals with disabilities also require training in skill areas that are requisite to living in the available housing (Liberman, DeRisi, and Mueser 1989), and others argue further that programs are required which move the individual through a series of settings or programs which provide decreasing support as the individual demonstrates increased competence (Vorspan 1988). The assessment of competence is called *functional assessment* and is a basis for both program planning and research to determine the most effective means of meeting the community living needs of individuals with disabilities resulting from mental illness (Farkas and Anthony 1987).

One purpose of this chapter is to describe the rehabilitation model and its application to residential programs for individuals with mental disorders. The rehabilitation model is presented as an alternative to the medical model. A second purpose is to depict the development of one functional assessment instrument and to describe and evaluate a self-report version of the functional assessment instrument. This instrument was developed with the rehabilitation model in mind.

## The Rehabilitation Model

Functional assessment is a cornerstone of the rehabilitation model, which provides the operating principles for many community-based programs. Reportedly there is a wide use of the rehabilitation model in residential programs, and for this reason alone it is important to review the principles of rehabilitation as a step toward assessing whether the model is indeed being applied and whether it is ultimately effective in meeting the residential needs of individuals with mental disorders as well as the needs of other populations with disabilities.

The rehabilitation model is a product of the World Health Organization. The model proposes that an individual with a handicapping condition has three levels of difficulty which can benefit from intervention by rehabilitation professionals. The first level is *impairment*, which refers to an anatomic abnormality. The second is *disability*, which is a limitation in activity or functioning on the part of the individual that results from an impairment. The third, *handicap*, refers to the inability of the individual to fulfill age-appropriate roles of choice. Impairment exists at the organ level, disability exists at the person level, and handicap exists at the societal level (World Health Organization 1980).

Interventions at the impairment level almost all involve changing the person who has the impairment. Surgery and medication are perhaps the most common forms of intervention. Unfortunately, surgeries performed in the past, such as lobotomies, have not been found effective in dealing with the major mental disorders. Conversely, the development of psychotropic medications and their usefulness in reducing major symptoms of mental disorders have had a profound effect. Medication, however, cannot teach new skills, and psychotherapy cannot substitute for rehabilitation (Wallace et al. 1980).

Interventions at the level of disability resulting from mental disorders are only recently becoming systematized. Rehabilitation programs for individuals with physical disabilities have developed specialties that focus almost exclusively on disability, for example, physical and occupational therapy. The intervention first involves a careful assessment of strengths and limitations (functional assessment) in relationship to the overall rehabilitation goal. Interventions include:

1. Education and training, for example, teaching someone new skills or teaching skills previously learned but lost as a result of the impairment.

2. Use of prosthetic devices; replacement of a lost limb with an artificial limb, for instance.

3. Use of aids, such as a wheelchair for someone who is unable to ambulate.

4. Changing the environment, as in widening doorways or lowering a sink for someone in a wheelchair.

Generally some combination of these interventions is required to reduce the level of disability. For example, someone who uses a prosthetic device or aid frequently requires training in its use. Considerable training in transferring is required for individuals who are wheelchair bound. However, what is noteworthy is that only the first intervention, training, requires changing the individual. Each of the other possible interventions involves changing the individual's environment in some manner. To accept this requires an important philosophic leap from the interventions most often taught in preprofessional programs. Even in physical medicine one can encounter resistance to interventions that do not actually effect change in the individual, rather only the environment. For example, should someone with dexterity problems be encouraged to use shirts with Velcro fasteners or rather be trained to use conventional buttons?

Interventions at the level of handicap are currently the least understood regardless of what field of rehabilitation we are discussing. In theory, an individual has a handicap if he or she is unable to fulfill a desired age-appropriate role as a result of disabilities. If someone is unable to work, go to school, participate in a family, or have friends, then he or she has a handicap. Conversely, regardless of whether the individual has disabilities, if he or she is able to fulfill all of the desired roles, then handicap does not exist. Someone may be visually impaired, hearing impaired, or unable to dress himself and yet not have a handicap if able to fulfill these roles. The mission of a rehabilitation program is to reduce handicap.

The identification of barriers to role fulfillment has generally focused on the individual and the disabilities and not on the environment in which the individual displays abilities and disabilities. This is evidenced by the fact that we generally mix the two terms *disability* and *handicap*. In the United States at the present time the terms *disabled* and *handicapped* are even included in legislation and standards, as if synonymous. There are other barriers that increase handicap which do not relate to disabilities or even to the individual. For example, the absence of barrier-free access to public buildings reduces the likelihood that individuals with ambulation disabilities will be able to fulfill certain social roles. Social attitudes that discriminate against individuals with disabilities, particularly in employment settings, are likewise barriers that increase handicap.

The intervention strategies for eliminating barriers and reducing handicap could include the individual with the handicapping condition. For example, counseling or education might be used to facilitate role relationships within the family. Such an intervention would naturally be more effective if it involves the family, as well. Interventions with employment have been an important component of rehabilitation programs, but only recently, with the advent of supported employment programs, have these interventions attempted to change the environment as well as the individual (Ibister and Donaldson 1987). Another level of intervention which is completely outside the individual involves changing public attitudes and changing legislation or public policy that discriminate against individuals with disabilities. Chapter 2 proposes that effort should be devoted to increase the availability of housing for individuals with disabilities. Such activity is completely consistent with the rehabilitation model if indeed, lack of availability of affordable housing is a barrier to community integration and role fulfillment. Carling presents a convincing case that it is.

Many of the interventions to reduce handicap are considered outside the responsibility of the mental health professional and have become the responsibility of advocacy groups. However, there are two principles that are considered essential to an effective rehabilitation program which serve to link professional interventions at the impairment and disability level to intervention at the handicap level. The first is the principle of *least restrictiveness*, and the second is the principle of *empowerment*. Least restrictiveness, in simple terms suggests that a professional intervention, however effective at reducing impairment, should not restrict the freedom of the individual to pursue chosen roles (Turnbull et al. 1981). As an example, the medication used to reduce behavioral symptoms of brain damage violates the least restrictiveness principle if it significantly limits the individual's interactions with others. The principle of empowerment relates to the *choice* component of role fulfillment. To experience no handicap means that the individual is fulfilling his or her *chosen* life roles. The implication is, to the extent possible, the individual must be informed and involved in every rehabilitation decision including assessment and intervention.

## The Application of the Rehabilitation Model to Mental Health

Anthony, Cohen, and Farkas (1986) provided a blueprint for the characteristics of a psychiatric rehabilitation program. The five essential ingredients are listed below:

1. *Functional assessment* of individual skills in relation to environmental demands.

2. *Consumer involvement* in the rehabilitation assessment and intervention phases.

3. *Systematic individual rehabilitation plans.*

4. *Direct teaching and programming* of individual skills.

5. *Environmental and resource assessment and modification.*

Functional assessment plays a key role in establishing the rehabilitation plan with the individual and refers to a systematic evaluation of the limitations in activities considered necessary for daily living. The World Health

Organization (1980) outlined a minimum list of 17 such activities and included the ability to walk, talk, hear, read, and carry objects. Most of these are not limited for individuals with mental disorders. The primary focus of functional assessment for individuals with severe and persistent mental disorders should be activities of daily living because these are commonly limited for this population and because they serve as the primary impediments to living in a less restrictive setting. Assessment is completed relative to the overall rehabilitation goal.

The ideal functional assessment instrument has undergone appropriate psychometric testing (i.e., it has identified reliability coefficients and some indications of validity) ánd is normed to the population in question. Normative data in this instance refer to the need to have some indication of the minimum levels of functional independence required for various levels of restrictiveness or support in the residential program. A number of years ago we became involved in designing and testing a functional assessment instrument for individuals with mental disorders who were residing in a community residential program. This instrument, called the Community Living Assessment Scale (CLAS) will be described in more detail later; however, it is important to note that we designed the scale precisely because there were few available assessment instruments for this purpose. Functional assessment also implies a need to evaluate environmental demands. If we are determining the ability of individuals to prepare their own meals while the residential program staff actually prepares them then there is no *environmental demand* on the individual to learn this task. The absence of opportunity to express skills is an important component of restrictiveness. In designing the CLAS we struggled with this issue from a measurement standpoint and concluded that *if the individual is unable to express a specific behavior, regardless of the reason, then the individual is scored 0 on that behavior item.* Staff in residential programs have argued with us that this is unfair to the client, that if he or she is capable of expressing a skill but not given the opportunity to express it, then the score should still reflect the client's abilities. Our response is that indeed *it is unfair to the client to not be afforded the opportunity to express a skill,* and this unfairness should be reflected in the measurement.

The second characteristic of a rehabilitation program is meaningful involvement of the consumer in the rehabilitation process. This is perhaps the most significant difference between the rehabilitation model and the medical model. In the medical model the problem or disorder is assumed to rest within the individual, and the treatments are aimed at changing him or her. In the rehabilitation model it must be determined whether the problem rests in the individual or in the individual's environment. Participation of the individual is important to making this determination.

Determining the extent to which individuals are involved in their rehabilitation is very difficult. Individuals with mental disorders are, almost by definition, disenfranchised. The diagnosis of mental disorders is often determined by the level and extent to which the individual has *poor judgment*. How do we involve those with poor judgment in assessing their own needs or in determining appropriate goals? Anthony and colleagues would ask, what have we gained if we do not?

Individual treatment plans are basic to a good treatment program whether the program is based on the medical model or the rehabilitation model. Individual plans should spell out specific interventions attached to specific (behavioral) goals and ideally, a time period when the goal should be accomplished. Several important components separate a *rehabilitation plan* from a (medical) treatment plan. The long-term goal of a rehabilitation program is to reduce the level of handicap experienced by the individual. Long-term goals should reflect role performance specifically and should identify barriers to expression of certain roles. There should be an indication that the individual with a mental disorder has had some say in what role activities may be enhanced.

The short-term objectives of an overall rehabilitation goal plan must reflect specific skills that, if developed, should decrease barriers to overcoming handicap. Again, the role of the consumer in the selection process should be explicit. In addition, a functional assessment procedure with collaboration between the staff and the individual should be used to assist in setting priorities among skill development steps. The interventions used to reduce disabilities—that is, to accomplish the short-term goals—should reflect both the change in the individual and the teaching techniques needed to accomplish this and also the change in the environment to increase the opportunity and demand for the expression of the skill.

Evaluation of the rehabilitation plan should reflect the extent of goal attainment, improvement in functional skills and satisfaction of the individual with a mental disorder. Evaluation of individual rehabilitation plans is not equivalent to evaluation of a rehabilitation program (Fuhrer 1987).

There are three teaching situations for individuals with mental disorders. First is the situation in which the client has never learned the skill and therefore must be taught a *new* skill. Second is teaching a skill that was learned previously but was either lost (generally after a period of decompensation or a long period of institutionalization) or is not expressed to the degree required by the environment. Third is the situation in which individuals with disabilities must be taught skills that would not normally have to be learned except as compensation for these disabilities. In developing the CLAS we compared the living skills of individuals who had mental disorders with other individuals who had never been diagnosed as mentally ill. The results indicated that many who have never been diagnosed as mentally ill had little occasion to learn how to manage the public transit system or to develop an awareness of the side effects of their medications.

Although the teaching of new skills is only one part of the rehabilitation intervention process, Anthony and colleagues emphasized this factor because it is so often overlooked in programs that claim to be rehabilitative in nature. Programs that emphasize teaching set aside specific times for this purpose. The individual rehabilitation plans reflect the skills to be taught, and the teaching strategy is specific to the type of skill to be taught.

An important aspect of teaching skills is to recognize the importance of generalizability. In most instances we attempt to teach skills in one location with the assumption that use of the skills will carry over to other locations. Thus, the individual may be taught banking skills in a day a treatment program with the hope that the individual will use those skills the next time he or she deposits a check or pays a bill. We know from research that individuals are most likely to retain a skill and use it most effectively if the skill is learned in that setting in which it is expected to be expressed. This principle of limited generalizability is especially true with young children and with individuals who may have impairments of cognitive functioning. Individuals with severe and persistent mental disorders often have behavioral characteristics and neurophysiologic indicators of impaired judgment and cognitive dysfunction.

The principle of limited generalizability has important implications for planning effective rehabilitation services. Supported employment programs have proved to be reasonably effective at encouraging learning of new skills and more successful placement of individuals with handicapping conditions (Danley and Anthony 1987). These programs operate, in part, on the principle that skills learned on the job site will be retained more effectively than skills learned in some other site such as a sheltered workshop. There is a growing recognition that supported residential programs may be more effective than transitional residential programs for some clients (Blanch, Carling, and Ridgway 1988). In supported residential programs, skills are taught in the setting in which the individual is expected to continue to live.

As pointed out earlier the rehabilitation model encourages the examination of the individual's functional skills along with a clear assessment of the environmental context within which the skills are expressed. The rehabilitation model is described by some as exceedingly practical. If the end result of living in a less restrictive environment and the reasonable fulfillment of desired roles can be obtained by changing the environment, then so be it. If the individual who is wheelchair bound cannot work because there is no way to get out of his house then we consider it perfectly appropriate to build a ramp. Environmental change strategies within psychiatric rehabilitation programs are sometimes regarded as taking the easy way out.

Consider the following example. A young man with brain damage resulting from an auto accident lives on his own in a small apartment. He is extremely routinized, and if nothing interferes with that routine he gets through the day in fine fashion, including attending his place of employment. Every morning he gets up, pours a bowl of cereal, eats, dresses, and catches the bus. One morning he found he was out of milk for his cereal. He proceeded to the nearby corner store to purchase milk, but the fact that he was still wearing his pajamas created some embarrassment in the store. The resolution to this problem could have been to *teach* the young man new skills, for example, what to do when he runs out of milk. However, he would then also have to be taught what to do when he runs out of cereal. The supported living coach resolved the problem, in consultation with the young man, by having him begin sleeping in a jogging suit rather than pajamas. For this situation and for this individual the solution worked. It was the least restrictive and most effective intervention that addressed a limitation for him.

## The Development of a Functional Assessment Scale

The development of the CLAS (Willer and Guastaferro 1989) required several generations of the instrument, each undergoing systematic psychometric assessment. Initially, a list of areas of functioning essential to living successfully in an unsupervised or semisupervised facility was developed. Anthony and Margules (1974) and others provided lists of skill categories that are considered essential. Instruments to assess the functional living skills of people with mental retardation, especially the Mid-Nebraska Independent Functioning Scale (Schalock 1976), provided an array of potential skill catgories and specific items. Interviews with the staff of the residential program added further to the listing of necessary skills. All versions of the CLAS were based on staff ratings of skills.

The initial CLAS listed 368 behavioral skill items in eight categories and was used to assess 157 residents of Transitional Services, Inc. Assessments were completed by two independent raters. After correlational analysis, items that did not correlate highly with other items in the same skill category and those displaying poor interrater reliability were eliminated. The final version of the CLAS contained 68 items in nine subscales, each representing a relatively distinct skill category. The mean score for each subscale is 50 with a standard deviation of 10.

The instrument was assessed for split-half and test-retest reliability and for internal consistency of subscales. Predictive validity and instrument sensitivity were assessed at three-month and two-year follow-up, using ratings of general improvement in independence and life satisfaction as dependent variables. In addition, construct validity was assessed by administering the CLAS to a nonpsychiatric sample and a sample from the population of interest matched on age and sex. Face validity was assessed by residential staff.

Several observations are worthy of note on the nature of functional assessment and the prediction of outcome after the transition through a residential program for individuals with disabilities resulting from mental disorders. First, functional assessment results were not only predictive of community living skills two years after assessment but were also reasonably good predictors of independent living and life satisfaction. However, functional scores on community living skills were generally not good predictors of rehospitalization. The only functional area that related to rehospitalization was the inability of the individual to manage his or her finances effectively. An informal check into the relationship between financial management and rehospitalization revealed a domino effect: poor financial management defined as the inability to pay the rent at the end of the month greatly increased stress and the need for asylum (the need for a less stressful environment and a place to live).

The comparison of community living skills of individuals with mental disorders and a matched sample of individuals without mental disorders revealed unanticipated results. Individuals with mental disorders were less functional than individuals who reportedly did not have disorders, but the magnitude of the difference was not as dramatic as one might expect. In fact, in functional areas more familiar to individuals with mental disorders, such as use of the health care system and management of medication, individuals with mental disorders were generally more capable.

## The Development of the Self-rating Form of the CLAS

For the purpose of the current chapter and because of the growing belief that individuals with mental disorders should be actively involved in their own rehabilitation process we created and tested a self-report version of the CLAS. To create the self-rating version of the CLAS, each item of the staff rating version was rewritten to reflect the tense and first-person nature of each statement to which an individual could answer *true* or *false*. We consulted with a group of consumers who were members of a psychosocial club and had them review the items for relevance and clarity of statement. We administered a pilot version of the self-rating scale to a sample of consumers and eliminated items that were always answered in the affirmative. This led to a reduction of approximately one third of the items including all of the items in the personal management subscale. Regardless of the hygiene habits one has, it seems that everyone reports personal cleanliness as impeccable. A second generation of the self-rating version was created. There are 43 items, and each is associated with one of eight areas of community living skill (see the appendix for a copy of the instrument).

The two principal questions we looked at with the next two samples of consumers who tested the self-rating version of the CLAS were: How do the staff ratings of an individual correlate with the self-ratings? and How do individuals with mental disorders compare with individuals who do not (apparently) have mental disorders?

To answer the first question, the self-CLAS was administered to a sample of 43 individuals (21 males and 22 females) currently residing in a community residential program for individuals with mental disorders. Each had a primary mental illness diagnosis. The average age of this sample was 32.5. These individuals were also assessed on the CLAS by mental health workers who were trained in the use of it.

To answer the second question, the self-CLAS was administered to a sample of individuals who worked in the mental health field and reportedly did not have mental disorders. These individuals did not work in the program that served the first sample of individuals, nor were they familiar with the CLAS or self-CLAS. This sample consisted of 24 individuals with an average age of 33.3 (8 males, 16 females).

Pearson correlations between subscales on the self-rating of the CLAS and the staff ratings averaged .57 across each of the skill areas for the 43 individuals with mental disorders. All of the Pearson correlation coefficients were significant at the $p < .01$ level.

Table 3.1 presents the mean scores of individuals with mental disorders on the self-CLAS and the mean scores for the mental health professionals. The results indicate that individuals with mental disorders perceived themselves at the same level or above that of mental health workers in the various areas of community living.

Table 3.1. Means and ANOVA F-Values for Community Living Skill
Categories for Individuals with Mental Disorders and for Mental
Health Professionals

| Community Living Functional Skill Area | Individuals with Mental Disorders (N = 43) | Mental Health Professionals (N = 24) | ANOVA F-Value (Probability) |
|---|---|---|---|
| Nutritional management | 31.8 | 32.5 | 0.03 (.86) |
| Money management | 32.6 | 35.4 | 0.65 (.42) |
| Home management | 35.4 | 25.0 | 10.08 (.01) |
| Medical management | 40.4 | 29.7 | 10.94 (.01) |
| Time management | 32.8 | 34.2 | 0.16 (.68) |
| Community use | 29.7 | 22.5 | 3.94 (.05) |
| Problem solving | 34.3 | 37.0 | 0.55 (.46) |
| Safety management | 37.5 | 27.7 | 5.47 (.02) |

These findings would have been more surprising if we had not conducted the earlier study on the staff-rating version of the CLAS. First, it appears that individuals with mental disorders are capable of assessing their
own skill levels and deficits and that their assessments do not vary significantly from those of the staff of the residential training program in which
they live.

The other important observation and conclusion are that individuals
with mental disorders may, indeed, have more skills in some areas of community living than do individuals who do not have mental disorders because the former group is in a residential living program in which these skills
are specifically taught and reinforced. It is also possible that individuals
with mental disorders *must have greater skills* to compensate for other deficits. For example, many of our mental health professional sample scored
very low on home management, which means that either someone else
looks after the cleaning and maintenance of the home or it is not getting
done. Individuals with mental disorders rarely have the opportunity to have
natural supports manage these aspects of their lives (unless they live in an
institution).

These data and the finding that individuals with mental disorders appear
to be functioning at a higher level in some areas of community living skills
point to one other possible conclusion. The individuals in the current study
all reside in a community residential program and may have developed sufficient skill levels to live in less supervised or less restrictive settings. This

may reflect the tendency for the mental health system to be overprotective and to restrict the movement of individuals to better integrated residential alternatives.

## Conclusions

The rehabilitation model has been applied very well with other disability groups and is highly applicable to individuals with severe and persistent mental disorders. The medical model represents considerable inertia, but as programs adopt the characteristics of rehabilitation programs, that is, have systematic functional assessment, involvement of the consumer in assessment and goal setting, have individual habilitation plans, provide goal-directed interventions with both the consumer and the environment, the ideology of rehabilitation is likely to follow. This ideology is best represented by its purpose: to enable the individual to function successfully in chosen environments with the least amount of professional intervention required *despite the presence of disabilities.*

The development of a functional assessment instrument has been informative about the process of community integration. This is especially true of the development of the self-report version of the scale. First, it appears that functional skill deficits are better predictors of outcome than diagnostic categories or psychiatric symptoms. For example, the ability to handle one's personal finances may be more critical to living independently than the absence of hallucinations. Second, it is possible that individuals with severe and persistent mental disorders must be *more skilled* in some areas of community living than are individuals who have not experienced mental illness. Individuals who have mental disorders may be less likely to have a relationship with someone else who, for example, manages their financial affairs or keeps the home up to standard.

Following the rehabilitation model, it is possible that many individuals with severe and persistent mental disorders living in residential programs already have sufficient skills to live independently. If there is available affordable decent housing, as pointed out in Chapter 2, these individuals could and perhaps should be living more independently. If their environment, or more precisely, someone in their environment, *compensated* for their disabilities (even if temporarily until the individuals adopt the skills themselves) then independent living could be a reality.

The rehabilitation model represents potentially a more effective and more humanistic approach to the provision of community-based services for

individuals with severe and persistent mental disorders. However, more research is required on the efficacy and benefit costs of programs that adopt the
model.

## Appendix

The following list of activities is considered important to independent
living. As part of the process of including you in your own rehabilitation
program, we would like to know whether you *regularly complete* each activity *without the assistance of others.*

Circle T (TRUE) if you regularly complete the activity, on your own,
without having to be reminded by others.

Circle F (FALSE) if you do not complete the activity.

Circle F (FALSE) if someone else completes the activity for you.

Circle F (FALSE) if someone else has to remind you to complete the
activity.

Circle F (FALSE) if the activity is not completed.

|  |  |  |
|---|---|---|
| 1. Prepare a list before going shopping. | T | F |
| 2. Make deposits and withdrawals at the bank. | T | F |
| 3. Make my bed each day. | T | F |
| 4. Remain on the same medication until it is changed by my doctor. | T | F |
| 5. Allow enough time for each planned activity. | T | F |
| 6. Am familiar with services provided by community agencies. | T | F |
| 7. Have planned escape route from my house in case of a fire. | T | F |
| 8. Follow a list when buying groceries. | T | F |
| 9. Ask for help to resolve banking problems. | T | F |
| 10. Change the bed sheets (once per week). | T | F |
| 11. Plan fun activities throughout the week. | T | F |
| 12. Am aware of the various services provided by the post office. | T | F |

13. Discuss personal problems without anger.                    T   F

14. Substitute cheaper items when shopping.                    T   F

15. Pick up clothes from floor and furniture (every day).       T   F

16. Fill my prescriptions before they run out.                  T   F

17. Keep activities written on the calendar.                    T   F

18. Am familiar with services provided by local                 T   F
    rental agencies.

19. Look for assistance when I am unable to solve               T   F
    a problem or conflict.

20. Disinfect and bandage minor cuts.                           T   F

21. Check expiration dates on foods.                            T   F

22. Pay debts and bills on time.                                T   F

23. Vacuum the carpets (once per week).                         T   F

24. Set an alarm clock to wake up (each day).                   T   F

25. Read a bus schedule.                                        T   F

26. Discuss personal problems with a friend.                    T   F

27. Clean the toilet bowl (once per week).                      T   F

28. Keep emergency numbers by the phone.                        T   F

29. Cook entire meal (each day).                                T   F

30. Follow money saving tips for groceries.                     T   F

31. Clean the sinks (once per week).                            T   F

32. Arrive on time for all appointments.                        T   F

33. Plan activities with others.                                T   F

34. Discuss disagreements in a calm way.                        T   F

35. Follow recipe or package instructions to prepare food.      T   F

36. Scrub the floors (once per week).                           T   F

37. Attend scheduled health or day program.                     T   F

38. Keep aware of current events through newspapers             T   F
    or television.

39. Sometimes contact a local taxi service for transportation.     T    F

40. Complete recertification required by income source             T    F
    (Social Security, welfare, etc.).

41. Read a map of the city.                                        T    F

42. Throw away garbage (each day).                                 T    F

43. Clean the stove after each use.                                T    F

# 4

# Supporting People with Mental Illness Regardless of Their Environment

## The Wisconsin Experience

William Knoedler, M.D., Elaine R. Carpenter, M.S.N., S. Sinikka McCabe, M.S., Pat Rutkowski, M.S.S.W., and Deborah Allness, M.S.S.W.

In the United States the responsibility for providing treatment, rehabilitation, and basic services to people with psychiatric disabilities has traditionally fallen on the shoulders of state government, with most care provided in inpatient institutions. Only in the last three decades have policies and resources of this public system shifted toward mental health services in the community, particularly through such organized approaches as community support programs (CSPs; Stroul 1989).

A number of states have had long-term experience in providing comprehensive care in the community to people with psychiatric disabilities, usually through mental health programs that are administered and operated locally. In a few of these states, such as Wisconsin, these local programs have provided all or most of these services in the client's natural milieu, using this milieu to enhance treatment and rehabilitation outcomes. Because of their relative success in this area, the mental health systems of these states are often imitated in the development of services elsewhere. Unfortunately, such imitation too often focuses on the current and overt workings of these systems rather than the basic factors that have fostered them. An understanding of these factors is critical if the experience of these states is to be utilized effectively.

In this chapter, we describe and discuss three factors that have fostered the development of effective CSP services in Wisconsin. These factors, all with strong historical roots, include: (1) a public policy tradition of local control of mental health programs as well as of services in the least restrictive setting possible, under the umbrella of statewide mandated standards of care; (2) the timely availability of a practicable, comprehensive, and effective model of providing treatment, rehabilitation, and basic services to people with psychiatric disabilities in natural environments; and (3) the consistent provision of competent technical assistance by state government to counties to promote CSP development.

After discussing these factors we will show how they have worked together to develop effective CSP services in one specific county, a county that has itself participated in providing technical assistance statewide.

## Factor One. A Progressive Tradition of Providing Mental Health Services in People's Home Communities and within the Framework of Local Control and State Standards of Care

Several ingredients contributed to the emphasis by the Wisconsin mental health system on local control of services and on the least restrictive settings for persons with psychiatric disabilities. These ingredients are: (1) a tradition of county governments taking the responsibility to develop, provide, and fund services for elders and persons with disabilities; (2) a philosophy of community treatment which emphasized uniform quality of care and accessibility to treatment across the state; (3) the consistent leadership of state Division of Mental Hygiene (later state Office of Mental Health) staff who remained in key positions long enough to implement long-range plans and who had the power, authority, and tenacity to advocate for change with the legislature, state bureaucracy, and local agencies; (4) the involvement of many citizen organizations and governmental bodies in the planning process to ensure support and shared ownership; and (5) the development of an effective model of community treatment by the Training in Community Living/ Program of Assertive Community Treatment (TCL/PACT) research program at Mendota Mental Health Institute. Several key political, clinical, and fiscal decisions and opportunities fashioned these ingredients and had the greatest impact on the system.

Historically, the state hospitals were the pivotal locus of treatment for persons with psychiatric disabilities. Wisconsin's two state institutions, Mendota and Winnebago, were established more than 100 years ago to provide acute rather than long-term psychiatric care. In the late 1880s, the legislature decided not to build additional state hospitals when these two facilities were at capacity but rather to provide financial incentives to encourage counties to develop locally operated long-term care facilities for people with psychiatric disabilities. This decision, based on the belief that counties were in a better position to develop effective local services, had a long-lasting impact on how the mental health system of Wisconsin was shaped, and it prevented the development of the large state hospital campuses seen in other states.

By the early 1900s, 35 county-owned and -operated facilities were scattered across the state. Patients were transferred from the state hospital to these facilities after stabilization. With time, many facilities improved in quality so that they were able to admit acute care patients as well. Counties also received an increased amount of state funding as an incentive to plan for and move patients back to the community. These early decisions served as the first steps toward placing with county governments responsibility for inpatient and community mental health services.

The next step occured in 1959 when the state Council on Mental Health recommended legislation to require already existing maternal/child guidance clinics to broaden their mission and become all-purpose community mental health clinics for people with psychiatric disabilities. This recommendation reflected the first recognition at the legislative level that many people discharged from the state mental hospitals needed ongoing care in the least restrictive environment in the community.

This community mental health initiative was opposed by the existing private nonprofit maternal/child clinics. To counter this opposition the state Division of Mental Hygiene established a planning office at the state Department of Health and Social Services. This office began a three-year process involving more than 5,000 persons in local, regional, and state level committees to gain local support for, and participation in, this initiative. This process eventually led to the introduction of the progressive community mental health legislation, known as the Chapter 51, Wisconsin Mental Health Act. It took yet another four years and two legislative sessions before the law passed in 1972. At this critical time the consistency and tenacity of leadership at the state level were crucial in passing the legislation. This act has been the foundation for subsequent progress in the development of care for people with psychiatric disabilities. The objective of this act was to bring the full range of mental health and other services to people where they live through a community-based system of care. It placed responsibility with county governments to establish mental health, alcohol/drug abuse, and developmental disability service boards to ensure the least restrictive community treatment and rehabilitation services to residents of each county.

Most state hospital funding was shifted to local mental health boards, which became fiscally responsible for state hospital care. Stein and Ganser (1983) wrote that Wisconsin was one of the first states to recognize that the manner in which the mental health care delivery system is organized and financed is a powerful tool in shaping the actual services that are delivered. Because of the fixed point of fiscal responsibility, there is a natural incentive for the county governments to develop community-based alternatives to more costly institutional care.

Major changes in Wisconsin's involuntary civil commitment process were incorporated into the Mental Health Act in the early 1970s. These changes established standards for dangerousness and outlined a commitment process that ensured protection of civil rights. Further, commitment is made to the county mental health board in a way that guarantees the least restrictive and most appropriate treatment setting. This change further reinforced the effect and impact of the Mental Health Act.

In the early 1970s when the counties began shouldering an increasing fiscal responsibility for state hospital care, Mendota Mental Health Institute developed the Training in Community Living (TCL) model to treat in the community persons with psychiatric disabilities. Client outcome data provided substantial evidence that this model increased the community tenure of consumers and improved their level of functioning. Convinced that new and more effective approaches to community treatment were available, the state identified $876,000 of flexible inpatient funding in 1978 and shifted these dollars to the counties as "capacity building funds" to develop community-based services. Basic service components and client characteristics identified by TCL were incorporated by the state into Community Support Program guidelines that directed the expenditures of these funds.

During the next decade, the CSP guidelines became more detailed, and compliance was increasingly required by the state. In 1983 the Mental Health Act was amended to add CSP as a mandatory county mental health service. This legislation also directed the Office of Mental Health to promulgate CSP standards to guarantee more uniformity in program quality across counties. To ensure continued, solid funding for CSPs, the Wisconsin Medicaid Plan was amended in 1989 to reimburse CSP services through the rehabilitation option. The state Mental Health Act amendment, CSP standards, and Medicaid coverage for CSP have been crucial in making CSP a core community program component that cannot be erased by shift in political leadership or by the changing commitment of a particular county.

These ingredients that have shaped Wisconsin's progressive tradition in mental health policy and legislation are the collective expression of a shared vision of life possibilities for persons with psychiatric disabilities. In this vision, individuals are seen as capable of controlling the symptoms of their illness, working in regular jobs, and living in normal homes in their own communities, *if* competent, flexible, and individualized mental health treatment and rehabilitation services are provided to them. The vision is based on the philosophy of "least restrictive, most appropriate treatment" and is shared by state level policymakers, many local mental health administrators and clinicians, an increasing number of local and state level elected officials, family members, and consumers.

## Factor Two. The Development of a Viable Clinical Model: Training in Community Living

Within the Wisconsin public mental health system, a well researched and demonstrated model of comprehensive care for people with psychiatric disabilities was developed which provided a concrete and proven methodology for the statewide reorganization of CSP services. Further, the clinicians and researchers who developed this model have themselves provided consultation and technical assistance to the public system.

This model, the TCL, is the product of the Program of Assertive Community Treatment (PACT) of Mendota Mental Health Institute, one of two state inpatient mental health facilities. In the late 1960s a group of talented clinicians and researchers at Mendota conducted a series of treatment trials with inpatients who had extensive histories of hospitalization, all with the purpose of shortening hospital stays and improving symptomatology and functioning. This work, which arose primarily out of frustration with the institutional nature of care and low level of functioning of these patients, did not lead to successful treatment innovations in the inpatient unit itself but had the unexpected result of stimulating efforts to help patients readapt to their home communities. This in vivo work seemed more successful than the treatment provided on the inpatient unit and led to the construction of a set of ideas and practices which became the basis for the TCL model and its extensive provision of services in the community.

Although having a somewhat serendipitous beginning, the TCL model developed thereafter quite logically. Marx, Stein, and Test, the creators of the model, understood that three problems explained the historically poor functioning and high rates of rehospitalization of former patients: (1) low stress tolerance in a variety of practical life situations; (2) inadequate skills in critical life role areas; and (3) excessive dependence on support systems and institutions (Stein and Test 1980; Test, in press). It was clear to them that their new approach needed the following characteristics in order to address these problems directly: (1) a high degree of comprehensiveness of care with most essential clinical, rehabilitative, and basic service elements provided by a single treatment team that holds responsibility for a designated group of clients; and (2) provision of the majority of care in those community settings in which clients live, work, and recreate to minimize problems with transfer of learning. Additionally, in-community services should be provided assertively to lessen drop-out and to maximize involvement in care; and (3) a focus in psychologic and social therapies on teaching clients various coping and community living skills and on providing them with necessary emotional, cognitive, and practical supports (Stein and Test 1980; Test, in press).

By 1970 the basic TCL model was formulated and then applied in a small study to determine its feasibility and short-term efficacy (Stein, Test, and Marx 1975). This study showed the model to be both practicable and effective and led to an expanded research program in which the TCL model was investigated on a larger scale and for a longer period of time.

In this second phase of research the TCL model was compared with a more traditional model of care which, in 1972, consisted of short inpatient treatment followed by outpatient counseling, medication follow-up, and aftercare groups.

This research produced the following results, all in favor of TCL: (1) a marked decrease in number of days per year in psychiatric institutions and in hospital admissions; (2) greater sheltered employment and earnings from competitive employment; (3) more contact with trusted friends and more social groups belonged to and attended; (4) more time spent in independent living; (5) a greater satisfaction with life; and (6) a significant lessening of symptomatology (Test and Stein 1980; Test, in press).

Additionally, cost benefit analyses showed the TCL approach to be slightly less expensive than the traditional model, taking into account both direct and indirect costs of treatment as well as economic benefits gained (Weisbrod, Test, and Stein 1980). Social costs, as measured by stress on family and time in jail, were roughly equal between the two groups (Test and Stein 1980).

Two other smaller studies followed this major investigation, each focusing on different areas of practice within the TCL model itself (i.e., vocational rehabilitation and family psychoeducation). In 1978 the PACT staff began a longitudinal investigation to study the comparative efficacy of the TCL model as provided to young adults with schizophrenia spectrum disorders. This project, which uses the present Dane County system of care as the control group, is still in progress and will end in 1991. Results to date show the same advantages for the TCL method as demonstrated in the earlier study (Test, Knoedler, and Allness 1985; Test et al. 1985, 1989). Currently, the PACT staff is developing methodologies for serving young adult persons with a "dual diagnosis" of psychiatric disabilities and alcohol and/or substance abuse (Knoedler, 1988; Test et al. 1989).

The implementation of this model by the PACT program has been quite consistent throughout the last 20 years. It has remained a small (15 full-time staff) multidisciplinary team of mostly professionally degreed clinicians and rehabilitators who provide 24-hour, seven-day-a-week comprehensive care to a designated group of clients (currently 120) who have severe and persistent mental illnesses. Community support services that are usually referred to specialized agencies in other models of care, such as vocational rehabilitation, crisis intervention, and chemical dependence treatment, are provided by PACT itself. Guided by individualized treatment plans, this team meets each day to review the status of each client and then disperses into the community to carry out its work. Services are guaranteed to each client as long as needed and wherever he or she resides.

It is apparent that a primary thrust of the TCL model has been to provide comprehensive care in natural environments in order to enhance the effectiveness of services. This aspect of the TCL model, and the work of the PACT program, converged quite early with new mental health policy and legislation in Wisconsin to improve services for people with psychiatric disabilities. In essence, the TCL model arose at a time that was opportune for it to provide the evidential base for the early funding and development of the Wisconsin CSP program.

MODEL DISSEMINATION

In 1974, soon after it became clear that the TCL model was effective, the PACT staff began to provide informal consultation and technical assistance to local programs throughout the state. By 1976 consultation became more formalized and joined with similar efforts by the Wisconsin Office of Mental Health (Field, Allness, and Knoedler 1980). Since the mid-1970s the PACT program has consulted at one time or another with the majority of Wisconsin counties (Allness, Knoedler, and Test 1985).

Additionally, quite early the senior members of the PACT staff began collaborating with policymakers at the state level to assist in CSP development. These staff have been involved in a variety of critical ways, with the most recent example being their participation in the formulation of Wisconsin CPS standards and Medicaid plan described before (Allness, Knoedler, and Test 1985). In the United States and abroad the TCL model has also been used extensively in various clinical settings from rural to heavily urbanized areas. The PACT staff, because of their great interest in replicability of the model, have promulgated and assisted this dissemination through on-site consultation. In five of these replications the model has been subjected to controlled investigation. So far, these studies have confirmed the original results in Madison and have provided the basis for use of the model elsewhere (Witheridge and Dincin 1985).

PACT consulting staff found that to use the TCL model optimally, administrators and clinicians of most mental health systems must reconceptualize how they provide services to the seriously mentally ill and must have the patience and will to implement this new approach over a number of years. In particular, they must move away from viewing CSP services as an array of individual agency providers glued together by case managers and instead begin seeing that these services can be provided comprehensively and longitudinally by single teams. Most often local systems change by first developing one or more pilot TCL teams that then provide the experiential and evidential basis for further implementation.

## Factor Three. The Provision of Technical Assistance and Training to Ensure Quality Community Programming

Very early the Wisconsin Office of Mental Health recognized that the skills and knowledge of local service staff were critical in providing effective community treatment, rehabilitation, and support services. In the 1960s this office began employing clinicians in the field to develop policies and provide training and technical assistance. Furthermore, the Mental Health Act of 1972 broadened the role of state hospitals to include the provision of technical assistance and training to local programs.

When the state began funding County CSPs in the late 1970s, a considerable technical assistance effort was launched by the state Office of Mental Health. Clinician experts from the PACT program provided extensive consultation to the initial CSP pilot programs to improve staff clinical knowledge and skills whereas state staff provided assistance in program organizational development and in financing. Over the last decade this two-pronged format of providing both clinical and organizational-fiscal technical assistance has continued to prove its effectiveness.

Technical assistance to county CSPs has typically included the following activities: (1) overall assessments of the capacity of the local system to provide mental health services in the community, including evaluation of CSP and crisis intervention services and evaluation of the use of community resources to help consumers work and live in the community; (2) organizational development to restructure or strengthen the community support program operation; (3) identification of funding sources for CSPs, including shifting funds from restrictive services (group homes, sheltered workshops, day treatment, inpatient settings) to more community-based, flexible services (CSP, community work opportunities, normal housing); and (4) clinical consultation regarding: staff skills training in treatment and rehabilitation; program operations such as record keeping and Medicaid billing; and development and implementation of individualized community based treatment plans. Consultation is provided usually through side-by-side teaching and modeling with frequent (sometimes monthly) follow-up visits to review practices and to teach additional skills. Additionally, county CSP staff are encouraged to visit other successful CSPs.

The interrelatedness of clinical and organizational-fiscal technical assistance needs resulted in the development of a technical assistance staff pool that included the state Office of Mental Health policy and program development staff and clinicians who were working full-time in local CSPs. Although PACT and Green County CSP have been the main sources of clinical consultants, staff from Vernon, Columbia, Oneida, Outagamie, Winnebago, and Dane Counties have also provided consultation. Clinical consultation time has been provided without charge although when Wisconsin received federal CSP funds from the National Institute of Mental Health some of these funds were used to reimburse local clinicians or their employers for their consultation time.

For those counties that ask for technical assistance, the Office of Mental Health assembles a team of policy developers and clinician experts which is custom-designed to respond to the request. The assistance varies from systems assessments to clinical case consultation to assisting a local CSP to upgrade areas of weakness so it can be certified for Medicaid reimbursement.

Although free expert consultation at first glance seems like a good idea, at first many county CPSs did not request assistance. To counter this situation, the Office of Mental Health developed different approaches to increase the counties' receptivity to outside help. In one approach, to assist a reluctant but needy CSP, state staff initiate a site visit to monitor program compliance with legislatively and administratively mandated population and service component guidelines. These guidelines, and later the CSP standards, have enabled state staff to access local mental health programs in order to monitor and ensure program and fiscal compliance. The site visit is followed by a report that identifies areas needing improvement, offers technical assistance, and suggests sanctions for noncompliance. The second step is the provision of follow-up technical assistance (often by different consultants) to begin implementing the needed changes. In this "good guy–bad guy" routine, the team work between policy and program developers and clinicians has proven extremely successful, and has resulted in substantial systems improvement in some counties over several years.

For example, when the northern regional director designated CSP development as a priority initiative a team of Office of Mental Health policy staff and local clinicians conducted site visits in each county CSP. Specific written observations and recommendations were shared with the county mental health directors and the regional director. As a follow-up, specific assistance was provided to county mental health directors on contracting issues, and the CSP clinicians in several counties received monthly assistance in conducting mental health assessments and in developing treatment plans that focused on in vivo services. Another CSP received follow-up technical assistance in developing a community service plan for a 32-year-old man who for several years had lived at state mental health institutions and in highly staffed residential facilities. The service plan developed for him provided an apartment in the community and focused heavily on employment in a normal work setting. Consultation provided to this CSP also involved program development consultation to expand the CSP staffing to serve this man with the funds (about $60,000/year) that had been spent on his hospital care and could now be redirected to build CSP program capacity.

In another approach, often combined with the previous one, local CSP staff are invited to visit exemplary programs, especially the PACT program, the Green County CSP, and the Dane County Mental Health Center. These site visits demonstrate in a concrete way that effective, flexible, and ongoing treatment, rehabilitation, and support services can be developed in urban and rural areas. This approach was particularly necessary during the early work of CSP implementation and is still used to change the attitudes of new staff and decision makers such as local and state elected officials. Because the hosting of visitors from other counties requires considerable staff time by the host program, the Office of Mental Health has used federal grant funds to reimburse host sites for the staff time required for site visits.

Additionally, more traditional staff training approaches have been used including statewide conferences, regional meetings, and newsletters. Over the past two years, a concentrated effort has been made to develop basic skills training modules for CSP workers. The first such module trained staff statewide in 1989 in the use of the Brief Psychiatric Rating Scale (Overall and Gorham 1962). The Office of Mental Health is also working with the School of Social Work of the University of Wisconsin-Madison to develop curriculum and field placement experiences for social work students with a strong emphasis on serving persons with psychiatric disabilities in the community.

The benefits of these extensive technical assistance and training efforts include the following. (1) CSP staff attitudes have shifted from facility-based services to community treatment approaches. (2) Staff know from experience that persons with psychiatric disabilities can succeed in the community, and they develop and provide their services accordingly. (3) Staff have become increasingly knowledgeable and skilled in assessing the symptoms and effects of mental illness and in effective community treatment and rehabilitation methods. (4) Staff feel more confident in serving increasingly challenging individuals in CSP. (5) Policy decisions in the Office of Mental Health are increasingly relevant to the needs of consumers and programs because of the experience state staff have gained during county consultations. (6) The use of local CSP staff as consultants has allowed the Office of Mental Health to recognize and reward these often underpaid and underappreciated clinicians. (7) The involvement of clinicians in the development of policy and legislation has provided them with a much better understanding of the compromise-based political environment in which policymakers operate.

### GREEN COUNTY: AN EXAMPLE OF HIGH QUALITY LOCAL SERVICE IN A RURAL AREA

The Green County CSP is an example of how technical assistance led to the development of a model rural program that itself eventually became a provider of consultation and training. Green County is located directly south of Madison, with a rural population of 30,000 and an economy based on agriculture and dairy products. Monroe, a community of 10,000, is the county seat and the headquarters of all human services offices.

Before 1981 a formalized CSP did not exist in Green County. The only services available were provided by a half-time staff person, whose salary was paid by the state CSP capacity-building funds. The county's use of inpatient facilities was higher than the state average, using up a significant amount of the service budget. Outpatient services consisted only of medication checks by a psychiatrist who also directed the local general hospital inpatient psychiatric unit, crisis intervention, and limited posthospital followup by a single case manager. The participation of consumers in these outpatient services care was highly dependent on individual motivation to attend as well as access to transportation to the clinic. In addition, most consumers, regardless of history and need, were referred after acute hospitalization to the local sheltered workshop for work and/or to the single available group home for residence. Many individuals who experienced frequent or persistent symptoms were admitted to the county-operated nursing home for longer periods of nonacute inpatient care.

In late 1981 several factors merged to change the character of the Green County service delivery system. The local Social Services Department, responsible for providing child welfare services, economic assistance, and services to nondisabled adults, merged with the county Department on Aging and the county mental health board creating a single Department of Human Services, housed under one roof and administered by one director who had a strong commitment to serving people with psychiatric disabilities. In addition, a new staff position was created to provide vocational services to persons who had psychiatric or developmental disabilities or who received general relief. The first person hired in this position had worked in the community support program unit of the state Office of Mental Health and had trained at the PACT program in Madison. This background provided her with an understanding of TCL treatment and service delivery as well as with hands-on clinical experience that was used to reorganize county services for people with psychiatric disabilities. In late 1981 this person, the other half-time staff, and a student intern combined to form a CSP team to provide more individualized and comprehensive services. Consumers were seen more often, and treatment and services began focusing on improving functioning in the areas of independent living, employment, and management of symptoms. Initially the program targeted the 13 persons in the county who had the most extensive histories of hospitalization.

Most consumers obtained residence in an apartment or rooming house in which team staff saw them a number of times each week to give support and to teach practical living skills. All consumers were assessed by team staff for vocational capacity and preference and were given help with placement in and adaptation to community jobs in mostly normal work settings. Each consumer became "connected" to one or more staff with whom they began the long-term work of identifying and better managing the symptoms of their psychiatric illnesses, with the bulk of this work also occurring in community settings.

Although treatment and services were modeled on TCL principles, implementation was adapted to local needs and resources. Since the hours of operation were those of a typical county agency (8:30 A.M. to 5:00 P.M. Monday through Friday), part-time indigenous workers were hired to provide necessary supports and services after hours and on weekends. Intensive monitoring and better anticipation of crises led to effective planning of after-hours coverage. Staff traveled large distances throughout the county and provided virtually all treatment and other services out of the office. The CSP staff were able to enhance services by collaborating with other providers in the same "mother" agency, particularly in assisting with parenting, locating housing, and serving people with dual disabilities.

The success of the program in reducing inpatient utilization led to a major shift in county funding from institutionally oriented traditional services (i.e., inpatient, sheltered work, and residential facilities) to mobile, CSP-oriented ones. During the first two years of operation, the first 30 clients of the CSP had 12 admissions and 216 days in the hospital compared with 82 admissions and 2,080 days in the hospital during the two years prior to entering the CSP program.

In addition to reducing inpatient days and costs, the CSP stopped using the sheltered workshop and began providing individualized vocational services in the community; consumers living in the group facility were moved to independent living settings and provided with in-home supports. The majority of the costs of the more institutional services were gradually shifted to the funding of additional staff positions. A full-time vocational counselor was hired after two years of program operation to enhance vocational services. Several months later an occupational therapist was hired to focus more intensively on independent living skills training. Both of these staff had also been trained as students at PACT, lending further strength to rural TCL replication.

The new shift in the locus of services to the community and the influx of younger, more challenging clients created the need for a new consulting psychiatrist who could work more compatibly with the CSP team. The psychiatrist who directs the PACT program in Madison was, therefore, hired as consultant. This not only strengthened the capacity of the CSP to function as a rural TCL model, but allowed it to begin providing both programmatic and clinical, client-centered technical assistance to other programs. Eventually additional master's level staff were hired, resulting in a core group of staff trained and skilled in providing high quality treatment and services for people with psychiatric disabilities.

Program outcome continues to be positive through the end of the 1980s. Hospital admissions have declined for several years. Approximately 25 to 35% of these served are competitively employed at any one time, with the majority of this group requiring on- or off-job supports. Including those other clients who are involved in noncompetitive individualized community work experiences, approximately 70% of program clients are participating in work of some sort. Coordination with the local vocational rehabilitation office continued to improve and has enhanced vocational programming.

Ninety-five percent of all program clients live independently with visiting staff support. The other 5% live in individualized supervised settings such as adult foster care, paid roommate situations, or housing with attendant care. No county resident with a psychiatric disability lives in a state hospital, residential facility outside of the county, or in a psychiatric nursing home bed.

In 1983 the state Office of Mental Health hired the Green County CSP director as a part-time clinical consultant to provide technical assistance to other CSP programs in Wisconsin. This enabled the state to provide consultation with an additional "hands-on" CSP clinician who was also based in a county with rural characteristics similar to those of the rest of the state.

In the past six years the Green County CSP has become both a model for rural service provision and a training site for staff from other Wisconsin county CPSs as well as for programs in other states and countries. Program staff have provided training in areas such as vocational rehabilitation, treatment of persons with psychiatric disabilities and the substance abuse problems, independent living and basic community supports, treatment planning, symptom management, and other aspects of CSP service delivery.

## Conclusion

During the last quarter-century we have failed, generally, in providing adequate care for people with psychiatric disabilities. The experience in Wisconsin and in a few other states in which the care of these citizens has approached an adequate level can provide direction for other systems but only with the recognition that success has been gained because of progress in such critical areas as: (1) a strong values base that is expressed in a tradition in public policy of providing services in the least restrictive and most normal settings; (2) manageable and accountable systems of care that depend on local control and responsibility, enabling state legislation and consistent state administrative leadership and capacity; (3) effective and practicable intervention models; (4) a clear dissemination strategy, including technical assistance and consultation focused both on staff skills and on organizational development; and (5) an emphasis on outcome. It must also be recognized that these states have only touched the surface in a field in which much needs to be learned and accomplished and in which quality is quickly eroded by cutbacks in resources and by loss of key personnel. With these reservations in mind, we hope that Wisconsin's experience can be useful to improving public mental health systems throughout our country.

# 5

## Developing a Managed Service System for People with Developmental Disabilities

### A State Agency–University Partnership

Michael W. Smull, B.A., Michael L. Sachs, Ph.D., and Maureen M. Black, Ph.D.

Managers of service systems for people with disabilities face increasingly complex and interactive problems. The demand for services has increased faster than resources (Braddock 1986a, 1986b; Krauss 1986). The components of the service system are increasingly stressed, and actions (or inactions) taken by each component affect the others (Smull and Bellamy 1991). Although families continue to be the largest providers of care and support for persons with developmental disabilities, they receive little attention and few services (Krauss 1986; Moroney 1983). As a consequence families often experience recurrent crises that may result in a need for immediate out-of-home services. To develop an effective service system that is proactive, managers need to be able to:

—project the need for services, considering that most persons with developmental disabilities live with family members;

—determine the efficacy of each service delivery component; and

—assess the interactive effects of resource allocation.

Meeting these goals requires information on a complex set of issues. The need for services is affected by factors such as the number of persons requesting services, the availability and utilization of informal support, the responsiveness of generic services, and the perceptions of families regarding possible responses to anticipated needs. Service efficacy and the related issues of service quality have been the focus of recent concern yet there is no consensus regarding how quality may best be measured. Resources allocated in one area may affect the need for services in other areas. For example, adequate family support services or meaningful daytime activities (e.g., supported employment) may defer the perceived need for out of home services (Sherman and Cocozza 1984).

This chapter describes two efforts by the Applied Research and Evaluation (ARE) Unit of the Department of Pediatrics at the University of Maryland School of Medicine to meet some of the public policy information needs of the state agency responsible for services to people with developmental disabilities (the Developmental Disabilities Administration or DDA).

## Community Needs Surveys

### "HOW MANY PERSONS WANT RESIDENTIAL SERVICES?"

In 1982 the DDA received funds for community residential services for persons with developmental disabilities. The DDA wished to use these funds to reduce the demand for institutional placement and to determine the cost of ongoing funding necessary to provide community living arrangements for all eligible persons requesting services.

In Maryland each service provider maintained a list of persons with developmental disabilities who had requested services. The order in which people were served was determined by the length of time spent on that provider's waiting list. Knowledgeable caregivers and advocates applied to multiple providers, indicating an immediate need for services. This strategy increased the probability that they would rise to the top of at least one list when services were needed. As a result of these practices:

—A number of people were on more than one waiting list;

—Many people indicated an *immediate* need for services in order to secure a future position when they anticipated that their caregiving system may no longer be available;

—Persons with a developmental disability who had not come into contact with a service provider were not included on any waiting lists.

These duplications, inaccuracies, and omissions in the service system waiting lists vitiated their usefulness to planners who sought an effective strategy to identify and address the service needs of people with developmental disabilities in Maryland. Given the policy goal of reducing demand for institutional placements the DDA requested assistance from the ARE Unit to answer three critical questions: (1) How many persons are requesting residential services? (2) How soon do they want them? (3) What individual and family factors should be used to determine the order in which people receive services? These questions initiated a set of collaborative data collection and applied research activities which continue to the present.

The ARE Unit and the DDA recognized that in order to plan effectively for these service needs a survey should be completed by the persons requesting services and by their families. Because the majority of individuals with developmental disabilities have mental retardation, the ARE Unit first developed a survey of persons with mental retardation who were living in the community. Since most were adults living with family members, the identification of service needs had to include the needs of the families providing the care.

Long-term care presents stresses to a maturing family at a time when most families of their generation are beyond the caregiving phase (Seltzer and Krauss 1989). In comparison with parents of children with developmental disabilities, parents of young adults with disabilities are often more isolated from the service system and more in need of services (Suelzle and Keenan 1981). The stresses of caring for a dependent family member can be very real (Erickson and Upshur 1989; Harris and McHale 1989), yet family functioning may also be affected by perceived stress or the family's cognitive appraisal of the situation (Crnic, Friedrich, and Greenberg 1983; Turnbull, Summers, and Brotherson 1986).

Regardless of the source of stress, families who are no longer willing or able to provide care and support for their adult family member with a disability may be in a critical situation as they contemplate alternative living arrangements. Because a breakdown in family functioning undermines a family's ability to provide adequate care and supervision and frequently leads to a critical need for residential placement, a procedure was needed to measure the factors contributing to family dysfunction before total breakdown occurred and placement needs became emergencies.

Although the need to assess aspects of family stress has been well documented (Kazak and Marvin 1984; Sherman 1988), there are no reliable and valid questionnaires in the literature beyond the Questionnaire on Resources and Stress (Holroyd 1974) and three shortened versions of the original scale (Friedrich, Greenberg, and Crnic 1983; Holroyd 1974; Salisbury 1986). These scales were designed to measure general family stress among families caring for a disabled child rather than to inquire about specific needs. To incorporate the concepts of family stress and adaptation into the procedure for determining access to state-funded services and to anticipate future service needs, we developed the Community Needs Survey-Mental Retardation (hereafter CNS-MR), a 27-item questionnaire including both multiple-choice and Likert-type scales. In addition to demographic information, items representing individual and family variables were included. The individual variables were: independence skills, self-care skills, medical problems, behavior problems, and daytime activities. The family variables were: stressful family situations, urgency of request for services, services requested, and caregiver reason for requests.

Items were selected from a careful review of existing scales of adapative behavior (Nihira et al. 1974), family adjustment to raising a child with mental retardation (Farran, Metzger, and Sparling 1986; McCubbin and Patterson 1983), and clinical experience. Stressful family situations included items that were not related directly to the presence of a person with mental retardation, such as poor health of caregiver or financial problems. Families requesting day services, community living services, and support services rated the urgency of each of their requests into one of five categories: (1) urgent and in crisis; (2) urgent, but stable; (3) highly desirable; (4) wanted in the future; and (5) present situation available indefinitely. In addition, they indicated the reasons for their requests, ranging from independence and training for their son or daughter to caregiver relief or inability of the caregiver to provide care and supervision.

Several initial drafts of the CNS-MR were reviewed and modified by a group of clinicians, policymakers, and researchers. To locate all persons with mental retardation in Maryland requesting residential services, families were recruited from more than 200 agencies serving persons with mental retardation throughout the state, including developmental service providers, health departments, departments of social services, school systems, and advocacy groups. The CNS-MR was designed to be completed by the primary caregiver, but a central telephone number was provided in case caregivers wanted assistance in filling out the survey. Although attempts were made to be exhaustive, persons not known to the human service systems or not yet seeking services may not have been included.

To assess the reliability and validity of the CNS-MR, a random sample of 120 families who were requesting residential services was chosen. Sixty-six percent ($n = 79$) agreed to participate and were visited at home by a two-person interview team.

Reliability was determined by having the family complete the CNS-MR a second time. The internal consistency of the CNS-MR (using Cronbach's alpha; Cronbach 1951) exceeded .70 on all subscales except that for medical problems. Test-retest reliability of the procedure over a six-month period was calculated by Pearson product-moment correlations and ranged from .81 to .94. Thus, caregiver responses to the CNS-MR were shown to be highly reliable among and within families over a six-month period. Validity was measured by administering three externally corroborated scales of adaptive behavior and stress. Adapative behavior was measured by the survey form of the Vineland Adaptive Behavior Scales, stress associated with caretaking was measured by the Questionnaire on Resources and Stress short form (Friedrich, Greenberg, and Crnic 1983), and generic stress was measured by the Perceived Stress Scale (Cohen, Kamarck, and Mermelstein 1983). The correlations between the CNS-MR and the measurements of adaptive behavior and stress were significant, albeit in the moderate range (from .37 to .66). These findings demonstrated that families were able to use this survey format to provide reliable and valid information on the functioning level of a family member with mental retardation, stress within the family, and the need for services. Nevertheless, the survey process will always be limited by caregiver knowledge about the person with the disability and available services.

Once an ongoing system was developed to collect information on persons with mental retardation, the ARE Unit and the DDA expanded the procedure to include persons with other developmental disabilities. Based on the work of Gollay et al. (1978), a second community needs survey was implemented to determine the service needs of persons with epilepsy, cerebral palsy, head injury, multiple sclerosis, deafness, and more than 20 other categorical disabilities. A third community needs survey was developed to anticipate the service needs of students with developmental disabilities who would graduate or leave school within two years.

### THE APPLICATION FOR SERVICES

In 1987 the Maryland legislature adopted a variant of the federal definition of developmental disabilities as the single definition of eligibility for services funded through the DDA. This change in definition, combined with the difficulties in dealing with three separate data bases, made it advisable to consolidate the CNS efforts and use one basic form, the

### DEVELOPMENTAL DISABILITIES ADMINISTRATION APPLICATION FOR SERVICES (AFS).

The AFS continues the focus on basic demographic, functional, and service needs information but also includes questions that are relevant to specific disability groups (e.g., seizure type, frequency, and severity for persons with epilepsy; mobility issues for persons with cerebral palsy and head injuries). Expert panels were formed with providers and advocates concerned about autism, cerebral palsy, deafness, epilepsy, head injury, and multiple sclerosis. Disability-specific "trailers," with questions pertinent to each disability, were developed for the six disabilities and for students. These seven trailers supplement the basic AFS so that respondents could answer questions specific to their particular disability. All applicants for services complete the basic AFS. Applicants with a disability other than mental retardation complete the basic AFS and the disability-specific trailer.

The AFS incorporated many elements of the original CNS-MR so that it could be completed easily and reliably by caregivers. Questions were expanded to be applicable to a broader base of persons with developmental disabilities, including those individuals living independently without a caregiver. The family functioning component of the instrument was also expanded by incorporating additional measurements of family stress and coping (McCubbin and Patterson 1983). The content areas and number of items in each area are shown in Table 5.1.

An initial validity study was done on 100 participants who completed both the AFS and the Inventory for Client and Agency Planning (ICAP)

Table 5.1. Application for Services: Content Areas

| Content Area | Number of Items |
|---|---|
| *Basic demographics* | 11 |
| *Caregiver/family demographics and stressors* | 8 |
| *Functional skills/needs* | |
| Mobility | 2 |
| Communication | 1 |
| Self-care | 6 |
| Independence | 26 |
| Supervision | 1 |
| *Behavior* | 12 |
| *Applicant stressors* | 6 |
| *Service requests/urgency* | |
| Day services | 2 |
| Support services | 27 |
| Residential services | 3 |
| *Disability-specific trailers* | |
| Autism | 3 |
| Cerebral palsy | 9 |
| Deafness | 5 |
| Epilepsy | 24 |
| Head injury | 13 |
| Multiple sclerosis | 7 |

(Bruininks et al. 1986), a standardized assessment of diagnostic, demographic, functional, behavioral characteristics, and service needs which is easily answered and has adequate reliability and validity. Pearson product-moment correlations between ICAP and AFS scores exceeded .83 for adaptive skills and .70 for maladaptive behaviors. This degree of agreement supports the AFS as a valid assessment of individual status and service needs which can be completed by a parent.

To assess the validity of the family functioning component of the AFS, developmental disabilities professionals made home visits to 55 families (35 persons with mental retardation and 20 with other developmental disabilities). Family stress and functioning were measured by Holroyd's version of the Questionnaire on Resources and Stress short form (Holroyd 1974) and a modified version of the Daily Hassles Scale (Crnic and Greenberg 1985). Correlations between these scales and components of the AFS ranged from .58 to .63, indicating the validity of the measurements of stress and family functioning from the client- or caregiver-completed form when compared with standardized measurements taken in interviews. Without adequate reliability and validity, policy planners cannot be sure that their information is stable or accurate.

HOW ARE THE DATA USED?

The data from the CNS and AFS have been incorporated into both individual and statewide planning and enable the ARE Unit and the DDA to (1) make a preliminary determination of an individual's eligibility, service needs, and priority for services; (2) provide state and local planners with the information required to project service needs and the costs of meeting those needs; and (3) answer specific questions, such as the extent of need for accessible housing or the numbers of persons waiting for a service within a given legislative district.

The use of the AFS as the first step in obtaining services ensures that all persons interested in services begin with a uniform, statewide procedure to determine their eligibility and priority. Although the AFS provides valid and reliable data for determining eligibility, contact with a developmental disabilities professional is necessary to clarify the specific service recommendations for each individual and family.

As of January 1990 the data base contained information on 5,430 persons with a disability who indicated a current need for services. Seventy-one percent had mental retardation (44% also had at least one additional disability), and the remaining 29% had a disability other than mental retardation. The majority of the applicants for service (54%) were young adults,

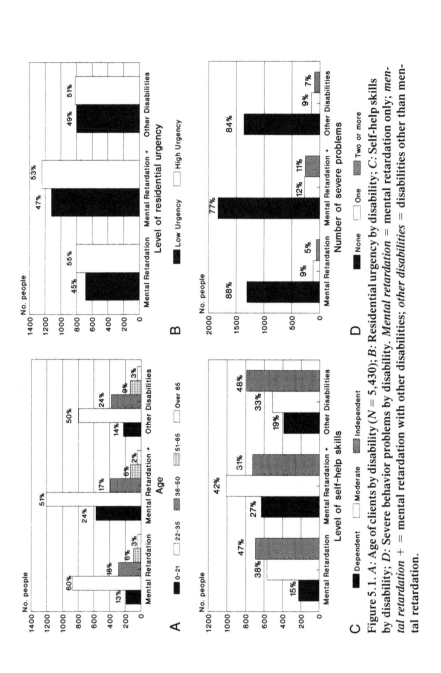

Figure 5.1. A: Age of clients by disability ($N = 5,430$); B: Residential urgency by disability; C: Self-help skills by disability; D: Severe behavior problems by disability. *Mental retardation* = mental retardation only; *mental retardation +* = mental retardation with other disabilities; *other disabilities* = disabilities other than mental retardation.

ages 22 to 35 (see Fig. 5.1*a*). They frequently lived with family members (56%), and many were cared for by aging caregivers (23% over age 65).

Families were asked to define their level of urgency regarding service requests. Slightly under half of the applicants in each disability area claimed that they had a current need for residential services (either urgent, in crisis or urgent, but not in crisis; see Fig. 5.1*b*). The self-help skills of the applicants varied from severely dependent (15–27%) to independent (42–48%). Applicants with mental retardation plus an additional disability were more likely to be dependent in self-help skills than were applicants with a sole diagnosis of mental retardation. As shown in Figure 1*c*, there did not appear to be a relationship between self-help skills and the urgency of the request for residential services. Severe behavior problems were uncommon among this population (17%; see Fig. 5.1*d*). However, applicants who displayed at least one severe behavior problem were more likely to express an urgent need for residential services, $\chi^2 = 163.58$, $p < .01$ than applicants without behavior problems.

Before these data were available debates about funding focused on how many people wanted specific services. The presence of these data has turned the debate to how the requests of these persons can be met and how quickly the waiting list can be reduced or eliminated. However, for the past several years the number of people asking for services has increased more rapidly than the resources to serve them. This trend has added a new dimension to the debate with officials, advocates, providers, and families seeking alternative ways to meet service needs.

The information from the AFS is also used to make refinements in the application process. For example, we recently surveyed families who advised us that they were no longer seeking state-funded services (Molaison et al. 1991). Most respondents (89%) were satisfied with the services they received. However, the best predictor of satisfaction was whether someone had facilitated the service acquisition process rather than an aspect of the services received or demographic variables. This information has assisted in refining the role of the professionals who make the home visits during the application process.

As the DDA increases its capacity to provide discrete support services to families the need for more precise information also increases. Maintaining an accurate data set that reflects changing service needs is a momentous undertaking that has required the close collaboration of the ARE Unit and the DDA. Where contact with the applicants is infrequent accuracy is degraded significantly. Individuals whose service needs become more acute tend to be reported as they seek funding whereas those individuals who have had their need for service met, have moved, or are deceased are less likely to be reported. In the short term these inaccuracies make the data set vulnerable to anecdotal criticism. In the longer term the bias toward overstating need adversely effects the advocacy potential of the data.

Efforts at maintaining the needed contact by mail are not cost effective. The low response rate and the need for extensive follow-up with those who do respond indicate that personal contact by phone or home visits is required. The frequency of contact depends on the rate at which the service needs change. For individuals with developmental disabilities annual contact or biannual contact appears sufficient to ensure aggregate accuracy. Were this methodology to be extended to other disability groups an assessment of the stability of service needs and functional skills of that group would assist in determining the resources needed to maintain a reasonably accurate data base. The results of the process can directly benefit persons with disabilities and their families because accurate and timely data are necessary for legislators and policymakers to determine correctly the distribution of resources and to allocate services.

## DD Definition

In 1983 the state of Maryland began to consider the implications of adopting the federal definition of developmental disabilities (see Table 5.2)

**Table 5.2. The Federal Definition of Developmental Disability**

The federal definition of developmental disability means a severe chronic disability of a person that:
- is attributable to a mental or physical impairment or combination of mental of physical impairments
- is manifested before the person attains age 22
- is likely to continue indefinitely
- results in substantial functional limitations in three or more of the following areas of major life activity: self-care, receptive and expressive language, learning, mobility, self-direction, capacity for independent living, and economic self-sufficiency
- reflects the person's need for a combination and sequence of special, interdisciplinary, or generic care, treatment, or other services which are of lifelong or extended duration and are individually planned and coordinated

*Source:* P.L. 100–146.

as the single eligibility criterion for persons to receive funding through the
DDA. Prior to 1984 Maryland operated with two definitions, the first for
mental retardation and the second for developmental disabilities other than
mental retardation (NRDD). The NRDD definition (Maryland Health General Article, 7.101.L, 1985) was a variant of the pre-1977 federal definition
of developmental disabilities which combined a categorical listing of disabilities and a functional impairment.

After receiving testimony from advocacy groups regarding potential
positive benefits of adopting the current federal definition, the governor's
office sought a fiscal impact estimate of doing so on the numbers of persons
eligible for services from the DDA. Available information indicated that by
using the federal definition the number of persons eligible for services would
depend on how its provisions were interpreted (Lubin, Jacobson, and Kiely
1982; Smull and Sachs 1983). In response to this information and the need
to revise an outmoded statute, the governor appointed a commission (the
Governor's Commission to Revise the Mental Retardation and Developmental Disabilities Law) to develop an eligibility definition and to revise the
existing statute. The ARE Unit was asked to serve as a technical advisor and
to determine the impact of adopting the federal definition.

METHODS

The methodology used provided the capacity to assess the varied effects
of alternative operational definitions of substantial functional limitations in
most of the life activity areas with a small, enriched sample. The sample
consisted of 1,915 students in special education programs funded by the
Maryland Department of Education and located either in Maryland or in
nonpublic school programs outside Maryland.

Three criteria were used to select the sample. First, students born in
1968 (15 years of age at the time of the study, in 1984) were selected. This
selection was based on the assumption that most individuals who are substantially functionally limited in several life activity areas are identified by
the school system and receive services from special education. In addition,
as a person becomes older, it becomes more likely that a disability that is
developmental in nature will be identified. Because by law individuals must
attend school until the age of 16, sample selection among 15-year-old children would yield a maximum likelihood of including the greatest number of
persons with developmental disabilities. This sample did have the limitation
of underrepresenting individuals with traumatic head injuries and other disabilities with onset between the ages of 16 and 22.

Second, consultation with officials at the state board of education indicated that students with developmental disabilities were most likely to be found in levels 3 through 6 of the seven-tiered system (level 3 students receive specialized services for primary academic services, level 4 students are in self-contained classrooms in community schools, level 5 students are in special schools, and level 6 students are in residential schools; COMAR 13A.05.01).

Third, students were selected from 9 of the 24 school jurisdictions in Maryland as well as from state-operated programs and nonpublic school placements. The 9 school areas account for more than 76% of the state's population and more than 80% of the state's special education students. The jurisdictions represent all regions and urban and rural sections of the state.

A stratified random sampling design was used, selecting half of all students in each cell in an 11 (jurisdictions) by 4 (levels) by 2 (disabilities) matrix. The 11 jurisdictions encompassed the 9 school areas plus the state-operated programs and the nonpublic school placements. The four levels were special education levels 3 through 6. The two disabilities were specific learning disability (SLD) and all other disability categories. Because students with an SLD label outnumbered students with all other disability labels combined, it was feared that a sample not stratified by disability would provide insufficient numbers of non-SLD students. This procedure provided a total sample of 1,915 students in which approximately half had SLD.

A survey instrument, the Special Education Survey Questionnaire (SESQ), was developed. The SESQ assessed the degree of functioning in the seven life activity areas specified in the federal developmental disability definition and was adapted from the CNS variants. The scales in the SESQ used ratings ranging from 0 (no special assistance needed) to 10 (completely dependent; no apparent functional ability). This format allowed assessment of a range of degrees of limitations in functioning.

The SESQ was designed to be completed by each student's special education teacher. Project coordinators managed the research project in each of the counties (e.g., distributing surveys, coding survey forms to maintain confidentiality, answering questions). Of the 1,915 questionnaires distributed, 1,602 usable forms were returned, a return rate of 84%.

RESULTS

The data obtained from the study provided estimates of the prevalence of developmental disabilities in the student population in Maryland. These estimates (see Fig. 5.2) illustrate the effects of differing interpretations of

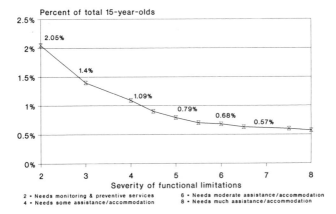

Figure 5.2. The prevalence of developmental disabilities by the severity of the functional limitations. 2 = needs monitoring and preventive services; 4 = needs some assistance/accommodation; 6 = needs moderate assistance; 8 = needs much assistance/accommodation.

*substantial* (as used in *substantial functional limitation*) on the numbers of persons who would be eligible for services.

The findings indicate that there is a core group of severely disabled persons (approximately 0.6% of the 15-year-old sample) who will meet almost any interpretation of substantial. The findings also demonstrate that as the interpretation is made less stringent the numbers rise on a curve with an increasing slope (see Fig. 5.2). The percent eligible increases from 0.57% at a scaled score of 7.5 to 0.63% at a scaled score of 6.5 (an increase of 11%) whereas it increases from 1.40% at a scaled score of 3.0 to 2.05% at a scaled score of 2.0 (an increase of 46%).

In order to assist the commission in determining the effects of a variety of interpretations of *substantial functional limitation*, a series of real life vignettes was prepared, representing an array of disabilities and functional limitations. A narrative was developed for each person which detailed the functional limitations in each life activity area, and each person was assessed using an adult version of the SESQ. Members of the governor's commission were asked to make a forced choice regarding each person's eligibility as developmentally disabled. This process enabled the members of the commission to recognize the necessity of having specific criteria to make judgments regarding disability eligibility.

Analysis of the results of the commission's choices indicated that the common theme that linked those persons who had been selected as having a developmental disability was a substantial functional limitation in the capacity for independent living. This criterion was consistent across all of the disabilities and also discriminated those persons found not to be eligible. The capacity to live independently is a variable comprised of items from three domains (household management, use of community resources, and personal care management; Gollay et al. 1978), each of which affects functioning in other life activity areas. The commission modified the federal definition and used the inability to live independently as a criterion for service eligibility as an individual with a development disability (Maryland Health General Article, 7.101.K, 1986) instead of substantial functional limitations in three of seven life activity areas.

The prevalence study data provided a means to project prevalence under the commission's definition as well as a variety of interpretations of the federal definition. The result of the analysis of the commission's definition was a prevalence of 1.7%, which is consistent with findings from other states (Jacobson and Janicki 1983).

## The University–Public Agency Partnership

The efforts of the ARE Unit and the DDA have demonstrated the potential contributons to public policy that a university-public agency partnership can offer. Although the collaborative relationship can be mutually beneficial, there are also potential conflicts. Both organizations seek to answer important questions; however, each has a unique set of resources to contribute to the process, and each presents its answer to a different audience.

Public agencies need information, often on critical issues, within specific time limits imposed by funding cycles. Moreover, they are often interested in "bottom line" answers and less concerned about issues of reliability, validity, or research. Universities may seek information on the same critical issues. However, their requirement that the processes conform to scientific standards of accuracy may hinder their ability to achieve results quickly. Partnerships require compromise, and in the case of the ARE Unit–DDA partnership, those compromises have been achieved through an active liaison. Fiscal resources from the DDA have been used to develop and maintain the management system necessary to determine eligibility and to track current services and requests for future services. When research-oriented questions have been raised, supplementary funds have been secured to pay for those investigations. Both the ARE Unit and the DDA have learned to appreciate the strengths in the partnership and both are committed to a common purpose—achieving equitable services for individuals with developmental disabilities and their families.

Note: Copies of the Application for Services and related documents may be obtained by writing to Michael W. Smull, Director, ARE Unit, University of Maryland, 630 West Fayette Street, Baltimore, MD 21201.

## 6

# Adults with Profound Mental Retardation and Multiple Handicaps

## Factors Associated with Mortality

Wayne P. Silverman, Ph.D., Warren B. Zigman, Ph.D., and Ellen Johnson Silver, M.S.

Over the past two decades, principles of normalization and social integration have strongly influenced models of service provision for people with developmental disabilities. There is now a clear consensus that deinstitutionalization and increased community integration of people with developmental disabilities have had, and will continue to have, a positive effect on their quality of life and adaptive competence (Jacobson and Schwartz, in press). Nevertheless, there is a small proportion of the population with mental retardation who have a constellation of disabilities so serious that risks of increased morbidity and mortality could be associated with community placement. Therefore, the present study was designed to examine survival in a subgroup of individuals representative of our most disabled clients while they were living either in a large service-intensive facility or small residences integrated within the community.

The individuals we included in our study all are adults with profound mental retardation, minimal adaptive competence, virtually no expressive language or independent mobility, and a history of serious medical problems. It was our suspicion that the health-related problems associated with the primary disabilities of these people, along with their inability to communicate effectively, could hamper timely intervention to address their acute health care needs if nursing and medical care were not immediately at hand. Thus, small community-based residential service models, typically not designed to include ready access to 24-hour-a-day medical services, may be unable to address all the needs of this population. Despite any risks that might have been associated with transfer of adults with profound and multiple handicaps to small community-based intermediate care facilities for the mentally retarded (ICF/MRs) there has been a strong feeling on the part of advocates that increasing community integration would improve their overall quality of life. Therefore, under the authority of the Willowbrook Consent Decree (see Beyer 1983), plans were developed during 1979 and 1980 to transfer a select group of persons with profound and multiple disabilities residing in a "specialty hospital," comparable in structure to a service-intensive skilled nursing facility (SNF), to small residences integrated within local communities. The specialty hospital, or SNF, provided comprehensive services to more than 100 people with developmental disabilities who were likely to require substantial daily medical care as well as habilitative programming. To monitor the status of these people, with regard to both physical health and adaptive competence, we initiated a longitudinal study in October 1980. Our original intention was to document the effects of community placement for this select population by: (1) collecting baseline data on a broad spectrum of individual characteristics while the people resided in the SNF; (2) reevaluating these persons shortly after their move to smaller, less service-intensive residential facilities located within the community; and (3) repeating the assessment after approximately one to two years to document changes in individual skills and physical condition. In addition to individual descriptions, our study focused on characteristics of the service environment.

Unfortunately, the original study design had to be altered because the development of placement settings proved to be exceedingly difficult. In fact, when our study concluded in November 1983, only nine of these persons had moved. Therefore, to address our original goals, we compared SNF residents with the adults with the most severe forms of disability who were already living in ICFs. Presumably, if people with characteristics similar to those of our select group of SNF residents already were coping successfully within the community, the anticipated service needs of our study group could be addressed. In contrast, if residents of small community-based facilities were not flourishing, it would suggest that additional service modalities would need to be developed before our SNF residents could be moved without placing them at relative risk. Finally, if the constellation of disabilities of even the community residents with the most severe disabilities indicated that they were less disabled than our SNF residents, then no firm conclusions could be drawn from the group comparison.

Our findings suggested that the majority of SNF residents' care needs could be addressed within community-based residential facilities (Silverman et al. 1986, 1987). However, conclusions had to be qualified because the two groups of adults, although overlapping substantially in their characteristics, were not matched perfectly. Although all services received by SNF residents were available for some community residents, the SNF group was more disabled overall, having substantially lower adaptive competence (Silverman et al. 1986) and greater physical involvement (Silverman et al. 1987). To determine with greater clarity the viability of providing services for the SNF residents within small community-based programs, we judged that it would be necessary to follow these particular clients into small residential facilities and evaluate outcome.

During the five years after our original study 40 of the SNF residents moved to smaller, community-based ICF/MRs. In addition, complete ascertainment data were available about the current status of our original study group with regard to survival. Therefore, we are now able to relate our prospectively collected data on individual characteristics to mortality during the five-year period after our original study and to determine if movement into the community and away from the intensity of services provided in the SNF was associated with increased mortality risk. These are the goals of the present set of analyses.

METHODS

Participants

Survival data were available for the 115 SNF residents with profound mental retardation and physical disabilities who participated in our original study. All study participants resided in the New York City vicinity and were representative of the persons who were the most severely disabled within the developmental disabilities service system. Participants' characteristics are indicated in Tables 6.1 through 6.3.

Assessment Procedures

The physical status of each study participant was documented using a highly structured interview format, the Health Status Indicator (HSI), developed by us for this purpose (Silverman et al. 1983, 1987). The HSI was composed of 102 multiple-choice items that focused on health and medical disorders experienced over the six-month period immediately preceding data collection. The HSI provided a summary of participants' status with respect to specific body systems (respiratory, cardiovascular, nervous, dental, musculoskeletal) as well as more general information typically recorded in a standard physical examination (e.g., height, weight, age, sex, history of acute infections). Further information summarized characteristics of the treatment program (e.g., frequency and types of medical services received,

Table 6.1. Demographic Characteristics (as of December 31, 1981) of the
Study Participants by Setting and Survival Group

| Characteristic | SNF Subgroup (N = 75) | ICF Subgroup (N = 40) | Surviving Subgroup (N = 95) | Deceased Subgroup (N = 20) |
|---|---|---|---|---|
| *Age (years)* | | | | |
| Mean | 25.85 | 25.23 | 25.61 | 25.79 |
| S.D. | 3.82 | 4.29 | 3.65 | 5.38 |
| *Sex* | | | | |
| % Male | 32.0 | 42.5 | 37.9 | 25.0 |
| % Female | 68.0 | 57.5 | 62.1 | 75.0 |
| *Height (cm)* | | | | |
| Mean | 144.5 | 141.2 | 144.2 | 141.3 |
| S.D. | 19.3 | 18.5 | 18.1 | 16.5 |
| *Weight (kg)* | | | | |
| Mean | 31.8 | 31.2 | 32.1 | 27.0 |
| S.D. | 7.3 | 7.0 | 7.2 | 5.3 |
| *Annual mortality (%)* | 2.78 | 2.11 | — | — |

special dietary needs). HSI information was provided by interviews with each participant's primary nurse, who was in daily contact with that individual. During each interview the participant's medical records were available for consultation.

Adaptive skills of study participants were assessed using the Minnesota Developmental Programming System Behavioral Scales, Alternate Form C (Bock 1979). The Form C was designed to provide an overview of the performance capabilities of individuals with severely limited adaptive competence. Information is provided by an informant well acquainted with a subject's characteristics during an interview with a trained data collector.

The Form C consists of four subscales that provide an overview of abilities in: (1) gross motor functioning; (2) eating behaviors; (3) environmental integration skills; and (4) language/communication skills. The 20 items of each scale consist of specific behavioral descriptions (e.g., *Sits unsupported for 10 seconds*), and respondents are required to indicate whether subjects can perform the behavior: *never, less than half the time, more than half the time,* or *always.* Each item receives a score of 0 to 3, corresponding to the frequency scaling of performance. The sum of items for each subscale is divided by the total possible (20 times 3 = 60) and multiplied by 100 to yield a percent competence score. These four subscale percent competence scores are used as an index of adaptive competence.

It must be noted at this point that percent competence scores provide a

Table 6.2.  Adaptive Competence, as Indicated on the Minnesota
Developmental Programming System Behavioral Scales, Alternate
Form C, of Study Participants by Setting and Survival Group[a]

| Form C Subscale | SNF Subgroup | ICF Subgroup | Surviving Subgroup | Deceased Subgroup |
|---|---|---|---|---|
| | | | % | |
| *Gross motor development* | | | | |
| Mean competence | 27.0 | 35.5 | 31.1 | 24.3 |
| Never can sit unsupported | | | | |
| for 10 seconds | 69.9 | 59.0 | 64.1 | 75.0 |
| Never can stand unsupported | | | | |
| for 30 seconds | 98.6 | 97.5 | 98.9 | 95.0 |
| *Eating behavior* | | | | |
| Mean competence | 40.0 | 47.0 | 44.3 | 33.4 |
| Never can use a spoon to | | | | |
| . . . eat food | 76.7 | 70.0 | 72.0 | 85.0 |
| Never can eat food with | | | | |
| fingers | 83.6 | 87.5 | 82.8 | 90.0 |
| *Environmental integration* | | | | |
| Mean competence | 37.2 | 45.5 | 41.3 | 34.2 |
| Never examines objects | | | | |
| placed in hands | 54.8 | 32.5 | 44.1 | 60.0 |
| Never rocks . . . to rhythm | | | | |
| of music | 72.6 | 72.5 | 72.0 | 75.0 |
| *Language/communication* | | | | |
| Mean competence | 32.5 | 35.3 | 34.3 | 29.6 |
| Never obeys a simple | | | | |
| instruction | 69.9 | 65.0 | 66.7 | 75.0 |
| Never can indicate *yes* or *no* | | | | |
| when questioned | 90.4 | 95.0 | 91.4 | 95.0 |

[a]Data were collected during 1981.

relative measure of behavioral functioning which is useful for comparing subgroups of study participants (i.e., those placed in ICFs with those remaining in the SNF). Because the Form C is intended for use with people who are
functioning at a level that would produce scores at or near the lowest extreme
of most adaptive behavior scales, even high percent competence scores reflect severe behavioral limitations. (See Table 6.2 for specific examples of
participants' abilities along with mean scale scores.)

Measures of participant movement and survival were taken directly
from their clinical records. For persons who had died the primary cause of
death was also recorded.

Table 6.3. Selected Physical and Medical Characteristics of Participants by Setting and Survival[a]

| Characteristic | SNF Subgroup | ICF Subgroup | Surviving Subgroup | Deceased Subgroup |
|---|---|---|---|---|
| | | % | | |
| *Musculoskeletal system problems* | | | | |
| No limb impairment | 5.6 | 7.9 | 5.3 | 11.1 |
| One arm impaired | 2.7 | 2.6 | 3.2 | 0 |
| Both arms impaired | 76.7 | 76.3 | 77.4 | 72.2 |
| One leg impaired | 0 | 0 | 0 | 0 |
| Both legs impaired | 94.4 | 89.5 | 93.5 | 88.9 |
| Quadriplegic | 76.7 | 76.3 | 77.4 | 72.2 |
| Daily physical therapy: | | | | |
| contractures | 81.9 | 79.5 | 84.9 | 61.1 |
| *Respiratory system problems* | | | | |
| Breathing difficulty | | | | |
| At least once a week | 5.5 | 5.1 | 4.3 | 11.1 |
| Less than once a week | 13.7 | 10.3 | 10.7 | 22.3 |
| Never | 80.8 | 84.6 | 85.1 | 66.7 |
| Pneumonia (once or more) | 8.2 | 5.1 | 4.3 | 22.3 |
| Required oxygen administration | | | | |
| At least once a week | 5.5 | 0 | 2.1 | 11.8 |
| Less than once a week | 4.1 | 2.6 | 2.2 | 11.8 |
| Never | 90.4 | 97.4 | 95.7 | 76.5 |
| *Seizure disorders* | | | | |
| No seizure history | 49.3 | 53.8 | 52.1 | 44.4 |
| Positive seizure history with | | | | |
| No seizures observed | 19.2 | 28.2 | 23.4 | 16.7 |
| Grand mal seizures | 19.4 | 15.4 | 17.0 | 23.5 |
| Only non–grand mal | | | | |
| seizures | 12.1 | 2.6 | 7.5 | 15.4 |
| Seizure frequency | | | | |
| Weekly | 4.1 | 7.7 | 4.3 | 11.1 |
| Monthly or less | 27.4 | 10.3 | 20.2 | 27.8 |
| No seizures observed | 68.5 | 82.0 | 75.5 | 61.1 |
| *Acute infections (two or more)* | | | | |
| Ear/nose/throat | 5.5 | 10.3 | 7.5 | 5.6 |
| Gastrointestinal | 1.4 | 2.6 | 1.1 | 5.6 |
| Eye | 6.9 | 7.8 | 6.4 | 16.8 |
| Urinary tract | 1.4 | 2.6 | 2.1 | 0 |

[a] Data were collected during 1981.

Procedure

The Form C data were collected at the SNF between December 1980 and February 1981. The HSI data were collected between May 1981 and September 1981. These data were collected as part of a larger study that included assessments of the characteristics of the residential program and staffing over a period of several years.

Data regarding participant survival and residential program were collected from files maintained in the medical records office of the SNF. These data were collected in January 1988 and were provided to us by medical records staff of the SNF.

RESULTS

Participant Movement

Overall, 40 (34.8%) of the original sample of 115 people moved from the SNF to various ICF/MRs within the New York metropolitan area between December 1980 and January 1988. Selected characteristics of the people placed in the ICF/MRs and those remaining in the community are given in Tables 6.1 (basic demographics), 6.2 (adaptive skills), and 6.3 (physical impairments).

Community-placed and SNF residents were compared on the large spectrum of measures included on the Form C and HSI, of which the data presented in Tables 6.1, 6.2, and 6.3 are representative. (For a more detailed description of the health status of the sample, see Silverman et al. 1987.) No significant differences were found between ICF/MR and SNF residents on any of the measures included in the study, suggesting that adaptive competence and physical conditions were roughly comparable across the two subgroups of study participants.

Mortality

Twenty individuals, 18 (24%) in the SNF subgroup and 2 (5%) in the ICF subgroup, died before January 1, 1988. The characteristics of the deceased participants compared with surviving individuals are also indicated in Tables 6.1, 6.2, and 6.3.

Deceased and surviving individuals were strikingly similar in their characteristics. The only variables that were significantly related to survival were: (1) *frequency of breathing difficulty,* with deceased people more likely to have had difficulties more than once a month (exact $p < .01$); (2) *frequency of receiving oxygen,* with deceased people more likely to have needed administration during the six-month period monitored ($\chi^2(1) = 5.6$, $p < .02$); (3) *incidence of pneumonia,* with deceased people more likely to have had pneumonia during the six-month period monitored ($\chi^2(1) = 7.6$, $p < .01$); and (4) *incidence of infected sputum* (exact $p < .03$).

Because previous discussions of mortality risk among people who have profound mental retardation and multiple handicaps have noted the significance of respiratory problems in this select population (Chaney, Eyman, and Miller 1979; Eyman et al. 1986; Richards 1976; Silverman et al. 1987), we planned a priori to examine the relationship between mortality (yes/no) and a subset of measures focusing on respiratory system vulnerability included in the HSI using a multiple-regression analysis. For the purpose of this analysis HSI measures were coded into dichotomous categories as follows: (1) *breathing difficulty,* at least one episode per month; (2) *oxygen administration,* at least once during the six-month assessment period; (3) *secretion-related breathing problems,* at least one per month; (4) *manual suctioning for secretions,* at least once during the six-month assessment period; (5) *chest physical therapy for secretions,* at least once during the six-month assessment period; (6) *episodes of wheezing,* more than one during the six-month assessment period; (7) *pneumonia,* at least once during the six-month period; and (8) *infected sputum,* at least three times during the six-month assessment period. These measures were significantly associated with mortality ($r = .430$; $F(8,100) = 2.83$; $p < .01$).

As indicated above, a primary goal of the present study was to determine if the movement of participants to an ICF/MR was or was not associated with an increased mortality risk. The most straightforward way to address this issue is to compare the frequencies of participants surviving (yes/no) in the two residential subgroupings (SNF versus ICF/MR). However, these data cannot be used directly for this purpose because movement from the ICF/MR did not occur at the beginning of the period monitored for all or even any members of the ICF/MR subgroup. In fact, for ICF/MR residents placements occurred throughout the period monitored in the present study, ranging from an earliest date of September 4, 1981 and a latest date of October 17, 1987. Because movement into ICF/MRs occurred gradually, the mean follow-up period elapsing between movement from the SNF and the end of our data collection was only 2.50 years across all members of this subgroup. In contrast, mortality was monitored over a full seven-year period for members of the SNF subgroup. When this difference was taken into account by calculating the number of deaths per person-year of observation within each subgroup, no significant relationship was found between residential setting and mortality. These rates, expressed as annual mortality rates (AMRs), were calculated based upon the total potential "resident years" spent in each facility using Equation 1:

$$AMR\ (\%) = d_k \div (\ y_{ik}) \times 100 \tag{1}$$

where $d_k$ equals the number of deaths occurring in each subgroup, and $y_{ik}$ equals the number of years of follow-up for each participant within that subgroup. These values are indicated in Table 6.1.

Although the ICF/MR and SNF subgroups did not differ significantly, there was a trend in the data suggesting that the ICF/MR subgroup may have been higher functioning (see Table 6.2) and therefore more physically robust initially. Thus, relative mortality risk among the ICF/MR subgroup may have been underestimated. To address this possibility, analyses were repeated on matched subsets of the ICF/MR and SNF subgroups ($N = 31$), with matching based upon (1) age (within three years); (2) whether a history of seizures was present; (3) whether an indication of respiratory problems was reported; and (4) whether a severe motor impairment was present. As found in the overall analysis, no measures differed significantly between the two subgroups, nor did annual mortality rate. Further, Form C data indicated quite comparable adaptive skills of the ICF/MR and SNF subgroups, which were, respectively: (1) gross motor, 31.8% and 24.1% ($p > .2$); (2) eating behaviors, 44.0% and 39.7% ($p > .5$); (3) environmental integration, 42.3% and 38.1% ($p > .7$); and (4) language communication, 33.8% and 36.8% ($p > .4$). These results verify that the matching procedure produced subgroups of comparable initial status.

Primary Causes of Death

The primary causes of death are indicated in Table 6.4; the three most prevalent among them were pneumonia, cardiopulmonary arrest, and aspira-

Table 6.4. Primary Causes of Death among 115 Adults
with Profound Retardation and Multiple Handicaps
over a Seven-year Period

| Cause of Death | N | Mean Annual Incidence (%) |
|---|---|---|
| Pneumonia | 6 | 0.74 |
| Aspiration | 4 | 0.5 |
| Cardiopulmonary arrest | 6 | 0.74 |
| Cardiac arrest | 1 | 0.13 |
| Intestinal obstruction | 1 | 0.13 |
| Undetermined | 2 | 0.24 |

tion, implicating respiratory system involvement. This finding is consistent with results of the HSI data analysis indicating that measures reflecting respiratory fragility were significantly associated with subsequent mortality.

## DISCUSSION

The primary goal of the present study was to determine if movement from a large, service-intensive living environment, equipped to provide comprehensive medical and therapy care, to a smaller and less service-intensive residence (an ICF/MR) would increase mortality risk among our select group of adults with profound retardation and multiple disabilities. Results indicated that this was not the case for those adults who changed residence. The annual mortality rate clearly was not increased among the subsample that moved to the ICF/MRs. This finding is consistent with earlier reports that residential setting is unrelated to mortality when the disability profile is controlled (Miller and Eyman 1978) and suggests that many adults who are profoundly developmentally disabled can live within a small community based ICF without being subjected to an increased risk of mortality.

However, this conclusion must be qualified. Placement decisions for SNF residents were not made randomly. Discussions with senior clinical staff at the SNF indicated that no placement was made unless the physical condition of the person was stabilized and the ICF service program was well equipped to address medical service needs. Therefore, the ICF/MR subgroup may have consisted of individuals who were more physically fit as compared with people remaining in the SNF. The analyses of matched groups was included to address this potential confound and replicated the overall results in all critical respects. Nevertheless, it remains likely that valid clinical considerations not quantified in the present analyses influenced placement decisions, and some members of the SNF subgroup might be placed at increased mortality risk if they were to move to a smaller, less service-intensive residential program.

Further, as we noted previously (Silverman et al. 1987), ICF/MR programs located within major metropolitan areas may have access to health care service networks not available elsewhere. Therefore, appropriate ICF/MR sites may be difficult to develop within regions that do not have such an extensive service network providing potential resources upon which to draw. Unfortunately, we were unable to study the ICF/MR programs, and we therefore cannot provide descriptions of their service regimens. Nevertheless, we can conclude that great care must be exercised during program development in order to ensure that the diverse and complex needs of these exceptional individuals are addressed satisfactorily.

Another limitation of the present findings is imposed by our initial sampling method. Although our sample indeed is representative of the adults with the most severe impairments who receive developmental disabilities services, it included individuals who had already demonstrated considerable survival ability. The most fragile members of the population with profound mental retardation and multiple handicaps would have been likely to die during infancy, childhood, or early adolescence, and we have therefore been examining a select subgroup of this overall population. The overall annual mortality rate of 2.70% was comparable to but slightly lower than that of 4.1% reported by Eyman and co-workers (1987) among 68 people who were profoundly retarded, non–toilet trained and nonambulatory, and 16 years of age and older. This also suggests that our study group may have been more robust physically as compared with their younger peers. On the other hand, the SNF service model provided an array of services which would be likely to reduce mortality to a minimum. Therefore, program characteristics rather than client characteristics may account for the slight difference in mortality rate estimates between our sample and that of Eyman and colleagues. In either case, although the present analyses indicate that placement into an ICF/MR environment may pose no additional mortality risks for many of the adult members of our study population, placement of younger people with profound retardation and multiple handicaps may entail mortality risk unaddressed by our analyses, and this issue should be investigated explicitly.

The primary causes of death confirmed other reports of respiratory weaknesses within the population of people with profound mental retardation (Eyman et al. 1986; Richards 1976). Respiratory difficulties were implicated in 70% of the mortalities observed during the study period. Further, prospective measures of respiratory problems were significantlyiy associated with subsequent mortality. This finding supports previously reported hypotheses that acute respiratory incidents, even when treated successfully, can cumulatively constitute a mortality risk.

The mean age at death for deceased study participants was 28.53 years. Thus, even among individuals who had survived to reach young adulthood, their life expectancy is severely restricted compared with that of the general population. Indeed, even in the population of persons who are severely mentally handicapped, Haveman and Maaskant (1989) reported five-year mortality rates of approximately 3% during early adulthood. Our mortality rate of 17.4% (over the seven-year period 1981–87) confirmed that our sample was representative of the most impaired subpopulation of individuals with severe mental retardation.

Overall, our findings support the conclusion that the majority of adults with profound mental retardation and multiple handicaps, most of whom require less intensive medical services than our study group, can reside in facilities integrated within the community without entailing an increased mortality risk as long as careful program planning and development precede relocation. The present data clearly indicate that these individuals should not be rejected for placement into ICF/MRs based upon a summary evaluation of their characteristics. However, there is likely to be a residual number of the most fragile individuals with developmental disabilities whose constellation of needs cannot be addressed effectively outside of a service intensive SNF program model.

## Acknowledgments

This research was supported by funds provided by New York State through its Office of Mental Retardation and Developmental Disabilities, as well as Grants P01 HD 22634 and R29 HD 24170 from the National Institute of Child Health and Human Development. Collection of the prospective data was also supported by a grant from the New York State Advisory Council on Mental Retardation and Developmental Disabilities. The authors thank the staff of the participating facility for their invaluable help and cooperation, and Drs. V. Bhushan, R. Sapin, and N. Schupf for their thoughtful comments on earlier versions of the manuscript. Ms. Silver is now at Albert Einstein College of Medicine, Bronx, NY. Address reprint requests to: W. Silverman, 1050 Forest Hill Road, Staten Island, NY 10314.

# 7

## Behavior Modification Procedures in Group Homes Serving People with Developmental Disabilities

John W. Jacobson, Ph.D., and Lee J. Ackerman, M.S.

This chapter examines the usage rates of restrictive interventions and of restrictive procedures in concert with major psychoactive (i.e., antipsychotic and antidepressant) medications to address the treatment needs of persons with developmental disabilities (Cataldo 1989; Thompson, Hackenberg, and Schaal 1989). A substantial body of literature has been developed which examines the extent to which use of more restrictive procedures is acceptable in treatment, usually by surveys of parents, personnel, or professionals (McMahon et al. 1984). In sum, this literature indicates that such use is considered justifiable by some professionals under limited circumstances whereas other professionals may consider these procedures to be inappropriate under any circumstances.

In publicly funded human services the role of government is often understood to involve not only assurance that the quality of the services provided is high but also that the civil and human rights of service recipients are protected. For administrators, regulations that prescribe or proscribe treatment practices constitute a means of protecting the human and civil rights of individuals. Clinicians, on the other hand, may view regulations that proscribe some treatment practices as interfering with the provision of effective services or may consider that regulations provide insufficient protections from harm, based on differing clinical perspectives. Readers may be familiar with these issues in the context of right to refuse medication or treatment, right to treatment, and the processes of voluntary or involuntary commitment in the field of mental health. In the developmental services sector, in which surrogates (i.e., family or correspondents) often provide consent for treatment procedures, controversy has existed for many years with respect to the use of behavior modification procedures as a treatment modality, particularly those that involve hindering access to reinforcement (e.g., timeout) or use of punishment (e.g., termed *restrictive techniques;* Thompson, Gardner, and Baumeister 1988).

Regulations have been developed in many states in response to concerns about the use of restrictive behavior modification procedures. These regulations, however, address principally processes by which procedures are selected, designed, implemented, evaluated, and authorized rather than specifying instances in which their use is inappropriate (Spreat and Lipinski 1986). Ironically, states typically lack meaningful information about the current practice in the settings that they regulate which would allow the determination of adequate and inadequate practices. Although clinical reports (e.g., Schalock et al. 1985) suggest that both restrictive and nonrestrictive behavior management procedures (the latter entailing positive consequences) are used in community settings, little information is available about the actual prevalence of these procedures (Schroeder, Rojahn, and Oldenquist 1989).

Given the controversial nature of some behavioral treatment procedures, it would be useful to know the extent to which these practices occur within a service system (Gardner and Cole 1987) and for which types of behaviors they are used. A review of the literature (e.g., Matson and Gorman-Smith 1986) may not indicate prevalent treatment practices as much as researchers' interests and publication policies. Although studies have examined specific treatment practices and the prevalence and typologies of specific behaviors in single facilities or throughout entire service systems (e.g., Griffin et al. 1989), data on both focal behaviors and treatment procedures considered together have been infrequent (see Altmeyer et al. 1987; Griffin et al. 1989). Despite the common assumption that punishment procedures are often applied to control severe problem behaviors of persons with mental retardation (Axelrod 1987), findings suggest that positive contingencies or "no formal program" (i.e., no professionially implemented behavioral intervention) has tended to predominate as an intervention (see Intagliata, Rinck, and Calkins 1986).

One study using data from community and institutional facilities in Missouri found low rates of use for behavior modification techniques in private community programs and slightly (although not markedly) higher use rates in public institutional units (Intagliata, Rinck, and Calkins 1986). Their study, however, did not address what procedures were used but rather described procedures in terms of *level of staff response.*

The collection of survey data reported here was stimulated by concerns of state policymakers about their lack of information on delivery of behavior modification services within a community residential system. Changes in regulatory content were being considered by the state agency which could include prescriptive guidelines for certain procedures and modifications in authorization, approval, and review processes. To inform the decision making of policymakers and interested clinicians, data were collected with regard to use of nonrestrictive procedures (using reinforcement), timeout (withdrawing attention or reinforcement), and restrictive interventions (involving specific, planned punishment procedures) in this state's community residences. The more restrictive procedures surveyed included both positive punishment (aversive stimulation, positive practice, overcorrection) and negative punishment (response cost) procedures (see Craighead, Kazdin, and Mahoney 1976 for further description of these techniques).

METHODS

Subjects

The subjects for this study were 295 group homes (community residences or CRs and Intermediate Care Facilities for the Mentally Retarded or ICF/MRs) serving 2,841 persons with developmental disabilities in New York State. These programs served an average of 9.63 persons, with a range of from 3 to 15 occupants. Approximately 97% of these persons were reported to have mental retardation as their primary disability. These programs represented 24% of the group home system and included privately (61.4%) and publicly (38.6%) operated homes.

The respondents were residence managers with an average 9.1 years of experience and an average of 2.4 years tenure. Managers and staff were required to participate in training provided by the state agency in a variety of topic areas including the terminology and procedures of applied behavior analysis (Knowles and Landesman 1986).

Instrument

Data were collected using a survey that permitted recording of demographic, resident, staff, and program information for group homes. The survey incorporated 19 questions about the use of behavior modification procedures; age, sex, and target behaviors for individuals subject to timeout and other restrictive procedures; characteristics of the procedures; joint use of restrictive and nonrestrictive procedures; joint use of psychoactive medications; and administrative practices. However, respondents were not re-quested to identify the individuals who were receiving treatment that in-volved any behavioral procedures. Use of timeout and restrictive procedures was documented separately (i.e., the categories are mutually exclusive).

Data on the relative prevalence of six predominant problem behaviors were extracted from the data base for the Developmental Disabilities Infor-mation System (DDIS; Janicki and Jacobson 1982). It was not possible to match individual data for all residents, but individual data were matched for at least 64% of the persons living in each of the residence categories used in this chapter.

### Procedure

The survey was mailed to a random, stratified sample of 500 residences in New York State. The sample was stratified according to public or private operation, certification, location in the New York City metropolitan area or elsewhere, and an opening date before 1983 or afterward. Within five months completed protocols had been received from 300 sites (60%) that were generally representative of each of the residence categories (i.e., strata). The prevalence of the three groups of behavior management tech-niques was identified, the target behaviors were specified, and details of be-havioral and related administrative procedures were reviewed.

### RESULTS

As Table 7.1 shows, the group homes served principally young to middle-aged adults, and a small majority of the residents were males. Both timeout and restrictive procedures were used more commonly in combina-tion with psychoactive medications than as sole intervention procedures. The use of timeout was more prominent in private than in public programs and more prominent in ICF/MRs as contrasted with CRs. Other restrictive procedures were employed less often than timeout, although the demo-graphic usage pattern was roughly similar. Of community residences, 34.3% had no current behavior management plans, 43.1% used positive procedures only, and 22.6% used positive procedures in combination with timeout or restrictive procedures with at least one resident, compared with 15.7, 45.1, and 39.2%, respectively, of the ICF/MRs. These patterns were significantly different, with more ICF/MRs using any behavior management procedure, and more ICF/MRs using restrictive procedures ($\chi^2$ (2) = 20.1, $p < .005$). Differences in use between private and public programs were not statistically significant. Overall, 22.0% of programs had no current behavior manage-

**Table 7.1.  Sample Characteristics**

| | Residence Category | | | |
|---|---|---|---|---|
| *Characteristic* | *Private* | *Public* | *ICF/MR* | *CR* |
| *Totals* | | | | |
| N sites | 181 | 114 | 157 | 138 |
| N residents | 1,740 | 1,101 | 1,512 | 1,329 |
| Mean residents/site | 9.6 | 9.7 | 9.6 | 9.6 |
| *Resident demographics (%)* | | | | |
| *Age* (years) | | | | |
| 0–21 | 11.6 | 9.2 | 15.0 | 4.3 |
| 22–45 | 65.7 | 59.2 | 60.3 | 68.1 |
| 46–55 | 11.7 | 12.9 | 11.2 | 14.6 |
| 56+ | 11.0 | 18.7 | 13.5 | 13.0 |
| *Sex* | | | | |
| Female | 42.3 | 44.0 | 43.5 | 43.1 |
| *Use of procedures* | | | | |
| *Timeout* | | | | |
| Timeout and medication | | | | |
| N/% sites | 41/22.7 | 19/16.8 | 41/26.1 | 21/15.2 |
| N residents | 70 | 39 | 80 | 31 |
| Timeout only | | | | |
| N/% sites | 10/5.5 | 9/8.0 | 14/8.9 | 6/4.2 |
| N residents | 45 | 50 | 81 | 19 |
| *Restrictive procedures* | | | | |
| Restrictive and medication | | | | |
| N/% sites | 20/11.0 | 11/9.7 | 20/12.7 | 11/8.0 |
| N residents | 31 | 19 | 34 | 16 |
| Restrictive only | | | | |
| N/% sites | 6/3.4 | 4/3.6 | 6/3.9 | 4/2.9 |
| N residents | 32 | 24 | 42 | 14 |

ment plans, 44.1% used positive procedures only, and 33.9% used positive procedures in combination with timeout or restrictive procedures with at least one resident.

Altogether, timeout was used with one or more residents in 26.8% of residences and more restrictive techniques in 13.9% of residences. With respect to persons who lived in the sampled residences, 7.2% ($N = 204$) received treatment that involved timeout, and 3.7% ($N = 106$) received treatment that involved more restrictive procedures. These patterns suggest that persons who received either of these procedures were not grouped in residences in which these treatment procedures were typical of the treatment provided.

However, there were 19 sites in which timeout was used without medication, accounting for 24.1% of sites in which time out was used and 46.5% of persons receiving timeout. Similarly, in 10 sites restrictive procedures were used without medication, accounting for 24.4% of sites in which these procedures were used and 52.8% of persons subject to restrictive treatment procedures. Use of these procedures without conjoint use of medication may be restricted to a small number of residences, within each of which an average of about 5.5 persons are subject to timeout or restrictive procedures.

Demographic patterns were also considered with respect to the use of timeout and restrictive procedures. The probability of receiving these treatments did not differ by sex. By inspection, children and adolescents in private residences and children in public residences (representing small proportions of the resident populations) evidenced the highest rate of treatment receipt. These individuals represented 12.1% (private) and 6.6% (public) of persons receiving timeout and 30.0% (private) and 5.0% (public) of persons receiving more restrictive treatments.

Target behaviors selected were reported for between 83.1 and 100.0% of uses of timeout across residence categories and for between 88.9 and 100.0% of uses of restrictive procedures. Six behaviors accounted for between 76.9 and 90.5% of uses of timeout depending upon the residence setting. These six behaviors were: physical assault, temper tantrums, self-injurious behavior, verbal abuse, property destruction, and resisting supervision (i.e., oppositional behavior in response to verbal request or physical prompt). These behaviors also accounted for from 43.7 to 78.3% of reported uses of more restrictive procedures across residence categories. Physical assault and temper tantrums were the behaviors for which timeout and restrictive procedures were most frequently prescribed.

Having identified which behaviors are the principal targets for timeout and restrictive procedures, it is also valuable to identify whether these behaviors are typically treated using these procedures. The data that addressed this issue are shown in Table 7.2. In this table frequencies of problem behaviors were extrapolated for the entire sample groups based on the proportion of cases which were matched to the DDIS data base. As shown, although timeout and restrictive procedures were, together, applied to about one fourth of the persons who were assaultive, use of this class of procedure was consistently less common for other severe behavior problems, at less than 10% of cases based on occurrence rates for behaviors. Even when severe behavior problems were present, in general, clinicians did not appear to be employing timeout or restrictive procedures as treatments of choice.

Table 7.3 shows six-month prevalences for procedures relative to the

Table 7.2.  Occurrence of Behaviors versus Use of Procedures

| Extrapolated Data | Residence Category | | | |
| --- | --- | --- | --- | --- |
| | Private | Public | ICF/MR | CR |
| *Physical assault* | | | | |
| N with behavior | 259 | 209 | 272 | 141 |
| % Timeout/restrictive | 17.0/5.8 | 16.3/7.7 | 19.2/9.2 | 18.4/5.0 |
| *Temper tantrums* | | | | |
| N with behavior | 315 | 186 | 257 | 193 |
| % Timeout/restrictive | 2.9/1.0 | 5.4/1.6 | 8.2/1.9 | 1.0/0.5 |
| *Self-injurious behavior* | | | | |
| N with behavior | 161 | 110 | 170 | 67 |
| % Timeout/restrictive | 5.6/2.5 | 6.4/1.8 | 8.2/3.5 | 6.0/0.0 |
| *Resists supervision* | | | | |
| N with behavior | 236 | 132 | 188 | 150 |
| % Timeout/restrictive | 3.8/2.5 | 2.2/3.8 | 4.8/4.3 | 2.0/2.0 |
| *Verbally abusive* | | | | |
| N with behavior | 232 | 140 | 156 | 182 |
| % Timeout/restrictive | 3.9/1.3 | 4.3/1.4 | 7.1/1.3 | 3.3/1.6 |
| *Property destruction* | | | | |
| N with behavior | 113 | 113 | 128 | 71 |
| % Timeout/restrictive | 7.1/2.7 | 6.2/3.5 | 10.9/6.3 | 2.8/0.0 |
| *Percent of cases matched*[a] | 64.4 | 68.4 | 79.4 | 62.2 |

[a] Percent of cases matched = percentage of persons in a residence category who could be matched to a data base containing information on these behaviors; "N with behavior" is extrapolated from these data. The table shows the percent of persons with each behavior subject to timeout or to a more restrictive procedure.

total numbers of persons in each program category. Most evident is that the usage of nonrestrictive, positive contingencies alone (used with 21–38% of program residents depending upon the category of group home) greatly exceeded usage of other procedures, including joint usage of positive procedures and either timeout or restrictive procedures (66.7% of CRs and 86.8% of ICF/MRs used some form of positive contingency with at least one resident). Joint usage rates shown for timeout and restrictive procedures are subsets of the overall timeout and restrictive procedures rates. However, across the residence categories, only between 15.9 and 25.7% of behavior plans involving timeout and between 19.2 and 26.9% of behavior plans involving restrictive procedures were modified during a six-month interval. Once instituted, such behavior plans typically remained in effect, unmodified, for periods in excess of six months. This finding may indicate that these procedures are relatively ineffective or that procedures remain authorized by the inter-

Table 7.3.  Types and Components of Procedures: Six-month Prevalences
as a Percent of Residents

| Procedure | Residence Category | | | |
| --- | --- | --- | --- | --- |
| | Private | Public | ICF/MR | CR |
| Positive contingencies only (estimated minimum/ maximum) | 29.3–31.4 | 25.0–29.3 | 34.4–38.5 | 21.6–23.5 |
| Any timeout or restric- tive procedures (minimum/maximum) | 6.6–10.2 | 8.1–12.0 | 11.0–16.2 | 3.9–6.2 |
| Timeout | 6.6 | 8.1 | 11.0 | 3.9 |
| Restrictive procedures | 3.6 | 3.9 | 5.2 | 2.3 |
| Joint usage with medication | | | | |
| Timeout | 4.0 | 3.5 | 5.5 | 2.4 |
| Restrictive procedures | 1.8 | 1.7 | 2.3 | 1.2 |
| Joint usage with positive contingencies | | | | |
| Timeout | 5.7 | 7.1 | 8.4 | 3.2 |
| Restrictive procedures | 2.1 | 3.9 | 4.2 | 1.8 |
| Percent of behavior plans modified[a] | | | | |
| Timeout | 25.2 | 23.1 | 25.7 | 15.9 |
| Restrictive procedures | 26.9 | 20.5 | 25.7 | 19.2 |

[a]Percent of behavior plans modified = of behavior plans in effect, percent substantially revised or altered over a six-month period. See text for explanation of "Joint usage" rates.

disciplinary team as the equivalent to a prn (i.e., as needed) order, regardless of the behavior change achieved, which may be infrequently invoked.

Characteristics of timeout and restrictive procedures were also surveyed.
Timeout procedures are, in regulation, limited to one hour in duration, and in
practice are used for much shorter periods (especially in-situation
timeout). Most frequently timeout was a formal intervention procedure entailing removal of the person from a situation (43.6–51.6%) and use of their
bedroom as a timeout area (56.8–66.0%). In general, special provisions
(physical modifications) were not made for use of a specific location for
timeout (6.0–13.7%). Instances of restrictive procedures most commonly
entailed response cost (e.g., loss of privileges or tokens; 27.4–40.0% of all
restrictive procedures) or contingent reprimand (e.g., verbal correction of
behavior or disapproval statements; 23.4–27.8%); positive practice
(19.3–23.6%), and overcorrection (11.1–21.0%). Aversive stimulation

Table 7.4.  Administrative Procedures

|  | % Distribution by Residence Type | | | |
|---|---|---|---|---|
|  | Private | Public | ICF/MR | CR |
| Timeout and restrictive[a] behavior plans reviewed by | | | | |
| Manager | 27.3 | 3.1 | 11.6 | 31.9 |
| Psychologist | 57.4 | 54.7 | 45.3 | 63.9 |
| Other staff | 14.8 | 45.2 | 43.1 | 4.2 |
| Positive contingency plans reviewed by | | | | |
| Manager | 36.3 | 8.0 | 10.0 | 32.9 |
| Psychologist | 32.5 | 51.8 | 44.1 | 59.9 |
| Educator | 25.5 | 40.2 | 42.5 | 5.3 |
| Other staff | 5.7 | 0.0 | 3.3 | 1.9 |
| Mechanism to coordinate psychologic and psychiatric services | 52.5 | 68.1 | 73.2 | 42.0 |
| Team process to approve behavior plans and psychoactive medications | 85.1 | 89.4 | 93.0 | 80.4 |
| Communication mechanism for psychologist and physician | 73.5 | 78.8 | 84.1 | 67.4 |

[a] Depending on the residence type, between 52.2 and 100.0% of respondents in each category indicated who reviewed behavior plans. The table shows percents of residences.

(e.g., water mist, unpleasant smells or tastes, faradic stimulation) accounted for only 8.1% of restrictive methods used in ICF/MRs and was applied to only 0.3% of CR and ICF/MR residents (e.g., nine persons, or a rate of roughly three per thousand). Although this rate (because it differs from zero) may concern persons who oppose any use of highly restrictive procedures, from a public policy standpoint it is far less of a concern than other treatment findings. For example, the rate of use of major psychoactive medications in these settings is 248 per thousand, or roughly 82 times as great (see Jacobson 1988b, 1990 for more detailed information on the use of psychoactive medications to treat psychiatric and behavior disorders in this state's community residences).

Administrative supports were also assessed (see Table 7.4). Consultants or private practitioners were seldom the source of behavior management services (accounting for services in 2.9–27.4% of sites depending upon the category). Most services were provided by psychologists who were employees of the private agency or the state agency for developmental services.

With the exception of ICF/MRs, a majority of the timeout and restrictive contingency plans were periodically reviewed by psychologists. Managers, educators, and unspecified staff provided a majority of the reviews of positive contingency behavior management plans. Many of the nonrespondents to the question regarding review of timeout or restrictive procedures plans were programs that did not currently use these procedures.

A large proportion of programs had team processes in place to monitor and authorize behavior plans and initiate or revise psychoactive medication regimens proposed by physicians and had mechanisms in place to promote communication between psychologists and psychiatrists or other medical specialists. However, mechanisms actually to coordinate the services of these disciplines were present in only half of these programs and were most frequently reported to be absent in private programs and community residences. Because these provisions were not mandated in regulations, the rates of implementation of methods and mechanisms can only be taken as an index of spontaneous efforts by providers to monitor and manage services.

In light of the possible sensitivity of the questions in this survey, the validity of the findings might well be questioned. It was not possible to conduct extensive reliability tests. However, expected associations of the use of procedures to other data were investigated to determine whether they were present. Use of timeout and other restrictive procedures tended to occur in the same program settings; the correlations between usage of these two procedural classes ranged from $r = .26$ to $r = .46$ (all $p < .001$), depending upon the operator and type of program. The mean resident intellectual level was correlated with the use of timeout ($r(259) = .12, p < .04$) but not with use of restrictive procedures. In addition, hours of psychologist services on site (per resident per month) were associated with usage of restrictive procedures in private ($r(172) = .15, p < .03$), public ($r(111) = .31, p < .001$), and ICF/MR programs ($r(155) = .23, p < .002$). In public programs the use of timeout was also associated with psychologist service hours ($r(111) = .38, p < .001$). Although the absolute magnitudes of the correlations were attenuated by skewedness in the data (i.e., a minority of programs used either class of procedure), the relationships found suggest convergent validation.

## DISCUSSION

The survey findings suggest the following in one state's group home system characterized by both public and private CRs and ICF/MRs. (1) A majority of programs provided behavior management services that were nonrestrictive in nature to a substantial majority of their residents. (2) The prevalence of such nonrestrictive procedures (and of programs that used them) greatly exceeded that of timeout or restrictive procedures. (3) Timeout and restrictive procedures were used more commonly in combination with psychoactive medication than as sole interventions. (4) Restrictive procedures were used more frequently in combination with positive contingencies than as sole interventions. (5) Restrictive procedures were used principally with young to middle-aged adults and to address highly disruptive or destructive behavior. (6) Restrictive procedures tended to remain in place for at least six months, and a majority were not altered substantially over this period. (7) A majority of instances of highly disruptive behaviors were addressed via procedures that entailed neither timeout nor restrictive procedures. (8) Aversive stimulation was very seldom used. (9) Administrative procedures were inconsistently in place to support or monitor behavior management services.

In general, the usage pattern found in this study suggests practices that appear acceptable and consistent with guidelines for effective behavioral treatment (Division 33 1989; Van Houten et al. 1988). However, several potential problems were noted. Although more restrictive procedures were used on a selected basis and for the treatment of severe behavior problems, the findings suggested that both timeout and restrictive plans were often in effect, without substantial alteration, for six months. Recent analyses indicate that the treatment effectiveness of more restrictive behavioral procedures can often be identified within 10 treatment sessions (Cataldo 1989). Extended duration of such treatment procedures could mean that procedures that are ineffective are often not altered in a timely manner and could contribute to decreased social (i.e., public) acceptability of the treatment procedure itself.

Public and social acceptability of behavioral theory and practice have been long-standing concerns of behavior analysts, and marked criticism has been voiced recently with respect to potential or real conflicts between some prevalent behavior modification procedures and the legal and civil rights of persons who are receiving them (see Gardner 1989; Wood 1975). Policymakers may choose either to regulate the provision of specific services (i.e., identify acceptable and unacceptable procedures) or to regulate the process by which various procedures are authorized. Central concerns involve whether potentially controversial procedures are used widely and whether the implementation of these procedures is authorized and reviewed in a manner that supports responsive treatment.

Restrictive procedures were not found to be used on a widespread basis and typically were employed in conjunction with other strategies as part of a comprehensive approach to treatment. However, timeout, restrictive, and nonrestrictive behavior plans were often reviewed by nonpsychologists, and many of these reviewers may be insufficiently trained to detect adverse effects or to redevelop interventions. Insufficient training could account for sustained implementation of behavior plans without substantial revision and could result in perpetuation of ineffective behavior plans that fail to promote skill development or may exacerbate problem behaviors. However, we collected no data to determine whether psychologists modified behavior plans more frequently or to verify the effectiveness of interventions.

Insufficient training is an important issue that public agencies can only partially address by making enhanced educational opportunities on topics of concern more available. However, the brunt of responsibility for training falls on the academic sector. The specification in regulation of the requirement for special competencies or certification for design and use of restrictive procedures would have the effect of preventing these procedures unless persons with the required competencies and knowledge were available. This reality indicates that to the (as yet undetermined) extent that such procedures may be required as components of some interventions for some individuals, both public higher educational and developmental services agencies have a responsibility to ensure that professionals receive adequate preservice preparation as well as competence-based in-service training in the full range of contemporary behavioral procedures. In addition, the availability of more adequate evaluative research on intervention effects and competencies for practice could constitute the foundation for more consensually valid regulatory practices with respect to the use of behavior analytic interventions involving persons with severe behavior disorders and developmental disabilities.

The data also suggested that insufficient provisions were made for the coordination of behavioral and psychiatric services. This could be another factor that contributed to extended intervention duration. This pattern could also reflect low rates of active participation within the team process for authorization of services or low rates of practitioner availability or accessibility, involving both psychologists and physicians. However, in most instances it appeared that the interdisciplinary team was deliberating with respect to differential treatment alternatives and that when restrictive procedures were employed these reflected one outcome of these deliberations.

The majority of persons with severe behavior disorders were not receiving behavioral services that entailed timeout or restrictive procedures despite the absence of regulations specifically limiting the use of such procedures. Contrary to some expectations that use of restrictive behavioral procedures is limited largely to public institutional settings, the data suggest that these procedures are also employed in public and private community residential settings with residents who present severe behavior problems and that the techniques employed are more frequently nonrestrictive rather than restrictive in nature. Particularly noteworthy was that even in instances in which residents had severe behavior problems, a minority of these individuals were subjected to restrictive behavioral procedures.

In addition to implications for policymakers, these data also offer a number of implications for practitioners. To date, the weight of scientific evidence has favored combined use of reinforcing and punishing treatment procedures to modify severe problem behaviors (when nonrestrictive procedures have been adequately demonstrated to be ineffective or inappropriate; Jacobson and Mulick 1989a). In practice, however, the organizational characteristics of community residential settings, the competencies of their staff, and the availability of sufficient clinical supervision will determine the feasibility of implementing restrictive procedures with the required fidelity (Jacobson and Mulick 1989b; Jacobson, Schwartz, and Janicki 1984).

Practitioners who carry extensive caseloads and cannot readily assign staff (e.g., skilled therapist extenders) to supervise procedures and who are willing to use restrictive procedures must limit the use of these procedures to highly selected instances in which they can supervise implementation personally (Jacobson and Mulick 1989b). Thus, the degree to which appropriately qualified clinicians are available, rather than the behavior and response to treatment of the people being served, may account for the usage rates for restrictive procedures, extended continuance of behavior plans, and reviews of plans by nonpsychologic personnel.

For the practitioner in community services, staff training, training of agency directors to assure increased attention to implementation, and training of managers to improve oversight and treatment fidelity are critical components of the clinical role (Jacobson 1989a). A skilled and well-trained work force is a necessary provision to ensure that appropriate target behaviors are selected, nonrestrictive procedures are tested properly for benefit, and that information gathered as part of a continuing assessment process is reliable and valid. The ability to develop and maintain this work force of staff and concerned professionals rather than regulatory strictures or ideologic debate may be the principal determinant of whether persons with developmental disabilities will have access to the most appropriate, effective behavioral treatment to assist their continued participation in community living.

# III
# SOCIAL ADJUSTMENT

The major efforts throughout this country over the past two decades on the part of policymakers, professionals, and advocates to implement programs and services to support the community integration of people with severe disabilities beg the questions, How well are they doing? How well is community integration working? What level of social adjustment and integration is achieved and how can it be improved? And, most important, How do service recipients view their social integration and adjustment? What is life like for the people with severe psychiatric or developmental disabilities who are experiencing "community integration?"

The following six chapters present original research and information in an attempt to answer these questions. Two chapters address the relationships of stress, support, and coping skills to personal adjustment; two chapters present self-reported information from people with disabilities (one describing the types and extent of social support they receive, the other, their preferences for the type of support they wish to receive); and the final chapters present the results of two longitudinal research studies on the community integration and adjustment of people with severe disabilities, adults with mental retardation, and adults with the dual diagnoses of developmental and psychiatric disabilities.

In Chapter 8 Joseph Hasazi and his colleagues present the results of original research that examines the relationship of life stress and social support to the behavioral adjustment and self-reported personal satisfaction of adults with mental retardation. The results of a cross-sectional study of individuals residing in three types of community living setting are used to illustrate the need to consider the experiences of stress and support as significant components of community life for people with disabilities, heavily influencing their social adjustment.

In Chapter 9 Sutherland Miller reviews the literature on stress, coping, and social adjustment and applies the findings to the needs of persons with severe disabilities. Miller presents a program for assisting individuals with psychiatric disabilities to learn effective coping strategies to counter the many pressures they meet in attempting to adapt to community living. The importance for these individuals for developing such strategies and skills is ably presented.

Sara Burchard and her colleagues present the results of original research that examines the social support, integration, and satisfaction of individuals with disabilities from their own perspective. Their Chapter 10 is a cross-sectional study of the social support networks and social activities of persons receiving agency services as compared with those living with their natural families. This chapter addresses the important issue of the extent of social integration which people actually experience, the constitution of their support systems, and their perceptions of the support they receive.

Chapter 11 presents the results of a statewide study of consumer-identified preferences and needs which was conducted by Beth Tanzman and her colleagues. The importance of designing and developing programs that actually serve the needs of consumers rather than the needs of providers or planners or established financing methods cannot be emphasized enough. This chapter presents empirical verification of the discrepancy between what we want to and are prepared to provide and what consumers want and need, which has significant policy implications.

In Chapter 12, Lawrence Gordon and his colleagues present the original results of a three-year longitudinal study of the community adjustment and integration of adults with developmental disabilities. The chapter is a comparative study between life in the community for individuals in supported living or small supervised group living and for individuals living at home. The results of this study emphasize again the need to examine consumer preferences for individualized and supportive living situations rather than to rely on site-based, group living programs generated by policymakers and providers who themselves do not live in such environments.

In Chapter 13, the final chapter in this section, James Kearney and Michael Smull present the results of a five-year postplacement outcome study of individuals with mental retardation who were placed under court order from mental hospitals to community settings. This study is unique among studies of deinstitutionalization in evaluating the outcomes for individuals presumably with dual diagnoses. The chapter shows once again the historic issue of how we place people into programs rather than designing programs to meet the needs of individual people (a large proportion of persons with mental retardation are placed inappropriately in mental hospitals), examines the factors associated with reinstitutionalization, and compares the community functioning of this sample with samples of deinstitutionalized persons from two other states.

Again, this series of chapters raises many policy issues with respect to providing needed supports to individuals with severe disabilities to enable them to live in the community and achieve some level of social adjustment there. These studies also demonstrate several different methods of conducting field research. The contributions of such studies to inform our policy, planning, and service providers as well as the limitations of such research are clearly illustrated in these chapters.

# 8

# Adjustment to Community Life

## The Role of Stress and Support Variables

Joseph E. Hasazi, Ph.D., Sara N. Burchard, Ph.D.,
Lawrence R. Gordon, Ph.D., Elia Vecchione, M.A.,
and Julie W. Rosen, Ph.D.

The ability of persons with mental retardation to live, learn, and work successfully within the mainstream of community life is more often limited by the presence of significant behavioral adjustment problems than by intellectual or skill deficits. In both community residential and vocational contexts, for example, such problems appear to be the primary factor associated with poor adjustment outcomes (Haney 1988; Parsons, May, and Menolascino 1984; Wehman, Moon, and McCarthy 1986). From that perspective alone there is a clear need to understand better the origins of these problems and to identify effective methods for their prevention and treatment. The importance of this need is underscored by the fact that as a group, persons with mental retardation experience significantly higher rates of emotional and behavioral problems than the general population (Matson and Frame 1986; Menolascino 1977; Parsons, May, and Menolascino 1984).

At the present time our understanding of the etiology of behavioral problems in children and adults with mental retardation is poor. For the most part applied research in the field has focused on the treatment of these problems and has ignored their etiology. To some extent this focus may be attributable to certain unfounded assumptions and beliefs about the adjustment processes of persons with mental retardation. For instance, it has often been assumed that the behavioral problems of persons with mental retardation develop in a manner different from those of persons of average intelligence, (e.g., that they stem from the same factors responsible for the retardation itself or are simply part of the syndrome; Menolascino 1983; Phillips 1971).

111

Insofar as a causal role was assigned to the presence of mental retardation, the need for any further study of etiology was largely obviated.

Recently there have been efforts to encourage basic research on the etiology of psychopathology in persons with mental retardation (e.g., Matson 1985; Menolascino 1977, 1983; Reiss and Benson 1985). At a basic level these efforts have urged the application of theories and models found to be useful in understanding the mental health problems of persons of average intelligence. In the absence of findings to the contrary it seems reasonable to assume that the same factors and processes contributing to the development of psychopathology in persons of average intelligence would apply as well to persons with mental retardation. If nothing else, this assumption is parsimonious and heuristic in that it suggests a direct application or extension of existing research methods and findings to persons with mental retardation.

Assuming that etiologic factors do not differ by level of intellectual functioning, Menolasacino's (1983, 36) contention that "increased exposure to psychological stress" may play a significant role in the etiology of behavioral adjustment problems in persons with mental retardation warrants consideration. There is widespread agreement that stress and coping processes are among the most important factors in the etiology of psychopathology in persons of average intelligence (e.g., Garmezy and Rutter 1983; Lazarus and Folkman 1985). Indeed, there have been literally thousands of studies relating the experience of stress to the development of both physical and behavioral adjustment problems in children and adults of normal intelligence. In contrast, the potential role of stress in the etiology of behavioral problems in persons with mental retardation has been, for the most part, ignored. It is unusual to find even a mention of the concept of stress in recent books on psychopathology and mental retardation. Within the field what research there has been on stress has emphasized the person with mental retardation as a *source* of stress to others rather than as an *experiencer* of stress.

The lack of attention to stress experience in persons with mental retardation is surprising in light of the long-standing belief that they have a reduced capacity to withstand stress (e.g., Cytryn and Lourie 1967; Menolascino, 1977) coupled with the observation that they may more frequently encounter stresses, frustrations, and conflicts in their daily lives than do other people (Heller 1988; Menolascino 1983; Reiss and Benson 1985). The failure to consider a possible stress adjustment link under these circumstances may represent a particular instance of the "overshadowing" phenomenon (Reiss and Szyszko 1983). Confronted with evidence that persons with mental retardation exhibit higher rates of emotional and behavioral problems, may encounter greater stress, and may have reduced coping abilities, it is difficult to dismiss the possibility that these factors are somehow related.

### LIFE EVENT STRESS AND ADJUSTMENT

Although a number of methodologies have been developed for the study of stress, by far the most widely used approach was pioneered by Holmes and Rahe (1967). This approach operationalizes stress in terms of life events that require adjustment or coping responses, such as the loss of a loved one or a change in living or working conditions. Studies using this approach assess the number of life events experienced by the individual over a period of time (for example, one year) and relate them to physical or behavioral outcomes observed at the end of that time period. Across age groups it has been found generally that as the number of such events increases, physical and behavioral problems of various kinds increase as well (Compas 1987a; Johnson 1986; Thoits 1983). The magnitude of the correlations between life events and such outcomes tends to be modest (around .30), however, suggesting that other factors may operate to potentiate or moderate the effects of stress. Among the factors that appear to be important in that regard are social support (Barrera 1981), gender (Compas et al. 1986), coping skills (Compas 1987b), and normative transitions (Compas et al. 1986). With respect to the last factor, Compas and co-workers (1986) suggested that people may be most vulnerable to the effects of life events during major life transitions (e.g., the transition from high school to college). Johnson (1986) argued that studies of stressful life events in individuals undergoing normative transitions are especially needed at the present time.

Based upon the general findings in the stress and coping literature, a significant, albeit moderate, association between life event stress and behavioral adjustment in persons with mental retardation would be expected if the processes involved are in fact similar across levels of intellectual functioning. One would expect as well to find an inverse relationship between life event stress and social support and more generally, for social support to moderate the relationship between stress and adjustment. Finally, one would expect to find that the experience of life event stress varies with both individual and environmental characteristics.

Some support for these expectations can be found in the literature on mental retardation. For example, Levine (1985) obtained self-reports of situational anxiety from adults with mild mental retardation under four conditions presumed to differ in stressfulness. He found that more anxiety was reported under conditions of higher stress, such as participating in a testing situation involving public performance and demonstration of competence under novel conditions. He also found that individuals who were unemployed or less socially active tended to report higher levels of anxiety across stress conditions. Ghaziuddin (1988) assessed life events among adults with mental retardation who were referred to an outpatient clinic for treatment of behavioral problems. He found that the onset of behavioral problems was associated with discernible life events, such as bereavement, in 44% of the sample. Persons in the mild range of mental retardation experienced a greater number of such events than persons in the severe range. Although Ghaziuddin's findings suggest a stress-adjustment relationship, he did not assess the frequency or severity of behavioral problems or test statistically the association between stress and adjustment. Furthermore, his sample consisted entirely of clinic-referred individuals without appropriate controls. As such, it is difficult to interpret his findings clearly or to relate them directly to general findings in the field. The extension of stress and coping concepts to the study of psychopathology in adults with mental retardation is supported further by the findings of Reiss and Benson (1985). They found that self-report and informant ratings of depression in adults with mental retardation were significantly and negatively correlated with measures of social support.

In our own research, we have been examining the relationship of life event stress to adjustment as part of a larger study of the community adjustment and integration of adults residing in group homes, supervised apartments, and family homes (Burchard et al., in press). In the study we assessed life events over a 12-month period and related them to both careprovider and self-reports of adjustment assessed at the end of that time period. In our initial analyses of these data we found that life events were significantly and positively correlated with careprovider reports of behavioral problem frequency ($r = .41$) and severity ($r = .51$) and were significantly and negatively correlated with self-reports of residential satisfaction ($r = -.18$) and personal well-being ($r = -.24$) (Hasazi et al. 1990). Both in direction and magnitude these correlations are consistent with general findings in the literature strengthening the contention that life event stress operates in the lives of persons with mental retardation similarly to persons of normal intelligence. We also found significant differences among residence types in both stress experience and adjustment. Persons in family homes experienced significantly fewer life events and were rated significantly lower in behavioral problem frequency and severity than persons in group homes and supervised apartments. Although these findings are open to a number of interpretations, they suggest that the experience of life event stress and its relationship to adjustment may be functions of particular characteristics of residential settings such as the number of cohabitants, availability of family support, and/or of personal characteristics such as level of mental retardation or nature of disability. In this chapter we explore these possibilities further. First, we examine the contributions of both personal and residential characteristics to the experience of life event stress. More specifically, we examine the contributions of personal characteristics, structural and organizational characteristics of the home, and social support variables to variations in life event stress. Second, we examine the contributions of life event stress and social support variables to adjustment outcomes controlling for both personal and residential characteristics.

METHODS

### Participants and Settings

The participants in this study included 133 adults with mental retardation ranging in age from 22 to 58 years. All resided in community settings: 54 in group homes providing 24-hour a day care and supervision to 3 to 6 persons; 41 in supervised apartments providing as-needed support and consultation generally to 1 or 2 persons; and 38 in family homes under the care and supervision of one or both parents.

Residents of group homes and supervised apartments were comparable in age, institutional history, and length of current residence whereas residents of family homes were significantly younger ($F(2,130) = 7.39$, $p < .001$), had significantly less institutional experience ($\chi^2(2, N = 133) = 10.16$, $p < .01$), and had resided in their current residence for significantly longer time periods ($F(2,130) = 17.90$, $p < .001$). Significantly more of the residents of supervised apartments and family homes were classified in the mild range of mental retardation compared with group home residents ($\chi^2(2, N = 133) = 14.83$, $p < .01$). Settings were comparable in the distribution of male and female residents.

### Procedure

Individuals were identified and recruited on a statewide basis with the assistance of mental retardation service providers and advocacy groups. Persons who met eligibility criteria were informed of the study and, if interested, initiated contact with project staff. Information was obtained from questionnaires and structured interviews with participants and parents (for those in family homes) or service providers (for those in group homes and apartments). Based upon this information, we quantified four sets of variables: life event stress, personal characteristics (age, gender, level of mental retardation, and disability status), residential characteristics (normalization practices and social integration), and social support variables (numbers of handicapped, nonhandicapped, kin, and total persons in support network, and satisfaction with support). Hierarchic multiple regressions were used to investigate the contributions of personal, residential, and social network characteristics to life event stress and of all variables to residential satisfaction and behavioral problem severity.

Measures

*Life Event Stress.* A 45-item scale based on the life events survey developed by Holmes and Rahe (1967) was used to quantify this variable. Items were modified, added, or deleted to fit the life circumstances of adults with mental retardation. For example, scale items concerning marriage or divorce were broadened to encompass beginning or ending a significant emotional relationship. The scale was completed by the individual's primary careprovider who was asked to endorse each item occurring within the previous 12 months. Endorsed items were summed to yield a single life events score. Test-retest reliability over a one-week period was relatively high, $r(15) = .89, p < .01$). Scores on the scale demonstrate moderate stability over a one-year period ($r(104) = .64, p < .01$).

*Personal Characteristics.* Age, gender, level of mental retardation, and disability status were determined on the basis of careprovider reports to a demographic questionnaire and review of historical records. The level of mental retardation was coded on a three-point scale corresponding to moderate, mild, and borderline levels. Disability status was defined by the total number of handicapping conditions and chronic health problems noted out of a list of 10 conditions, such as hearing impairment or seizure disorder.

*Residential Characteristics.* Careprovider interviews were used to assess two residential characteristics. (1) A measure of *life-style normalization,* was based upon a 34-item structured interview assessing the opportunities provided to the individual for age-appropriate activities, personal responsibility, and autonomy in decision making. Interrater reliability in scoring careprovider responses was $r = .87$. This measure has been found to differentiate group homes and intermediate care facilities for the mentally retarded (ICF/MRs) of equal size (Burchard et al. 1987) and to correlate positively with direct observations of age-appropriate activities and with ratings of residence normalization (Pine 1983). (2) A measure of *social integration* was obtained based upon careprovider reports about the number of activities engaged in by the individual in integrated, community settings with nonhandicapped peers over a two-week period excluding work or day program settings.

*Social Support.* Resident interviews were used to assess four social network characteristics. An 18-item structured interview was used to elicit the names of individuals upon whom respondents rely for social support. This interview was based on the social network questionnaire of Weinberg (1984) and was modified for use with persons with mental retardation (Rosen and Burchard 1990). Based upon interview responses, we calculated the total number of individuals in the network as well as the numbers of individuals determined to be peers with handicaps, nonhandicapped peers, or kin (as well as those in other categories not considered in this chapter). A measure of satisfaction with support (i.e., the proportion of persons in the network who were viewed as a source of support) was also computed. Test-retest reliabilities over a two- to six-week period were .73, .78, and .53 for size, relationship type, and satisfaction measures, respectively.

*Residential Satisfaction.* This variable was assessed using a 22-item scale assessing the individual's general satisfaction with his or her residential living situation with respect to physical characteristics, personal autonomy, and relationships. It was administered in interview format with each item calling for a *yes* or *no* response. Items are worded in both positive and negative terms to account for possible response biases or acquiescence sets. The percentage of items responded to in a positive manner (i.e., reflecting satisfaction) is calculated to yield a single score with a possible range of $0-100$. Test-retest reliability over a two-week period was relatively high ($r(15) = .78$, $p < .01$) (Burchard et al. 1987). The measure's internal consistency (coefficient $\alpha$) was .73 (Burchard, Pine, and Gordon 1990).

*Behavioral Problem Severity.* This variable was based upon careprovider responses to a 10-item scale reflecting general categories of behavioral problems such as self-injurious, aggressive, or socially withdrawn behavior (Bruininks et al. 1984). Informants were asked to identify no more than three behavioral problems and to then rate each on five-point scales of frequency and severity. Behavioral problem frequency and severity scores with possible ranges of $0-15$ were then derived. The interrater reliabilities for behavioral problem frequency ($r(48) = .83$, $p < .001$) and behavioral problem severity ($r(48) = .78$, $p < .001$) were both relatively high. The behavioral problem frequency and severity scores are themselves significantly associated ($r(133)$ = .84, $p$ < .0001). As such, only the behavioral problem severity scores were retained for analysis.

RESULTS

The results of the hierarchic multiple regressions on the life events, residential satisfaction, and behavioral problem severity variables are summarized in Table 8.1. Across analyses, personal characteristics were entered first as a set followed by residential characteristics as a set. In the analyses of residential satisfaction and behavior problem severity, life events were entered at the third step. Across analyses, social support variables were entered as a set at the final step. In the analysis of life events, the set of social support variables consisted of the numbers of peers with handicaps, nonhandicapped peers, kin, and total persons in the network. In the analyses of the residential satisfaction and behavioral problem severity variables, the set of social support variables consisted of the number of persons with and without handicaps in the network and support satisfaction. Analyses involved only those individuals for whom all variables were available.

Life Events

The regressions of personal characteristics alone and with residential characteristics were not significantly different from zero. In other words, the

Table 8.1. Summary of Hierarchical Multiple Regressions

| Dependent Variables | Independent Variables | $R^2$ | $F$ | $\Delta R^2$ | $F$ |
|---|---|---|---|---|---|
| Life events | Personal characteristics | .00 | 0.15 | .00 | 0.15 |
| | Residential characteristics | .06 | 1.02 | .06 | 2.74 |
| | Social support | .23 | 2.46* | .16 | 4.39** |
| Residential | Personal characteristics | .07 | 1.81 | .07 | 1.81 |
| satisfaction | Residential characteristics | .15 | 2.37* | .07 | 3.87* |
| | Life events | .21 | 3.23** | .06 | 6.64** |
| | Social support | .45 | 6.87*** | .24 | 12.23*** |
| Behavior | Personal characteristics | .02 | 0.47 | .02 | 0.47 |
| problem | Residential characteristics | .12 | 2.06 | .10 | 3.63* |
| severity | Life events | .34 | 6.31*** | .21 | 28.00*** |
| | Social support | .37 | 4.86*** | .03 | 1.29 |

*$p$ < .05; **$p$ < .01; ***$p$ < .001.

particular personal characteristics and residential characteristics examined did not contribute significantly to variations in the experience of life events and together accounted for approximately 6% of the variance in life events. When social support variables were added to the equation, the resulting regression was significantly different from zero ($F(10,84) = 2.46$, $p < .05$) with $R^2 = .23$. The change in $R^2$ was statistically significant ($F(10,84) = 4.39$, $p < .01$) with social support accounting for approximately 16% of the variance in life events after adjusting for the contributions of personal and residential characteristics.

### Residential Satisfaction

The regression of personal characteristics alone was not significantly different from zero, accounting for approximately 7% of the variance in residential satisfaction. When residential characteristics were added to the equation, the regression was statistically significant ($F(6,88) = 2.57$, $p < .05$) with $R^2 = .15$. The change in $R^2$ was statistically significant ($F(6,88) = 3.87$, $p < .05$) with residential characteristics accounting for approximately 7% of the variance in residential satisfaction after adjusting for the contributions of personal characteristics. When life events were added to the equation, the regression was statistically significant ($F(7,87) = 3.23$, $p < .01$) as was the change in $R^2$ ($F(7,87)$, $6.64$, $p < .05$). Life events accounted for approximately 6% of the variance in residential satisfaction after adjusting the contributions of personal and residential characteristics. When social support variables were added to the equation, the regression was statistically significant ($F(10,84) = 6.87$, $p < .001$) with $R^2 = .45$. Social support accounted for an additional 24% of the variance in residential satisfaction after adjusting for personal and residential characteristics and life events ($F(10,84) = 12.23$, $p < .001$).

### Severity of Behavioral Problem

The regressions of personal characteristics alone and with residential characteristics were not significantly different from zero. When life events were added to the equation, however, the regression was statistically significant ($F(7,87) = 6.31$, $p < .001$) with $R^2$ of .34. The change in $R^2$ was statistically significant as well ($F(7,87) = 28.00$, $p < .000$) with life events accounting for approximately 21% of the variance after adjusting for personal and residential characteristics. When social support variables were added to the equation the regression was statistically significant ($F(10,84) = 4.86$, $p < .001$), but the increase in $R^2$ of approximately 3% was not.

Table 8.2. Partial Correlations between Independent and Dependent Variables

| | Dependent Variables | | | | | |
| | Life Events | | Residential Satisfaction | | Behavior Problem Severity | |
| Independent Variables | r | t | r | t | r | t |
|---|---|---|---|---|---|---|
| Age | −.18 | 1.68 | .07 | 0.63 | .02 | 0.15 |
| Gender | −.05 | 0.50 | −.15 | 1.42 | −.05 | 0.43 |
| Level of mental retardation | −.13 | 1.23 | .05 | 0.46 | −.17 | 1.54 |
| Disability | −.03 | 0.24 | .04 | 0.41 | .03 | 0.24 |
| Normalization | .11 | 0.97 | .42 | 4.20*** | −.07 | 0.63 |
| Integration | .06 | 0.51 | .22 | 2.08* | .06 | 0.54 |
| Life events | | | −.29 | 2.77** | .49 | 5.17*** |
| Social support | | | .52 | 5.56*** | −.14 | 1.33 |
| No. handicapped | −.15 | 1.41 | −.29 | 2.76** | .11 | 1.03 |
| No. nonhandicapped | −.22 | 2.11* | −.02 | 0.16 | −.12 | 1.06 |
| No. kin | −.36 | 3.50*** | | | | |
| No. total | .26 | 2.47* | | | | |

$*p < .05; **p < .01; ***p < .001.$

Partial Correlations

At the final step of each regression, the partial correlations of each independent variable with the dependent variable were computed. These correlations represent the association between each predictor and the dependent variable with all of the other variables partialed out. With regard to life events, only the partial correlations with social support variables were significant. More specifically, significant negative correlations between the numbers of nonhandicapped persons ($r = −.22$) and kin ($r = −.36$) in the network and life events were found (see Table 8.2). As the number of such persons in the support network increased, the number of life events experienced decreased. In contrast, a significant positive correlation was found between the total number of persons in the network and life events ($r = .26$).

In the case of residential satisfaction, significant positive correlations with social integration ($r = .22$), life-style normalization ($r = .42$), and satisfaction with support ($r = .52$) were found. Significant negative correlations with life event stress ($r = −.27$) and the number of handicapped persons in the network ($r = −.29$) were also found. Persons who were more socially integrated experienced more normalized life-styles and were more satisfied with the social support available to them reported higher levels of residential satisfaction whereas those who experienced more life event stress or had a greater number of persons with handicaps in their support network reported less residential satisfaction.

Finally, behavioral problem severity was significantly correlated with only one variable, life event stress ($r = .49$). As life event stress increased, ratings of behavioral problem severity increased as well.

### DISCUSSION

The results of this study support the contention that life event stress and adjustment among persons with mental retardation are related in a manner comparable to that observed among persons of average intelligence (Ghaziuddin 1988; Hasazi et al. 1990). Life event stress contributed significantly to self-reports of residential satisfaction and to careprovider reports of behavioral problem severity even when the contributions of personal, residential, and social support variables were controlled statistically. The magnitude and direction of the obtained correlations were comparable to those found typically in children and adults of average intelligence (Compas 1987a; Johnson 1986; Thoits 1983). Furthermore, life event stress was significantly and inversely related to social support indices, consistent with general findings in the stress and coping literature (e.g., Barrera 1981). More specifically, the number of life events experienced by the individual tended to decrease as the number of handicapped peers and kin in the social network increased. The seemingly contradictory finding that life events were also positively correlated with the total number of persons in the social network may be the result of the confounding of this network characteristic with residence type. Network size was greatest among persons living in group homes which also include the greatest number of cohabitants (Chapter 10). On the basis of these findings, one cannot attribute a causal role to life event stress in the etiology of adjustment problems or to social support variables in the experience of life events, but the extension of the stress and coping model and methodology to the study of psychopathology in persons with mental retardation is strongly supported by them.

There is of course a need to replicate the present findings and to develop measures that may be more sensitive to the individual's idiosyncratic experience of stress and support. In developing the measure of life event stress for this study we selected items based upon the general literature and our own assumptions about potential sources of stress encountered by persons with mental retardation living in community settings. In assessing these events we relied upon careprovider reports rather than those of the individuals themselves. On both counts our approach has serious limitations. Research on the development of life event scales in children of average intelligence suggests that they are a better source of information about what may be stressful to them than parents or professionals (e.g., Johnson 1986). Likewise, among children, adolescents, and adults of average intelligence, their subjective appraisal of the stressfulness of particular events appears to be a better predictor of adjustment outcomes than the events themselves (e.g., Johnson 1986; Lazarus and Folkman 1985). Levine's (1985) work suggests that adults with mild mental retardation can identify sources of stress in their lives meaningfully. For this group especially, the development of more sensitive measures of life event stress may be possible and should be pursued. Furthermore, the study of stress and coping processes among persons with mental retardation need not and should not rely exclusively on the life events methodology. Other ways of conceptualizing and defining stress operationally are available (e.g., Levine 1985; Reiss and Benson 1985; Richardson, Koller, and Katz 1985), each of which provides a meaningful approach to the problem.

At another level the present findings support the view that variations in the experience of stress and support are inherent in the community life experience of persons with mental retardation (Emerson 1985) just as they are for people generally. With a few notable exceptions (e.g., Heller 1988; Menolascino 1983) we have failed to consider the potential importance of these factors in the overall community adjustment process or to recognize that particular care practices even if necessary and well-intentioned, such as movement from one residential setting to another, may contribute to stress or alter support. Although not reported in this chapter, we have found differences in the types of life events experienced by persons in different residence types which reinforce this contention. For example, we found that persons in group homes were more likely than residents of supervised apartments or family homes to experience events involving changes in significant emotional relationships resulting from staff turnover and relocation of fellow residents (Hasazi et al. 1990). Likewise, the lesser experience of life event stress by persons in family homes may be a reflection in part of the greater continuity in relationships associated with family living.

Although not the focus of the study, it is interesting to note that residential satisfaction was significantly associated with life-style normalization, social integration, and social support as well as stress. Indeed, the strongest contributions to residential satisfaction were made by social support variables. These findings contribute to the general literature on this topic (e.g., Heal 1988) and suggest that individuals' perceptions of the social support provided by a particular living arrangement may be an especially important factor in their overall evaluation of that arrangement. In that regard the support provided by other persons living with the individual, whether they are peers or careproviders, seems to contribute most to residential satisfaction. For instance, we have found that staff support contributes to residential satisfaction only among group home residents whereas peer support contributes to residential satisfaction among both group home and supervised apartment residents but not among persons in family homes (Chapter 10). The pattern of results obtained thus parallels the particular configuration of coresidents characteristic of each living arrangement.

Although this study was exploratory in nature, our findings may have important implications for theory, research, and practice. When viewed in context of related findings (e.g., Ghaziuddin 1988; Levine 1985; Reiss and Benson 1985; Richardson, Koller, and Katz 1985), they suggest that the study of psychopathology among persons with mental retardation may benefit from the application of conceptual models and research methods used widely in the study of psychopathology among children, adolescents, and adults of average intelligence. To the extent that we have assumed that the causes of psychopathology differ among persons with and without mental retardation we may actually have limited our ability to understand how the presence of mental retardation increases the risk of psychopathology. Within the context of general models of psychopathology the ways in which the behavioral characteristics, social experience, and living conditions of persons with mental retardation contribute to their greater experience of adjustment problems may be more amenable to analysis. With a broader perspective we may be better able to intervene in more effective and humane ways when adjustment problems occur. If nothing else, the present findings reinforce the importance of looking outside of the person to his or her social context when problems occur (in the same ways that we typically do when assessing and treating the emotional and behavioral problems of the "average" person). Were we ourselves to experience difficulties we would likely think very little of a clinician who failed to consider our experience of stress, the quality of our social relationships, or the adequacy of our resources in assessing and treating those difficulties. Yet in our work with persons with mental retardation we frequently fail to do so. Finally, the present findings suggest that our current policies and procedures may at times increase stress, disrupt support, or otherwise contribute to the adjustment problems of the persons we serve. By giving greater consideration to these possibilities, we may be able to formulate policies and procedures that contribute instead to the prevention of psychopathology among persons with mental retardation.

## Acknowledgments

This research was supported in part by National Institute of Disability and Rehabilitation Research Grant 1-33-GH-40203. The authors wish to acknowledge the assistance and support of the individuals with mental retardation and their parents and service providers who participated in this study.

# 9

## Stress Management Interventions with People with Psychiatric Disabilities

### A Key Support to Community Living

Sutherland Miller, Ph.D.

People with severe and persistent psychiatric disabilities do live successfully in the community, could live successfully in the community, and can use community living as a way of increasing their competence and self-esteem. But each environment has its pressures and hassles. Stress and its effects have become a general concern in society, and people with disabilities are not immune to them. In fact these people carry a double burden: not only the hassles of daily living but also the uncertainties and concerns about having a mysterious, long-term condition.

Is there a relationship between stress and long-term psychiatric conditions? If so, what can be done to enable people with these disabilities to cope with stress effectively? This chapter summarizes the relevant literature on stress and coping and on stress management interventions with individuals with a mental illness, and it presents recommendations for designing and implementing programs. It also explores why stress and coping for persons with psychiatric disabilities have been ignored at the systems, service organization, and individual provider level.

### Stress

Stress occurs when an individual is overwhelmed with the demands of a situation and believes that he or she has insufficient resources to deal with them. Stress is the product of a complex person/environment interaction that continues over time. For example, a stressor appears—some internal or external pressure. The person appraises the stressor and answers two ques-

125

tions: Is this situation a genuine threat to me? If so, can I handle it successfully? Depending on the answer to those questions, the person acts, and that
action affects the pressure, ending it or continuing it in some way. Thus, the
person and environmental stressors may proceed in their exchange until
there is a resolution. This simplified version of Lazarus's work (Lazarus and
Folkman 1985) provides the theoretical basis for much of the general research on stress today even though many definitional and operational issues
remain.

## Stress and Severe Psychiatric Conditions

Although there appears to be little crossover between the significant
amount of research on the theory and process of stress presented above and
research on severe psychiatric disabilities, stress has become an important
concept in mental illness. It is postulated that people with the schizophrenias
and bipolar disorders are predisposed to being vulnerable to stress (Nuechterlein and Dawson 1984; Strauss and Carpenter 1983). This vulnerability
may result in acute psychosis and continuing disabling conditions. Anthony
and Liberman (1986, 547) called the phenomenon "the vulnerability, stress,
coping and competence model of mental disorders."

Most of the evidence for this model comes from research on the relationship between stressful life events and mental illness (Lukoff et al. 1984)
or from research on expressed emotion in families (Leff and Vaughn 1985).
In the general population the relationships between major life events and
stress symptoms have not appeared to be strong (Rabkin and Struening
1976), and there are questions about how large a role critical life events play
in the stress experienced by people described as mentally ill.

### THE ROLE OF "HASSLES"

Over the years, however, the focus on life events in the literature has
diminished because research has demonstrated that daily hassles play a
greater role in producing stress and its effects than do life events (Kanner et
al. 1981; Monroe 1983). Although understanding the relationships among
life events, hassles, and stress requires more research, daily hassles appear
to be a critical factor in understanding stress in people's lives (Lazarus
1984).

It should be noted that in the research on both life events and daily hassles there have been methodologic problems (Spring 1981). One of the main
difficulties has come from the fact that the typical signs of stress have also
been the indicators of pathology, as in, "I am nervous a good deal of the

time" or "I keep thinking of death." Thus, there have been problems in confounding the two conditions (Dohrenwend et al. 1984). But even when the effects of pathology are controlled, hassles explain more of the stress condition than do life events (Monroe 1983).

Until recently there have been no studies on hassles among persons with severe psychiatric disabilities. Miller and Miller (in press) revised the Kanner Hassles scale (Kanner, et al. 1981) by removing all pathologic items and adding items relevant to the lives of persons with psychiatric disabilities. Sixty-nine people living in a community residence program and 35 non-disabled people completed the revised scale.

The results showed that although the community residence group checked far fewer hassles than the mainstream group, those that they did select were more bothersome to them, and many items were not relevant to the circumscribed lives they led. Furthermore some items had a strong middle-class bias. Most of the hassles that bothered the community residence group were related to stigma, violation of rights, medication, poverty, isolation, and a lack of supports. Therefore it would appear that instruments need to be applicable to both populations so that changes can be observed as psychiatrically disabled people move from social isolation into mainstream lives.

## Coping

*Coping* has been defined simply as "the things that people do to avoid being harmed by life strains" (Pearlin and Schooler 1978, 2) or more complexly as "the person's cognitive and behavioral efforts to manage (reduce, minimize, master or tolerate) the internal and external demands of the person-environment transaction that is appraised as taxing or exceeding the person's resources" (Folkman et al. 1986b, 571). In Hobfoll's new attempt at conceptualizing stress these coping actions would be called into play when there was a potential or actual threat to valued personal resources (Hobfoll 1989).

Research has suggested that many factors play a significant, interactive role in how coping actually works. Some of those factors are personality characteristics; social roles; economic, social, and psychologic resources; appraisal; the nature of the encounters; coping techniques or styles; the environment in which encounters occur; and time. Optimism (Scheier and Carver 1985), pessimism (Peterson, Seligman, and Vaillant 1988), hardiness (Banks and Gannon 1988), high attending to environmental cues (Miller, Leinbach, and Brody 1989), attributions, helplessness, and cognitive distortions (Brown and Siegel 1988; Mikulincer 1988; Smith 1986), response styles (Miller, Brody, and Summerton 1988), and self-deception (Jamner and Schwartz 1986) are all examples of personality traits that have been found to influence coping.

Pearlin and Schooler's research (1978) demonstrated the importance of social roles, and several studies (Perrucci and Targ 1982; Rabkin and Struening 1976) have highlighted the buffering effects of economic resources as well as social class. Social support networks have played a significant role in coping, and making use of them has been considered a powerful coping tool (Thoits 1986).

*Appraisal* refers to the process of evaluating the degree of threat and the resources available to a person when confronted with an encounter. The outcomes of these judgments contribute to the experience of stress and the effectiveness of coping. Appraisal has been shown to possess a degree of stability over encounters as well as to contribute significantly to the stress/coping process (Folkman et al. 1986b).

The research has also demonstrated that the type of encounter influences coping styles and effectiveness (Folkman et al. 1986a; Pearlin and Schooler 1978; Suls and Fletcher 1985). Furthermore Suls and Fletcher's (1985) metaanalysis of avoidant and nonavoidant coping strategies provided examples of research studies documenting that coping techniques can make things worse.

Another factor that has been explored rarely is the environment in which the encounter occurs. Nevertheless it is an important concern because environments are stress producing and can be changed (Krantz et al. 1988). Novaco and Vaux (1985) have demonstrated the importance of environment particularly if prevention of stress is a goal.

The last factor to consider is time. Suls and Fletcher (1985) found that avoidant strategies were helpful at the beginning of interactive encounters, but as time continued on and the stress-producing situation remained potent, avoidant strategies were less useful, and problem-solving strategies appeared of more benefit. Obviously, according to the person-environment interaction model, it would follow that as coping strategies were applied, other factors such as the environment and appraisal would change.

There are no examples of studies that have examined all these factors together and their interactions. Two reports by Folkman et al. (1986a, 1986b) come closer than most others in exploring a variety of variables such as primary and secondary appraisal, coping techniques, outcomes, types of encounters, and time.

One very important point emerges from reviewing the literature on coping. If a coping style is right for one person but not for another because of traits, resources, coping repertoires, and roles and if a coping technique that works for a person one time but not in another encounter because of the nature of the appraisal, the encounter itself, the environment, and the time, then flexibility of responding is essential.

## COPING BY PERSONS WITH PSYCHIATRIC DISABILITIES

Unfortunately, there is only one study reported which dealt directly with how persons with severe and persistent mental illness cope, and it did not use the theories, paradigms, and methodologies discussed above. Cohen and Berk (1985) asked 101 patients how they coped with 29 symptoms grouped within four categories: anxiety, depression-withdrawal, schizophrenia (talking to myself), and interpersonal. Nine coping styles were identified, and they included fighting back, time out, isolated diversion, social diversion, prayer, medical, drugs or alcohol, doing nothing-helpless, and doing nothing-accepting. They found that *fights back* and *accepts* were most frequently used, but that the kind of symptom, employment status, living arrangements, and gender all made a difference in the coping interaction patterns. Although this study provided useful new data, basic questions such as the degree of stress symptoms generated and the nature of primary and secondary appraisal were ignored.

Auerbach (1989) pointed out that most health care research on stress dealt with issues related to short-term adjustment, but for chronic diseases the person must not only deal with the daily hassles that occur for everyone but also with the context of chronicity, which is characterized by continuing uncertainty and threat to well-being. An analogous situation may apply to persons with chronic psychiatric disorders. It has already been noted that rather than the number of hassles—a measure for people in the mainstream—it is the intensity of reaction which is important for people with psychiatric disabilities (Miller and Miller, in press). Perhaps there are other special issues for this population such as the fact that many stressors may be generated internally (e.g., hearing voices). Leete (1989) described what it is like living with schizophrenia and trying to cope with the stress that is produced. Her description of coping may even contain strategies not contained in current coping assessments. Auerbach (1989, 388), for example, noted that "The stimulus complex confronting the individual has rarely been conceptualized in terms of the nature of coping demands it poses for that individual, and intervention strategies have not often been formulated to match those demands."

## Stress Management Effectiveness

*Stress management* refers to a variety of interventions which can be learned. These interventions include relaxation, self-instruction, monitoring stress cues, knowing what your typical stresses are, information gathering, changing primary and secondary appraisals, changing beliefs and illogical thinking, problem solving, rehearsal, seeking support, physical training, and expanding the size of coping repertoires. There is ample evidence that these techniques can reduce such symptoms as anxiety, anger, depression, pain, and reactivity. Conditions such as cancer, childbirth, hypertension, bereavement, surgery, and arthritis have all seen applications of such strategies. Examples of cognitive approaches can be found in the work of Meichenbaum (1985), and his stress inoculation concept emphasizes regulatory self-talk and preparing for stressful situations by rehearsing the appropriate responses for each stage of an encounter. Janis (1983) conducted some of the early studies on the role of information as a coping strategy, and D'Zurilla and Goldfried (1971) are known for their demonstrations of the value of learning problem solving. Studies that have shown the effectiveness of relaxation are numerous (Borkovec et al. 1987; Foa and Kozak 1985). The role that physical exercise can play in managing stress can be seen in the work of Sinyor et al. (1983).

Typically, multiple techniques are applied in a group setting, as was illustrated in Roskies's work with Type A individuals (1983). Combined approaches have been used successfully to reduce cardiovascular reactivity (for a review see Jacob and Chesney 1986) and to reduce stress for people with chronic physical conditions such as multiple sclerosis (Foley et al. 1987).

Regardless of the data supporting the effectiveness of stress management in reducing anxiety and other symptoms, there are some very significant concerns. Sometimes programs are based on myths about the natural course of stressful events (see Wortman and Silver's work on loss, 1989). As Roskies (1983) pointed out, all too frequently stress mangement programs aim a shotgun at an unknown target and hope that something is hit. She stated, "Rather than developing a rationale to guide the choice of treatment techniques and outcome measures, the tendency has been to apply, more or less haphazardly, a variety of currently fashionable therapies (anxiety management, relaxation, psychotherapy, cognitive therapy, exercise training) to type A individuals in the hope that these treatments would change something in the person's physiological, emotional or behavioral functioning that would somehow reduce his or her coronary risk" (265–66). The result is that researchers do not know what has changed, what made the change, or how to effect flexible responding. The question is, now that there is evidence of bits and pieces of techniques working in some situations, how can stress management be put together to teach people the best ways to *manage* stress in their individual lives?

## Stress Management for Persons with Psychiatric Disabilities

If reports in the psychologic literature are an indicator of applying stress management techniques to people with severe and persistent psychiatric disabilities, then little has been happening despite the logic for doing so. Occasionally there have been articles on using stress reduction strategies with depressed people (Rehm, Kaslow, and Rabin 1987; Reynolds and Coats 1986) and on the coping deficits, such as reduced problem-solving skills, which characterize "psychotic patients" (Schotte and Clum 1987). Also, some case examples have been reported. Stein and Nikolic (1989) reported on teaching a man with a schizophrenic disorder to use muscle relaxation and biofeedback to decrease his anxiety and to cope with stress. Alford (1986) worked on treating schizophrenic delusions with a cognitive intervention that was designed to modify the strength of the belief in delusional ideas. He used a single subject experimental research design and found persistent therapeutic gains.

Since 1980 there have been three studies on stress management among people with persistent mental health problems. All three studies reported successful results. The most recent study, by Long and Bluteau (1988), used the term *chronic* to describe its clients; however none of them had a psychotic diagnosis, and they were dissimilar to those people typically seen in community living programs. Using a wide range of coping strategies, 50% of the group reduced symptoms and maintained their progress at one-year follow-up. Lukoff and co-workers (1986) provided 28 male chronic schizophrenic patients with either a social skills training program or a holistic stress management program which consisted of exercise and yoga sessions as well as a meditation. Both groups made improvements in reducing psychopathology, and the holistic approach was favored although on follow-up it was discovered that no one continued the holistic approach on his or her own after the program stopped. There were no differences in relapse rates between the two groups.

In the final study, Brown (1980) provided 10 90-minute sessions of progressive relaxation, anxiety management, social skills, and self-reinforcement procedures to 20 persons with psychiatric disabilities at a community mental health center. Diagnoses were not given, but the participants had at least one hospitalization, and the mean was close to three. Fewer people who received the program were hospitalized than controls, and they scored in the healthy direction on measures of anxiety, fear, self-concept, and assertiveness. Questions about this study's design were raised and included contamination of the trainer-evaluator's role, self-selection, and nonrandomization of the experimental group, the heavy reliance on self-report, and the effects of novelty.

### DESIGNING STRESS MANAGEMENT PROGRAMS

Even if we had better information about hassles, demands, coping styles, and training strategies relevant to these individuals, it is not likely that we would find a one-to-one relationship between a given form of coping and outcome. If, as noted earlier, many factors influence effective coping, the key word in stress management programs becomes *management*. How can people be taught to manage themselves in stress-related encounters so that after checking out their status, reviewing their appraisals, analyzing the encounter and the phase that the process is in, they select the most appropriate coping technique?

Meichenbaum and Cameron (1983) addressed the design of stress programs for individuals and suggested that the procedures first should help the client learn to assess what is going on through data collection, situational analysis, and self-monitoring. The client also needs to understand how stress works and what the therapist and client will do collaboratively. This phase is called *conceptualization*. Next the focus is on developing a coping repertoire that meets the specific client's individualized needs. Skills training and rehearsal make up the second phase. The objective of the final phase is to give the client confidence in coping and to encourage the utilization of what has been learned.

Although Meichenbaum and Cameron's (1983) recommendations are directed toward therapists working with individual clients, their ideas are applicable to group psychoeducational programs. Properly designed group stress management courses have the advantage of including more people, requiring less skilled personnel, capitalizing on the strengths of a large number of people learning from each other, and developing group support. Individual programs permit more tailoring to the specific client and usually allow more time. Group programs can compensate for these advantages through individualized homework, a rich variety of stress scenarios, and multiple feedback from all the group members.

Two examples of stress management courses for persons with psychiatric disabilities which address program issues and implementation strategies are GET WISE (Miller 1988) and the ABC's of Handling Hassles (Wilder et al. 1989). GET WISE is an 11-session course that was reviewed by a panel of consumers as it was being developed. Piloting occurred with people living in a community residence program. The course was designed to be comprehensive and to be taught by either a consumer or direct service staff. Trials demonstrated that little instructor preparation was required.

Each session focused on a specified competence so that the student could do something better when the lesson was over. The course covered learning a simple stress model, discovering which situations bothered each participant, and identifying individual stress cues. Next, students were taught to recognize and combat dysfunctional cognitions and to learn about a variety of coping techniques. Problem solving, getting help from others, starting a self-help group, developing strong beliefs, and rehearsing anticipated negative situations were additional areas of focus. Throughout, students learned relaxation and concentration.

The ABC's of Handling Hassles met many of the implementation criteria discussed in the next section and, with only three sessions, required little time commitment. To respond to different demand characteristics three versions of the course were developed by creating stress scenes typical of hospitals, outpatient programs, and community residences.

IMPLEMENTATION ISSUES

If stress management works and if this approach has high relevance because of the vulnerability to stress of people with severe and persistent psychiatric disabilities, why are stress reduction programs not widely used? First, there are the larger social issues of stigma, power, and poverty. *Stigma* reinforces the notion of improving coping skills for people who have a chance at success and ignoring those for whom we have no expectations. Second, as *self-efficacy* is a key concept in dealing effectively with stress, it also follows that developing personal competencies leads to power. People with psychiatric disabilities who learn how to choose, solve problems, stand up for their rights, and withstand pressure can also demand changes in the way service systems and communities treat them.

The third factor, *poverty,* greatly influenced the early rehabilitation and community support system emphasis on providing those basic supports which poor people do not have: jobs, housing, health care, education, and access to other services. Although the promise of providing material improvements has not been realized, it may be time for the leaders in mental health care to add an internal focus. That focus is one of capitalizing on the strengths that survivors of institutionalization, stigma, fear, and internal chaos have demonstrated.

At the organizational level, there are a variety of factors which must be dealt with for successful implementation to take place. Introducing courses or group programs can be seen as added work. If stress management comes in, what goes out? In some institutional settings in which little active programming of any kind exists and in which direct service staff who could teach courses often appear idle, attitudes against doing more work hinder changes. One representative of direct service staff indicated, "These are lousy jobs. Doing nothing is a fringe benefit. You can't take it away." Furthermore, to switch from a therapeutic model to an educational and collaborative one changes personal status, making collaborators more equal. Such alterations are often not desired in hierarchic organizations. Where instructors of stress management programs are clients or former clients, resistance to adoption can come from fears of giving clients more control in areas traditionally reserved for staff.

Financial concerns can also play a role in implementing stress reduction programs. Will there not be substantially higher costs if additional, well-trained, highly paid staff are added? What about the costs associated with training the staff? And if the intervention is educational and not clinical, who will pay for it? Certainly, third party payers will not provide reimbursement in most situations.

There are attitude problems as well, some of which relate to favoring traditional treatments over rehabilitation, long-term interventions over short-term, and current modes of behavior, even if they appear ineffective, over new behavior even if they may produce success in the future. There are administrators and staff who do not perceive clients as being able to learn new approaches readily and who question the worth of stress management, seeing it as frivolous.

Ignorance is another major barrier to implementation. Some caregivers may not know the relationship between stress and mental illness and what can be done to teach people better coping skills. They may not know how to design a program and train clients. Some clients may not understand the benefits and initially may be uneasy switching to the role of student. Also, clients may not want to make a significant time commitment to taking a course about which they are unsure.

STRATEGIES FOR REDUCING BARRIERS

Some strategies for dealing with these organizational barriers are to design courses that are easy to teach so that either direct service staff or clients
can serve as instructors. Courses should be designed which are short so that
neither instructor nor student makes a large investment before discovering
the value, and they should be fun. The same curriculum should be used in
many settings, and one should start with settings whose staff want to have a
program. It is important to demonstrate the effectiveness and ease of teaching through presentations in which audience members teach on the spot.
Both instructors and participants should be rewarded for their participation.
Their use of these courses should be encouraged in client-run programs or
self-help groups. The curriculum should be used as a part of staff training to
meet their own needs and to provide them with a structure for understanding
stress and their client's issues with stress.

## Evaluation of Stress Management Programs

Evaluation of stress management programs requires assessment of increased competence in specific skill technique areas; utilization of those
skills in real life situations; competence in stress management—employing
the right techniques at the right time in a flexible fashion; and effectiveness
of both stress reduction and stress prevention interventions. Such complexity makes evaluation a difficult task. Nevertheless, there are some useful examples. One evaluation model with predictive power in working with people
with alcoholism was reported by Chaney, O'Leary, and Marlatt (1978).
After a skill training program, students were asked to respond to a simulated
situation associated with relapse. They had to indicate how they would deal
with the encounter. The length of time to respond, the number of words in
the response, and the extent to which the response could clearly guide someone else in what to do were predictive of duration and severity of relapse.

Summative evaluation approaches are likely to mask the true effectiveness of psychoeducational programs. Therefore formative methods are recommended, particularly when the interventions are complex and when the
process of interactions is critical. From the perspective of designing interventions, formative approaches provide feedback on what components of the
program are working for whom and in what circumstances.

Challenging the assumption that learning follows the same linear path
for all people is also important. Studies of stress program effectiveness need
to measure intraindividual change. It is unrealistic to assume that everyone

will be at the same competence level initially, place equal emphasis on the same parts of the content, and will learn at the same rate.

## Summary and Recommendations

Stress management for persons with severe psychiatric disabilities who are living in the community is a critical but largely unresearched area. There is little knowledge about what hassles this group of people confronts, what the coping demands of those hassles are, how the people cope, and what coping works best under a variety of circumstances. Although it is assumed that feeling overwhelmed with the demands of daily living can lead to relapse, that hypothesis itself bears testing.

Although we know how to improve competence in specific stress management techniques, how to teach flexibility in the management of stress is unclear. For researchers and trainers to "go it alone" in this area reflects both arrogance and ignorance. Collaborative relationships with potential recipients of training are required to enable cautious program development to proceed even though we have so few of the answers.

# 10

# A Comparison of Social Support and Satisfaction among Adults with Mental Retardation Living in Three Types of Community Residential Alternatives

Sara N. Burchard, Ph.D., Julie W. Rosen, Ph.D., Lawrence R. Gordon, Ph.D., Joseph E. Hasazi, Ph.D., James T. Yoe, Ph.D., and Laurie C. Dietzel, M.A.

The numbers and types of community living alternatives for persons with mental retardation have proliferated over the past 15 years as states have attempted to provide environments that promote acquisition of independent living skills and life-style normalization (Bruininks et al. 1987). Providing opportunities for persons with disabilities to live, work, and recreate alongside and in the same manner as their peers without disabilities has become a major goal of social policy (Heal, Haney, and Novak-Amado 1988). The creation of these community living situations has stimulated numerous research efforts to evaluate their effectiveness (for a recent review see Heal 1988).

Life-style normalization (Burchard et al. 1987; Hull and Thompson 1981a, 1981b), adaptive behavior (Kleinberg and Galligan 1983), community use, and leisure activities (Aveno 1987; Burchard, Pine, and Gordon 1990), and resident behavioral adjustment (Hill and Bruininks 1984) have been examined to evaluate these services. However, the need to evaluate the quality of life, particularly social life, has become a major concern (Heal 1985; Landesman and Butterfield 1987). Social life (i.e., social support; social integration; and satisfying interpersonal relations with family, friends, and community members) has been identified as among the most critical aspects of life-style related to the quality of life (Edgerton 1984; Landesman 1986; O'Connor 1983).

Previous studies that have examined the social life of persons with mental retardation have used careprovider estimates of social contacts and activities (Aveno 1987; Hill and Bruininks 1981b) or observations of social

137

contacts in the community residence or sheltered work setting (Landesman-Dwyer and Berkson 1984; Romer and Berkson 1980a, 1980b). These measures are restricted in scope, the latter excluding information about activities and social contacts outside the segregated residential and work settings. In addition, these do not necessarily reflect aspects of personal choice as to preferred or valued social contacts, support, or friendships. In fact, when persons are asked about their friendships and preferences, their responses are not congruent with careprovider reports or observations in these closed settings (Romer and Berkson 1980a, 1980b).

Program and policy issues have evolved rapidly, determined largely by professionals and advocates, that is, by persons other than the consumers of services. It is imperative to obtain information from individuals themselves with regard to their life-styles and quality of life. This has not been widely done, perhaps partly because of the ease with which policymakers have accepted families and professionals as the spokespersons for individuals with disabilities and partly because of the constraints of obtaining information from many individuals with mental retardation (Sigelman et al. 1981; Willer and Intagliata 1982). Nevertheless, obtaining information from consumers has been recognized as essential in determining quality of services (Edgerton 1984; Halpern, Close, and Nelson 1986; Heal 1985), and methods for doing so reliably have been developed (Burchard, Pine, and Gordon 1990; Heal and Chadsey-Rusch 1985).

This chapter presents a study that uses a social network research methodology to obtain information on social support and friendships directly from individuals with mental retardation who are receiving community services (Rosen and Burchard 1990; Weinberg 1984). Information on their quality of life and social integration is obtained directly from them and not inferred by others' observations.

Participants were adults with mental retardation living in two types of publicly supported residential alternatives commonly available through developmental service systems: small group homes providing 24-hour supervision, and semiindependent living situations, for example, apartments with drop-in or periodic staff supervision and support. Studies of community residential alternatives frequently lack comparison groups (Heal 1985; Landesman and Butterfield 1987) making interpretation of results problematic. In the present study, adults with mental retardation living with their own families were included as a comparison group for measures of social support, satisfaction, and well-being.

This chapter describes the social support networks and social contexts of community activities of adults with mental retardation living in the three settings. Characteristics of social life are examined in relation to self-described residence satisfaction and well-being. Previous research has shown that satisfaction with the family living situation and with social support is important to feelings of personal well-being and happiness for persons in general (Deiner 1984). The extent of community-based integrative activities and positive interpersonal relations with housemates has been found to be highly related to the residence satisfaction of adults with mental retardation living in small group homes (Burchard, Pine, and Gordon 1990). Therefore, those persons with more active social lives in the community and greater social support were expected to report greater residence satisfaction and personal well-being.

METHODS

### Setting

The study was in Vermont where community residences for individuals with mental retardation serve no more than six residents and subscribe to a normalization philosophy and a developmental model of service provision. This study focused on three community residential settings. (1) *Group homes* (GHs), which provided room, board, 24-hour supervision, and habilitation services for three to six persons in residential neighborhoods, were staffed by one or two persons at a time. (2) *Supervised apartments* (SAs), multiunit residences in residential neighborhoods, were occupied generally by one or two individuals with staff supervision and training on an as needed basis, but there was no 24-hour supervision provided (residents were responsible for meal preparation, housekeeping, and basic living skills). (3) *Family homes* (FHs) were private residences in which adults lived with their parents or relatives. Nationally, family homes constitute the principal resource for supervision and care for adults with mental retardation (Bruininks et al. 1987).

### Participants

Participation was limited to unmarried adults with mild and moderate mental retardation who were between 23 and 55 years of age, who were able to respond to structured interviews, and who had no major behavioral or physical restrictions that would prohibit access to the community. These criteria were chosen to control for individual characteristics that could differentially affect the outcomes examined (Seltzer 1984) and to include individuals who could provide information from their own perspective.

Recruitment was statewide via parent associations and agencies responsible for developmental services. Of the 157 persons identified who met the

Table 10.1. Comparison of the Personal Characteristics of 133 Persons Living in Group Homes, Family Homes, and Supervised Apartments

|  | Residence Type[a] | | | |
|---|---|---|---|---|
| Characteristic | Family Home (N = 38) | Group Home (N = 54) | Supervised Apartment (N = 41) | $F^1/\chi^2$ |
| Age (years) | | | | |
|   Mean | 29.2$^x$ | 36.6$^y$ | 34.9$^y$ | 7.39*** |
|   Range | 23–49 | 22–58 | 28–54 | |
| Gender (female) | 19 | 31 | 26 | 1.45 |
| Years in residence | | | | |
|   Mean | 9.0$^x$ | 2.9$^y$ | 2.7$^y$ | 17.9*** |
|   S.D. | 8.0 | 2.0 | 1.6 | |
| No. previously | 4$^x$ | 32$^y$ | 23$^y$ | 10.16** |
|   institutionalized | (11%) | (60%) | (56%) | |
| Years since discharge | | | | |
|   Mean | 9.23 | 7.6 | 8.4 | 0.27 |
|   S.D. | 2.3 | 6.3 | 3.8 | |
|   Range | 8–12 | 3–28 | 3–15 | |
| LMR | | | | |
|   Mild | 30$^x$ | 32$^y$ | 36$^y$ | 14.83** |
|   Moderate | 8 | 22 | 5 | |

[a]Group home level of retardation (LMR) is significantly different from family home and supervised apartment ($\chi^2 = 3.93$, $p < .05$; and $\chi^2 = 13.80$, $p < .01$, respectively). Different superscripts (x, y) denote significant differences between group means.

**$p < .01$; ***$p < .001$.

criteria, 133 agreed to participate. Fifty-four lived in group homes, 41 in supervised apartments, and 38 lived with their relatives. One group home resident, 7 apartment residents, and 14 families declined to participate. The demographic characteristics of the participants are shown in Table 10.1.

Procedure

Primary careproviders and study participants were interviewed separately and in private by trained interviewers who made home visits. Interrater reliabilities were obtained by having a second interviewer score approximately 20% of the interviews. Participants were given a small cash honorarium for participating.

Measures

*Community Activities.* Primary careproviders provided information about out-of-home activities based upon a retrospective report of the previous two weeks. Activities were coded for location (physically integrated or nonintegrated), initiation (self or careprovider), companionship (accompanied by a careprovider, by peers, by peers without disabilities). A list of activities (e.g., went to the bank, movie, ballgame, shopping for groceries) from previous research (Hill and Bruininks 1981b) and calendars were used to prompt informants for recalling out-of-home activities. Work or a day program was not included. The mean interrater reliability based on percent agreements for each category was 88%.

*Resident Satisfaction.* A structured interview designed to minimize response biases measured residence satisfaction from the perspective of the individual with mental retardation (Burchard, Pine, and Gordon 1990; Seltzer 1980). Twenty-two items assessed satisfaction with the residence, with the physical setting, activities, personal responsibility, autonomy, and interpersonal relations in the home. The score was the percent of items which could be scored unambiguously and which reflected positive aspects of the residence. Reliabilities were .96 (interrater) and .73 (internal consistency) (Burchard et. al., in press).

*Personal Well-being.* This measure included 18 forced choice items that required self-evaluation of behavior, feelings, and interpersonal relations (Seltzer 1980). The score was the percent of responses which were positive. Positive and negative responses were alternated to control for response bias. Questions were of the following form: "Do you feel lonely or do you have plenty of friends?" "Do you feel you control your temper, or do you think you lose your temper too often?" Reliabilities were high, interrater reliability, .98, test-retest reliability, .80 (Burchard et al., in press).

*Social System Self-assessment* (SSSA) (Weinberg 1984). This 18-item questionnaire assessed social networks by eliciting the names of individuals upon whom respondents relied for social support. Original items were adapted to meet language and comprehension requirements of participants, and a structured interview format rather than a questionnaire was used.

The SSSA yielded five scores: (1) *size* (the number of persons named as providing support); (2) *multiplexity* (the relationships of the individuals named, i.e., kin, staff, friend, service provider, employer); (3) *stress/support balance* (the proportion of network members who were viewed as providing positive support versus stress); (4) *satisfaction with contact* (the proportion of members with whom frequency of contact was seen as sufficient); and (5) *reciprocity* (the number of relationships in which there was mutual initiation of social contact and support).

The questions used to elicit network members names were variations of the following: "If you wanted to be sure that your (*self-identified important possession*) was kept safe while you were away (on vacation, out of town, visiting relatives) who would you ask to take care of it? Is there anyone else you would ask?" (*prompt for more names*).

Respondents were asked to indicate for each individual if he or she was supportive or stressful ("makes you happy or makes you upset?") and whether they had contact with that individual as often as they desired. The queries were in alternating forced choice format to eliminate response bias.

Interrater reliability (percent agreement) was obtained for each derived score. The mean reliability was 98%. Test-retest reliability based on read-ministration of 11 interviews was .73 for size, .78 for relationship types, .55 for stress/support balance, .53 for satisfaction with frequency of contact, and .93 for reciprocity. All were significant ($p < .05$).

RESULTS

Personal Characteristics.

Family home members differed from persons in the other settings: they were younger, had lived in their homes longer, and few had a history of institutionalization (see Table 10.1). However, all participants had been living in their current residence for at least six months prior to the initiation of the study. There were no group differences in the rate of community employment. About 25% were engaged in work in nonsegregated settings on a regular basis. Another 64% (85 persons) attended sheltered workshops or day activity programs. Only eight persons had no regular daily activity.

More individuals in GHs were classified as moderately mentally retarded than were those in FHs or SAs. In cases in which the level of retardation or age was associated with variables in a manner that could be confounded with residential setting, forward regression analyses were performed with the level of retardation and age entered first as control variables (Seltzer 1984) followed by residence type. This procedure is equivalent to an analysis of covariance with residence setting as "treatment," controlling for level of retardation and age as covariates (Howell 1987).

Size and Composition of Social Support Networks

Group home residents reported the largest networks. They had more peers and more staff in their networks than did persons in SAs or in FHs, reflecting the greater number of cohabitants and staff associated with their residences (see Table 10.2). Persons from FHs and SAs had similar sized networks, but persons in FHs had more kin and fewer peers. Less than half of the sample named a peer without disabilities as a source of support. There

**Table 10.2. Group Comparisons of Size, Composition, and Reciprocity of Social Networks**

| | Residence Type[a] | | | | | | |
|---|---|---|---|---|---|---|---|
| | Group Home (N = 54) | | Supervised Apartment (N = 41) | | Family Home (N = 38) | | |
| Network Variable | Mean | S.D. | Mean | S.D. | Mean | S.D. | F(2,130) |
| Size (no. of individuals) | 10.8$^x$ | 3.2 | 8.4$^y$ | 3.4 | 8.5$^y$ | 4.0 | 7.55*** |
| No. of kin | 1.2$^x$ | 1.2 | 1.1$^x$ | 1.2 | 4.1$^y$ | 2.2 | 49.12*** |
| No. of staff | 3.6$^x$ | 2.0 | 2.8$^y$ | 1.4 | 1.1$^z$ | 1.2 | 28.68*** |
| No. of peers | 5.7$^x$ | 2.3 | 4.0$^y$ | 2.3 | 2.9$^z$ | 2.6 | 17.10*** |
| No. of non-handicapped peers[b] | 0.4$^x$ | 0.7 | 1.0$^y$ | 1.3 | 1.0 | 1.7 | 3.09* |
| No. of handi-capped peers | 5.3$^x$ | 2.1 | 3.0$^y$ | 1.9 | 1.9$^z$ | 1.6 | 39.43*** |
| No. of others[c] | 0.3 | 0.6 | 0.6 | 1.0 | 0.4 | 0.8 | 1.49 |
| No. of reciprocal relationships | 0.7 | 1.0 | 0.7 | 1.0 | 0.8 | 1.1 | .07 |

[a] x, y, and z superscripts denote differences between group means.

[b] Only 52 persons named a peer without handicaps in her or his social network, 16 in GHs, 21 in SAs, and 15 in FHs.

[c] Advocates, generic service providers, and work supervisors.

$*p < .05; **p < .01; ***p < .001.$

were eight persons with no peers in their networks, two from GHs and six from FHs, and 40% of the persons from GHs and SAs failed to identify a relative as a source of support even though they had contact with relatives at least yearly. Finally, few persons in any setting reported reciprocal relationships with members of their network.

The composition of networks was similar for persons in GHs and SAs; half were peers and a third staff. The difference was in composition of peer networks. Group home peer networks were almost entirely composed of friends with disabilities whereas more than 20% of peer networks of persons in SAs were nonhandicapped individuals. Peer networks of persons in FHs were also comprised of a relatively greater proportion of friends without handicaps (more than 25%) than were those of persons in GHs. These results are shown in Table 10.2. Since the number of peers without disabilities was correlated with mild retardation as well as with living in SAs and FHs, a forward regression analysis was used. Entering level of retardation and age as control variables made a small but significant contribution to group differences ($R^2 = .065$, $F(2,114) = 3.97$, $p < .05$). Residence setting made an additional, similar contribution to group differences ($R^2$ (change) $= .07$, $F(4,112) = 4.54$, $p < .01$).

### Network Support and Desire for Contact with Network Members

All groups reported a very high proportion of supportive network members (more than 85%). However, perceived supportiveness and desire for more contact with network members were inversely related to their relative proportion in the network. Relationships that were less heavily represented were those that were perceived as more supportive and those with whom more contact was desired. For persons living in FHs, this was peers; for those in agency settings, it was kin. Although staff constituted a large proportion of GH and SA persons' networks, they were seen as equally and highly supportive by all groups, and all groups wished to see about half the staff in their networks more often. Table 10.3 shows these results.

### Special Relationships

All persons living in SAs were able to identify a best friend whereas seven from GHs and eight from FHs were unable to, a significant group difference ($\chi^2$ (2, $N = 133$) $= 8.98$, $p < .05$). Peers were named most frequently as best friends by all groups, more than 60% of the time, but almost all of these friends were peers with disabilities. Persons without disabilities (nonstaff or kin) were identified as best friends rarely (9% by GH residents, 17% by SA residents, and 16% by persons in FHs). Staff were named as best friends one third of the time by persons in GHs and SAs whereas persons living in FHs named kin and staff equally often (10% each).

The relationships of the individuals named most frequently throughout the interview as providing support, companionship, and assistance are shown in Table 10.4. Relatives were named most frequently by persons in FHs whereas staff and peers were named with almost equal frequency by GH and SA persons. Best friends were cited most frequently by about 40% of GH and SA residents but infrequently by persons living in FHs in which kin were providing most of their companionship and support.

Approximately 55% in each setting reported having a romantic relationship. However, significantly fewer individuals living at home engaged in actual dating ($\chi^2$ (2), $N = 133$) $= 15.95$, $p < .001$) than did those in GHs and SAs, where careprovider reports of dating corresponded to reports of having

Table 10.3. Comparisons of Composition, Support, and Desire for Contact
in Social Network Groups

| Network Variable | Residence Type[a] | | | | | | |
|---|---|---|---|---|---|---|---|
| | Home (N = 54) | | Supervised Apartment (N = 41) | | Family Home (N = 38) | | |
| | Mean | S.D. | Mean | S.D. | Mean | S.D. | F(2,130) |
| | Mean % | | | | | | |
| **Network** | | | | | | | |
| Supportive | 86 | 17 | 86 | 14 | 87 | 20 | 0.02 |
| More contact | 52 | 31 | 46 | 29 | 46 | 36 | 0.65 |
| **Kin** | | | | | | | |
| Network | 11$^x$ | 12 | 12$^x$ | 14 | 53$^y$ | 24 | 82.44*** |
| Supportive | 94 | 20 | 98$^x$ | 10 | 79$^y$ | 31 | 5.72** |
| More contact | 83$^x$ | 37 | 60$^x$ | 49 | 36$^y$ | 41 | 10.95*** |
| **Staff** | | | | | | | |
| Network | 34$^x$ | 18 | 34$^x$ | 14 | 13$^y$ | 14 | 25.30*** |
| Supportive | 90 | 24 | 87 | 27 | 90 | 25 | 0.27 |
| More contact | 54 | 41 | 52 | 38 | 53 | 45 | 0.01 |
| **Peers** | | | | | | | |
| Network | 53$^x$ | 18 | 47$^x$ | 16 | 30$^y$ | 20 | 18.44*** |
| Supportive | 80$^x$ | 24 | 82$^x$ | 25 | 94$^y$ | 19 | 3.63* |
| More contact | 44 | 32 | 38$^x$ | 32 | 60$^y$ | 41 | 3.88* |
| **Peers without handicaps** | | | | | | | |
| Network | 4$^x$ | 6 | 12$^y$ | 16 | 8$^y$ | 13 | 6.24** |
| Supportive | 100 | 0 | 88 | 25 | 95 | 14 | 1.94 |
| More contact | 69$^x$ | 40 | 36$^y$ | 45 | 68$^x$ | 46 | 3.35* |
| **Peers with handicaps** | | | | | | | |
| Network | 49$^x$ | 17 | 34$^y$ | 16 | 21$^z$ | 18 | 29.40*** |
| Supportive | 79$^x$ | 24 | 82$^x$ | 25 | 95$^y$ | 19 | 4.36* |
| More contact | 42$^x$ | 34 | 38$^x$ | 33 | 65$^y$ | 41 | 5.32** |

[a] x, y, and z superscripts denote differences between group means.

*$p < .05$; **$p < .01$; ***$p < .001$.

a boyfriend or girlfriend. Only one fourth of persons in FHs were reported as
actually dating.

### The Social Context of Community Activities

Persons in SAs enaged in a greater number of activities in the community in integrated settings on a weekly basis, more of which were independently initiated and unaccompanied by staff or kin, than did persons in GHs

Table 10.4. Relationship of Network Members Most Often Cited for Support[a]

| Relationship (% Identified) | Residence Type[a] | | |
| --- | --- | --- | --- |
| | Group Home (N = 54) | Supervised Apartment (N = 41) | Family Home (N = 38) |
| | | % | |
| Kin | 7 | 5 | 82 |
| Staff | 54 | 49 | 5 |
| Peers | 39 | 44 | 13 |
| with handicaps | 35 | 39 | 13 |
| without handicaps | 4 | 5 | 0 |
| Other[b] | 0 | 2 | 0 |
| Best friend[b] (most often cited) | 43 | 39 | 16 |

[a]Groups differed in composition of person most often cited for support, $\chi^2$ (2, N = 133) = 77.76; p < .001. GHs did not differ from SAs, $\chi^2$ (2, N = 95) = .65, p > .05. GH and SA combined did differ from FHs, $\chi^2$ (2, N = 133) = 77.17, p < .001.

[b]Advocate, generic service provider, and work supervisor are combined with peers for analysis.

[c]Groups differed in identification of best friend as most frequent source of support, $\chi^2$ (2, N = 122) = 6.94, p = .03.

or FHs. They engaged in more activities with peers than did persons in FHs and more activities with peers without disabilities than did persons in GHs. Fifty percent of community activities for persons in SAs and GHs were in the company of peers whereas only one fourth were for persons living with their families. Community activities of individuals living in GHs and in FHs were very similar in rates and in the numbers independently initiated and unaccompanied by a careprovider. About 50% of their activities were not structured by careproviders (see "independent initiation" in Table 10.5) and were unsupervised in the community. Persons living in FHs differed from those in GHs only in the proportion of activities which were in the company of friends, which was about half that of persons in GHs.

Residence Satisfaction and Well-being

Persons living in GHs reported lower residence satisfaction and personal well-being than the other groups ($F(2,130) = 8.82$, p < .01; $F(2,130) = 5.97$, p < .01). Persons in FHs and in SAs had similar and high reports of residence satisfaction (77 and 80% positive compared with 69% for GH residents) and high and similar attributions of personal well-being (84 and 82%

**Table 10.5. Mean Number of Weekly Activities by Type and Residential Setting**

| | Residence Type[a] | | | | | | |
|---|---|---|---|---|---|---|---|
| | Group Home (N = 54) | | Supervised Apartment (N = 30) | | Family Home (N = 37) | | |
| Activity Type | Mean | S.D. | Mean | S.D. | Mean | S.D. | $F(2,118)$[b] |
| Total activities | 8.4[x] | 5.5 | 13.4[y] | 9.2 | 8.2[x] | 2.2 | 6.80** |
| Location | | | | | | | |
| (integrated) | 7.6[x] | 5.1 | 13.0[y] | 9.2 | 7.8[x] | 5.1 | 7.95*** |
| Social context | | | | | | | |
| Independent | | | | | | | |
| initiation | 5.4[x] | 5.8 | 11.4[y] | 9.0 | 5.2[x] | 5.6 | 8.99*** |
| Unsupervised | 4.4[x] | 5.0 | 10.9[y] | 9.2 | 4.5[x] | 5.5 | 11.45*** |
| Including | | | | | | | |
| peers | 4.2 | 4.2 | 6.8[x] | 5.3 | 2.2[y] | 4.2 | 3.55* |
| Alone with | | | | | | | |
| peers | 2.2[x] | 3.2 | 6.2[y] | 6.2 | 1.4[x] | 2.5 | 13.36*** |
| Including non-handicapped | | | | | | | |
| peers | 0.9[x] | 1.6 | 3.1[y] | 4.1 | 1.2 | 2.4 | 6.94** |

[a] x, y, and z superscripts denote group means that are significantly different. Weekly numbers are based upon average of two weeks reported.

[b] Information from SAs is based on $N = 30$; 11 careproviders said that resident out-of-home activities were too numerous to report.

*$p < .05$; **$p < .01$; ***$p < .001$.

positive compared with 73% positive for GH residents). Residence satisfaction was correlated with personal well-being for persons in each setting ($r = .51$ for FH; .54 for GH, .58 for SA, $p < .01$ for each).

Neither the size nor the composition of the social network was related to satisfaction or well-being. However, the proportion of network members who were seen as supportive was significantly correlated with both. Because network composition was different for the different residence groups, relationships of these variables to residence satisfaction and well-being were examined separately for each residence type. As shown in Table 10.6, percent staff supportive was significantly related to well-being and residence satisfaction for persons in GHs only, where staff have continuous daily contact and responsibility for the residents. Staff supportiveness was unrelated to residence satisfaction and well-being for persons in SAs (to whom they pro-

**Table 10.6. Pearson Correlations of Social Network Characteristics with Satisfaction and Well-being**

| Network Characteristic | All Persons (N = 133) | | Group Homes (N = 54) | | Supervised Apartments (N = 41) | | Family Homes (N = 38) | |
|---|---|---|---|---|---|---|---|---|
| | Satisfaction | Well-being | Satisfaction | Well-being | Satisfaction | Well-being | Satisfaction | Well-being |
| Total no. | -.12 | -.16 | -.16 | -.14 | .10 | .08 | .06 | .14 |
| % Supportive | .38*** | .39*** | .43*** | .48*** | .42** | .40** | .35* | .33* |
| No. of kin | .07 | .06 | -.11 | -.07 | -.02 | .08 | .11 | -.22 |
| % Network kin | .09 | .17 | .06 | .02 | -.09 | .06 | .02 | .02 |
| % Kin supportive | .15 | .13 | .15 | .28[a] | .02 | .04[b] | .29[c] | .19 |
| No. of peers | -.13 | -.08 | -.12 | -.02 | .01 | .09 | .16 | .16 |
| % Network peers | -.04 | .10 | -.04 | .09 | .03 | .06 | .24 | .18 |
| % Peers supportive | .30*** | .36** | .27[c] | .46*** | .48*** | .36** | .02 | -.01 |
| No. of staff | -.14 | -.23* | -.03 | -.14 | .10 | .08 | -.22 | -.30 |
| % Staff supportive | .21* | .09 | .32* | .30* | .14 | -.08 | .19[d] | -.03 |

[a] N = 32: only 32 persons had kin named in their network.

[b] N = 24: only 24 persons had kin named in their network.

[c] p < .10.

[d] N = 22: only 22 persons in FHs had staff named in their networks.

* p < .05; ** p < .01; *** p < .001.

vide supervision on an as needed but not continuous basis) and in FHs, where individuals encounter staff primarily at day or vocational training programs.

Percent peers supportive was related to the well-being of persons in GHs and SAs, those groups whose networks included sizable numbers of peers. For SA residents, the more supportive the peer network was perceived, the higher the residence satisfaction. In networks of persons in FHs where peer representation is relatively small, there was no relationship between peer support and well-being or satisfaction. Dating, although unexpectedly unrelated to well-being in any setting, was significantly related to residence satisfaction for persons in SAs ($r = .31$, $p < .05$). The relationship of kin supportiveness to well-being and residence satisfaction for persons living in FHs where most of their support is derived from kin was positive but only statistically significant for residence satisfaction. The relationships of community activities to satisfaction and well-being were also examined. For persons in GHs and FHs, the rate of integrated community activities was related positively to residence satisfaction ($r = .25$, $r = .33$, $p < .05$, one-tailed) but not for persons in SAs who could access the community much more independently and at will.

The rate of social integration was related to residence satisfaction only for persons living in FHs ($r = .37$, $p < .02$). For persons living in GHs who had almost no social integration, the number of community activities with peers with disabilities was significantly related to well-being ($r = .29$, $p < .03$). The results for persons living in SAs indicated that a high rate of community access, particularly on a solitary basis, was associated with low scores on satisfaction and well-being ($r = -.51$ and $-.47$ respectively, $p < .01$).

### Community Activities and Network Characteristics

Examination of the relationships between careprovider information and the social composition of support networks obtained from self-report was performed as a means of cross-validation of measures. There were a number of logical consistencies. The number of peers with handicaps reported in the network was correlated with the number of activities in the community with peers with handicaps reported by careproviders ($r(131) = .24$, $p < .01$). The number of nonhandicapped peers in networks corresponded to the number of activities including nonhandicapped peers ($r(131) = .19$, $p < .02$). Finally, frequencies of activities with a careprovider correlated with both the number of kin ($r = .17$, $p < .06$) and number of staff ($r = .16$, $p < .08$) reported in networks.

DISCUSSION

Community services for adults with mental retardation established throughout the country are based on the principle of normalization and are intended to promote normative, age-appropriate activities and life-styles for individuals alongside their nondisabled peers in the community (Landesman and Butterfield 1987). However, few studies have examined these aspects of life in the community extensively or related them to social support and satisfaction (Halpern, Close, and Nelson 1986; Kennedy, Horner, and Newton 1989; Rosen and Burchard 1990).

Activities in the Community

The majority of participants in this study were neither inactive nor socially isolated in the community. They averaged at least one community activity outside home and work each day. Activities took place in integrated settings in which contact with community members without disabilities was highly probable. However, the results also show that they rarely engaged in these activities with friends who were nondisabled other than staff persons or relatives. In that respect, one could say that they were socially isolated from friendships with nondisabled peers in the community. In FHs, contrary to an assumption of higher integration (Willer and Intagliata 1982), companionship was provided mainly by kin. Persons living in SAs were the most active, independent in the community, and had peer companions without disabilities. However, the number and proportion of activities with peers without disabilities were extremely low for all groups. Many individuals reported none at all, indicating a lack of social integration. This replicates an earlier study of semiindependent living programs (Halpern, Close, and Nelson 1986).

The social policy goal of promoting social integration through community residential alternatives was not achieved to any degree. Persons living with their own families were similarly limited in the degree to which they actually participated with nondisabled peers outside of their homes and were the most isolated from engaging in activities with peers.

Social Networks

Social network composition reflected the social context of participants' community activities. Networks of persons living in FHs were mainly kin whereas those of persons in SAs and GHs were mainly other adults with mental retardation and staff. Participants saw their networks largely as sources of support rather than of stress and although they were satisfied with contact with half of their network, they wished to have more contact with the rest. The proportion of networks which included peers from the community without disabilities was small, less than half had any in their network, reflecting the general lack of social integration in any setting.

Persons in SAs and GHs cited staff and peers most frequently as a source of support even though 90% had contact with kin. In contrast, persons living in FHs relied on their families for a majority of their activities and social support and reported not receiving as much support and contact with peers as they wished.

The majority of persons in SAs and GHs were dating and had privacy in their residences for these relationships as had been reported by Halpern, Close, and Nelson (1986). Few persons living at home, however, were dating. This could reflect either more restricted opportunities for peer contact or overprotection. Although having an active romantic relationship has been highly related to self-esteem and satisfaction in other groups (Deiner 1984), dating was related to satisfaction only for persons living in SAs in this study.

Another striking finding was the virtual absence of reciprocal relationships between participants and their network members. They were engaged in one-way dependence relationships in which they viewed themselves as recipients rather than providers of emotional and practical support, even with their peer network members who were also individuals with mental retardation and often their best friends. This suggests that more needs to be done to assist individuals to develop an appreciation of what they themselves can and do provide for their friends and relatives.

### Satisfaction and Well-being

Study participants expressed a high degree of well-being and residence satisfaction. Having a supportive social network was related to well-being as consistently found in studies with other groups (Caplan 1974).

Persons in GHs were more dissatisfied with their residence and less happy than people living in the other two settings. They had, however, more persons living with them, staff and peers, and they had less autonomy in choosing activities, choosing companions, and perhaps in choosing housemates, than persons in SAs (see Burchard et al., in press). In addition, individuals were not randomly assigned to the type of residence in which they lived. Therefore, other factors may have contributed to the residence-related group differences in satisfaction and well-being. The factors in these group living situations which contribute to lower satisfaction need further study.

The composition of social networks had implications for which relationships had the most impact on well-being and satisfaction. For persons in GHs with networks that were comprised primarily of peers and staff with whom they lived, the perceived supportiveness of both network components was related to their well-being, and staff supportiveness was related to residence satisfaction, confirming an earlier finding (Burchard, Pine, and Gordon 1990). For those in SAs, the support of peers was related to well-being and residence sataisfaction. Staff, although providing support, did not live with them. These results can be interpreted in light of the literature that has shown that relationships in the immediate family (i.e., those with whom you live) are the among the most essential determinants of feelings of well-being and happiness (Deiner 1984). This certainly has implications for individuals with mental retardation if they must live in congregate settings in which they have no control over either staff or peers with whom they live. Greater control in this regard may be contributing to the greater personal and residential satisfaction of those who are living in supportive settings, either alone or with one or two other individuals.

The relationship of frequency of integrated activities to well-being and satisfaction in earlier studies of group homes (Burchard, Pine, and Gordon 1990) was replicated here for persons in group home settings only. The absence of this relationship for persons in SAs may be due to the fact that they are virtually free to access the community as frequently as they wish.

## Summary

The life-styles of the persons living most independently in the community were those of persons residing in SAs, a form of supported living. They were not isolated, nor were they lonely as had been thought (O'Connor 1983). They expressed a high degree of well-being equal to that of persons living at home, and they were the group that experienced the most social and physical integration in the community.

This setting clearly represents an environment that most closely approximates the widely accepted policy goals of providing services in the least restrictive setting which maximize life-style normalization, community integration, and independence (Burchard et al., in press). The advantages, opportunities, and personal satisfaction of persons who receive services in this type of setting have also been reported by Halpern, Close, and Nelson (1986). Networks were similar to those of GH persons and included considerable staff support. They did not appear to rely emotionally on staff, however, as much as GH persons but instead looked to their peer friends.

Every SA person reported a "best friend," and as a group they had the most peer activities in the community. They had not become isolated from peers with disabilities. Persons in SAs may have had greater well-being and satisfaction because they were not living in structured group situations and had more autonomy in choosing where to go and with whom while maintaining contact with friends and staff.

Although many persons may require the degree of supervision provided in small group home settings. it is also evident that these settings also serve persons who might well be benefitting from living in more individualized and more independent supportive living settings such as supervised apartments (Burchard et al., in press; Halpern, Close, and Nelson 1986).

Regardless of the setting or how active individuals were, life-styles were characterized by a lack of social integration. When one considers that only 30% of the study sample was involved in daily work in nonsegregated settings and 70% was at home or in segregated settings daily, the lack of social integration looms even larger. Social integration, the development of friendships and activities with community members at large rather than with service providers or other individuals with disabilities, has been a major goal of advocates which is reflected in social policy. These results show that this goal is far from attainment even by persons who have been residing in the community within their own families most of their lives. Outside of family support, their social lives appear to be just as circumscribed as those of individuals in small group homes and even more circumscribed with respect to peer contact.

Opportunity, proximity, and shared interests are major determinants of friendships in the community at large (Selman 1980). The issue of whether best friends and associates are by personal choice in this situation or are a result of a lack of opportunity for contact with others or a need for more training in social skills (O'Connor 1983) is a question that needs further exploration. Neither social policy nor advocates should determine personal goals and friendships over personal preference and choice. The key issue is whether current social networks reflect personal choice or limited opportunity and limited skills.

Although this study attempted to examine life-style and satisfaction of individuals who were similar with respect to their skill levels and disabilities and who happened to live in three different community residential alternatives, individuals were not assigned randomly to those settings. There were group differences in level of retardation and age which had to be controlled by statistical procedures. Family home participants were those whose families chose to participate and were known in some fashion to service agencies; persons in agency settings were all within one state system. These factors may limit the generalizability of the findings. Nonetheless, the study provides a descriptive analysis of activities and support networks from which to draw a more complete picture of the life-style of persons in community settings.

The congruity of the information from careprovider reports and participants with mental retardation shows the value of using respondents to provide information directly about their lives, friendships, needs, and wants so that they, like persons in other service systems, may speak for themselves. Developing ways to obtain more complete information about the extent and personal meaning of physical and social integration for persons with mental retardation is essential for evaluating life in the community, the effectiveness of community services, and for supporting reasonable and personally chosen consumer goals. Although there appears to be a need to identify ways to assist persons in developing and maintaining social support from community members, consumer information, experience, and personal choice should be the basis for these efforts.

## Acknowledgments

This research was supported in part by National Institute of Disability and Rehabilitation Research Grant 1-33-GH-40203 and is based in part on the dissertation of the second author. The authors wish to acknowledge the assistance and support of individuals with mental retardation, their families, and state and local mental retardation service providers throughout Vermont whose cooperation and participation were essential, and the assistance provided by Diane Simoneau, Elia Vecchione, and Haydee Toro.

# 11

# Mental Health Consumers' Preferences for Housing and Supports

## The Vermont Study

Beth H. Tanzman, M.S.W., Susan F. Wilson, Ph.D., and James T. Yoe, Ph.D.

Throughout the United States most individuals with psychiatric disabilities now live in community settings rather than in institutions (Goldman, Gatozzi, and Taube 1981). Generally they reside in typical, generic community housing and not in specialized residential treatment facilities (e.g., Ohio Mental Health Housing Task Force 1986). In part, this shift in locus has occurred as a result of the ideology of deinstitutionalization which holds that "community care and freedom of choice are better for the chronic mentally ill than the paternalism and restrictiveness of the state hospital" (Minkoff 1987, 945–46). This shift is also a result of the welfare reforms of the 1960s which, through Social Security Disability Insurance (SSDI) and Supplemental Security Insurance (SSI), provide some income for people who are unable to work as a result of psychiatric disabilities (Mechanic 1987) and therefore enable some access to generic housing.

One consequence of this shift is that people with psychiatric disabilities are forced to compete with other low-income groups for the rapidly shrinking stock of affordable housing in our communities. Because of a combination of poverty, the social stigma associated with psychiatric disabilities, and the virtual disappearance of inexpensive housing in our communities it is becoming increasingly difficult for these individuals to "find and maintain decent, affordable and appropriate housing" (Boyer 1987, 72).

Complicating these housing problems is the confusion that exists between the federal and state government and between local mental health and housing providers about which system is responsible for addressing the housing needs of people with psychiatric disabilities. Public housing agencies view these housing needs as a mental health system responsibility. On the other hand, mental health agencies have historically viewed housing as a social welfare problem and have narrowly defined their role as the provision of residential "treatment" but not housing per se (Blanch, Carling, and Ridgway 1988). With regard to support services, the health system currently finds itself funding two different approaches, psychiatric hospitals and community services, often without sufficient integration of these locally (Hall, Nelson, and Fowler 1987). So while mental health systems have implemented a policy of deinstitutionalization, in reality community programs remain under funded, and in most cases, institutions still receive the great majority of mental health financing (Torrey and Wolfe 1986).

In spite of these constraints, state departments of mental health, community mental health centers (CMHCs), Alliance for the Mentally Ill (AMI) family groups, consumer/former patient groups, and communities across the country continue to struggle with the challenge of providing stable and affordable housing with supports for citizens with severe psychiatric disabilities (consumers and former institutional residents).

For these various systems to share the responsibility for housing and supports they must be informed about the specific needs of the people who live in our communities and have psychiatric disabilities. More explicitly, if the housing and supports are to be used and if consumers are to be satisfied with them, the systems must have a clear idea of what consumers and former patients themselves want in these areas.

Increasingly, research is being conducted which directly and systematically surveys consumers and former patients rather than using the traditional approach of surveying only mental health service professionals (Conte et al. 1989). Data suggest that professionals and consumers/former patients often have different perceptions concerning mental health services and housing (Prager 1980; Lord, Schnarr, and Hutchison 1987), and there is growing evidence that consumers' perceptions of what they need and want in the way of housing and support are associated with success in housing (Ridgway 1988a, 1988b; Wilson, in press).

In recognition of the importance of consumer preferences the Vermont Department of Mental Health contracted with the Center for Community Change Through Housing and Support, located at the University of Vermont, to survey a sample of the state's citizens with psychiatric disabilities to assess their housing and support preferences. The results of the survey were incorporated into the department's statewide housing plans and policies.

## METHODS

### Target Population

One hundred nineteen people with psychiatric disabilities were interviewed in three Vermont counties (Chittenden, Rutland, and Washington Counties) during the months of August and September 1988. These counties were selected from the 14 counties in Vermont since they contain the largest populations of consumers with psychiatric disabilities in the state and comprise a range of geographic settings from larger towns to rural environments. There were three target groups within the study sample: (1) a random sample of community rehabilitation and treatment clients (CRT clients) diagnosed as having a major mental illness ($N = 73$); (2) individuals within these three counties identified by service providers as having a major mental illness and as being either homeless or only temporarily housed ($N = 30$); and (3) nonforensic, nonnursing home inpatients at the Vermont State [psychiatric] Hospital (VSH) ($N = 16$).

### Instrument Development

The consumer preference survey instrument used in this study was an expanded and revised version of an earlier instrument (Ridgway and Carling 1988). An advisory group of consumers/former patients, family members, and service providers was consulted on drafts of the survey instrument. The instrument was organized around six major content areas including demographic information, income level and housing costs, stability of housing, satisfaction with current housing, housing preferences, and community supports and services.

### Procedures

*Interviewer Selection and Training.* The survey was conducted through face-to-face interviews. All interviews were performed by current or former mental health consumers or former patients trained specifically for the task. Hiring consumers/former patients as interviewers (rather than community mental health staff or research assistants) offered unique advantages: it helped to ensure that respondents replied to the survey questions without potential role bias which might have been present in the professional-client relationship; it provided employment for mental health consumers/former patients while giving them an opportunity to learn new skills; and, at the same time, it fostered a sense of their involvement in the complex issues of housing in Vermont. Several additional advantages emerged during the study. For example, the interviewers were not intimidated by symptoms of mental illness. They noted if a respondent seemed sedated or distracted and dealt well with this by keeping the interview focused. Altogether, 19 consumers/former patients were hired as interviewers on this project.

*Interviewer Interrater Reliability.* During each interviewer's first two interview sessions, interrater reliability was checked by having two interviewers attend the same session. One person (called the *interviewer*) asked the questions and recorded the respondent's answers while the other person (called the *shadow partner*) listened to the respondent and recorded the answers only. The interviewer and the shadow partner were instructed not to compare recorded responses. The average agreement between interviewer and shadow partner was 96.8%.

*Data Analysis.* The analyses of these data are descriptive and cross-sectional in nature since no variables were manipulated experimentally and no control groups were used. However, it was convenient to treat variables such as age, gender, present living situation, target population, and county as pseudoindependent variables and variables such as housing and support preferences and most-preferred housing situations as pseudodependent variables. Based on the study design, causal interpretations of the data are not warranted.

RESULTS

Sample Characteristics

A total of 119 individuals were interviewed in the study. More than half of the respondents were from the community mental health center sample (CRT), 14% were patients at the VSH, and one quarter were from the homeless population. Slightly more than half of the respondents surveyed were male, and nearly three quarters of the respondents were between the ages of 18 and 50.

The makeup of the three target groups differed with respect to gender and age, but the samples were each representative of their particular target group. The CRT group included fewer males (41%) than either the VSH (56%) or homeless groups (83%). In fact, the high proportion of men in the homeless sample led to an overrepresentation of men in the overall sample. The target groups also differed across age. Although 27% of the CRT respondents were 35 years or less, 40% of the VSH respondents and 62% of the homeless respondents were in this age group.

The survey respondents lived in a variety of different residential situations, with apartments or houses being the most common and homelessness (because one quarter of the overall sample was homeless) as the second most common situation. Very few of the 119 individuals surveyed were living in mental health-sponsored congregate living situations even though all respondents were labeled as having a psychiatric disability. Sixteen (13%) of the respondents were living in the VSH, and only five respondents (4%) were living in community mental health group homes. This is representative of the current living situations of people labeled as mentally ill in Vermont because only 3% of all CRT clients live in community mental health center-operated congregate living arrangements.

Income and Expenses

A summary of the monthly income and expenses of the overall sample is shown in Table 11.1. Fifteen percent of the sample reported having no income whereas half of the respondents received between $401.00 and $600.00 per month. Of those who had an income their mean monthly income was $524.22. This figure suggests that most respondents fell into the very low-income category, having only about 20% of the mean yearly income in their respective counties. Slightly less than one fifth of the sample earned some income from employment, and the same percentage reported receiving financial assistance from their family (Table 11.1).

**Table 11.1. Overall Income and Housing Costs**

| | |
|---|---|
| Monthly Income (N = 106) | |
| No income | 15% |
| $200 or less | 7% |
| $201–$400 | 10% |
| $401–$600 | 50% |
| $601–$800 | 8% |
| $800 or more | 10% |
| *Source of Income* (N = 119) | |
| Employment | 19% |
| Family support | 19% |
| Monthly Housing Cost (N = 118) | |
| None | 24% |
| $100 or less | 20% |
| $101–$200 | 21% |
| $201–$300 | 13% |
| $301–$400 | 8% |
| More than $400 | 14% |
| *Receive rent subsidy* (N = 114) | 28% |
| Section 8[a] | 79% |
| Other | 21% |

[a]Section 8 = federally funded housing subsidy.

Table 11.1 also shows that the most frequently reported amount spent on housing was between $100.00 and $200.00 whereas nearly one quarter spent more than $300.00 per month on housing. The mean monthly housing cost was $225.81, which represents about 43% of the respondents' mean incomes. This is well above the accepted rate of affordability (30%) set by the federal Department of Housing and Urban Development and the Vermont Department of Housing and Community Affairs. Just over one quarter of the sample reported receiving a rent subsidy although 80% appeared to be eligible, and more than three quarters of those who received a rent subsidy described it as a Section 8 certificate.

The most common source of income for the respondents in all target groups was the federal SSI benefit, which was $414.20 per month at the time of these interviews. In general, the CRT respondents were more likely to receive income from employment (26%) than were respondents in the other target groups. CRT respondents also reported the highest monthly incomes of all target groups. Individuals who were homeless at the time of the interviews were the most likely (46%) to report having no income and were the least likely to receive financial assistance from their families.

Stability of Housing

More than half (54%) of the sample had lived in their current housing for less than a year. However, CRT respondents were more likely to have lived there for more than three years (42%) than were either VSH respondents (16%) or homeless respondents (7%). Half of the homeless respondents reported having been homeless for less than three months.

More than half (63%) of the sample said that they could continue to live where they were at the time of the interview, but given the choice, a majority (61%) said that they would prefer to move. Common reasons cited for wanting to move were to find a better physical setting (better location, more space, better repair) or a less crowded place, and to have more freedom and autonomy.

The desire to stay in one's current housing or to move to a new situation varied somewhat with age and the respondents' current housing. All of the people living in single room occupancy housing and those who were homeless at the time of the interview wanted to move, and most (80%) of the respondents at the state hospital expressed the same preference. Respondents in the youngest age group, those 18–35 years, were more likely to want to move (81%), and those 65 and older (65+) were the least likely to want to move (38%).

### Satisfaction with Current Housing

The best liked aspects of the respondents' living situations were that their basic needs (food and shelter) were met and that the location, freedom and autonomy, and the comfort of the physical space were agreeable. Conversely, lack of comfort was the least liked aspect (27%).

Levels of satisfaction with current housing varied significantly by current living situations, $F(6,111) = 4.74$, $p < .01$. Those who lived in their own apartments or houses were the most satisfied (mean = 1.80) whereas those living in single room occupancy situations were the least satisfied (mean = 3.43).

### Housing Preferences

A summary of the housing preferences reported by the overall sample of respondents is presented in Table 11.2. A majority of the respondents reported that an apartment or house would be their ideal living situation whereas the least preferred living arrangement was a mental health program such as a hospital or group home. One tenth of the respondents named a community care home (boarding home) as their ideal living situation, and a similar number said they would prefer to live in their family's home. More than one third of the respondents cited freedom and autonomy as the most important aspects of their ideal living situation whereas permanence, security, and privacy ranked as the second most important characteristics.

The majority of respondents preferred not to live with other mental health consumers, usually because it was difficult to live with other people's problems or because they simply preferred to live alone. Of those who preferred to live with other mental health consumers, most cited the mutual support and understanding that such a relationship might provide as the reason for their preference. The most frequently stated roommate preference was a romantic partner or spouse. Slightly more than one quarter of those surveyed said that they would prefer to live alone.

### Supports and Services

Table 11.3 presents the frequency with which respondents reported needing certain material and social supports. Most respondents said that they needed more income to live successfully in the housing of their choice. The majority also said that they would require money for rental, furniture, and household supplies. In addition, most reported needing a telephone and help with transportation. Less than half expressed a need for assistance with

Table 11.2. Overall Housing and Roommate Preferences

| | |
|---|---|
| What would be your ideal living situation? ($N = 116$) | |
| Mental health facility | 3% |
| With my family | 9% |
| Community care home | 10% |
| Apartment/house | 70% |
| SRO/temporary housing | 8% |
| What is the most important aspect of your ideal living situation? ($N = 113$) | |
| Freedom/autonomy | 38% |
| Meals, caring for home | 11% |
| Proximity to support network | 11% |
| Size of physical space | 11% |
| Permanence/security/privacy | 29% |
| What would be your living area preference? ($N = 118$) | |
| City/town | 62% |
| Rural | 33% |
| No difference | 5% |
| Who would you like to live with? ($N = 116$) | |
| Family | 19% |
| Friends | 15% |
| Romantic partner/spouse | 38% |
| No one | 28% |
| Would you like to live with other consumers? ($N = 118$) | |
| Yes | 19% |
| No | 63% |
| Why do you feel this way? ($N = 102$) | |
| I want to live alone | 13% |
| I don't want to live with others' problems | 33% |
| There is mutual support between consumers | 24% |
| No reason | 30% |

activities of daily living (such as shopping, budgeting money, cooking, and laundry).

The majority said that they needed help avoiding emotional upsets and crises and would like to be able to reach mental health staff any time of the day or night by telephone. However, only 12% said that they would need to have staff live with them to be successful in the housing of their choice. Survey respondents reported using a variety of specific services when in a crisis situation (Table 11.4). Most said that they used community mental health centers and natural supports such as family and friends although the supports and services generally used by respondents did vary by respondent type. CRT respondents were more likely to use natural supports and community

**Table 11.3. Supports Needed to Live in Desired Situation**

| | |
|---|---|
| More income, money, benefits | 79% |
| Rent deposit | 73% |
| Furniture | 67% |
| Household supplies | 61% |
| Telephone | 80% |
| Transportation | 73% |
| Help in finding place to live | 72% |
| Roommates/housemates | 40% |
| Finding roommates | 26% |
| Making friends | 47% |
| Getting along with people | 50% |
| Reach staff by phone day or night | 73% |
| Staff come to me day or night | 55% |
| Staff live with me | 12% |
| Staff come regularly during the day | 36% |
| Managing medications | 39% |
| Avoid emotional upsets, crisis | 77% |
| Budgeting money | 49% |
| Shopping | 46% |
| Housecleaning | 33% |
| Cooking | 29% |
| Doing laundry | 25% |

**Table 11.4. Supports Used in a Crisis by Target Group[a]**

| Respondent Type | Total N | CMHC | VSH | Community Hospital | Natural Supports | Consumer Self-help | Crisis Clinic |
|---|---|---|---|---|---|---|---|
| | | | | % | | | |
| CRT | 73 | 96 | 27 | 59 | 97 | 34 | 56 |
| VSH | 16 | 69 | 75 | 75 | 88 | 31 | 63 |
| Homeless | 30 | 80 | 27 | 47 | 63 | 37 | 37 |

[a]This table reports percentages for those respondents who said *yes*, they use the support or services.

mental health centers. VSH respondents were more apt to seek hospitals and crisis clinics and were the least likely to use community mental health services. Homeless respondents were the most likely to use generic community services such as shelters, churches, and legal services but were the least likely to use community hospitals, crisis clinics, or natural supports.

DISCUSSION

The results of this study have direct implications for the manner in which housing and support services should be delivered to citizens with psychiatric disabilities. If community services are to be successful they must reflect the preferences and desires of the people who are to receive them.

Most persons interviewed in this study would prefer to live in their own apartment or house rather than in a mental health-operated facility or program, single-room occupancy hotels, with their family, or in a community care home. This finding is to be expected for the community mental health clients because almost all of them already live in this type of housing. This finding, however, was consistent for all three respondent types—community mental health clients, residents of the state hospital, and people who were homeless. Because of this a primary responsibility of the mental health system must be to enhance the availability of regular, affordable housing for people with psychiatric disabilities in local communities.

Housing availability can be increased through a variety of mechanisms at the state, local, and individual levels. First, the state mental health authority can work with other state agencies directly involved in housing finance, planning, and development to advocate for the needs of people with psychiatric disabilities. In addition, coalition building can serve to further the agenda of all state citizens who have unmet housing needs. These same strategies can be applied at the local community level and can be enhanced by the clear direction and support provided by the state mental health agency. Neither of these strategies will be successful, however, unless the housing arrangements and support services provided reflect the unique needs of the individuals being served.

One of the most blatant needs detailed in this study was the lack of adequate income to access housing and to pay for other basic needs. Almost one sixth of the respondents reported no income, and although a disproportionate number of these respondents were homeless, this was not always the case. Of those who did report an income, the average amount reported was only 20% of the mean yearly income for their respective counties. In addition, the average respondent spent 43% of his or her mean income on housing—far above the recommended 30% maximum standard of affordability. Consequently, people with psychiatric disabilities in Vermont are very poor in comparison with their fellow community members and are in the position of spending far too much of their limited resources on housing.

The findings point to several ways in which this issue of poverty could be addressed. First, only one fifth of the respondents had income from employment; thus, increasing opportunities for gainful work might assist in housing accessibility. Second, only 28% of the respondents were receiving some form of rent subsidy. The availability of such subsidies to people with mental illness could be enhanced through increased state and local advocacy with housing finance authorities for Section 8 certificates or by increasing the available resources in mental health-operated housing subsidy programs. In addition, assistance must be provided to those respondents who reported having no income, either by hiring them or by connecting them with government assistance programs.

Along with assistance with income, the specifics of the living situations must be taken into account when planning or accessing housing. More than three fifths of the respondents expressed a desire to move from their current living situation, primarily because they wanted to live in a better location, have more space that was in better repair, and experience more freedom and autonomy. It is interesting to note here that although all people living in single-room occupancy hotels or who were homeless wanted to move, as did most of those living in the state hospital, people living in single-room occupancy hotels reported the least amount of satisfaction of all respondents, including those in the state hospital or who were homeless. Thus, the poor living conditions of most single-room occupancy hotels seem to make them the least satisfying of all settings even though the most important aspects of the preferred living situations were freedom and autonomy, permanence, security, and privacy. These environmental qualities are not unlike those valued by most people in our society, and there is no reason to assume otherwise for people with a psychiatric disability.

Traditionally, mental health systems have assumed that many people with psychiatric disabilities need live-in staff to assist them during crisis situations or to teach them daily living skills. A premise underlying this assumption is that people are unable to articulate their needs for assistance well enough to secure adequate services on their own. The findings of this study indicate that individuals with a psychiatric disability can articulate their individual needs both reasonably and clearly. Only one tenth of the respondents reported needing live-in staff. Instead, most people preferred that staff be available by telephone or in person if necessary on a 24-hour basis. These findings imply that the mental health system should organize its support services to be responsive on a flexible, as-needed basis.

Another interesting finding of the study was that a majority of respondents preferred not to live with other mental health service consumers, primarily because they felt that it was difficult to live with other people's problems as well as their own. This preference is in direct conflict with current practices in segregated and congregated mental health residential programs and with the apparent assumption that mental health consumers prefer to live with each other, or that this may, in fact, be therapeutic. Although this may be the case for some individuals, this study suggests that we must pay much more attention to individuals' preferences concerning who they live with if we want to maximize their possibility for success.

Finally, the crisis supports and services used by the three respondent types varied substantially. It is unclear, however, whether this variation is a result of preference, availability, or familiarity. These patterns need further study in order to develop a more responsive crisis service system capacity which might ultimately avert such situations before they occur.

Ultimately, the goal of mental health services is to assist people to live full and meaningful lives. The premise of this study was that the first step toward assisting people in this way is to ask them about their needs and preferences; only then is there a firm foundation on which to build. In doing this kind of research, Vermont and other states that have undertaken similar efforts (Daniels and Carling 1986; Keck 1990) have not only acquired information about how to develop more responsive housing and supports but have also established the importance of consumers' own voices in the development and provision of housing and services.

# 12

# Stability and Change in the Life-style and Adjustment of Adults with Mental Retardation Living in Community Residences

Lawrence R. Gordon, Ph.D., Sara N. Burchard, Ph.D.,
Joseph E. Hasazi, Ph.D., James T. Yoe, Ph.D.,
Laurie C. Dietzel, M.A., and Diane Simoneau, B.A.

The adoption of normalization philosophy and deinstitutionalization policies on a national basis (Landesman and Butterfield 1987) has resulted in an enormous growth in community services for individuals with developmental disabilities (Bruininks et al. 1987). With this growth, interest in evaluating community residential alternatives in terms of the goals of the new social policy has also grown. The focus of these evaluative efforts is on the extent to which these new community residential alternatives promote the acquisition and performance of independent living skills, provide normalized life-styles including employment for adults, and enhance physical and social integration within the general community (Burchard et al., in press; Heal 1988; Landesman-Dwyer 1985).

Previous research on community residential alternatives has often been cross-sectional or retrospective in nature (Burchard et al., in press; Eyman, Demaine, and Lei 1979; Halpern, Close, and Nelson 1986; Intagliata and Willer 1982; Kleinberg and Galligan 1983) and has defined *community adjustment* narrowly in terms of remaining in the community or of acquiring greater daily and community living skills (Hill and Bruininks 1984; Kleinberg and Galligan 1983; Schalock, Harper, and Genung 1981). Although some studies have used a more extensive array of variables to represent community adjustment, few have been both prospective and comprehensive in their examination of variables that represent life-style and adjustment (Heal 1985).

Prior research has also often failed to take into account the importance of personal and social factors related to quality of life and adjustment of persons in community living situations (Heal 1988; Landesman 1986; O'Connor 1983). Particularly, examination of these issues from the point of view of the consumers themselves has rarely been included (Burchard, Pine, and Gordon 1990; Halpern, Close, and Nelson 1986; Seltzer 1981). Examining life-style, satisfaction, and social support from the perspective of the person being served is critical for determining quality of life, community adjustment, and ultimately, the success of publicly supported community living arrangements.

This chapter summarizes selected findings from a three-year longitudinal study conducted throughout Vermont which examined the quality of life of adults with mental retardation who were living in three types of community settings. The relevant variables included personal characteristics and environmental factors that are known or suspected to influence personal performance, life-style, and adjustment of individuals with mental retardation (Burchard et al., in press; Campbell and Bailey 1984; Landesman and Butterfield 1987). We also examined a broad range of variables which represented individual outcomes that would reflect desired social policy goals and personal satisfaction (Borthwick-Duffy 1989; Heal 1988).

One important environmental factor is the type of residential alternative in which participants live. We examined the life-style and adjustment of adults with mental retardation who resided in three types of residential alternative commonly available throughout the nation: semiindependent living situations (supportive apartments), small group home settings with continuous staff supervision, and family homes in which individuals reside with their own families or relatives. Because every state is actively engaged in planning and providing an array of community living alternatives for persons with disabilities it is important to examine the type of opportunities, life-styles, and personal satisfactions which these publicly funded residential alternatives are providing (Landesman and Butterfield 1987). Living with family or relatives is the situation that is the most common throughout the nation and the most likely or only option available to many individuals, but it is one that is infrequently studied and contrasted with the other settings (Bruininks et al. 1987).

To avoid the major confounds of comparing persons with different disability statuses across environments which, by their inherent organization and staffing provide quite different levels of support and opportunity (Campbell and Bailey 1984), we included individuals with similar abilities in our study: individuals who performed a specified level of daily living skills, who had no physical or behavioral disability that would prevent their access to the community, and who would be able to respond to simple interview formats so that we could obtain their perspective on their own life-style, satisfaction, and adjustment (Burchard et al., in press). The importance of obtaining information and direction directly from service consumers is a widely recognized policy among other disability groups, but persons with developmental disabilities have been given little opportunity to evaluate directly or to have an effect upon the services they receive.

METHODS

Setting

This study was conducted in Vermont, where group homes and supportive apartments are operated by nonprofit agencies regulated by the state. Services subscribe to a normalization philosophy and a developmental model of service provision. We focused on three community residential settings available to persons with mild and moderate retardation not only in Vermont but also nationally: group homes, supportive ("sheltered") apartments, and the individuals' own family homes.

*Group Homes.* Group homes (GHs) are residences that provide 24-hour supervision and habilitation services for three to six persons. The homes are located in residential neighborhoods and are staffed by one or two persons at a time. There were 20 group homes in the state at the time of the study.

*Supportive Apartments.* Supportive appartments (SAs) are located in residential neighborhoods and are usually occupied by one or two individuals. Staff provide supervision and training as needed but do not provide 24-hour supervision. There were 35 SAs at the time of the study.

*Family Homes.* Family homes (FHs) are private residences in which the individual with mental retardation lives with parents or other family members. These residences are not regulated by the state, do not necessarily subscribe to any philosophy of service, and provide the level of care and supervision which they individually deem essential.

Participants

Participation in the study was limited to unmarried adults with moderate and mild mental retardation, who were between the ages of 23 and 55, and who were able to respond to simple interviews. Recruitment was done statewide through mental retardation service agencies. Individuals living in all of the GHs and SAs throughout the state were contacted to participate, and families having adult members with mental retardation were located in every region of the state. Altogether, 157 persons meeting the study criteria were

Table 12.1. Comparison of the Personal Characteristics of Persons Living in Group Homes, Family Homes, or Supportive Apartments[a]

| | Residence Type | | | |
| Characteristic | Family Home (N = 34) | Group Home (N = 42) | Supportive Apartment (N = 38) | |
|---|---|---|---|---|
| Age | | | | |
| Mean | 30.5$^x$ | 38.6$^y$ | 36.4$^y$ | *** |
| Range | 24–51 | 24–59 | 29–56 | |
| Gender | | | | |
| Female | 16 | 25 | 23 | N.S. |
| Male | 18 | 17 | 15 | |
| Years in residence | | | | |
| Mean | 21.1$^x$ | 3.7$^y$ | 4.1$^y$ | *** |
| S.D. | 6.1 | 1.8 | 1.8 | |
| Years previously institutionalized | 4$^x$ | 25$^y$ | 23$^y$ | *** |
| Years since discharge | | | | |
| Mean | 11.8 | 9.2 | 10.0 | N.S. |
| S.D. | 3.6 | 6.3 | 3.8 | |
| LMR | | | | |
| Borderline | 5 | 1 | 8 | * |
| Mild | 22 | 25 | 26 | |
| Moderate | 7$^x$ | 16$^y$ | 4$^x$ | |

[a]Overall tests use analysis of variance or $\chi^2$ square procedures. x and y superscripts denote significant differences between residence types. LMR, level of mental retardation.

*$p < .05$; **$p < .01$; ***$p < .001$; N.S., not significant.

identified. Of these, 54 in GHs, 41 in SAs, and 38 in FHs agreed to participate (85% of the individuals identified). More than one third of the families reported an annual income less than $25,000.

This report is based on information about the 114 individuals (86% of the original sample) who remained in the same residence type throughout the three years. Of these persons, 42 lived in GHs, 38 lived in SAs, and 34 lived with their families. Their demographic characteristics are shown in Table 12.1.

Design and Procedure

Participants were followed from 1985 through 1988. Analyses of variance and covariance were performed to examine differences among residential alternatives. The variables included in our study design (personal

**Table 12.2.  Predictors and Quality of Life Indicators for Persons with Mental Retardation Living in Community Settings**

| *Predictors* | *Indicators* |
|---|---|
| *Personal characteristics* | *Life-style* |
| Age | Performance of adaptive behavior |
| Sex | Life-style normalization |
| Level of retardation | Physical integration |
| Disability status | Social integration |
| | Community employment |
| *Environmental factors* | |
| Residence type | *Adjustment* |
|   Family home | Residence satisfaction |
|   Group home | Work satisfaction |
|   Supportive apartment | Social network characteristics |
| Careprovider attitudes/competencies | Personal well-being |
| Location (access to community) | Severity of maladaptive behavior |
| Opportunities provided | |
| *Social factors* | |
| Recent life events | |
| Frequency of contact | |
|   with family | |
|   with advocate/benefactor | |

characteristics and environmental and social factors, and variables representing client life-style and adjustment) are displayed in Table 12.2.

Information was obtained (1) from questionnaires and structured interviews with a knowledgeable informant and (2) by structured interviews with the participants themselves which were conducted in private at their homes by trained interviewers. Second interviews were scheduled approximately 12 months later and the third 6 to 8 months following. Interviews were audiotaped, or a second observer was present to score interviews for reliability analyses independently. A second informant provided independent scores for the questionnaire measures to allow reliability assessment. For all measures interrater or interscorer reliabilities were above .80 (Burchard et al., in press).

Measures

*Personal Characteristics.* These were obtained from a demographic questionnaire filled out by the primary careprovider.

*Community Adjustment Scale.* Developed by Seltzer and Seltzer (1976), this is a careprovider questionnaire measuring independent performance of daily and community living skills.

*Life-style Normalization Interview.* This structured interview with the careprovider (Burchard et al. 1987) provided a measure of life-style normalization in the residential setting and a measure of community integrative activities in which the resident had engaged. The former provided a score for the degree of age-appropriate rhythms, activities, responsibilities, and autonomy of the individual. The latter supplied information on the number, type, and structure of the participant's community activities during the prior two weeks.

*Resident Satisfaction Interview.* This is a structured interview adapted by Burchard and her colleagues (1987) from Seltzer (1981), which measures normalization practices, residence satisfaction, work or day program satisfaction, and personal well-being from the perspective of the participant. It also provides a single rating of how well each participant likes his or her home. The interview is constructed to eliminate response and acquiescence biases (Burchard, Pine, and Gordon 1990).

*Severity of Problem Behavior.* This measure (Bruininks et al. 1984) was completed by the careprovider and reflects the frequency and severity of any behavior adjustment problems.

*Social System Self-assessment.* Adapted from Weinberg (1984) by Rosen (1988), this is a self-report measure obtained by a structured interview with the resident which documents the size, nature, supportiveness, and reciprocity of the participant's social network.

Information on the construction, reliability, and validity of these measures is reported elsewhere (Burchard, Pine, and Gordon 1990; and Burchard et al., in press).

RESULTS AND DISCUSSION

This study examined the life-style, adjustment, and satisfaction of participants who lived continuously in the same community and residence type over a two and one-half- to three-year time span. Comparisons were made among the three residence types on the specific measures already described.

Personal Characteristics

Because persons were not assigned randomly to residence settings, persons with similar personal characteristics were selected for participation. Nevertheless, there were some differences among individuals living in the three settings which were consistent over time. The persons living with their

own families did not include many people over 50 years old, and yet age was
not systematically related to outcome variables within residence types. The
most important difference between individuals across settings was their level
of retardation. Group homes had a greater proportion of persons with moderate retardation than did the other sites (see Table 12.1). The level of retardation, however, was *not* related to factors of personal satisfaction, behavioral
adjustment, or characteristics of social support networks. Level of retardation *was,* however, consistently related to performance of skills, life-style
normalization, and social integration (e.g., having friends without disabilities actively involved with them). These relationships were also highly
associated with residence setting, particularly with SA living, which provided much greater opportunities for all of these outcomes (Burchard et al.,
in press). Using covariance and regression techniques to control for group
differences in the level of retardation, the latter finding became clear: the
setting characteristics were strongly and consistently related to differences in
life-style outcomes such as normalization, community (physical) and social
integration, and employment in the community (Table 12.3, *overall* means
across the three years).

### Residence Settings and Community Adjustment

*Supportive Apartments.* Supportive apartment residents showed an advantage on most life-style measures related to the identified goals of social
policy: performance of independent behavior, life-style normalization, and
community integration. These differences were consistent over three years
(see Table 12.3). Ratings of maladaptive behavior decreased significantly
the second year to levels similar to those of family home members (Table
12.3). These differences were not attributable to differences in level of retardation between persons in SAs and persons in FHs as there were none, and
covariance techniques were used to control for level of mental retardation in
comparisons including persons from GHs. The differences appear to be
related to the advantage provided by community access and individual
opportunities afforded by their location and the necessity for independent
performance of many skills of daily and community living for persons in
apartments (Burchard et al., in press). Supportive apartment residents' rate
of community use was consistently the highest of the three groups over three
years (Table 12.3).

The level of satisfaction with the social support of network members
was similar to that of persons living in other settings and was highly positive
(see Table 12.4). The participants had as many people in their networks and
as many nondisabled peers in their activities as did persons in FHs. None,

**Table 12.3.** Life-style Measures for Persons in Three Types of Residences across Three Years[a]

| Indicator | Residence Type | | | |
| --- | --- | --- | --- | --- |
| | Family Home (N = 34) | Group Home (N = 42) | Supportive Apartment (N = 38) | |
| | | % | | |
| Performance (N = 94; 26,31,37) | | | | |
| Year 1 | 49 | 51 | 71 | LMR *** |
| Year 2 | 50 | 52 | 73 | Residence type *** |
| Year 3[b] | (35) | (45) | (79) | Time *** |
| Overall | 44.6[x] | 49.3[x] | 74.3[y] | |
| Life-style normalization (N = 111; 34,40,37) | | | | |
| Year 1 | 73 | 79 | 88 | LMR ** |
| Year 2 | 79 | 84 | 88 | Residence type *** |
| Year 3 | 79 | 85 | 90 | Time *** |
| Overall | 77[x] | 83[y] | 88[z] | |
| Physical integration[c] (N = 101; 34,39,28) | | | | |
| Year 1 | 7.3 | 7.4 | 12.3 | LMR * |
| Year 2 | 7.4 | 6.5 | 11.0 | Residence type ** |
| Year 3 | 8.0 | 7.6 | 9.6 | |
| Overall | 7.6[x] | 7.2[x] | 11.0[y] | |
| Social integration[d] (N = 101; 34,39,28) | | | | |
| Year 1 | 1.3 | 0.7 | 2.8 | LMR * |
| Year 2 | 2.2 | 0.8 | 3.7 | Residence type * |
| Year 3 | 1.6 | 0.7 | 1.7 | Time * |
| Overall | 1.7 | 0.7[x] | 2.7[y] | |

however, had many contacts or frequent association with peers without disabilities (see Table 12.3, social integration).

Supportive apartment residents had levels of self-reported adjustment on personal and social indicators similar to FH members, with both groups having higher scores than persons living in GH settings on most measures. These outcome variables were not related to the level of retardation and were consistent over the three years (Table 12.4)

*Group Homes.* Individuals in GHs had the largest social support networks (see Table 12.4). Their networks included more peers with disabilities than did persons in the other settings, reflecting the larger number of peers

**Table 12.3.** *Continued*

| Indicator | Residence Type | | | |
|---|---|---|---|---|
| | *Family Home* (N = 34) | *Group Home* (N = 42) | *Supportive Apartment* (N = 38) | |
| *Community employment[e]* (N = 112; 33,41,38) | | | | |
| Year 1 | 26 | 12 | 39 | Year 1 *** |
| Year 2 | 24 | 12 | 34 | Year 2 N.S. |
| Year 3 | 21 | 19 | 47 | Year 3 * |
| Overall | 24 | 14 | 39 | $\chi^2$ * |
| *Behavior rating: Severity[f]* (N = 106; 32,36,38) | | | | LMR N.S. |
| Year 1 | 2.0[x] | 5.8[z] | 4.0[y] | Residence type *** |
| Year 2 | 2.7[x] | 6.2[y] | 2.5[x] | Time * |
| Year 3 | 1.5[x] | 4.6[y] | 3.2[y] | Residence × time ** |
| Overall | 2.1[x] | 5.5[y] | 3.2[x] | |

[a] Analysis of variance (three times by three residence types) with level of mental retardation (LMR) covaried to control for differences in level of retardation. x, y, and z mean superscripts indicate significant differences between mean scores.

[b] Performance measure in year 3 is on a new scale not directly comparable to previous years.

[c] Average weekly activities in the community.

[d] Average weekly community activities with nonhandicapped peers.

[e] Paid work in nonsegregated settings part or full time. Percent scores. $\chi^2$ analyses.

[f] Severity of maladaptive behaviors ranges from 0 to 15.

* $p < .05$; ** $p < .01$; *** $p \leq .001$; N.S., not significant.

who lived with them (Chapter 10). This advantage was reflected neither in personal adjustment or satisfaction nor in higher rates of activity in the community. These persons had higher reported rates of behavior problems than did others (Table 12.3), and they consistently reported lower rates of residence satisfaction over the three years. This measure includes satisfaction with interpersonal relations with staff and cohabitants and with autonomy (see Table 12.4).

Selection factors may be keeping less well-adjusted persons in the GH settings. In the initial sample of 133 persons there was no difference in behavior ratings between individuals in SAs and GHs although there was a significant difference between their residence satisfaction and personal well-being (Burchard et al., in press). The present sample includes 10 fewer GH residents who moved into supportive apartments during the study. Nevertheless, the

Table 12.4. Personal Satisfaction Indicators for Persons in Three Types of Residences over Three Years[a]

| Indicators | Family Home (N = 34) | Group Home (N = 42) | Supportive Apartment (N = 38) | |
|---|---|---|---|---|
| | Residence Type | | | |
| | % positive ratings | | | |
| *Home rating* | | | | |
| *(N = 105; 32,36,37)* | | | | |
| Year 1 | 93 | 75 | 75 | LMR N.S. |
| Year 2 | 94 | 72 | 78 | Residence type*** |
| Year 3 | 93 | 71 | 81 | Time N.S. |
| Overall | 93[x] | 72[y] | 78[y] | |
| *Residence satisfaction* | | | | |
| *(N = 110; 33,42,35)* | | | | |
| Year 1 | 77 | 69 | 81 | LMR N.S. |
| Year 2 | 80 | 76 | 84 | Residence type*** |
| Year 3 | 83 | 73 | 84 | Time*** |
| Overall | 80[x] | 72[y] | 83[x] | |
| *Work satisfaction* | | | | |
| *(N = 89; 23,38,28)* | | | | |
| Year 1 | 86 | 83 | 94 | LMR N.S. |
| Year 2 | 92 | 84 | 90 | Residence type N.S. |
| Year 3 | 92 | 86 | 94 | Time N.S. |
| Overall | 90 | 84 | 93 | |
| *Personal well-being* | | | | |
| *(N = 110; 33,41,36)* | | | | |
| Year 1 | 85 | 74 | 83 | LMR N.S. |
| Year 2 | 87 | 76 | 85 | Residence type* |
| Year 3 | 88 | 82 | 85 | Time*** |
| Overall | 87[x] | 77[y] | 84 | |

behavior ratings of persons remaining in GHs were not high, and they decreased to the rate of those in SAs by the last year (Table 12.3); residence satisfaction was consistently lower in GHs than SAs throughout the study (Table 12.4). It is reasonable to assume that living in a group setting with a number of peers and staff whom one has not chosen could create more stress and present a greater challenge for personal adjustment as it undoubtedly does for any adults who have multiple housemates. The opposite finding, however, that SA resdients did not report great loneliness or lack of activity and support because of their more independent living is quite notable.

*Family Homes.* Individuals in FHs reported considerably less life-style

**Table 12.4.** *Continued*

| Indicators | Residence Type | | | |
|---|---|---|---|---|
| | *Family Home* (N = 34) | *Group Home* (N = 42) | *Supportive Apartment* (N = 38) | |
| *Support network satisfaction* (N = 111; 32,42,37) | | | | |
| Year 1 | 86 | 88 | 86 | LMR N.S. |
| Year 2 | 91 | 87 | 90 | Residence type N.S. |
| Year 3 | 88 | 90 | 93 | Time N.S. |
| Overall | 89 | 88 | 90 | |
| | | *No. of people* | | |
| *Support network size* (N = 111; 32,42,37) | | | | |
| Year 1 | 8.2 | 10.7 | 8.6 | LMR N.S. |
| Year 2 | 8.6 | 11.3 | 8.8 | Residence type*** |
| Year 3 | 8.8 | 10.3 | 9.1 | Time N.S. |
| Overall | 8.5$^x$ | 10.8$^y$ | 8.8$^x$ | |

[a] Analysis of variance (time × residence type) using (LMR) as a covariate to control for differences in level of retardation. x and y superscripts indicate significant differences in mean scores. There were no significant interactions of time × residence type.

*p < .05; **p < .01; ***p < .001; N.S., not significant.

normalization than did persons living in other settings, and they engaged in independent activities of daily and community living significantly less often than did individuals living in SAs. However, indicators of well-being and adjustment were very high for this group, including residence satisfaction and positive home ratings. Few, however, had ever experienced any other sort of living situation.

*Integration.* Information on community activities suggests a general absence of social integration for persons living in all three types of settings. Community activities in the company of peers without disabilities were infrequent (none or one to three times a week) and were virtually zero for people in GHs (Table 12.3). As presented in Chapter 8 one third of FH members had *no peers* in their networks, and three-quarters did not date. Group home residents relied on housemates and staff for companionship in community activities and for support, FH members relied primarily on kin, and persons in SAs relied equally on peers and staff and experienced the most normative involvement in the community from the perspective of num-

**Table 12.5.** Comparisons of Life-style and Adjustment Outcomes for Persons Residing in Community Settings for Three Years[a]

| Outcome | Year 1 | Year 2 | Year 3 | |
|---|---|---|---|---|
| *Careprovider report* | | | | |
| Performance (%) ($N = 94$) | 58[x] | 60[y] | N.A. | *** |
| Life-style normalization | | | | |
| (%) ($N = 111$) | 80[x] | 84[y] | 85[y] | *** |
| Physical integration | | | | |
| (weekly rate) ($N = 101$) | 9 | 8 | 8.4 | N.S. |
| Social integration | | | | |
| (weekly rate) ($N = 101$) | 1.5 | 2.1[x] | 1.3[y] | * |
| Community employment | | | | |
| (%) ($N = 112$) | 25.7 | 23.3 | 29 | N.S. |
| Behavior rating: severity | | | | |
| ($N = 106$) | 4.0[x] | 3.8[x] | 3.2[y] | * |
| *Self-report* | | | | |
| Home rating (%) ($N = 105$) | 80.4 | 80.7 | 81.2 | N.S. |
| Residence satisfaction (%) | | | | |
| ($N = 110$) | 75[x] | 79[y] | 80[y] | *** |
| Personal well-being (%) | | | | |
| ($N = 110$) | 80[x] | 82[y] | 85[y] | *** |

[a] Main effect of time based upon $3 \times 3$ analysis of covariance with level of retardation controlled. x, y, and z superscripts indicate significantly different means.

$*p < .05; **p < .01; ***p < .001$; N.S., not significant; N.A., not applicable.

bers and types of activities and companionship in activities (see Chapter 10 and Rosen and Burchard 1990).

Time and Community Adjustment

*Changes.* For those measures of adjustment and integration which changed, most indicated increased adjustment with time (see Table 12.5). Performance of daily and community living skills, life-style normalization, and residence satisfaction increased from the first to second year. Behavior problems decreased first for persons in SAs and then for persons in GHs (see Table 12.3). Self-reported well-being increased consistently over the three years (Table 12.5). The only measure showing a decrease was social integration (i.e., participating in community activities with a nondisabled friend). This decreased from the second to third years to rates that were similar to those in the first year (see Table 12.5).

*Stability.* The most impressive set of results is the stability of the picture of life-style, adjustment, integration, and satisfaction for these individuals. There is no indication of a loss of support over time for persons in agency settings with respect to the size of their social networks, perceived support from network members, personal satisfaction, well-being, or behavior adjustment.

Other indicators notable for their stability were rates of employment and community integration, neither of which changed appreciably over the three-year period (Table 12.5). Most gains in community adjustment, including community integration, were not lost, as some research has suggested they might, after the initial experience of being in the community (Bell, Schoenrock, and Bensberg 1981; Kleinberg and Galligan 1983).

Most measures of life-style, adjustment, and satisfaction were consistent across the three years within residence types and for the sample as a whole. Where changes in outcomes occurred, they were mainly in a positive direction, indicating increased community adjustment over time. There was also continuing stability with respect to the relative strengths and weaknesses of the three living settings over time.

However, it needs to be noted that the life-style and personal stability found for study participants were of the people who remained in their original type of community living alternative for the three-year period. Individuals who moved from one alternative to another were not included in these analyses. The stability of the life-styles, personal satisfaction, and support of the individuals who moved to new programs, 10% of the original sample, is not known. The majority of those individuals moved from GHs to more independent living in SAs. Therefore, the results of this study are limited to individuals who remain within one type of living arrangement and do not apply to individuals who are experiencing major changes in their living situations.

## CONCLUSIONS

An examination of the status of individuals living continuously in three types of community residential alternatives over a three-year period showed that those settings, as distinct environments, were systematically related to the life-style and adjustment of the persons who lived in them. Although personal characteristics (e.g., ability level) had some influence on life-style factors such as independence, autonomy, and social integration and possibly influenced the type of setting in which persons were placed (there was a greater proportion of individuals with moderate retardation living in GHs than in SAs or FHs), characteristics of the settings themselves were significantly and consistently related to indicators of community adjustment.

The environmental demands for personal responsibility and the variations in the concomitant opportunities for autonomy and independence
which are part of SA living (Burchard et al., in press) clearly affected the
level of performance, life-style normalization, and community integration
these individuals experienced. Personal characteristics were not a sufficient
explanation of the pervasive differences in the indicators of adjustment and
integration between persons in SAs and GHs. There were many persons with
moderate retardation in SAs and persons with mild retardation in GHs, and
setting differences persisted when statistical methods were used to control
for level of retardation. The importance of organizational characteristics of
residences, such as whether the resident, parent, or staff person is in control
of the residence, has been shown previously to affect the opportunities for
independence and skill performance for persons residing in them (Burchard
et al., in press; Campbell and Bailey 1984). In this study, life-style and residence satisfaction were related to residence type as well.

Persons in FHs who were as functionally capable as individuals living in
SAs were far less autonomous, performed fewer skills of independent living,
and had fewer responsibilities. They were assuming fewer of the adult roles
related to maintaining themselves and their household, which was reflected
in lower scores for life-style normalization. These outcomes may be related
to the individual's role in the family as well as to the family's perception of
the individual's retardation. The roles and responsibilities of nonretarded
adult children as well might be somewhat circumscribed were they as adults
to continue to live at home.

The results point very strongly to a general failure in the promotion of
social integration by existing community residential alternatives. In general,
activities out of the home in which persons with mental retardation participated with nondisabled friends other than staff or relatives were very rare.
However, persons in the agency-supported residences, at least those in SAs,
were no more isolated from nondisabled friends than were persons living in
their own FHs. Surprisingly, growing up at home in one's own community
with one's family has not apparently resulted in opportunities for participation in community activities with nondisabled friends to any greater degree
than has living in community alternative settings. For persons in all settings,
active participation with individuals from the community at large is quite
restricted even though access to the community is not. These analyses replicate and extend findings from more detailed analysis of social integration,
and they support findings for the full sample during the first year of the
study, which are presented in Chapter 10.

In this study the community living alternatives are clearly defined and differentiated by their structure, the number and type of cohabitants, and the degree of supervision exercised. They are also similar to options existing throughout the country. The differential demands of these settings for independent behavior (or alternatively, the differential allowance for personal control within these settings), the differential degree of supervision provided, and the different numbers and roles of individuals in the residence setting clearly promote different life experiences and opportunities for the individuals living in them. One interesting result is that the apparently greater social support provided within a supervised group living situation does not appear to promote greater social or personal satisfaction and adjustment among the residents. The individuals living with family or in semiindependent situations expressed the greatest residence satisfaction whereas the life-style of persons in semiindependent living most closely approximated the program goals of human services policies.

These results underscore the importance of environmental factors such as opportunity for independent performance of behavior and community access, as exemplified by SA living, in promoting life-style normalization, performance of adaptive behavior, community integration, and personal adjustment of individuals with mild and moderate retardation. The results emphasize the importance for persons, including persons with mental retardation, to have control in their lives. Those persons living most independently show reasonable success and personal satisfaction, as also shown in other research (Halpern, Close, and Nelson 1986).

It is important for public policy analysts and social planners who promote supports for persons with disabilities to use information obtained from the individuals themselves with respect to the success of their supports and their resulting life-styles and satisfactions. It is also clear that those in a position to plan and assist should be very concerned to provide opportunities for control, choice, and independence for the persons they serve. Finally, the results also point out the necessity of examining means of assisting individuals to increase their actual social integration into communities. Approximating this goal of social policy will continue to be a major challenge both for service systems and for the larger society.

## Acknowledgments

This research was supported in part by National Institute of Disability and Rehabilitation Research Grants 1-33-GH-40203 and 1-33-MH-50078.

The authors wish to acknowledge the assistance of individuals with retarded development, their families, and state and local community mental health providers throughout Vermont whose cooperation and participation were essential.

# 13

# People with Mental Retardation Leaving Mental Health Institutions

## Evaluating Outcomes after Five Years in the Community

F. James Kearney, J.D., Ph.D., and
Michael W. Smull, B.A.

For some individuals with mental retardation public policy dictates where they will live. This chapter focuses on a group of people relocated, under court-approved consent decree, from public mental health institutions in Maryland to community residences. Descriptive data concerning outcomes of this policy initiative are examined. When postplacement data were collected in 1987 most of these individuals had been in the community for four to six years. The study looks at residential and day program status, medications, adaptive behavior, and factors associated with risk of rehospitalization.

## Moving from Institutions to the Community

There have been a number of investigations of the effects of deinstitutionalization on persons with mental retardation (Bruininks et al., 1981; Conroy and Bradley 1985; Craig and McCarver 1984; Eastwood and Fisher, 1988; Landesman-Dwyer 1981). Gains have been consistently seen in adaptive behavior domains whereas little or no improvements have been noted for maladaptive behaviors. Heller (1984) wrote that methodologic problems such as lack of random assignment to treatment groups and selection bias may influence these findings.

Studies on alternatives to long-term institutional care for persons with persistent mental disorders are inconclusive. Reviews indicate, however, that individuals living in alternative programs had outcomes equal or superior to those of controls remaining in institutions (Braun et al. 1981; Kiesler

1982a, 1982b). Again, cautious interpretation is warranted. Control groups remaining in institutions may have experienced conditions affecting developmental growth which individuals now in alternative programs did not. Furthermore, community placement environments are not uniform. These and other factors complicate interpretation of nonexperimental data.

Most, if not all, of the investigations regarding individuals with mental retardation report on individuals leaving mental retardation institutions. We are aware of no published investigation of the residential stability of persons with mental retardation leaving mental health institutions. Estimates suggest that about 10,000 individuals with mental retardation reside in mental health institutions (Krantz, Bruininks, and Clumpner 1982; Landesman and Butterfield 1987). Continued placement of these individuals in mental health facilities is, in many cases, clinically inappropriate and continues to provide a basis for litigation.

## Reasons for Returning to an Institution

The literature on reinstitutionalization suggests that the presence of adaptive skills and the absence of serious problem behaviors are predictive of community residential stability. A survey of superintendents of institutions for persons with mental retardation indicated that physical aggression, verbal aggression, and rebelliousness were the major problems leading to the failure of community residential placements (Scheerenberger 1981). An examination of admission records for a random sample of persons readmitted to public mental retardation residential facilities indicated that the most frequently stated reason for readmission to these institutions was unmanageable or intolerable behavior (Lakin et al. 1983).

## Study Background: Administrative Structure and Statutory Reform

Before 1972, there was no administrative separation of the mental health and mental retardation service systems in Maryland. Persons with mental retardation were admitted to and received treatment in the state's mental health institutions. One investigation estimated that there were 382 persons with mental retardation in state psychiatric hospitals who were inappropriately placed (Maryland Humane Practices Commission 1975).

Administrative separation of Maryland's mental health and mental retardation service systems took place in 1972. The purpose of this change was to "remove all references to mental retardation from the Mental Hygiene laws of this state and to make clear that the Mental Hygiene laws do not apply to the mentally retarded; [and] to provide for the organization . . . of the Mental Retardation Administration" (Maryland Laws 1972, Chapter 345).

Another important legal change was the exclusion of mental retardation from the statutory definition of mental disorder. Mental retardation was no longer a sufficient diagnostic basis for admission to a state psychiatric hospital. To be admitted involuntarily to a psychiatric facility in Maryland in 1979 an individual had to be found: (1) to have a mental disorder; (2) to be in need of inpatient psychiatric treatment; and (3) to represent a danger to his own life or safety or the life and safety of others (Code of Maryland Regulations 1979, 10.21.01.04). In theory at least, individuals with mental retardation who did not also have a diagnosed mental disorder could no longer be legally admitted to or retained in state mental health institutions. Responsible officials were still, however, faced with the task of relocating individuals who were inappropriately placed.

Progress in resolving this clinical and legal dilemma was slow. Three years after the statutory reforms a report estimated the number of inappropriately placed residents of state hospitals (Maryland Humane Practices Commission 1975). In 1979 Maryland's attorney general outlined a plan to end the continued "detention" of persons with mental retardation in mental health facilities (Sachs 1979). Progress in implementing this plan was not, however, sufficient to avoid litigation. In 1980 the state's designated protection and advocacy agency filed a class action lawsuit on behalf of these individuals in federal court (*Knott v. Hughes* 1980). Herr (1988) summarized the legal theories and procedural history of the case.

A consent decree settling the lawsuit called for interdisciplinary evaluations of all class members and placement of many individuals in community residential settings operated by private, nonprofit agencies. By August 1983, placement decisions had been implemented for the vast majority of class members. Of the 356 class members, 135 (38%) moved to community residences for persons with mental retardation, and 85 (24%) transferred to mental retardation institutions. Other placement decisions included: 40 persons (11%) placed on a dual disability unit, 50 (14%) retained in mental health facilities, and 46 (13%) discharged from their mental health facility of origin.

## Questions Addressed

Descriptive data on two types of questions are presented. First, policy outcome questions are considered. How many *Knott* class members were still residing in community placements at follow-up? How many were rehospitalized? Descriptive information on class member characteristics—for example, changes in behavioral medication levels—is also provided. Second, more general research questions are considered: What factors are associated with rehospitalization? How important were community living skills in successful community placement for *Knott* class members?

One note of caution is warranted concerning these analyses. The data presented are almost exclusively descriptive. Limitations, and in some cases strengths, of the evidence will be noted.

### PARTICIPANTS

This study spotlights a subset of the class members in the *Knott v. Hughes* litigation. The *Knott* class, as a whole, was made up of individuals residing in public mental health institutions and who were diagnosed as having mental retardation. Some had diagnoses of both mental retardation and mental illness. Our focus was individuals moving directly from a mental health institution to community residences. The interdisciplinary evaluations mentioned above played an important factor in determining where an individual moved.

Independent consultants conducted evaluations of class members to determine, among other things, appropriateness for community placement. Evaluations included standardized assessments of intelligence, adaptive behavior, and residential independence. Based on these and other considerations, such as age and health status, evaluation teams made placement recommendations. The subset of the *Knott* class on which our study focused included: (1) individuals placed directly from state mental health institutions to community placements in, primarily, the developmental disabilities service system; and (2) individuals placed in the community after a transitional placement at a state mental health facility unit serving individuals with mental retardation and significant behavior problems. *Knott* class members not included in our study included: (1) individuals initially transferred from state mental health institutions to state mental retardation institutions; (2) individuals not discharged from state mental health institutions; and (3) individuals discharged from mental health facilities without service system placements.

Of the 356 *Knott* class members, 150 (42%) met the criteria for participation in this study—what we will call the *Knott* class community placement group.

### METHODS

To locate potential participants and obtain their consent to participate, each class member's initial community service provider was contacted. If no longer receiving services from this agency, individuals were tracked using information from service providers and state data bases. The process resulted in the location of all but 24 (16%) of the 150 class community placement group members. Once located, the individual's service provider was given a consent form and asked to discuss the project with the individual. Included with the consent form was a straightforward narrative describing the study and emphasizing the voluntary nature of participation.

Between September 1986 and July 1987, consent to participate was obtained, and interviews were completed on 79 (53%) of the *Knott* class community placement group members. Reasons for potential participants not taking part in the study were: consent refused (9%); location undetermined (16%); no response to request to participate (10%); incomplete data (9%); and individual deceased (4%). Follow-up data collection was completed on approximately three fourths (79 of 107) of the *Knott* class community placement subject group on whom data could have been gathered. These sample restrictions limit the generalizability of our findings to the *Knott* class as a whole. Individuals who were unwilling to participate and those whom we were unable to locate may have differed in significant ways from the individuals included in the sample.

Although project staff did speak informally with a number of participants, systematic subject interviews were not conducted. Methodologic problems, such as response bias and acquiescence, in interviewing persons with moderate or severe mental retardation were an important consideration (see Sigelman, et al. 1981). It was determined that collecting reliable interview data from a sufficiently representative sample of participants was beyond the scope of the project.

Information reported here comes primarily from: (1) comprehensive evaluations of *Knott* class members conducted between 1979 and 1982 while the individuals were residing in their facility of origin; and (2) follow-up interviews and file reviews conducted in 1986 and 1987 with the participant's then-current service provider. Preplacement records of 67 (89%) of the 79 participants were obtained. Evaluation reports were reviewed and coded by project staff to extract demographic information, diagnoses, intelligence quotient test scores, previous institutional history, and medication information. Field data collection involved a project staff member interviewing at least one current service provider who knew the participant well. Information was also obtained from participant files.

Interviews with service providers, ranging from approximately 1 hour to 2½ hours in length, consisted of: (1) completion of the Inventory for Client and Agency Planning (ICAP; Bruininks et al. 1986), a standardized third-party informant instrument designed to collect service need information and measure adaptive and maladaptive behavior; and (2) completion of a supplemental follow-up data collection instrument.

The adaptive behavior section of the ICAP assesses motor skills, social and communication skills, personal living skills, and community living skills. Items measuring these four constructs, or domains, are statements describing a particular behavior rated on a four-point scale from *does very well* to *does never or rarely*. Items that vary in difficulty cover a broad range of adaptive skill development. The adaptive behavior section yields four domain scores and one broad independence score. Problem or maladaptive behaviors are subdivided into eight categories that generate four maladaptive behavior indexes: internalized maladaptive behavior (e.g., hurtful to self); asocial maladaptive behavior; externalized maladaptive behavior (e.g., hurtful to others); and a composite general maladaptive behavior index.

Bruininks et al. (1986) reported a median split-half reliability coefficient for the ICAP's four adaptive behavior domain and composite broad independence scores of .94 ($N = 1,200$). For a sample of 159 adults, most of whom had moderate or severe mental retardation, maladaptive index test-retest coefficients ranged from .70 to .85 (median = .78; see Bruininks et al. 1985, 1986 for further information on the development, standardization, reliability, and validity).

The supplemental data collection instrument included questions in areas in which the ICAP did not gather sufficient information. Residential placement history and current medications are two such areas.

RESULTS

Participant Characteristics

Participants included 62 men and 17 women with an average age of 51 years (range = 26 to 78 years, S.D. = 13). Table 13.1 outlines disability and health characteristics. About one third of the community placement sample had severe mental retardation.

One misconception about persons with mental retardation residing in mental health institutions is that most if not all of these individuals have a mental disorder. Of the 79 participants, only 58% had both mental retardation and mental health diagnoses at follow-up. The other most frequently reported diagnosis was some form of epilepsy (27%). Almost all of these individuals (19 of 21) were taking seizure medications.

Records for 92% of the participants were sufficiently detailed to determine the number of years of institutionalization prior to the preplacement

Table 13.1.  Disability Characteristics of Knott Class
Member Participants

| Characteristic | N | |
| --- | --- | --- |
| *Level of mental retardation* | | |
| Borderline | 4 | (5%) |
| Mild | 29 | (37%) |
| Moderate | 20 | (25%) |
| Severe | 25 | (32%) |
| Profound | 1 | (1%) |
| Additional diagnoses | | |
| Mental health | 46 | (58%) |
| Epilepsy | 21 | (27%) |
| Physical health | 25 | (32%) |
| Health limitations | | |
| No limitations | 60 | (76%) |
| Slight limitations | 16 | (20%) |
| Many limitations | 3 | (4%) |
| *Total* | 79 | (100%) |

evaluation. The average was 22.4 years (range = 0.8 to 53, S.D. = 15.2), and 73% had been institutionalized for more than 10 years.

Residential Status

At follow-up, a substantial majority of the participants were still residing in their original community residential program (see Table 13.2). Another tracking effort was conducted by Service Coordination Systems, Inc. (SCS), a private corporation providing service coordination services to the some class members. SCS determined the placement status of 93 class members who lived in central and western Maryland in mid-1986. Although the groups of *Knott* class members included in our study and the SCS tracking are not identical, just over three fourths of the class members in each sample were living in their original community residential programs. A class member was considered still in his or her original program if he or she: (1) was still being served by the residential provider agency with which the participant was originally placed; and (2) had at no time been reinstitutionalized. Of the 62 still with their original residential program, 88% were still in their original residential location, and 12% had moved at least once to another setting managed by the same agency. Such a move might, for example, be

**Table 13.2. Reinstitutionalization and Residential Movement of Knott Class Members at Follow-up**[a]

| Characteristic | N |
|---|---|
| Living in original community residential program, no reinstitutionalization | 62 (78%) |
| Has lived in more than one community residential program, no reinstitutionalization | 6 (8%) |
| Reinstitutionalized and returned to community residential placement | 3 (4%) |
| Reinstitutionalized and residing in institution at survey date | 8 (10%) |
| Total survey size | 79 (100%) |

[a]Reinstitutionalization defined as placement in a state mental health or mental retardation facility.

from a group home to a smaller community living situation with fewer hours of staff supervision.

The number of class members reinstitutionalized is one indication of success or failure of the *Knott* community placements. Eight of the 79 participants (10%) were currently reinstitutionalized at follow-up data collection.

The vast majority of participants (90%) were residing in the community at the time of data collection. Fifty-six percent were residing in alternative living units (ALUs) that serve between one and three persons, usually in a supervised apartment setting. Another 24% were living in group homes in which between four and eight individuals with disabilities resided. Five percent were residing in a large group residence in which 29 persons with mental retardation lived. Other residences included foster homes, a boarding home, and a nursing care facility. No class member in our sample was considered to be living independently.

Day Program Status

As Table 13.3 indicates, participants were being served in a variety of day placement settings. These ranged from day activity centers—providing social, leisure, and prevocational activities—to full-time paid employment. As with residential settings, most participants (65%) remained in their original day program setting. Another 27% had two-day settings since leaving their facility of origin. Almost half (48%) were reported to have been in paid employment at some time since entering the community.

Table 13.3.  Types of Day Placements by Percent Currently in Paid
Employment, *Knott* Class Community Placements

| Type of Day Placement | N (%)[a] | Paid Employment[b] | Not Paid Employment |
|---|---|---|---|
| No formal day program or activity | 8 (10%) | 0% | 100% |
| Day activity center | 20 (25%) | 25% | 75% |
| Work activity center | 35 (44%) | 40% | 60% |
| Sheltered workshop | 10 (13%) | 80% | 20% |
| Supported employment | 3 (4%) | 100% | 0% |
| Other | 3 (4%) | 0% | 100% |
| Total | 79 | 38% | 62% |

[a]Column percentages.

[b]Row percentages.

Although 38% were in paid employment, many made only nominal wages and worked part time. For individuals in paid employment, the average monthly pay was $63, and 30% of these individuals made less than $40 per month. The highest reported earnings were for three persons who made between $200 and $280 per month. Half of the participants in paid employment worked less than 20 hours per week, and only 7% worked more than 30 hours per week.

Behavioral Medications

Preplacement medication information was available on 85% of the participants. Sixty percent of these individuals were on either neuroleptic medications or lithium at preplacement evaluation. Medication information was available on all 79 individuals in the follow-up sample; two thirds were taking prescribed behavioral medications.

Changes in medication levels were assessed by converting prescribed daily dosages of neuroleptic medications to thorazine equivalent units (TEU). Too few participants were prescribed lithium ($< 2\%$) to warrant analysis of dosage change data on this type of medication; prn or "as needed" prescriptions were also not examined. Preplacement TEUs were subtracted from postplacement TEUs to determine amount and type of change in neuroleptic medication dosage.

No distinct pattern of changes in neuroleptic medication levels emerged. Almost as many participants had increased dosages at follow-up as had decreased dosages (22 and 24, respectively). For the 47 participants who were prescribed neuroleptic medications at either preplacement or postplacement data collection the mean change in TEU was $-116$ (S.E. $= 71$). This figure indicates an average decrease in medication levels, but this difference was not statistically significant.

### Reinstitutionalization and Respite Rehospitalization

An individual's residential placement history reflects both the attributes and behavior of the individual and the service system's responses to those attributes and behaviors. Here we consider placement history data relevant to the following questions: What were the characteristics of those participants who were rehospitalized, and do those characteristics differ significantly from those of participants who remained in the community?

Based on information collected concerning residential placement history, participants were assigned to one of two rehospitalization categories. The first category included those who had been placed in an institution, intensive behavior management unit, or respite care psychiatric hospital or unit at any time since their original community placement. The second category included participants who had lived in none of these settings since leaving their facility of origin.

Of the 79 participants, 21 (27%) had been rehospitalized as defined above (see Table 13.4). As a group, the participants *not* rehospitalized were significantly older and more cognitively impaired. The no-rehospitalization group was also significantly less likely to have a diagnosed mental disorder than were those individuals who had been rehospitalized.

Examination of mean adaptive behavior scores and associated correlation coefficients indicated that higher motor skill scores were associated with a risk of being rehospitalized. Less severe mental retardation was also associated with a higher probability of reinstitutionalization. A subject's proficiency in social, communication, personal, or community living skills did not, however, appear to be related to rehospitalization. Comparison of mean maladaptive index scores showed that rehospitalized participants displayed significantly more externalized (i.e., hurtful to others) and general maladaptive behavior that did their counterparts who remained in the community. To summarize, individuals who were at some time rehospitalized were, as a group, significantly younger, less cognitively impaired, more likely to have a mental health diagnosis, and displayed more maladaptive behavior than their *Knott* class counterparts who remained continuously in the community.

**Table 13.4. Knott Class Participant Characteristics: Rehospitalized Versus Never Rehospitalized**

| Variable | Mean Class Member Scores[a] | | Correlation[c] with Outcome Measure |
|---|---|---|---|
| | Institutional, IBMP, IBU, or Respite Re-hospitalization[b] (N = 21) | Never Re-institutionalized (N = 58) | |
| Age (years) | 46 ± 2.7 | 53 ± 1.7* | −.23 |
| Level of retardation[d] | 2.4 ± 0.21 | 3.0 ± 0.12** | −.28 |
| Mental health and mental retardation diagnoses[e] | 0.81 ± 0.09 | 0.50 ± 0.07** | .28 |
| Years of previous institutionalization[f] | 18 ± 3.5 | 24 ± 2.1 | −.15 |
| Adaptive behavior domain scores[g] | | | |
| Motor | 471 ± 7.9 | 453 ± 4.1* | .23 |
| Social/communication | 462 ± 9.0 | 461 ± 3.2 | .01 |
| Personal living | 494 ± 5.5 | 489 ± 3.3 | .07 |
| Community living | 474 ± 7.5 | 468 ± 3.7 | .08 |
| Broad independence | 475 ± 7.0 | 468 ± 3.1 | .12 |
| Maladaptive index scores[h] | | | |
| Internalized | −12 ± 1.8 | −13 ± 1.7 | .04 |
| Asocial | −16 ± 2.9 | −12 ± 1.4 | −.17 |
| Externalized | −14 ± 3.5 | −7 ± 1.3* | −.29 |
| General | −19 ± 2.8 | −12 ± 1.4* | −.26 |

[a]Mean ± standard error of mean.

[b]Participants who were, at any time since leaving their facility of origin: (1) reinstitutionalized to a state mental health or mental retardation institution; (2) sent to an intensive behavior management unit; or (3) sent to a mental health hospital or unit for respite rehospitalization.

[c]Point biserial correlation unless otherwise noted.

[d]1 (borderline) through 5 (profound).

[e]1, both mental retardation and mental illness diagnoses; 0, no mental health diagnosis.

[f]Number of years institutionalized prior to preplacement evaluation (N = 73).

[g]As assessed on the ICAP. A higher score indicates more ability.

[h]As assessed on the ICAP. A higher score indicates less problem behavior.

*t-test, $p < .05$; **t-test, $p < .01$. Phi coefficient, $\chi^2 (1) = 6.07$, $p < .01$.

DISCUSSION

"If the political and administrative system has committed itself in advance to the correctness of its reforms, it cannot tolerate learning of failure. . . . We must be able to advocate without that excess of commitment that blinds us to reality testing" (Campbell 1969, 410).

Such observations on the conflict between advocacy and a realistic appraisal of public policy outcomes point out the need for, and the inherent problems with, policy evaluation efforts such as the instant study. The data presented here in this descriptive, postplacement outcome study must be interpreted carefully. Campbell (1969) pointed out the dangers in interpreting the results of evaluation studies of this type. Pitfalls include confounding of selection and treatment variables. Applied to the *Knott* class follow-up effort, the problem might be stated as follows: If we are to generalize the success—that is, community residential stability—of study participants to persons with developmental disabilities leaving other mental health institutions, does the manner in which the original class members were selected or the methods used to determine whether an individual would be included in the follow-up bias the samples in such a way as to produce misleading results?

Attributing community residential stability to any particular factor is problematic. There are at least three viable explanations. First, these individuals received adequate preparation to move and adequate support and programming once in the community. Second, these individuals did not need any more than the most basic support services and succeeded despite inadequacies in their preparation to leave institutional environments. Third, only individuals with a high potential for success were moved to community placements, thereby biasing the success rate.

It follows then that we cannot definitively address why some *Knott* class members were successful and others unsuccessful in the community on the basis of these data. Furthermore, no evidence is presented on important components of placement success. Appropriateness of and need for services received, the role of characteristics of diverse community placement environments, and participant perspectives on these living situations have not been considered.

With these limitations in mind, let us reconsider the issues addressed. Overall, the *Knott* class participants have shown substantial residential placement stability. More than three fourths of them were, some five years after leaving institutions, still in their original residential placements. The vast majority were living in small community settings in the mental retardation service system. They do attend a variety of day programs but, as a group, have made little progress in securing paid employment. Analysis of preplacement and postplacement neuroleptic medication levels indicates no significant increase or decrease in the use or dosages of behavioral medications.

Two broad categories of *Knott* class follow-up participants emerge. The larger group is composed of older, more cognitively impaired individuals who display little evidence of current mental health problems. This may be because they never had a mental disorder or because a mental disorder that precipitated institutional admission is no longer present. These individuals' lengthy prior institutionalization—an average of 22 years—has not prevented continued stability in community residential and day placements. The other broad category is a group of younger, less cognitively impaired individuals. This group is more likely than their older counterparts to have a diagnosed mental disorder and are at greater risk of rehospitalization.

Rehospitalization data show three statistically significant differences between participants who have been reinstitutionalized and those who have had not been rehospitalized since their initial *Knott* class placement. As a group, the older, more cognitively imparied participants, who *do not* have mental health diagnoses, have not been rehospitalized. On this criterion, participants with these characteristics have been more successful, or less unsuccessful, in their community placements than their younger, less cognitively impaired counterparts with diagnoses of mental disorders.

This result is quite different from that found by Schalock and Lilley (1986). These investigators found less impaired individuals to be more successful in maintaining their residences in independent settings. This does not appear to have been the case with our sample. Schalock, Harper, and Carver (1981) found having practical behavioral skills to be predictive of placement success. For the *Knott* participants behavioral skills were not predictive of placement success. The only adaptive behavior measure that differed significantly between reinstitutionalized and other participants was the motor skills index. Rehospitalized participants had significantly higher rated proficiency in adaptive motor skills than those remaining in the community; no significant differences were found in other adaptive behavior domains.

Maladaptive or problem behavior appeared, as one might expect, to play a role in rehospitalization. Participants who had been reinstitutionalized had significantly higher rated levels of maladaptive behavior—specifically externalized (i.e., destructive, disruptive, or hurtful) problem behavior—than did individuals with no rehospitalization. This finding is consistent with the thesis put forth by Scheerenberger (1981) and Lakin et al. (1983) that

maladaptive behavior is a primary factor in reinstitutionalization of persons
with mental retardation.

CONCLUSION

It appears that most of the *Knott* class community placement group did
not require, and continue not to require, institution-based care. Those individuals who were rehospitalized were younger, less cognitively impaired,
more likely to have a mental health diagnosis, and displayed more maladaptive behavior.

The evidence presented here indicates that many *Knott* class members
were, as the result of this public policy initiative, afforded an opportunity to
live in apparently appropriate community residential settings. The strength
of that evidence is best assessed in the context of continued efforts to systematically evaluate the outcomes of such policy initiatives.

## Acknowledgments

This chapter is based in part on James Kearney's doctoral dissertation,
"Persons with Mental Retardation Leaving Mental Health Institutions: An
Empirical Follow-up Study after Five Years in the Community" (1988).
Dr. Kearney's contribution to this chapter was undertaken in his private ca-
pacity; no official support by the Office of the Attorney General of Maryland
is intended or should be inferred. This research was funded in part by the
Maryland Developmental Disabilities Administration and the University of
Maryland at Baltimore. The authors wish to acknowledge the contributions
of the following individuals and thank them for their efforts: Toni Tyndall,
Andrea Kaiser, Michael Millemann, Alison Loughran, Sally Gorman,
Timothy Quinn, and Bradley Hill.

# IV

# CHANGING STAFF ROLES

The radical and persisting movement to shift the focus of service provision for individuals with severe disabilities from institutional and congregate settings to more normalized and natural community settings has resulted in the creation of new service "industries" (Castellani 1986). Community-focused services have created a new work force, new service organizations, and new organizational structures. The following chapters provide some perspective and substantive information about the constitution of this work force, their new roles, the new organizational structures that constitute their "work place," and the needs and challenges inherent in replenishing and sustaining this new work force and the new work settings.

Michael Nagy and Heather Gates present a clear and compelling picture of the changing roles, job descriptions, and competencies of the work force needed to provide community supports for persons with persisting psychiatric disabilities. In Chapter 14 they use a residential program case example to identify how the shift from providing services in fixed residential programs to providing supportive housing causes changes in the organization, activities, and skills of the work force and the agencies providing the supportive services. The refocus of staff energy to actively promoting social integration and independence creates significant changes in the work force.

In Chapter 15, Betsy Galligan reports the results of a field study designed to examine the quality of work life and job satisfaction of staff members who move from institutional to small residence work settings that serve individuals with developmental disabilities. This research compares baseline to postmove self-reports of institutional staff members with reports of staff members remaining in the institution or already working in small community group homes. The relation between changes in the quality of staff work life and corresponding changes in quality of life of the individuals receiving services is also described.

John Jacobson and Lee Ackerman present an empirical organizational analysis of group homes for persons with developmental disabilities as a work place in Chapter 16. With high rates of turnover, high demands for staff, and an aging population, personnel issues will be of tremendous importance to policy planners and providers during the next decade. This chapter contributes to the process of identifying management practices and organizational characteristics that can affect staff attitudes, practices, and retention.

Charlie Lakin and Sheryl Larson provide a comprehensive review of the current literature on staffing issues in the field of community mental retardation services in Chapter 17. A presentation of the results of a national prospective survey of staff retention and turnover conducted by the University of Minnesota Center for Residential and Community Services in the early 1980s is followed by a critical analysis of subsequent findings to identify areas for improvement in management practices and organizational strategies and to define areas needing further research.

Human resources are equally important for persons involved in providing community services and support for individuals with severe psychiatric disabilities as for those providing services for persons with developmental disabilities. As David Shern and his colleagues report, 75% of the cost of mental health services is personnel costs. In Chapter 18, these authors present a heuristic model for developing important human resources data. They examine the results of a statewide study of the relationship of environmental contexts, staff characteristics, and consumer characteristics to rehabilitation outcomes based upon this model.

In the final chapter Valerie Bradley and Mary Ann Allard examine the results of their recent national survey of stability and change in community residences. Using a three-tiered survey method they identify regulatory, reimbursement, and state and federal policies that influence the long-term viability of privately operated community residential services, and they look at information about the degree of physical and fiscal stability of current community programs across the nation. As reliance on community programs continues to increase, the importance of identifying factors that contribute to program viability and assuring continuity for consumers and workers cannot be overestimated.

These six chapters present a range of recent empirical research examining the work force needs and current status in the new community service industry or industries. These service systems are continuing to change and evolve, creating demands for new staff roles, new organizational structures, and research on policy initiatives that support effective services.

# 14

# Decongregating Residential Programs in Mental Health

## The Impact on the Staff and Clients

Michael P. Nagy, Ph.D., and Heather M. Gates, M.B.A.

This chapter examines a number of issues related to the "decongregation" of mental health residential programs (i.e., changing from a traditional group living facility to supporting individuals in a variety of living situations). It summarizes the problems with traditional residential programs in mental health, focusing on the impact of decongregation on staff and residents by describing an actual scenario that took place in Holyoke, Massachusetts, at Maple House, Inc. (now Foundations, Inc.), which successfully made the transition from the "old" to the "new" model.

New models place significant demands on the internal structure of agencies as well as the system as a whole. Relationships among agencies, the funding source and the agency, and with other stakeholders (e.g., family members) change as new ways of conducting business are introduced to the various players. Programmatic, fiscal, and work force implications arise as new models are implemented. The policy implications of change, discussed below, are also significant.

## The Transitional Residential Model

As described by Budson (1978, 4), psychiatric community residences developed "in response to the abominable conditions of the typical state hospital." Psychiatric community residences retained the same goals as inpatient units, only they were located in community. As such, residential services were designed to be psychotherapeutic, inclusive of client social and physical needs, and transitional. Clients would come into the residence, receive therapy (in the residence as well as through outpatient services), training, and, upon making insight-based progress, they would leave the residence and the program and begin living independently.

According to Budson, psychiatric community residences would supplant state institutions and their "abominable conditions" by replacing largeness with smallness, a universal medical model with a family model, a closed setting with an open setting, and isolation from the community with residence in the community.

The family model of operation was coupled with an assimilation approach which saw the psychiatric community residence as a sort of ethnic enclave, a haven, offering respite and support to people in transition between the hospital and the community (Fairweather 1964; Gumrukru 1968; Jansen 1970; Sandall, Hawley, and Gordon 1975). The guiding image is one of the gradual incorporation of individuals with psychiatric disabilities into the community in a fashion similar to the assimilation of immigrants to the United States (Budson 1978). As compared with institutions, therapeutic community residences constituted a major innovation. But, as Black (1987, 5) more recently maintains, "I doubt that many of the Fairweather Lodge societies that I have seen quite meet this purpose [i.e., integration or assimilation], and I don't believe that any of the psychosocial clubs do at all."

The reaction to the shortcomings in current residential programs has been a fundamental rethinking of residential services for people with psychiatric disabilities (Carling, Daniels, and Ridgway 1985; Carling et al. 1987; Carling and Ridgway 1989; Carling and Wilson 1988a, 1988b). The new models being developed stress helping people with psychiatric disabilities find "places of their own" and emphasize people's individual choice of housing. This chapter examines the positive and negative aspects of these new strategies by focusing on a program that is moving through a model transition that mirrors in practice the debates that rage in theory.

## History

Maple House was a transitional residence that had been in operation for more than 14 years (since 1976). The program was started through the coordinated efforts of the Department of Mental Health, the Holyoke Housing Authority, the Junior League of Holyoke, and a local landlord. Residents first moved into a newly renovated building at 450 Maple Street in April 1973. Potential members of the program had all experienced psychiatric hospitalizations of varying durations, required considerable support to maintain life in the community, and lived on limited resources. When the program first opened, there were 30 residents and a live-in resident director. Over a period of time, the number of people being served dropped to 22.

Of all the changes that have taken place in the agency, decongregation of the program has been the most dramatic. Foundations has been deinstitutionalized. Formal program support had always been tied to residence at 450 Maple Street. Support ended with the person's "graduation" from the program. Maple House was to be a three-quarterway house, a dress rehearsal for independent living, but what happened over the course of time was, as one former staff person put it: " [that] they still called it a 'transitional residence,' but nobody ever moved." Maple House had become a miniinstitution in the community.

The "new" model at Maple House, engendered by an increasing awareness of problems with traditional programs, was instituted through a task force process, consisting of the executive director, the clinical supervisor, a resident, a former resident, two counselors, two members of the board of directors, and two outside consultants with expertise in providing services in the community. The task force met biweekly throughout autumn 1985, examined the Maple House model through the use of model coherency from the PASS (Program Analysis of Service Systems) evaluation tool (Wolfensberger and Glenn 1975), and recommended the new model that has been created at Foundations. In April 1985, the board of directors voted unanimously to proceed with the restructuring of Maple House.

In autumn 1985 residents began moving out of 450 Maple Street into their own apartments with support from the program. This was accomplished on a person-by-person basis, never at the convenience of the program or the larger system. By January 1988 approximately half of the residents had moved. An accidental fire occurred on January 29, 1988 and left Maple House uninhabitable. The remaining 10 people were left homeless, and the next nine months were spent helping them locate suitable housing and reestablishing program operations. The previous articulation of the new model made it significantly more feasible to adjust to this radical change in circumstance without major program disruption even though incremental change had always been honored as a guiding principle.

## Homes, Not Housing: The Moral Imperative to Change

The home/housing distinction can be approached by exploring what makes a place to live a *home* rather than simply *housing*. What does living in one's *home* as opposed to being a resident in *housing* mean to the individual and the community? How do roles that are available when one is living in a *home* help create positive social definitions for the individual in contrast to the ways that being a resident of *housing* affords roles that lead to negative social definitions by others and even by the individual?

The "old" model at Maple House provided housing for the people who lived there. At best, half of the residents participated in extensive inhouse programming. This programming led to participants feeling that they were a part of a community even if it was a segregated, deviant one, which isolated them from the larger "normal" community. Thus, they were subjected to social definitions that matched and maintained their deviant and powerless status. Under the old model, Maple House actually discouraged people from reintegrating into the community by being overprotective.

In the new model, clients live in housing they have selected, within the constraints of their income or housing subsidies. The support services they receive from the program are independent of where they live. They do not have to live in a program residence to be part of the program; they reside in their own homes.

The cornerstone of the new model involves separating housing from service needs and then providing program members with the necessary support so that they can become socially integrated into their community. Because living in a congregated setting is no longer a requirement of program membership, clients and program staff as well as families and the public are able to view as the client's home where he or she actually lives. This view establishes a new set of expectations and expanded possibilities for social roles for all parties involved.

### AN EXPECTATION OF PERMANENCE AND EXIT BY CHOICE

Residents of homes can stay there as long as *they* want to. Interestingly, residential programs that have abandoned time limits also claim, in some cases, that people can stay as long as they want to. Given the scarce commodity that residential programs represent, however, and considering the pressures to have more and more disabled individuals use those places, such a promise of stability may be transitory at best. By way of contrast, residents of homes can assume valued social roles as tenants, neighbors, and friends as opposed to devalued social roles as clients or program members, subject to program demands rather than their own decision about when to move.

## CONTROL OVER THE ACCESS OF OTHERS

Maintaining control over others' access to your property is a necessary condition of being a "host" and having "guests" rather than "visitors." From the start, apartments at Maple House have officially been the responsibility of the residents, who had their own keys, came and went as they wished, and paid their rent directly to the landlord. Nonetheless, the split between housing and support was not a reality for residents. The program interceded for residents when the building needed repairs. Residents' first contact about housing was the program, not the landlord. Thus, the program was still in a clear dependence-making role.

Access by staff to residents' apartments was, at times, a matter of some controversy. Residents, asserting their right to privacy, complained of staff walking into their apartments without warning in nonemergency situations. Generally, residents have not seen themselves, and have not been seen by staff, as having the same control over physical premises as would be the case in one's *home*.

## CONTROL OVER THE PHYSICAL FEATURES OF APPEARANCE AND RESPONSIBILITY FOR MAINTENANCE

Maple House apartments were always furnished, with very little resident input. Rules prohibiting overnight guests and pets limited residents further. On the other hand, residents always had the responsibility of maintaining their apartments. There was intervention, generally, only at the point of health endangerment.

As the new model has been implemented, there are indications that clients have become more committed to maintaining the appearance of their homes than they were to their housing. For example, one older man who moved to a place of his own decided to put up curtains. His neighbors all had them, and he thought they would make his place look better. In another case, a resident who had been notoriously messy in her housing kept her new apartment clean and neat. When questioned about her new-found tidiness, she replied, "Well, it's my place now."

## A "TERRITORIAL ATTITUDE"

People develop a territorial attitude based on their level of control over the environment. In turn, a sense of territoriality among residents appears to generate a respect for territory on the part of staff. New model apartments are treated by clients as "my place." This attitude forms an important aspect of the changing context of relationships between staff and clients.

## Changing Context of Staff Work and Relationships

### COUNSELORS

Counselors are being asked to change their daily work routine: where they go, when they need to be on the job, and what the main focus of the job is. Several important concerns have been raised by counselors about the changing context of their work.

#### Loss of Control of the Face-to-face Situation

Staff perceive themselves being treated as guests and friends, with a concomitant decrease in their power. Although a central purpose of the new model is to empower clients, this process requires a redistribution and a re-negotiation of relationships.

#### An Increase in the Chances of Personal Embarrassment

As the locus of service delivery moved from within Maple House to a broad variety of settings in the community, interactions between staff and residents became more public. What once took place within the confines of a controlled environment now occurs in someone's home, a restaurant, the local YMCA, or on the street. Counselors have found themselves in em-barrassing situations and ones in which they are not in total control of outcomes.

#### Others' Perception of Staff Roles vis-à-vis Clients

The role change for clients, from program member to independent citizen, means that staff should no longer act like staff. But, staff-who-are-not-to-be-seen-as-staff find themselves at risk of unwanted role attributions. A female staff member who regularly visits a male client in his home may feel herself unwillingly cast as the girlfriend. Imputations that might be made based on sex and age characteristics of clients with regard to staff may be uncomfortable.

#### Blurring of Personal and Professional Roles

Maintaining a relationship with clients in the community rather than at Maple House subverts the underpinnings of the professional role. At issue is the genuineness of what may look for all intents and purposes like a friend-ship relationship. It is unfair for staff to pretend to be a client's friend when they are paid to be in the client's life. It is acceptable and desirable to be friendly, warm, giving, and caring. Clear, ongoing communication between staff and clients is necessary to avoid such confusion.

An Increase in Perceived Personal Responsibility for the Client

Generally, the primary counselor is the staff member who has the most regular contact with the client, as contrasted with the congregate setting in which all staff and residents were together, which permitted client monitoring by more than one person and confirmation of perceptions. Staff now feel more individually and personally responsible for clients. In addition, the clinical supervisor and executive director have less of an opportunity to interact with residents and simultaneously confirm counselors' perceptions.

Anxiety about Social Integration

A central focus of the new model is for staff to promote freely given relationships. Integration into the community means integration into a social network of friends, family, and acquaintances which increasingly provides social, emotional, and instrumental support for people as program support decreases and finally ends completely. Building social networks for others brings to the surface staff insecurities about their own social abilities and certainly presents the prospect of failure to support clients in becoming interdependent.

SUPERVISORY STAFF

"Leading from the Front"

It is critical for leadership to be visible if major organizational change is going to succeed: staff are being asked to make significant changes in their work roles, and supervisory staff must set the example. This may involve supervisory staff taking on unusual roles and functions for a period of time (e.g., locating suitable housing and promoting social integration in order to demonstrate their commitment to the changes).

Distinctions between Counselor and Supervisor Positions

Staff have noted inherent differences in the organizational positions of supervisors and themselves as supervisors try to demonstrate their extra commitment to change. For example, supervisors do not need to worry what the boss might say about decisions in working with a client. Also, the greater experience of supervisors enables them to display deliberate naturalness in their work as opposed to staff's greater difficulty presenting an acceptable interactional style. Finally, because supervisors are not directly responsible in their job for any individual client, they are seen as having less need to maintain a working relationship with any individual client, and as such can "push" issues with clients further.

Maintaining a Casual Approach

Supervisors must be careful not to undercut staff's autonomy in the eyes of clients while taking a more active part in day-to-day relations with clients. The model change should proceed as a routine feature of agency operations, empowering staff and residents as a matter of course. The benefit of supervisory visibility will be lessened if staff feel that they are being devalued and in turn pass on this impression to clients.

## Effecting Change and Planning for More: How Do You "Flip the Priorities"?

The process of change has raised concerns for staff, supervisors, and the agency as a whole. The agency adopted several approaches to promote the success of the change effort.

### PROMOTING FREELY GIVEN RELATIONSHIPS

As we have seen, the new model makes new and, for most staff, intimidating demands on their social skills. To deal with the issue of expanding clients' social networks in the community, the agency needs to develop an organizational mechanism that will motivate staff to do the groundwork necessary for promoting client integration and also will provide program staff with personal support and relevant information.

One mechanism that was implemented early on was an expectation that everyone, including the executive director and clinical supervisor, would make at least one contact each week which might be useful in promoting freely given relationships between clients and other citizens. At a weekly meeting everyone would discuss their contact for the week. Disclosing these efforts and their results would provide an incentive for doing the work on the one hand and a supportive atmosphere for discussing outcomes and suggesting new approaches on the other.

The meetings were suspended when the fire destroyed the building. They were never reestablished, due in part to the hiring of two part-time counselors whose jobs focused specifically on social and recreational integration.

The importance of social integration was highlighted by including it as a section in the counselor evaluation tool. The evaluation tool is reviewed with staff when they are hired, and this area is stressed from the first day on the job.

## DESIGNING A "DEINSTITUTIONALIZED ORGANIZATIONAL STRUCTURE": REINVENTING THE ROLES

Changing where work is done raises issues for staff about their roles and relationships with clients and each other. To facilitate a conscious choice of new organizational structures that would promote people living independently, with natural support networks, two committees were established. Each committee made recommendations for changes in the organizational structure. One proposed replacing the assignment of individual clients to individual counselors, making counselors responsible for functions rather than clients, for example, locating homes, advocating with government agencies, developing opportunities for clients' social integration. Another suggestion was for administrative offices to be moved out of Maple House before all the clients left as a demonstration of commitment to the new model.

The fire intervened in this process as well. All discussions had focused on how to achieve the change in model incrementally, with as little disruption to individual lives as possible. Because of the fire, significant gains were made in a very short period of time. One of the gains was funding from the Department of Mental Health to hire an additional counselor. When the needs of the program were examined closely it was clear that more time and energy were necessary to create viable options for people socially. Two half-time people were hired to focus on recreational activities and social integration. It was hoped that by relieving them of traditional job duties they would be free to develop relationships with participants which could focus on socially and culturally normative activities. This, in turn, could lead to opportunities for real friendships to develop.

Of equal importance in furthering those goals is the need to address the cultural and social deprivation experienced by many members of the program. Individuals need to talk about something other than their experiences as clients of the mental health system. Since friendships usually develop out of common interests, helping individuals develop or rekindle their interests is important, not only because of the intrinsic value in having interests but also because they create opportunities for interaction and friendship.

### COMMUNITY OUTREACH AND PUBLICITY

#### Provider Network

The network of other mental health service providers is an important part of the larger community. The fact that changes made by Maple House, as part of a community mental health delivery system, would affect other providers necessitated educating them about the model change. Thus, Maple House maintained a constant, ongoing dialogue with other providers over a three-year period. This dialogue was carried out in four different ways: (1) visiting other agency staff meetings to speak about the model change; (2) meetings about individual clients with their other service providers; (3) memoranda describing the new model; and (4) memoranda describing the progress of the change as it occurred.

As could be expected, other agencies tended to attribute any difficulty that developed to the model change. Although there were varying opinions about the likelihood of success, it was clear that everyone was watching. In the long run, other providers were more resistant to the change than any other single group.

### Community as a Whole

Numerous channels for educating the community as a whole were used, including: (1) Holyoke/Chicopee Area [service system] Newsletter; (2) articles in the local newspapers; (3) meetings with local officials and housing authorities; (4) board of directors' members explaining the changes to friends; (5) informal contact with shopkeepers, bus drivers, bank tellers, and so forth. Word of mouth communication, especially, plants the thought that the new model can succeed. People begin to see it as reasonable and natural for people with psychiatric disabilities to be living in their own places rather than in congregate, segregated settings.

Maple House has developed strategies for education, suggesting ways to present the message regardless of the particular mechanism used. It is helpful to use specific examples of why the old model did not work and why the new model should work. The point of reference is always the people being served. Individualized comparisons are the most powerful demonstration of the differences between the two models. It has also been helpful to be persistent and honest and not to promise more than could be delivered. For example, landlords should not be guaranteed absolute quiet or the ideal tenant because this is a setup for failure. No one could meet those demands, including the people we serve.

### Staff Training: Building the Program

The process of conceptualizing the idea was the easy part; it was much more difficult to translate concept into action. Maple House found it easier, for example, to locate suitable housing than to redirect staff energies toward social integration. One of the major distinctions between the old and the new models was to develop permanent homes and social networks that consist of "real people." We wanted to create interdependence with others, not independence that may really be isolation.

Staff Skills under the Old Model and the New

Working with clients in their homes involves a complex array of knowledge and skills. Some of the substantive areas in which counselors need to be knowledgeable include: (1) the various types of medications clients use and their effects; (2) the larger service system and the agency's place in it; (3) regulations governing the program; (4) emotional problems and how to deal with them; (5) agency policies and procedures.

Some of the skill areas counselors must develop in order to provide effective services include: (1) being empathetic; (2) planning leisure activities with clients; (3) coordinating other necessary services; (4) developing a treatment plan; (5) dealing with someone in a crisis; (6) mediating disputes with landlords and others.

For the new model to be successful, staff must learn a whole new set of skills while continuing to keep track of their more mundane, day-to-day responsibilities. New skills must be developed, for which there is little in the way of previous training or experience to draw upon.

In a supported housing program, being able to negotiate with landlords is invaluable; it requires a delicate balance of advocating for clients with landlords without becoming their overseer and thus increasing their dependence on the program.

Rather than planning noninteractive activities such as movies or shopping, a new expectation is inserted into the counselor's job. Activities need to be planned to facilitate social integration. For example, rather than go to the local YMCA to play basketball one on one, it is important to go when there are team games. This is done in the hope that a friendship will develop with a nonhandicapped individual. It is no longer enough just to entertain members of the program; recreation must have an associated goal of social integration.

Overall, in terms of their orientation to their job, counselors must become more resourceful and confident operating alone. This adjustment has been facilitated through peer support as well as ensuring backup from the clinical supervisor via a 24-hour on-call system. Recognition of new or other needs does not mean the old ones go away. The model change means added responsibilities for staff.

New Demands on Staff Training

An important part of staff training in the context of the model change is developing a common sense of purpose and a mission. Initially this was accomplished through the use of the task force; several staff participated in these meetings. In turn, they spoke to other staff, quickly generating support internally. The idea of the new model was and is introduced in job interviews and continues to be emphasized through orientation, in weekly supervision meetings, staff meetings, and informal discussions. Programmatically, staff evaluations and job descriptions were revised to reflect the mission of the agency and to reinforce the skills required to implement that mission.

An additional staff training resource is the use of consultants. Until recently, a consultant came once a month to talk about the need for friends and how to have an impact on individual situations. This proved very useful in terms of motivating both staff and leadership, as well as allowing staff to hear the same ideas from someone other than their supervisor. Staff retreats, weekly supervision, staff meetings, and formal training (both inhouse and out) all contributed toward the necessary knowledge, skills, and support that counselors needed to work under the new model.

## STAFF RECRUITMENT: WHAT SHOULD WE LOOK FOR? NOT WHO CAN WE GET?

The recruitment process is critical because different program models require different kinds of staff. Recruitment for the new model demands attention to the personal characteristics of individual staff members and also to the staff mix to establish an overall balance. Personal characteristics that are particularly important include: independence, energy, emotional balance, the desire to be a team player, being established in the local community, and not wanting to control the clients. At the organizational level, desirable staff mix characteristics include a broad age range, mixed educational backgrounds, broad ethnic backgrounds, and a male/female balance. By the same token, there is a desire to avoid people who are comfortable with the medical model or the status quo of congregated residential services or who are very emotionally needy people lacking self-confidence.

## DIVERSIFICATION OF FUNDING SOURCES AND POLITICAL SUPPORT

Broadening the financial base of the agency will help guarantee the ongoing existence of the new model. As long as any agency is solely dependent on one funding source it will remain precariously subject to the political tides of the times. Efforts are being made to diversify while retaining the strengths of a small agency. In addition to cultivating stability through diversifying funding sources, it is also desirable to have a strong board of directors that provides the agency with political power in the local community. The members of the board should be well connected locally and in full support of the program direction. They are critical to remaining viable and autonomous.

### THE INITIAL ASSUMPTIONS: VALID OR NOT

We have examined the value-based reasons for change, the change process itself, and some expectations about areas of the new model which might be problematic. This section contrasts the actual experience with these expectations and presents developments that we did not anticipate. The major characteristics of the organizational change were as follows.

#### Facilitation by Staff Turnover

The expected turnover of direct service staff was supplemented in this case by the model change and the fire. Individuals for whom the model change proved too stressful left the agency. They were replaced by staff whose personal and professional manner and expertise are more suited to the new model.

#### Increasing Subtlety of Client Adjustment

Although issues of clients really taking control of places of their own and of changing roles for clients in the new model were considered at the inception, how they have played out in practice has proven elusive and difficult. How can clients be induced to behave more proactively and assertively? The dilemma is similar to that posed by trying to get someone to behave spontaneously. To instruct or order them destroys spontaneity. Similarly, *requiring* proactive behavior makes the behavior, by definition, *not* proactive. Merely waiting for proactive behavior to occur, on the other hand, may mean that it never does and that clients become isolated. Continuing the same dependence-producing relationships with clients obviates the purpose and values of the model change.

We had anticipated a significantly changed context for staff and relationships. How this actually transpired is described below.

#### Loss of Control of the Face-to-face Situation and an Increase in the Chances of Personal Embarrassment

Counselors do have less control in their face-to-face meetings with clients. This potential problem has been dealt with for the most part by hiring counselors whose personal style is more consistent with the operation of the new model.

There have been some casualties. For example, one woman who was considered a good counselor but is visually impaired recently left the agency. She had difficulty with the increased travel required. She also had greater difficulty in face-to-face situations in public.

### Others' Perception of Staff Roles vis-à-vis Clients and Blurring of Personal and Professional Roles

Judicious hiring practices, taking into account the kind of staff characteristics needed for the new model, have facilitated changing roles. Individuals have been hired who all have "lives outside the agency." Staff are, in general, older than previously. Others' perceptions are less of a problem for them.

Counselors do perceive a shift in the locus of power in the relationships they maintain with clients. The positive and negative features of the shift are illustrated in the following observation by a staff member: "It's an equalizer. It forced me to become more respectful of the client. . . . It forces us to think twice before invading somebody's space and trying to manage them. I think that that part is good, however, sometimes being inhibited in that way, [we] didn't act in the client's best interest."

A blurring of personal and professional roles has clearly taken place. The agency's clinical director reports she now is dealing with the problem of counselors sharing too much of their personal life with clients rather than being too distant.

### An Increase in Personal Responsibility for the Client

The increase in personal responsibility for clients which counselors report, as the person's sole link with the agency, has been greatly mitigated by adjustment in supervision, having more staff visit clients, and then sharing perceptions. Most clients see, at minimum, three different counselors at least briefly during a week. Perceptions are shared among counselors, and decisions for frequency of monitoring are made. There has been some change in the role of the clinical supervisor. Since the agency has been decongregated, she does not see every client. She reports summarizing and tying counselor perceptions together rather than making the definitive clinical judgment she was expected to make in the past.

### Roles of Supervisory Staff

Before the model change, counselors were concerned that supervisors evidence personal commitment to the model change in such a way as to assure counselors that they were willing to make equivalent levels of sacrifice. As counselors became more adept, this became irrelevant.

### Increasing Subtlety of Client Adjustment

The area in which the model change has been less clear relates to clients taking actual, operating control of their own places. In some ways the counseling technology is underdeveloped. Counselors at Foundations are not clinical therapists, do not see themselves as such, and do not attempt to provide clinical therapy; their focus is on practical problem solving. They are community living skill teachers, and they need to develop teaching methods that do not demean or embarrass the client. As Foundations' clinical director puts it, "The way you teach . . . is really important, because otherwise, you're just being another one of those people who impose stuff on them."

There is a fine line between just waiting (perhaps forever) for people to find out things for themselves and imposing ways of being on them. Ways of facilitating clients' discovery of how to be owners and to be socially integrated, without imposing or neglecting, are developing as part of the technology of effective rehabilitation.

The issue is not only helping people make their place belong to them physically but assisting them to be owners cognitively and personally. Cooking at home leads one to discover what cooking utensils one wants to buy. Looking at magazines helps a person determine how to decorate. Effective incidental instruction has turned out to be a very elusive strategy, one characterized by a myriad of activities which are the taken-for-granted aspects of independence.

The new model also represents another trade-off: Foundations' clients are more prey to the real world than are their counterparts in congregated residences. So far, that trade-off has cost clients some knocks; but the hard knocks of the real world have been seen by clients as preferable to the insulation of a congregated residence.

## Broader Policy Implications

Programmatically there are several major concerns from a system perspective. Admission to the program needs to be timely to avoid unnecessary lengths of stay in psychiatric inpatient units caused by locating suitable housing every time an individual is accepted by the program. In areas of the country in which housing is scarce, and usually expensive, the program needs to provide some form of intermediate housing to guarantee timely placement into the program. It is unacceptable for an individual to remain needlessly in an inpatient unit if the predominant need is a home rather than secure psychiatric treatment. The search for permanent housing is more easily undertaken from the community than from a hospital. In many cases, the availability of adequate rent subsidies can make this intermediate step unnecessary.

As individuals terminate services and retain their housing, the program needs to help new program members locate suitable areas in which to live. Unlike the traditional transitional group home which is owned and/or controlled by the provider, under the supported housing model the control over housing rests with the individual. Therefore, the provider and funding source need to develop relationships with the generic housing community. This means meeting with landlords, local officials, and politicians as well as aggressively pursuing creative sources of financing constantly to replace housing that stays with the individual. Agencies need to broaden their understanding and role in the development of affordable housing. We are no longer just in the business of delivering mental health services.

The funding source should be concerned about the intensity of services and should specify its expectations in the service delivery contract. It is easier to measure intensity in a group residence in which the number of staff and residents can be counted at a point in time to arrive at a staff:client ratio. Supported housing is, by design, more flexible but also needs to be quantified. Activities and tasks should be delineated clearly and a minimum number of hours of service per client negotiated. As with any program model, there will be a tendency for the program to cling to the individuals who are the most independent. This is particularly true where the search for housing is difficult, since termination of services to the client means a renewed housing search for the staff.

A policy should be developed regarding evictions. Although it is often desirable for individuals to experience the consequences of their actions, homelessness is a high price to pay. The system and its various components need to be prepared to deal with this eventuality in accordance with their mission. Individual situations will require individually tailored plans, but they should be consistent with an overall policy.

Fiscally there is a need to shift resources from fixed capital expenditures to more flexible sources. It may be necessary to provide security deposits, to pay for damages, or to lend money for the purchase of furniture. Costs are less predictable initially, but over time historical patterns will develop. The primary concern is to build flexibility into the budget so individual needs can be addressed to the greatest extent possible.

Despite initial impressions, the supported housing model is not more expensive than a staffed residence. Unlike a staffed residence in which staffing is present regardless of individual need at one point in time, support to individuals in their own homes is provided as needed. The tendency in group homes is to staff for the worst case scenario. This means there are times when staff presence is nothing more than a precaution for a possible future occurrence. Whether or not a problem actually occurs, the staffing is still provided. Over time this becomes a wasted resource. In addition, a great deal of time is devoted to managing the group rather than addressing individual needs.

Finally, there are implications for the work force. The characteristics of the job are different, and the qualities of the workers may differ. As mentioned earlier, the professional boundaries are not always clear, thereby necessitating the hiring of individuals who can operate autonomously, who have clear personal boundaries and know how to negotiate within their communities. Organizationally, less on-site supervision is provided, and a more consultative approach is used. This increases the need to define outcomes clearly since monitoring is more difficult. Given less direct supervision, it is desirable to hire more highly skilled workers. Obviously this has fiscal implications since these individuals will demand higher salaries. However, it is possible to have flatter organizations by eliminating some of the supervisory positions. There is no longer the need for house managers, assistant house managers, and shift supervisors because relationships are established with individuals directly. The tasks generated by managing a group and capital investments no longer exist.

One of the unexpected outcomes of shifting residential services from fixed staffed residences to supported housing throughout an entire system is the fluidity between programs. If the individuals retain control over their living situations but need a different intensity of service, it is relatively easy to change that intensity by referring to another program or adapting the existing services. The change occurs in the service delivery rather than in the place of residence.

Finally, it should be noted that the stable living model of service delivery is intended to return control over their lives to people receiving services. What is to be accomplished is not something that occurs primarily inside the individual. Rather, through reconstructing social relationships and social definitions, people with psychiatric disabilities can begin to be valued for their ability to participate fully in our communities. Research examining the process through which clients develop social relationships in the community and the effects of the stable living model on clients will be critical as systems seek to improve their effectiveness in achieving the goal of community integration.

# 15

# Changes in the Quality of Work Life for Staff Members Transferred from Institutional Units to Small Residential Units

Betsy J. Galligan, Ph.D.

This chapter summarizes the quality of work life changes for staff who transferred from an institutional setting for developmentally disabled people to smaller residential units. This is a critical area of concern since the focus of residential service delivery to developmentally disabled people has shifted dramatically over the past 15 years. Since 1975 the number of people living in New York State institutions has decreased from about 25,000 to less than 10,000. By 1991 New York plans to reduce that number to 7,000 and to increase the number of community beds past 25,000. A decade ago it was common for competent professionals to advise parents to institutionalize their child with a developmental disability. Today, it is all but unheard of.

The theory of normalization (Wolfensberger et al. 1972) underlies this major shift. A variety of studies offer empirical support for this theory by showing that functional skills are more likely to develop if people live in smaller, more homelike settings (e.g., Felce et al. 1986; Jacobson and Schwartz 1983; Landesman and Butterfield 1987; MacEachron 1983).

However, living in a smaller community setting is not necessarily more normalizing and does not always result in greater functional gains (Butler and Bjaanes 1977; Silverman et al. 1986). Moreover, several authors have found that some of the initial increases in adaptive functioning after a move to a more homelike setting are lost over time (Hemming 1986; Hemming, Lavender, and Pill 1981; Kleinberg and Galligan 1983).

Clearly, then, the issues are complex. Although living in a more homelike setting facilitates habilitative growth, it does not guarantee it. Thus, the nature of the relationship between normal environments and functional growth needs to be investigated to strengthen the factors that promote growth. The factor highlighted in this chapter is the influence of the direct care worker, whom Thaw and Wolfe (1986, 88) describe as the most important figure in clients' lives, actually their "linkage with life."

Just as living in a smaller homelike residence is a profound change for someone who has lived in an institution, working in a community residence is a profound change for someone who has worked in an institution. Contemporary research suggests that staff who work in smaller, more homelike settings enjoy a higher quality of work life and are more likely to interact with clients in a therapeutic manner (Jacobson and Schwartz 1983; Mac-Eachron, Zober, and Fein 1985). If it is true that quality of work life is better in smaller work sites and that this is reflected in staff behavior toward clients, quality of life is indeed an important factor in determining whether moving to a community home will enhance residents' skill development.

Although its relationship to quality care is the primary issue to be addressed here, there are additional implications of the quality of work life. Estimates of turnover rates in public residential facilities have ranged from 14 to 55% (Lakin and Bruininks 1981; Lakin et al. 1983). Thus, staff turnover is a significant issue in this field. It results directly in heavy administrative costs while hindering program continuity. Furthermore, because of anticipated needs for increased numbers of staff to work in integrated community settings for persons with developmental disabilities (Panel on the Future of the Work Force 1987), investigation of work life issues is justified to increase our understanding of staff role responsibilities, role performances, and preferences.

### AIMS OF THE STUDY

In the present study longitudinal data were collected on a group of staff and clients who moved from a traditional institution to one of six small residential units (SRUs). The SRUs were all located in the same small rural community as the institution. However, they were dispersed among the other homes in the community, on three separate sites, rather than being located on the same grounds as the institution. The organization that operates these facilities is one of the 20 developmental disabilities service offices (DDSOs) in New York State's Office of Mental Retardation and Developmental Disabilities. The DDSO of interest provides direct services to more than 700 individuals with developmental disabilities in three western New York rural counties and overseas services for another 1,000 individuals in privately operated residential, day, and support services.

For a variety of reasons, this venture was critical. SRU development at several DDSOs had caused a statewide political controversy because the homes were to be located on the periphery of institutional grounds. As well, the logistics were formidable as the DDSO had never opened six homes concurrently. Finally, the people moving into these homes had more severe intellectual and functional impairments than did the majority of people who preceded them into the community.

This chapter describes the changes in quality of work life which occurred for staff who transferred to the new SRUs. Although the relevant data will not be discussed here, concurrent changes in the quality of life for the SRUs' residents were also found: they made significant progress in their functional skills, their general nutritional status improved, their rate of respiratory infections decreased, and their daily routines were more individually oriented than those in the developmental center (Galligan, McArdle, and Zazycki 1989). These concomitant changes are critical to note, particularly as they relate to the public policy issues reviewed previously.

RELEVANT LITERATURE

There is a vast literature on employee attitudes and the organizational characteristics that might be associated with those attitudes. A small subset of that literature is related to human services, and a smaller subset is related to staff who work in developmental disabilities service settings. The underlying argument in this literature is that better quality of work life encourages better staff performance. However, it is unclear how far this argument can be generalized to the developmental disabilities field because most of the relevant occupational literature is focused in the business sector or upon nursing personnel whose actions are in part guided by ethical codes and special training (MacEachron, Zober, and Fein 1985; Spector 1985).

Several studies directly address quality of work life for staff who work in developmental disabilities program settings. Sarata (1974) found that employees with more client contact were less satisfied with their work setting. Other investigators, however, have found no relationship between satisfaction and level of client contact (Bersani and Heifetz 1985; Silver, Lubin, and Silverman 1984) or a positive relationship (Holburn and Forrester 1984). Lakin and co-workers (1983) found that satisfaction with extrinsic job elements was related to staff stability, but satisfaction with intrinsic elements was not. They also found that older staff and staff who had worked in the organization longer were less likely to leave their jobs. No relationship was found between job stability and client functioning level or ratings of the treatment environment. Thompson (1980) studied burnout in group home parents and found significant differences by sex. For men, burnout was related to higher salaries and having no decision-making power in accepting clients. Women were more likely to burn out if they screened clients or ran group meetings. MacEachron, Zober, and Fein (1985) found that a move to a more homelike setting was associated with increased staff decision making and performance as well as increases in residents' functional skills. Other investigators have also found relationships among participatory decision making, job satisfaction, and quality of care in developmental disabilities service systems (Browner et al. 1987; Holland 1973; King, Raynes, and Tizard 1971; Pratt, Luszcz, and Brown 1980; Raynes, Pratt and Roses 1977).

Thus, a variety of relationships have been found among quality of work life, staff, and resident characteristics in developmental disabilities program settings. Clearly, the quality of work life is part of a complex interaction between employees and their organizations. Most studies of the quality of work life in the developmental disabilities field consider job satisfaction and participatory decision making as critical components. These constructs have thus been included in the present study. Before describing this study's methodology, the manner in which these constructs have been quantified in the literature will be reviewed.

It is generally accepted that job satisfaction subsumes a set of domains. Although the exact number of domains varies, many authors postulate an intrinsic (e.g., work role, advancement, and recognition) and an extrinsic component (e.g., salary and policies). Various studies have provided factor analytic verifications for these two main components (Hauber and Bruininks 1986; Sluyter and Mukherjee 1986; Zautra, Eblen, and Reynolds 1986). Most studies have measured job satisfaction with the Job Descriptive Index (JDI; Smith, Kendall, and Hulin 1969) or an instrument that has been validated against the JDI (e.g., Sluyter and Mukherjee 1986; Spector 1985; Weiss et al. 1967). Thus, although an exact and universal definition of job satisfaction does not exist, it is safe to generalize across the literature because most studies use highly related instruments, and many distinguish between intrinsic and extrinsic job satisfaction components.

Intuitively, the construct of participatory decision making refers to the level of staff involvement in decisions about their work. However, because measurement tools vary so widely across studies, different studies are probably measuring different domains within the construct (see Cherniss and Egnatios 1978; MacEachron et al. 1985; Raynes, Pratt, and Roses 1977). Thus, no standard definition of the construct of participative decision making has emerged nor has a standard means for measuring the construct. This is a serious shortcoming because this construct is emerging as a critical factor associated with living environments and the functional growth of persons with developmental disabilities.

METHODS

### Subjects and Settings

The subjects were the direct care staff who transferred into the SRUs during spring 1987. For comparison purposes, the direct care staff who worked in the institution and those who worked in the already existing community homes were also included as subjects. Job satisfaction surveys were completed when the SRUs opened and again one year later. Because of different response rates at the two administrations, there were a different number of subjects at the baseline and the follow-up. For the SRUs, there were 87 responses at baseline (100% response rate) and 49 at the follow-up (56%). For the institution, there were 65 responses at baseline (39%) and 80 at the follow-up (48%). For the community homes, there were 73 responses at baseline (56%) and 65 at the follow-up (50%). Overall, there was a 59% response rate at baseline (225 responses) and a 51% response rate at the follow-up (194 responses).

In the institution, each employee cared for 20 to 24 individuals on a living unit. Residents attended a day program and ate their meals in the same building in which they lived. Centralized departments provided dietary, housekeeping, medication administration, and maintenance services. In the SRUs, an employee cared for 12 residents in a home that was located among the other homes in the surrounding community. Residents attended a day program at a community site. The SRU staff worked with clients to prepare meals, do housekeeping, and administer medications. Most maintenance services were provided by community vendors. In the institution, a staff person could, and often was, asked to work on other living units to replace absent staff. However, SRU staff only covered for other staff in their own home. Duties of SRU staff were similar to those of staff in already existing community homes although there were fewer clients in those homes (average = 9.1; range = 8 to 12).

### Job Satisfaction

All SRU direct care staff completed a job satisfaction survey before starting work at the SRUs in the spring 1987 and then again a year later. For comparison purposes staff in the institution and community homes were also asked to complete a survey within the same time frames. Sluyter and Mukherjee's (1986) Job Satisfaction Survey was used. This instrument was chosen because, unlike other available instruments, it had been designed for use with, and its reliability and validity had been established with, a large group of employees in congregate mental retardation facilities. The instrument has six subscales related to extrinsic job aspects and six subscales related to intrinsic job aspects. Sluyter and Mukherjee (1986) found a significant canonical correlation between their 12 subscales and the JDI's five variables, suggesting that the two instruments measure similar information about job aspects. In the present study, a principal components factor analysis with varimax rotation was used to confirm the extrinsic and intrinsic factor structures.

Influence in Decision Making

When the staff in the institution, SRUs, and community homes completed their follow-up Job Satisfaction Survey in the spring 1988 they also completed a modified version of Tannenbaum's Employee Influence Scale (EIS, 1968, 1974). Unfortunately, Tannenbaum and co-workers (1968, 1974) offered no empirical measures of the scale's reliability and validity. However, they did present logical arguments for the reliability (i.e., the scores would likely be stable if averaged across a reasonably large number of respondents) and validity of the instrument (i.e., the instrument reflected organizational differences that were confirmed by observational data). It should be noted that reliability and validity data are also lacking for the other decision-making instruments discussed earlier (Cherniss and Egnatios 1978; MacEachron, Zobers, and Fein 1985; Raynes, Pratt, and Roses 1977). For purposes of this study, the EIS was modified by deleting items inapplicable to the civil service system, which governed many personnel decisions and by adding items related to working with clients, providing a total of 14 items in the measure. A principal components factor analysis and varimax rotation yielded three factors: working with clients (five items, for example, deciding which individuals move into the residence, deciding which individuals move out, setting treatment goals); staff scheduling (five items, for instance, deciding staff schedules, specific tasks to be done, when breaks occur); and career mobility (three items: getting promoted, transferred, or approval for inservice training).

RESULTS

Job Satisfaction

In each of the following analyses the intrinsic and extrinsic factors were treated separately as dependent variables. In all cases, the intrinsic factor was more sensitive than the extrinsic factor to the work life aspects studied.

To investigate job satisfaction changes over the course of the year, a two-way analysis of covariance was used with length of employment as the covariate. The two factors were time of administration (baseline or follow-up) and work location (community versus SRU versus institution). This is not the ideal analysis because pairing each staff person's baseline score with his or her own follow-up score would provide a more powerful test of changes over time. However, respondents were not asked to identify themselves because of the sensitive nature of the information requested. Thus, data could not be paired at the individual level.

This analysis yielded a significant interaction of work location and time of survey administration when using either the intrinsic, $F(2, 305) = 4.8$, $p < .01$, or the extrinsic factor, $F(2, 312) = 3.0$, $p = .05$, as the dependent variable. Although the job satisfaction of SRU and institution staff tended to increase over the year, that of community staff tended to decrease (see Table 15.1). There was nothing in the design of the study to explain these overall organizational trends. Thus, the issue was investigated further by looking at the baseline and one year follow-up information separately.

Using analysis of covariance with length of employment as the covariate, work environment and length of employment were the keys to explaining the results. In these analyses a significant relationship was found with the intrinsic factor as the dependent variable but not with the extrinsic factor. At baseline, community staff reported higher intrinsic factor scores than institution staff (in this analysis, SRU staff were included with the work location that they were leaving because their scores did not differ from their previous cohort). There was also an interaction of work location and length of employment so that differences across work location became more pronounced as length of employment increased, $F(1, 149) = 4.2$, $p < .05$. Thus, the

Table 15.1. Average Job Satisfaction Scores at Baseline and One-year Follow-up for Different Work Locations[a]

| Follow-up Work Location | Baseline | | | | | | One Year | | | | |
| | | Intrinsic Factor | | Extrinsic Factor | | | Intrinsic Factor | | Extrinsic Factor | |
| | N | Mean | S.D. | Mean | S.D. | N | Mean | S.D. | Mean | S.D. |
|---|---|---|---|---|---|---|---|---|---|---|
| Institution | 65 | 3.0 | 1.1 | 3.5 | 1.0 | 80 | 3.3 | 1.3 | 3.7 | 1.1 |
| SRUs | 87 | 3.0 | 1.1 | 3.8 | 1.0 | 49 | 3.4 | 1.1 | 4.0 | 1.0 |
| Community homes | 73 | 3.3 | 1.2 | 3.9 | 1.0 | 65 | 3.1 | 1.0 | 3.7 | 1.0 |

[a]The instrument was based on a seven-point scale (e.g., 1 = not satisfied; 4 = satisfied; 7 = completely satisfied).

**Table 15.2. Average Intrinsic Factor Scores for Staff with Different Lengths of Employment**

| | Baseline | | | | | | One-year Follow-up | | | | | |
| | Fewer Years of Employment[a] | | | More Years of Employment | | | Fewer Years of Employment | | | More Years of Employment | | |
| Work Location | N | Mean | S.D. | N | Mean | S.D. | N | Mean | S.D. | N | Mean | S.D. |
|---|---|---|---|---|---|---|---|---|---|---|---|---|
| Institution | 56 | 2.9 | 0.9 | 50 | 3.2 | 1.3 | 32 | 3.8 | 1.3 | 33 | 3.1 | 1.3 |
| SRUs (included in previous work location) | | | | | | | 25 | 3.2 | 1.3 | 20 | 3.8 | 0.9 |
| Community homes | 36 | 3.2 | 1.0 | 22 | 4.1 | 1.3 | 40 | 3.0 | 0.8 | 19 | 3.4 | 1.3 |

[a]The average length of employment was 7.7 years. People who had worked less than 7.7 years were included in the "fewer years of employment" group. Those who had worked 7.7 years or longer were included in the other group. Years of employment was dichotomized around the mean for illustrative purposes only. All analyses included length of employment as a continuous variable.

difference between community and institution staff who worked in the DDSO longer was much larger than for staff who had not worked as long. A similar picture was found at the one year follow-up. Again, the interaction of work location and length of employment was the key to explaining the results, $F(2, 154) = 3.3$, $p < .05$. For less experienced staff, institution staff had higher intrinsic scores than SRU and community staff. For more experienced staff, the SRU and community had higher scores than the institution (see Table 15.2).

### Influence in Decision Making

Table 15.3 shows that SRU staff felt they had more influence than institution staff in all three decision-making areas (staff scheduling, $t(119) = 2.8$, $p < .01$; working with clients, $t(120) = 2.9$, $p < .01$; career mobility, $t(118) = 3.5$, $p < .01$). They also felt that they had more influence over client-related issues than did community staff ($t(101) = 2.5$, $p < .05$). Again, length of employment was an important variable: there was a positive relationship between length of employment and influence in the staff ($r(159) = .43$, $p < .001$) and client domains ($r(154) = .29$, $p < .001$). However, length of employment was not related to the career mobility domain.

LIMITATIONS OF THE DATA

As in all field research, there are significant limitations to the inferences that can be made from this study. First, since the study was limited to one organization, the dynamics of that organization were embedded in the findings. An important characteristic of the organization studied was its location in a very rural region. Thus, the relative lack of choices for comparable jobs in the area and the related low turnover rate may well limit the generalization

Table 15.3. Average Participation in Decision-making Scores for Different Work Locations[a]

| | Decision-making Domains | | | | | |
| | Staff Scheduling | | Working with Clients | | Career Mobility | |
| Work location | Mean | S.D. | Mean | S.D. | Mean | S.D. |
|---|---|---|---|---|---|---|
| Institution | 1.9 | 0.9 | 2.0 | 0.9 | 1.9 | 0.8 |
| SRUs | 2.4 | 1.0 | 2.5 | 0.9 | 2.4 | 0.8 |
| Community homes | 2.4 | 1.2 | 2.1 | 0.7 | 2.6 | 0.9 |

[a]The instrument was based on a five-point scale (1 = none; 3 = some; 5 = a great deal).

of findings to employees in more urban work settings. However, this factor may facilitate generalization to many modern facilities that continue to be located in rural areas.

Second, because staff were not asked to provide identifying information beyond their work location and years of employment, the relationships among employee characteristics and quality of work life could not be investigated fully. Most importantly, how the staff who remained in the institution may have differed from those who transferred to the SRUs could not be thoroughly examined. Although the SRU staff had comparable job satisfaction scores and lengths of employment with their previous cohort in the institution, they undoubtedly had meaningful reasons for changing their work location. Those reasons might be critical to the inferences that can be made from these findings. For example, if the people who chose to remain in the institution were less open to enhanced decision-making opportunities, they may not have found the SRUs to be as positive an experience as those who had moved to the SRUs. The relative lack of staff demographic information may thus limit the generalization of findings. However, the sensitivity of the requested information required anonymity, otherwise a very low return rate was likely.

Last, the exact nature of job characteristics was not addressed in the study design. Thus, it is not possible to determine the particular aspects of SRU staff's jobs which made them feel more satisfied and more involved in decision making than their colleagues in the institution. Likewise, the available data do not provide a clear basis for hypotheses about why SRU staff felt more involved in client-related issues than staff in already existing community homes.

DISCUSSION

The present study supports existing literature in that a significant relationship between more homelike residential settings and higher quality of work life was found. In regard to job satisfaction, the current study confirms that work environment is related to job satisfaction and that staff are generally more satisfied in more homelike environments. However, this study also indicates that the relationship between the work environment and job satisfaction is complex. In particular, the interaction of work location and length of employment emerged as an important factor in job satisfaction reports. For staff who had worked in the organization longer, community and SRU staff reported greater job satisfaction than institution staff. However, for staff who had not worked as long there was either a minimal difference based on work location, or institution staff actually reported greater satisfaction than staff in community sites.

In regard to staff influence in decision making, SRU staff reported that they had significantly more influence than did institution staff in all areas studied. Also, they reported that they had more influence than community staff in issues related to residents. Again, length of employment was critical in that staff who had worked in the organization longer saw themselves as more involved in decision making.

The present study also provides information about each of the constructs of interest. The study confirmed that there are two critical components to job satisfaction as typically measured in human services: an intrinsic and an extrinsic factor. The intrinsic factor was found to be more sensitive to differences in work settings than was the extrinsic factor. This study also found that influence in client-related issues is a separate domain within the construct of participatory decision making. This is a critical notion for the human services field and should be considered in future evaluation and research activities.

The present study included a variety of components beyond the quality of work life. Concurrent with changes in quality of work life, separate analyses found that daily routines were more individually oriented than those in the institution; residents made significant progress in their functional skills; their general nutritional status had improved; and their rate of respiratory infections had decreased. Thus, the enhanced quality of work life for staff was associated with enhanced adaptive and health status of residents in the smaller homes (Galligan, McArdle, and Zazycki 1989).

## IMPLICATIONS OF FINDINGS

This study's major implication is a confirmation of the relationship between quality work life and quality care. There are, however, several more detailed implications. First, length of employment appeared as a critical mediating factor. MacEachron, Zober, and Fein (1985) also found a relationship between the quality of work life and length of employment although they found a negative relationship whereas a positive relationship was obtained in the present study. Thus, although it seems to be an important variable, the nature of the relationship is unclear. There is a variety of rival explanations for the importance of length of employment. It may be the effect of developing a strong social support system over time, the effect of a particular hiring or age cohort, the effect of finding the area in the organization which best suits one's talents over time, or a change in how the organization is perceived over time. In any event, because it has emerged as an important factor in this study, it requires administrative attention and further attention in the literature.

Second, this study showed that of the two job satisfaction factors the intrinsic factor (i.e., job aspects such as recognition and achievement) was most strongly related to differences in work setting. Because the extrinsic factor (i.e., job aspects such as salary and policies) is generally not amenable to administrative discretion in the public sector, it is heartening to find that the work life areas studied here are more strongly related to the intrinsic factor.

A final implication is a confirmation of the importance of staff participation in decision making and empirical evidence that it is a multi-faceted construct. Because it is a critical factor, the relatively low scores on this dimension are discouraging. In this sample, the highest scores attained were for SRU staff in regard to client-related issues and for community staff in regard to career mobility. In both cases the average scores were halfway between "a little" and "some" influence.

Thus, the major implication for public policy formulation and day-to-day administration is that development of smaller, more homelike settings is not enough. Unless there is a commitment to make those settings places in which staff and clients work together to shape individualized treatment, major strides forward will not occur. Without the administrative commitment needed, individualized treatment may happen in spite of, rather than because of, the major policy changes underlying community development.

Beyond the specific implications that follow from this study, there are several policy questions that the study highlights. First, there is the general issue of establishing group homes on the periphery of institution grounds. As mentioned previously, SRU development was strongly opposed by many advocates of normalization and social integration. Although the homes reviewed in this study were not actually on the same grounds, they were in the same extremely rural community as the institution. Even so, there were documented improvements in quality of work life, resident skills, and individualized routines. However, this study cannot resolve whether community development in neighborhoods more removed from the institution might have been even better for staff and residents. The kinds of neighborhoods and program practices which are more conducive to social integration of people with developmental disabilities is still an empirical question that needs continuing attention in political and programmatic arenas.

The second major policy question that this study highlights is the difficulty of improving the quality of work life within the highly regulated environments surrounding developmental disabilities program settings. The structure imposed by these regulations may well be counterproductive to the management practices supported by this study's findings. We need to ask whether the current regulations allow enough flexibility for managers to improve the quality of work life, particularly participatory decision making and the intrinsic aspects of job satisfaction (e.g., advancement and recognition). If not, we need to consider reinterpretations or revisions of regulatory provisions to allow that flexibility.

# 16

# Staff Attitudes and the Group Home as a Workplace

John W. Jacobson, Ph.D., and Lee J. Ackerman, M.S.

This chapter presents findings from an organizational analysis of group homes using staff attitudes toward their work and to a lesser degree, attitudes toward the persons they served as a basis for defining the social environment, or culture, of these settings (Pratt, Luszcz, and Brown 1980). After residences were grouped according to more and less positive attitudes a number of additional elements of the work environment were investigated to determine how they might relate to these attitudes and assist in a description of the group home as a work and service setting.

From the standpoint of a public agency that operates and oversees a complex system of residential alternatives for persons with chronic disabilities and which may employ tens of thousands of personnel directly or indirectly through contracts, administrative concerns exist as to the nature of prevailing attitudes of workers toward the difficult tasks inherent in the direct care work role and toward the persons whom they serve. Concerns about personnel and management practices become especially acute if issues such as high staff turnover, an endemic problem in direct care services, is believed to be adversely affecting staff who remain on the job (Lakin et al. 1989).

A small but significant body of research has considered the attitudes of personnel serving people with disabilities, not only with respect to the people they serve but also with respect to the work that they do. These attitudes are anticipated to affect the behavior of personnel toward people living in residences and to affect the performance of their duties. For example, two studies have shown that providing normalizing experiences and working cooperatively with others (i.e., consistent with attitudes favoring such processes) are group home manager competencies associated with program and resident management practices and with resident satisfaction and community integration (Burchard, Pine, and Gordon 1990; Burchard et al. 1987).

Considerable research has indicated the legitimacy of studying situational factors that could affect positive and negative job attitudes. For example, work roles and the nature of the work itself have been investigated to ascertain how they impact employee outcomes such as satisfaction and performance in a range of occupations (Hackman and Oldham 1980).

In the developmental services field, job satisfaction has been the construct most often studied among group home staff, as for example in Zigman, Schwartz, and Janicki (1982), who found that positive job attitudes and restriction of occupant autonomy were somewhat reflective of occupant functional level. Organizational features of group homes such as job satisfaction have usually been studied in isolation or in the context of few other aspects of the settings. For example, Fimian (1984) studied role conflict and ambiguity, and Bersani and Heifetz (1985) studied satisfactions and stressors, in community residences. Fimian's findings suggested that role conflict and ambiguity contributed to both stress and burnout whereas Bersani and Heifetz noted that aspects of both the workplace and occupant functioning constituted sources of stress and satisfaction. Management activity has also been studied in selected institutional research reports (e.g., Holburn and Forrester 1984) but much less often in group homes (for exceptions see Thousand, Burchard, and Hasazi 1986).

The community residence has not been well studied in terms of its organizational design. Organizations may be defined as *systems of knowledge* (e.g., cultures or social environments) wherein there is a network of subjective meaning (including attitudes) that members share and which appears to define expectations for conduct (Smircich 1983). An organizational analysis entails measurement of multiple aspects of the work environment including workers' appraisals of aspects of their work, workplace, and co-workers: participation in decision making, job satisfactions, commitment, social support, leader behavior, staff relations, operational issues, and burnout (Cherniss 1981). In a comprehensive study organizational characteristics should be considered with respect to the normative social structure of the residence (Cherniss 1981). Social structure has been defined in past research by social environment measures that categorize settings as having practices reflecting the needs and abilities of the persons living there rather than the convenience of the people working there (e.g., Pratt, Luszcz, and Brown 1980).

In this study the social structure of residences was characterized according to the attitudes of staff toward their work and toward the people they serve. The dominant staff attitudes, we suggest, should contribute to and reflect the dominant culture of the residence and the norms for staff behavior (e.g., overprotective staff members may deny occupants valid opportunities to exercise greater autonomy in selection of activities and routines). Positive attitudes should be associated with other positive work group characteristics, and multiple negative work group characteristics should be found in the presence of negative attitudes.

METHODS

Subjects

The subjects for this study were 269 staff and managers of 35 group homes located in New York State and serving people with mental retardation and developmental disabilities. Residences were selected as a stratified sample of all community residences in the state in 1987. Strata were defined by operator (public or private), type (group home or intermediate care facility for the mentally retarded [ICF/MR]), and location (metropolitan or nonmetropolitan). Five sites were selected from each cell, for a total of 40 sites. Data from 35 residences were available for these analyses.

Of the staff who participated, 73.8% were female, 62.5% were age 30 years or older, 40.6% had a high school education, 63.6% worked in group homes that were certified as ICF/MRs, and 42.8% worked in publicly operated residences. From 3 to 12 persons lived in each residence.

Instruments

Data were collected through completion of a general survey by the resident manager, completion of questionnaires by staff and the manager, and structured interviews with each manager and one or two staff at each residence. From 3 to 15 staff completed a questionnaire at each location. A total of 100 personnel completed an interview.

Questionnaires contained a commitment measure (Wicker, Kirmeyer, and Alexander 1976), an understaffing and a social support measure (Yoe et al. 1986), the Job Descriptive Index (or JDI; Smith, Kendall, and Hulin 1969), the Job Diagnostic Survey (or JDS; Hackman and Oldham 1980), the Community Residence Employee Opinion Scale (or CREOS; Living Alternatives Research Project 1981), and the Leader Behavior Description Questionnaire (or LBDQ; Halpin and Winer 1957). Questionnaires provided information about commitment, social support from co-workers and supervisors, job satisfactions, job characteristics, attitudes toward work and persons living in the residence, and supervisory behavior. Structured interview forms included the Maslach Burnout Inventory (Maslach and Jackson 1981), providing an assessment of dimensions of burnout.

Procedure

Staff attitudes (i.e., from the CREOS) were scored using the factor solution obtained by Zigman, Schwartz, and Janicki (1982) and yielded five scores: positive job attitudes, lower staff control, positive job demands, staff-resident affiliation, and supporting development, with higher scores representing more positive attitudes. The mean scores for the sites were then classified for each score as above or below the median. Residences and associated staff were then assigned to a group depending upon whether either none to two or from three to five of the scores fell at or above the median. Two groups were formed, with 19 residences characterized as more positive and 16 residences characterized as less positive. *t*-tests verified that the groups differed on three job-related scales: positive job attitudes, staff control, and job demands (all $p < .004$), and one resident-related scale: supporting development ($p < .001$) but did not differ on the resident-related scale of staff-resident affiliation. Characteristics of the resulting staff groups are shown in Table 16.1.

Staff in residences wherein staff held more positive attitudes were younger, had less experience in human services, were more likely to be public employees, worked with residence occupants who had less marked intellectual limitations, and were more likely to respond to the research questionnaires. Several staff demographic characteristics were modestly associated with features of the organizational context (see Jacobson 1988a).

A composite of the scale scores was factor analyzed for the questionnaire instruments using principal components analysis with varimax rotation. Based on a preliminary solution, scale scores were standardized, assigned to a scale according to their primary factor loadings, and restandardized as parcels. These scales were intercorrelated and a model derived for the residence sample, similar to that which can be obtained through structural equation modeling. Intercorrelations were also conducted separately for staff in homes with prevailing positive and negative attitudes and separately for staff in homes with higher and lower management scores. Management scores were drawn from the LBDQ for initiation (i.e., assisting staff in structuring their work activities) and consideration (i.e., showing interest in staff as individuals).

*T*-tests were used to establish differences in the organizational features between the two attitude groups. Of concern was whether relationships (i.e., correlations) among organizational variables might differ in the context of

**Table 16.1. Characteristics of Groups of Staff with More and Less Positive Attitudes**

|  | Attitude Groups | | |
|---|---|---|---|
| Characteristic | More Positive | Less Positive | Statistics |
|  | % | | |
| Age (years) | | | |
| 18–29 | 42.5 | 26.2 | $\chi^2(3) = 8.92$ |
| 30–39 | 26.1 | 31.5 | $p < .05$ |
| 40–49 | 18.3 | 28.5 | |
| 50+ | 13.1 | 13.8 | |
| Sex (female) | 74.2 | 73.4 | N.S. $(\chi^2)$ |
| Years of education | | | |
| ≤ 12 | 33.9 | 42.8 | N.S. $(\chi^2)$ |
| 13–16 | 44.8 | 34.7 | |
| 17+ | 21.3 | 22.5 | |
| Years of human services experience | | | |
| 0.0–1.99 | 16.9 | 7.0 | $\chi^2(2) = 38.07$ |
| 2.0–3.99 | 38.0 | 11.8 | $p < .001$ |
| 4.0+ | 45.1 | 81.2 | |
| Years of tenure | | | |
| 0.0–1.99 | 49.1 | 40.5 | N.S. $(\chi^2)$ |
| 2.0–3.99 | 23.7 | 33.1 | |
| 4.0+ | 27.2 | 26.4 | |
|  | N | | |
| Works in a CR | 44.6 | 40.5 | N.S. $(\chi^2)$ |
| Works in an ICF/MR | 55.4 | 59.5 | |
| Public employee | 44.3 | 27.9 | $\chi^2(2) = 7.78$ |
| Private employee | 55.4 | 72.1 | $p < .01$ |
| Residents/site[a] | 9.11/2.2 | 7.31/3.4 | N.S. (t-test) |
| Resident functional deficits (maximum = 7) | 3.22/1.3 | 3.46/1.2 | N.S. (t-test) |
| Resident intellectual level | | | $t(267) = 2.60$ |
| (1–5, 5 = PMR)[b] | 3.38/1.2 | 3.76/1.2 | $p < .01$ |
| No. of residences | 19 | 16 | |
| No. of employees | 140 | 129 | |
| Percent of all employees in these | | | $\chi^2(1) = 8.63$ |
| residences | 85.9 | 77.9 | $p < .01$ |

[a]Mean and standard deviation shown for residents per site, resident functional deficits, and resident intellectual level.

[b]PMR = profound mental retardation.

more or less positive prevailing attitudes. Concurrent validity of the data was assessed via comparison of disparate satisfaction measures and emulation of Hackman and Oldham's (1980) job characteristics model. Reliability and validity analyses, presented in Jacobson (1988a), indicated generally that the data were internally consistent when expressed in scale scores and were consistent across respondents within residences.

RESULTS

Table 16.2 shows the norms for service occupations and the scores for staff of private and public residences on the JDS scales. Service occupations include those in which, as in human services, there is frequent contact with persons to whom services are rendered and includes restaurant workers as well as direct care personnel (e.g., mental health, day care) but excludes managerial, technical, clerical, and sales occupations. Although restaurant and kindred work is not similar to work in group homes, educational requirements are similar, and both job groupings involve variable effort and demand characteristics.

Staff of private programs scored higher than the norms on autonomy, feedback from agents (e.g., supervisors, peers, and the persons served), meaningfulness of the work, knowledge of results of the work, and general satisfaction and were lower than the norms on skill variety. Staff of public

**Table 16.2 Comparison of Job Diagnostic Survey Norms and Staff Scores**

| Variable | Service Norms[a] | | Private Staff | | Public Staff | |
|---|---|---|---|---|---|---|
| | Mean | S.D. | Mean | S.D. | Mean | S.D. |
| Skill variety | 5.0 | 1.4 | 4.5* | 1.3 | 4.3* | 1.3 |
| Task identity | 4.7 | 1.2 | 4.8 | 1.2 | 4.8 | 1.3 |
| Task significance | 5.7 | 1.0 | 5.7 | 1.1 | 5.7 | 1.1 |
| Autonomy | 5.0 | 1.2 | 5.2* | 1.0 | 5.0 | 1.3 |
| Feedback from the job | 5.1 | 1.1 | 4.9 | 1.3 | 4.6* | 1.2 |
| Feedback from agents | 3.8 | 1.6 | 4.9* | 1.4 | 4.7* | 1.5 |
| Dealing with others | 6.0 | 1.0 | 6.1 | 0.92 | 5.9 | 1.2 |
| Motivating potential score | 154 | 55 | 132 | 60 | 123 | 65 |
| Experienced meaning | 5.2 | 1.1 | 5.5* | 1.0 | 5.3 | 1.2 |
| Experienced responsibility | 5.6 | 0.86 | 5.5 | 0.84 | 5.4* | 0.91 |
| Knowledge of results | 5.0 | 1.1 | 5.2* | 1.1 | 5.2* | 1.0 |
| General satisfaction | 4.6 | 1.2 | 5.0* | 1.1 | 5.0* | 1.2 |
| Internal motivation | 5.7 | 0.76 | 5.6 | 0.81 | 5.4* | 0.89 |

[a]Norms for service occupations drawn from Hackman and Oldham (1980).

*Differs significantly from service norms at $p < .05$ or greater ($t$-test, $df = 398$).

Table 16.3. Comparison of Two Attitude Groups on
Organizational Measures

|  | Attitude Group Mean Scores | | | |
| --- | --- | --- | --- | --- |
| Organizational<br>Characteristics | More Positive<br>(N = 138) | Less Positive<br>(N = 123) | t | p |
| Leader initiation | 41.4 | 39.6 | 2.4 | .02 |
| Leader consideration | 35.6 | 33.3 | 4.1 | .001 |
| Skill variety | 14.2 | 12.9 | 2.5 | .02 |
| Task identity | 15.0 | 14.0 | 2.3 | .03 |
| Task significance | 17.8 | 15.9 | 2.3 | .03 |
| Autonomy | 16.2 | 14.7 | 3.6 | .001 |
| Feedback from agents | 15.3 | 13.6 | 3.2 | .002 |
| Dealing with others | 18.6 | 17.8 | 2.1 | .04 |
| Motivating potential score | 3,911 | 3,246 | 3.2 | .002 |
| Meaningfulness of work | 5.6 | 5.3 | 2.6 | .02 |
| Responsibility for work | 5.7 | 5.4 | 2.6 | .01 |
| Knowledge of results | 5.3 | 5.1 | 2.0 | .04 |
| Social support (co-workers)[b] | 31.4 | 39.3 | 3.4 | .001 |
| Social support (supervisor)[b] | 31.6 | 40.7 | 3.6 | .001 |
| Satisfaction with supervision | 17.6 | 16.5 | 2.9 | .004 |

[a]Groups did not differ on understaffing, work commitment, job feedback, or satisfaction with
work, co-workers, pay, or promotions.

[b]In social support, lower scores = greater social support.

programs scored higher than the norms on feedback from agents, knowledge
of the results, and general satisfaction and were lower than the norms on
skill variety, feedback from the job, experienced responsibility for the work,
and internal work motivation. In both public and private residences these
personnel indicated higher than expected general satisfaction with their work.

On the other hand, staff reported that their skills were not utilized in the
performance of their work (i.e., skill variety) to the degree that would be
expected. Need for job redesign was also indicated for public personnel to
enhance the level of feedback received from the completion of job tasks and
the extent to which they perceive (or have) responsibility for work outcomes.
Job redesign was indicated in both public and private residences to make
better use of the skills that staff can bring to bear.

Table 16.3 compares mean scores on organizational measures for the
two attitude groups. The group with more positive attitude scores rated their
managers as more initiating (e.g., structuring) and considerate (e.g., showing interest), their jobs as better defined and more motivating, their satisfaction with supervision greater, and their degree of social support received

from both co-workers and supervisors as greater. Groups did not differ, however, on commitment to the work or on most aspects of job satisfaction. Because of the number of statistical comparisons that were made, differences between these groups shown in Table 16.3 on variables other than leader consideration, autonomy, feedback from agents, motivating potential of the work, social support, and satisfaction from supervision should be viewed as suggestive and as bearing further study.

Burnout data for the two attitude groups were also compared ($N_1 = 57$; $N_2 = 43$). The two groups were not found to differ in degree of staff burnout. Burnout measure scores suggested that high degrees of emotional exhaustion and depersonalization were present in both groups, accompanied by marked feelings of personal accomplishment. *Exhaustion* and *depersonalization* reflect expected effects of stressors in care settings serving people who are chronically dependent whereas *sense of accomplishment* may reflect an appraisal that one's work is of value and that one performs the work well. Because burnout did not differ between the two groups it appears that the impact of stressors (e.g., unpredictable work tasks and schedules, frequent overtime, and multiple shifts) was not mediated by the presence of more positive attitudes.

To reduce the number of variables, identify the underlying dimensions measured, and more completely describe the dynamics of the residence workplace, the questionnaire data were submitted to factor analysis. A five-factor solution (see Table 16.4) accounted for 57% of measured variance and provided factors of: (1) positive work characteristics and commitment; (2) management practices and social support; (3) positive work orientations; (4) satisfaction; and (5) response to dependence. Substantial overlap of the JDS and CREOS scores was not apparent, suggesting that in general, they are measuring distinctly different constructs.

Correlation coefficients between standardized scores are essentially similar to path coefficients as employed in structural equation modeling. Figure 16.1 shows one possible model that emerges from the correlations among the factors derived in this study. When these correlations were computed using data from staff of all of the residences, scores for the management and social support factor were not significantly related to any of the other factor scores. However, in this general model, a strong triad of relationships emerges among positive work orientations, positive work characteristics, and job satisfaction.

When residences were partitioned into those with staff holding positive or negative attitudes, the management and social support factor remained unrelated to the work characteristic and orientation factors in both groups

**Table 16.4.  Primary Loadings in Factor Analysis of Questionnaires Completed by Staff**

|  | Primary Factor Loadings | | | | |
|---|---|---|---|---|---|
| Scale or Measure[a] | 1 | 2 | 3 | 4 | 5 |
| 6. Understaffing | .62 | | | | |
| 1. Staff-resident affiliation | .46 | | | | |
| 2. Skill variety | .67 | | | | |
| 2. Task significance | .74 | | | | |
| 2. Autonomy | .38 | | | | |
| 2. Feedback from the job | .65 | | | | |
| 3. Leader initiation | | .70 | | | |
| 3. Leader consideration | | .75 | | | |
| 4. Social support (supervisor)[b] | | −.65 | | | |
| 4. Social support (co-workers)[b] | | −.82 | | | |
| 1. Positive job attitudes | | | .58 | | |
| 1. Lower staff control | | | .79 | | |
| 1. Positive job demands | | | .77 | | |
| 5. Intrinsic satisfaction | | | | .78 | |
| 5. Extrinsic satisfaction | | | | .80 | |
| 1. Supporting development | | | | | .75 |
| 2. Task identity | | | | | .53 |
| Percent of Variance | 24.1 | 9.7 | 8.9 | 7.6 | 6.9 |

[a] 1, CREOS score; 2, JDS score; 3, LBDQ score; 4, social support measure score; 5, JDI score (intrinsic = work itself; extrinsic = sum of supervision, pay, co-workers, and promotions). 6 = Understaffing is a single score.

[b] In social support, lower scores = greater social support.

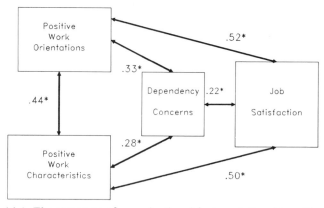

**Figure 16.1.  The structure of organizational factor relationships. N = 166. *p < .002. Management factor rs not significant.**

but weakly related to the dependence response and job satisfaction factors ($r(97) = .18$ and $r(95) = .21$; both $p < .05$, respectively) in the residences in which more positive attitudes prevailed. When residences were split into two groups according to high or low median factor scores for management and social support in residences with lower management scores, the management scores were not correlated with the other factor scores. However, they were significantly correlated with job satisfaction, work characteristics, and work orientations in residences with higher management scores.

DISCUSSION

The analyses presented in this chapter demonstrate the complexity of the group home as a small work setting. However, interpretations should be tempered by the facts that there were some demographic differences between the samples (although these did not account for all of the observed intergroup differences) and that the research design was correlational, and no cause-effect relationships can be specified.

From a management science standpoint it may be important that both public and private agency staff rated the nature of their work and the outcomes of their work in ways that were similar in many features to those typically found for workers in other service occupations. Although some significant differences from the norms were noted, the overall similarity of combined public-private employee ratings to the norms suggests that findings from applied research on job design with other types of service workers may be applicable to people who work in small residential settings.

The findings also merit some consideration from the standpoint of the literature on organizational culture. Wilkins and Ouchi (1983) characterized one type of culture as a *clan*. Clans are settings in which there are broadly shared goals of activity and expectations through which, with cooperation, collective interests will be satisfied. Clans seem more likely to develop in small work groups and may be especially effective at attaining collective goals under conditions of external environmental uncertainty (Wilkins and Ouchi 1983). It is valuable to consider at least whether some of these residences resembled clanlike work groups; this type of culture would be evidenced by work group cohesion and worker interdependence and would possibly be predisposed to lower staff turnover. Relationships identified in the foregoing analyses suggested that clanlike cultures may be formed in residences in which more positive attitudes prevailed. Job motivation and social support findings, in particular, suggest the presence of a clanlike culture.

Although the findings are not reported here (see Jacobson & Ackerman 1989a, 1989b), more desirable scores on job-related concerns were positively associated with a wide array of organizational features. Attitudes involving staff-resident affiliation and support for resident development (person-related concerns) were less consistently associated with organizational characteristics. How managers acted toward the staff and how decisions were made in the residence, for example, were more reflective of attitudes concerning the nature of the work than of staff's desire to spend time with the residents or beliefs that residents required constant supervision and direction. It appears that staff preparation for the manager or direct care role should address interpersonal skills and values-based skills (see Burchard and Thousand 1988).

Results of this study suggest that management practices involving the structuring of subordinate responsibilities and showing interest in staff appear to be related to more positive staff characterizations of the nature of their work. These findings indicate the practical value of providing managers and potential managers with training in supervisory skills prior to their undertaking of supervisory responsibilities.

Finally, indications of burnout did not differ between programs in which staff reported more positive or more negative attitudes. Both groups generally reported high levels of burnout, suggesting that efforts would be usefully directed to training in stress management and time management as integral components of staff development programs.

What are the implications of research on staff attitudes and management practices in group homes for public policy? First, the study and dissemination of research on staff attitudes and management in itself constitute a type of intervention. By conducting and disseminating this type of research a public agency demonstrates its commitment to support field personnel and to improve management and personnel practices.

Second, this type of research assists a public agency in identifying areas of management improvement or support. Several general findings have immediate policy implications, including: (1) the probable utility of a job design perspective in analyzing the direct care work role in ways that may assist retention; (2) the potential importance of developing structural supports for reliably interdependent (i.e., clanlike) work groups; (3) the possibility that values-oriented attitudes do not appear to be related to management practices and thus might be the focus of preservice training; and (4) that both supervisory skills and training in stress management and time management appear to be of potential importance.

Such findings assist public agencies in times of fiscal constraint, whether acute or chronic, in deciding which present activities will or should be discontinued and which new efforts should be championed despite greater cost. Findings also assist managers of residences and managers of agencies in making many of the same decisions at the local level.

Personnel issues that often have been treated in a cavalier manner in local human service agencies will be of great importance in the coming decade as the population grays and the number of potential entry level employees (the principal source of direct care staff) diminishes. Policymakers, together with academicians, will have a key role to play in the formulation of supports for personnel recruitment, retention, and development which will enable emergence of the expanded systems capacity that is being demanded by consumers. Such supports should be developed on a foundation of accurate information about existing personnel management issues, processes, problems, and successes.

# 17

# Satisfaction and Stability of Direct Care Personnel in Community-based Residential Services

K. Charlie Lakin, Ph.D., and Sheryl A. Larson, M.A.

## Public Policy Dimensions

Community services for persons with mental retardation in the United States are a large, complex, and costly social enterprise. Total costs for community-based services in fiscal year 1988 were an estimated 5.65 billion dollars (Braddock et al. 1989) with personnel costs (wages, fringe benefits, and payroll taxes) accounting for almost two thirds of those expenditures (Lakin 1988) or about 3.5 billion dollars. The community direct care labor force is estimated at about 120,000 full-time equivalent positions, 80,000 of which are held by persons without college degrees (paraprofessionals) (Lakin 1987). As community residential services have continued to evolve toward less restrictive, better integrated settings, services have become decentralized, and increased responsibilities are being given to paraprofessionals. Recognition of this increased responsibility has recently brought increased attention to the training of community direct care personnel. But the personnel issues in community services are far more complex than mere training. For training to have its desired effect agencies must be able to recruit people who can acquire the necessary job skills and who find satisfaction in applying them, and they must retain effective staff members so that their skills and familiarity with the needs, desires, and abilities of service recipients can contribute to the well-being of those individuals. The importance of developing a better understanding of the content and demands of direct care work, the people who do it, their problems with and perceptions of the role, and ways to improve personnel policy to meet the needs of staff is hard to overstate.

244

It is the nature of the community-based services "industry" that concern for meeting the needs of the care receivers cannot be isolated from concern for meeting the needs of the caregivers. Yet there is little evidence that we have been successful at meeting the needs of staff members. Recruiting, selecting, training, and retaining effective personnel in direct care roles are among the most consistently noted problems facing community services programs (Bruininks et al. 1980). In the past decade there has been growing acknowledgment that personnel studies should be an important part of human services research. In this chapter we examine personnel research done in residential settings on two key "outcome" variables: job satisfaction and job stability.

## Basic Concepts

### JOB SATISFACTION

Job satisfaction is a common outcome variable in personnel research. It has been defined as the degree to which the members of a social system have a positive affective orientation toward membership in the system in which they work (Price 1972). However, the components of a positive affective orientation are not well established, and many self-report questionnaires have been developed to measure job satisfaction. These questionnaires generally overlap on key, essentially intuitive job aspects, yet they differ on strategies to gather, organize, and summarize job satisfaction ratings. These instruments address areas such as satisfaction with: opportunities to use abilities, recognition received, relationships with co-workers, job demands, opportunities to participate in decision making, and a chance to do something important. Items are typically aggregated to produce composite scales of overall job satisfaction, and subscales such as extrinsic or intrinsic satisfaction.

The study of job satisfaction has been justified by researchers in four primary ways. First, it has been argued that quality of life for people in residential programs is largely determined by the job performance of staff and that expressed job satisfaction and job performance are interrelated (Bersani and Heifetz 1985; Hauber and Bruininks 1986; Lakin 1988; MacEachron, Zober, and Fein 1985; Sarata 1974). However, a recent authoritative meta-analysis by Iaffaldano and Muchinsky (1985), which examined 74 studies of the job satisfaction-job performance link in a wide range of occupations, resulted in an estimated composite correlation between these variables of only .17. In the highly interpersonal direct services role, worker satisfaction may be more highly related to performance than in other settings, but little objective evidence of this exists. Second, it has been contended that satisfaction with aspects of the job may operate as a buffer between work irritants and other withdrawal behavior, especially turnover (Holburn and Forrester 1984; Lakin and Bruininks 1981; Mobley et al. 1979; Zaharia and Baumeister 1979b). In other words, satisfied workers may be less likely to quit their jobs. Third, researchers argue that job satisfaction is an important outcome variable in its own right but that it has not been studied adequately in residential environments (Bersani and Heifetz 1985; Holburn and Forrester 1984; Sarata 1974). Finally, job satisfaction is sometimes studied because managers believe it to be the outcome of good management.

### TURNOVER

Recent reevaluation of the job satisfaction construct has shown remarkably little consistent association between measures of job satisfaction and more concrete measures of the effectiveness of organizations. Staff turnover, on the other hand, has had the benefit of being a behavioral referent that is easily observed and has clear organizational implications. *Turnover* is basically the rate at which persons in the employ of an organization leave that organization. Turnover has been widely studied among organizations in general (Price 1977) and, more specifically, among residential environments for persons with mental retardation (Ganju 1979; Lakin and Bruininks 1981; Zaharia and Baumeister 1978b). Ongoing study of turnover is important because it is hypothesized to have many negative effects on organizational effectiveness in community services including the discontinuity of treatment and care; withdrawal of important relationships from the lives of dependent people; low productivity and staff shortages; consumption of administrative and financial resources in the personnel replacement process; increased formalization in the rules of staff conduct; lower participation of staff in primary group relationships; increased job stress; and reduced job satisfaction of staff (Bersani and Heifetz 1985; Lakin 1988; Price 1977; Zaharia and Baumeister 1978a).

## A National Study of Community Direct Care Staff

In 1979 the Center for Residential and Community Services at the University of Minnesota undertook a large national prospective study of job satisfaction and job turnover within a national sample of approximately 1,000 direct care staff members from a total of 263 public and private residential facilities (Lakin and Bruininks 1981). This chapter will focus on the findings from the 161 private residential facilities in the study. This study was one of the earliest efforts in the area of residential services to use multivariate and longitudinal approaches in the study of turnover. In this study job satisfaction was both an outcome variable in its own right and a predictor variable for job leaving. This study gathered (1) retrospective data on staff turnover in the previous year; (2) data on all terminating staff during a one-month period; and (3) one-year follow-up data in which self-reported demographic, job satisfaction, and other data were used to predict voluntary job leaving.

### METHODS

The 161 private facilities in this study were drawn from a stratified national random sample based on size and region of 4,427 private, non–foster care facilities identified in the 1977 National Census of Residential Facilities. These facilities were defined as any licensed non–government-operated living quarter(s) providing 24-hour, 7-days-a-week responsibility for room, board, and supervision of persons with mental retardation (Hauber et al. 1981).

In study 1 administrators in 161 community facilities retrospectively reported their facility's 1978 crude separation rate (i.e., the number of employees who left during the year divided by the total number of positions $\times$ 100). Predictor variables used in descriptive and multiple-regression analyses included: facility size, starting pay, per diem costs, facility location, facility type, staffing ratios, year of opening, area unemployment rate, and percent of residents with severe/profound mental retardation.

In study 2 administrators of 104 community facilities recorded basic demographics, work history, job performance, and reason for leaving for each staff member terminating during a 30-day period in early 1979. The median and mean length of service by facility type, size, employee factors, and geographic location was determined. Those who left were described in terms of education, age at the time of initial employment, size of the facility, and facility location. The reported reasons for separation and supervisor evaluations of separating were also examined.

In study 3, a random sample of residents was selected from each facility. For each resident the administrator provided the name of the staff member who was responsible for daily care or supervision of the resident. In all, 316 paid employees and 33 owner-operators were interviewed. These staff provided detailed information on the sampled residents' characteristics; on the services provided; on their own personal background, training, and reasons for accepting their current position; and on their satisfaction with their job, using the Minnesota Satisfaction Questionnaire-Short Form (MSQ-SF; Weiss et al. 1967). Of the interviewees 224 were followed up one year later, including 174 people who had completed the MSQ-SF. The one-year follow-up data included the current job status and, for those who left, why they left and their subsequent type of employment. Both $\chi^2$ and discriminant function analysis were used to discriminate between stayers and leavers on a range of factors including age, sex, education, special training, length of service, facility location, personal geographic stability, shift versus live-in staff, reason for accepting the job, major work frustrations, resident characteristics, and reported job satisfaction (people leaving for uncontrollable reasons such as pregnancy and transfer of spouse were excluded).

RESULTS

Job Satisfaction

The MSQ-SF is a self-report instrument containing 20 components of general job satisfaction. It yields three separate aggregated scores: general job satisfaction, intrinsic job satisfaction, and extrinsic job satisfaction, with intrinsic and extrinsic scales derived from factor analyses of responses of thousands of workers. Short-term test-retest reliability of these scales is reasonably high, ranging from .80 to .90 (Weiss et al. 1966) whereas reported two-year test-retest reliability is more volatile, ranging from .58 for general satisfaction to .52 for extrinsic satisfaction (Anderson and Weiss 1971). A factor analysis of MSQ-SF responses suggested that the intrinsic and extrinsic scales, previously described, were applicable to the direct care role (Hauber and Bruininks 1986).

Table 17.1 shows the mean MSQ-SF satisfaction scores on a scale of 1 (*not at all satisfied*) to 5 (*extremely satisfied*) for 174 community staff members. Means ranged from 2.79 on satisfaction with job advancement to 4.44 on satisfaction with social service. A statistically significant association was found between age and extrinsic job satisfaction. However, the ratio of residents to direct care staff, years of education, and length of employment were unrelated to intrinsic, extrinsic, or general job satisfaction. Four aspects of job satisfaction (see Table 17.1) predicted those still on the job a year later. These will be discussed later.

Turnover

Turnover was examined in several different ways. In study 1, the mean annual turnover rate reported retrospectively by administrators was 54.2%, and the median turnover rate was 40.4% (see Table 17.2). Study 1 also examined variables associated with the reported turnover rates for private facilities serving 64 or fewer residents. Contextual variables including the proportion of residents with severe/profound mental retardation, urban versus rural location, and county unemployment rate were unrelated to turnover.

Organizational variables including the ratio of residents to staff, year of opening, number of staff, cost of care, and raw starting salary were also not related to turnover. At the same time three organizational variables were associated with turnover, including starting salary indexed to county per capita income ($r = .27$, $p < .02$), ratio of direct care staff to administrative staff ($r = .21$, $p < .04$), and the ratio of residents to administrative staff ($r = .23$, $p < .03$). A multiple-regression analysis of the variables in study 1 showed that the indexed starting salary and the number of staff employed accounted for a statistically significant 9% of the variability in turnover.

In study 2, the adjusted annual turnover rate based on a one-month recording of all separations was 80.3% for all facility sizes (see Table 17.2). The rates were almost twice as high for facilities of six or fewer residents as for facilities with seven or more residents. Among the 33 owner-operators, only 6% were not providing care after one year. An examination of the cumulative percent of staff leaving showed that 17% of staff left after two or fewer months of employment, 51% left within 12 months, and 74% left within 24 months. Exit interviews recorded the expressed reasons for separation of 213 direct care employees leaving private residential facilities over a one-month period. Table 17.3 summarizes those reasons separately for men and women. Half of all separations relate to reported efforts to improve employment, especially through a better job or a job with higher pay. Women were quite likely (24%) to express family-related reasons for leaving (e.g., schedules that interfered with family life and pregnancy). Discharges were likely among men (19 of 52 separations, or 37%).

In study 3, a number of contextual, organizational, and employee variables measured during the data collection for study 1 were examined to determine if they predicted actual job staying or leaving for individual employees of private facilities over a one-year follow-up period. One contextual variable, adaptive behavior of the residents, did not predict whether staff members would stay or leave. Another contextual variable, size of the town, did significantly predict turnover, with staff stability more common in rural areas ($p = .02$). The selected organizational variables (live-in versus shift staff and quality of the treatment environment) did not predict subsequent turnover. Of the employee variables other than job satisfaction, gender and race were not significantly related to voluntary turnover. Employee variables that were related to increased turnover included more formal education ($\chi^2 = 45.54$, $p < .0001$), younger age ($\chi^2 = 47.52$, $p < .0001$), shorter length of service ($\chi^2 = 127.69$, $p < .0001$), younger age at hiring ($\chi^2 = 10.41$, $p < .015$), more specialized training before being hired ($\chi^2 = 24.53$, $p < .0001$), and taking the job for professional reasons rather than for economic or interest

**Table 17.1.  Mean Scores on the Minnesota Job Satisfaction Questionnaire Items and Their Relationship to Turnover Rates**

| Areas of Job Satisfaction | Mean[a] | S.D. | Signifi-cance[b] | I/E[c] |
|---|---|---|---|---|
| 1. Activity; being able to keep busy all of the time | 4.05 | 0.96 | N.S. | I |
| 2. Independence; the chance to work alone on the job | 3.63 | 1.14 | N.S. | I |
| 3. Variety; the chance to do different things from time to time | 3.90 | 1.07 | N.S. | I |
| 4. Social status; the chance to be "some-body" in the community | 3.44 | 1.03 | N.S. | I |
| 5. Supervision-human relations; the way my supervisor handles his or her workers | 3.51 | 1.28 | N.S. | E |
| 6. Supervision-technical; the competence of my supervisor in making decisions | 3.62 | 1.20 | N.S. | E |
| 7. Moral values; being able to do things that do not go against my conscience | 3.90 | 0.97 | N.S. | I |
| 8. Security; the way my job provides for steady employment | 4.05 | 0.93 | N.S. | I |
| 9. Social service; the chance to do things for other people | 4.44 | 0.78 | N.S. | I |
| 10. Authority; the chance to tell people what to do | 3.26 | 1.00 | N.S. | I |
| 11. Ability utilization; the chance to do something that makes use of my abilities | 3.99 | 1.05 | N.S. | I |
| 12. Company policies and practices; the way the facilities' policies are put into practice | 3.00 | 1.24 | .005 | E |
| 13. Compensation; my pay and the amount of work I do | 2.80 | 1.30 | .017 | E |
| 14. Advancement; the chances for ad-vancement on this job | 2.79 | 1.24 | .005 | E |
| 15. Responsibility; the freedom to use my own judgment | 3.74 | 1.02 | N.S. | I |
| 16. Creativity; the chance to try my own methods of doing the job | 3.81 | 1.05 | N.S. | I |
| 17. Working conditions[d]; the working conditions | 3.47 | 1.14 | N.S. | |
| 18. Co-workers[d]; the way my co-workers get along with each other | 3.57 | 1.14 | N.S. | |
| 19. Recognition; the praise I get for doing a good job | 3.21 | 1.24 | N.S. | E |

**Table 17.1.** *Continued*

| Areas of Job Satisfaction | Mean[a] | S.D. | Signifi-cance[b] | I/E[c] |
|---|---|---|---|---|
| 20. Achievement; the feeling of accomplishment I get from the job | 3.97 | 1.11 | .047 | I |
| Intrinsic satisfaction | 46.17 | 8.23 | .033 | |
| Extrinsic satisfaction | 18.93 | 5.96 | N.S. | |
| General satisfaction | 67.40 | 12.80 | N.S. | |

*Source:* Parts of this table appeared previously in Hauber and Bruininks (1986) and are reprinted here with permission.

[a]On a scale of 1 to 5 with 5 indicating extremely satisfied and 1 indicating not at all satisfied.

[b]N.S. (not significant) is noted when $p > .05$ for correlation to turnover rate.

[c]I means this item relates to intrinsic satisfaction; E means this item relates to extrinsic satisfaction.

[d]Item 17 (working conditions) and item 18 (co-workers) were not part of either the intrinsic or extrinsic subscales.

**Table 17.2.** **Annual Turnover Rates for Private Facilities**

| Size | Study 1: Rates of Crude Turnover Reported | | Study 2: Estimated Turnover Based on 1 Month | |
|---|---|---|---|---|
| | No. of Facilities | Mean % | No. of Facilities | Mean % |
| 1–6 | 21 | 86.7 | 29 | 147.7 |
| 7–16 | 25 | 45.4 | 35 | 132.0 |
| 17–64 | 24 | 46.2 | 30 | 60.4 |
| 65+ | 31 | 45.5 | 32 | 77.4 |
| Total 1–65+ | 101 | 54.2 | 126 | 80.3 |
| Owner-operated | 33 | 6.0[a] | | |

*Source:* Portions of this table appeared previously in Lakin et al. (1982) and are reproduced here with permission.

[a]Represents owner-operators who closed during the year.

Table 17.3. Reasons for Separation of Direct Care Employees
in Nonpublic Settings

| Reason | Female (N = 161) | Male (N = 52) | Total (N = 213) |
|---|---|---|---|
| | | % | |
| Quit for better job, higher pay, job related | 48.4 | 51.9 | 49.3 |
| Family-related | 24.2 | 5.7 | 19.7 |
| Fired, discharged | 9.9 | 36.5 | 16.4 |
| Illness, death | 5.6 | 1.9 | 4.7 |
| Further education | 3.7 | 1.9 | 3.3 |
| Leave of absence | 1.9 | 0 | 1.4 |
| Retirement | 0.6 | 1.9 | 0.9 |
| Layoff, position closed, temporary position | 1.2 | 0 | 0.9 |
| Other | 2.5 | 0 | 1.9 |
| No reason given | 2.5 | 1.9 | 2.3 |

Source: Lakin et al. (1982).

reasons ($\chi^2 = 12.16$, $p < .002$). A discriminant analysis of the variables in study 3 indicated that younger care providers, fewer years lived in the county, shorter length of employment, more favorable treatment environments, shift work status, family members living in the home, receiving special training before taking the job, and accepting the job for professional advancement predicted a statistically significant 22% of the variability in individual job leaving.

Relationship between Job Satisfaction and Turnover

The relationship between job satisfaction and staff separations was explored by using responses to the MSQ-SF. The three items with the lowest average satisfaction, (1) chances for advancement, (2) compensation, and (3) organizational policies and practices, were most predictive of staff separations (see Table 17.1). Higher satisfaction with achievement (a feeling of accomplishment from one's work) was significantly associated with staying. Discriminant analysis showed that job satisfaction ratings predicted a statistically significant 9% of turnover during the year.

DISCUSSION OF FINDINGS

Staff stability was relatively low among the community facilities in this study, and the factors that best predicted staff turnover (e.g., relatively low wages and relatively few opportunities for advancement) were those that are most difficult to improve in a decentralized and inadequately funded system.

On the whole, direct care staff were found to be as satisfied with their jobs as persons doing similar work. Workers who left their jobs usually did so when jobs with better compensation or advancement opportunities became available. Supervisor ratings indicated that excellent performers (28% of leavers) were as likely to leave as poor performers (24% of leavers) so job leaving did not constitute a purge of ineffective employees.

Although findings on the basic predictors of job stability were congruent with research in other areas, other outcomes raised important questions. If most aspects of reported job satisfaction are unrelated to job tenure, are they related to any outcomes of importance? For example, are satisfied employees more productive? The metaanalysis of Iaffaldano and Muchinsky (1985) raised doubts about the strength of that relationship. A *Fortune* article (Kiechel 1989) was entitled and considered How important is morale [job satisfaction], really? In it scholars discussed the general lack of relationship between job satisfaction and productivity, saying "the effects of job satisfaction on productivity are indirect rather than direct. . . . [S]pecific things . . . increase productivity, and separate things . . . improve satisfaction . . . [and] today what experts look for among employees, and what they find in high performing outfits, is commitment to the organization and its goals" (Kiechel 1989, 122). To increasing numbers of experts organizational commitment rather than satisfaction is the important outcome to examine.

Our research experience made us aware of how little we had learned about the quality of the organizations in which people worked. Understanding job satisfaction and ultimately job tenure requires additional information on the attitudes, expectations, experiences, work milieu, organizational integration, and sense of shared purpose of the staff. To borrow a term from Robert Kahn (1974), it seems important to study direct care work as a *humanized* role including (1) fulfillment of the instrumental purpose of having a job (e.g., making a living, providing social status); (2) avoidance of negative emotions (e.g., boredom, uselessness); (3) provision of a sense of interest and accomplishment; (4) use of skills and abilities and development of new ones; (5) recognition of skills and abilities; (6) enhancement of other important roles (e.g., wife, parent, community member); (7) membership in an organization and activities that are gratifying; and (8) allowing one to be a respected, valuable and well-integrated member in an organization. In the research disseminated since we undertook our study we have found useful examples of data collection on virtually all aspects of a humanized work role but few examples of efforts to incorporate all of these into a comprehensive framework.

## The Evolving Literature on Community Services Personnel

Over the recent past, the literature on personnel providing community services to persons with mental retardation has grown considerably in size and diversity. Eighteen recent studies of job satisfaction and job turnover among residential services personnel included 203 distinct predictor variables, 68 outcome variables, and 22 separate instruments to assess characteristics, attitudes, and satisfactions of staff. The predictor variables identified in these studies included both manipulable and nonmanipulable variables. Three categories of nonmanipulable predictor variables included client variables such as age, level of mental retardation, and functional limitations; setting/locational descriptors such as cost of care, local economic conditions, and facility size; and employee variables such as age, previous experience, and recruitment source. Two more manipulable categories of predictor variables included employer variables such as administrative structure, compensation, and training provided; and job characteristics such as job content, manager behavior, and organizational climate. The outcome variables identified in these 18 studies included employee outcomes such as burnout, quality of staff work life, and stress; resident outcomes related to the quality of life such as desire for control over residents, quality of the treatment environment, and staff-resident affiliation; satisfaction outcomes such as intrinsic or extrinsic satisfaction, satisfaction with pay, and overall satisfaction; and finally, turnover and withdrawal indices such as the crude separation rate, adjusted tenure, and retention rate.

Table 17.4 summarizes information on nine studies involving institutional direct care personnel, four involving both community and institutional residential services personnel, and five involving community residential services direct care personnel which specifically measured satisfaction and/or turnover as outcome variables. Table 17.4 is representative but not exhaustive. Studies that exclusively examined employee outcomes or quality of life variables were not listed, nor were the many unpublished studies of turnover and job satisfaction carried out by individual agencies over this period. Table 17.4 notes the setting of the research, the number of settings examined, the number of staff involved, the categories of predictor variables examined, and the outcome variables addressed for each study.

Several important characteristics of personnel studies in residential settings can be identified from the information on Table 17.4. Earlier studies tended to examine institutional settings whereas the later studies focused on community settings or on a combination of settings. Studies that included both community settings and institutions involved more staff and more facil-

ities than either of the other two types. Several studies looked at more than
one outcome variable (e.g., job satisfaction and job turnover) and reported
on the relationships between those variables. Studies in community settings
typically examined a more comprehensive range of outcome variables. A
higher proportion of the studies done in the community or combined settings
included comprehensive sets of predictor variables than studies done in institutional settings, but few studies included even one variable from each of
the different categories of predictor and outcome variables which research
suggests should be studied. The most troublesome characteristic of these
studies is a lack of integration in conceptualization and instrumentation
among them which makes it difficult to argue that much closure has been
obtained except in the areas of compensation, recognition, and accomplishment, each of which is associated with overall satisfaction and stability and
in the broader literature, performance.

### REVIEW OF RECENT JOB SATISFACTION LITERATURE

Thirteen studies, eight in community settings and five in institutional
settings, attempted to identify variables associated with 20 different aspects
of staff satisfaction. A total of 119 different potential correlates of staff satisfaction was examined: 96 in one study, 11 in two studies, and only 12 in 3 or
more studies. At least one statistically significant association was found in at
least one study for 96 variables. Of the 23 variables included in at least two
studies, 10 were found to have mixed or no association with job satisfaction
in the majority of studies examining them. There were 13 variables for
which a majority of studies found statistically significant associations in the
same direction. Those variables, the number of studies reporting results, and
the range of significant correlation coefficients were: staff age (five studies; $r$
$= .19-.47$); feedback on performance (five; $r = .18-.46$); autonomy (four;
$r = .31-.59$); skill variety (four; $r = .21-.67$); task identity (three; $r =$
$.24-.43$); task significance (three; $r = .23-.50$); staff-occupant affiliation
(three; $r = .12-.32$); manager consideration shown toward staff (two; $r =$
$.20-.67$); staff control in decision making (two; $r = .30-.55$); clarity of
instructions (two; $r = .40-.44$); rewards for staff (two; $r = .30$); level of
manager initiation of structure (two; $r = .19-.36$); and staff tenure, to be
examined separately. In sum, only 20% of the variables hypothesized to be
related to job satisfaction were examined in more than one study, and statistically significant associations were seldom established in more than one
study.

The most commonly stated reason for studying staff satisfaction was
that it has not been adequately (i.e., often) studied in community settings.

**Table 17.4. Predictor and Outcome Variables Studied in the Reports Reviewed**

| Study (Date) | Setting[a] | No. of Settings | No. of Staff | CV | SL | EEV | ERV | JC | Empl. | Qual. | Sat. | Turn. |
|---|---|---|---|---|---|---|---|---|---|---|---|---|
| | | | | Predictor Variables[b] | | | | | | Outcome Variables[c] | | |
| Cope et al. (1987) | 1 | 1 | 288 | | | × | | × | | × | | × |
| Ganju (1979) | 1 | 11 | | × | × | × | × | × | | | × | × |
| Holburn and Forrester (1984) | 1 | 1 | 154 | | | | × | × | | | × | |
| MacEachron, Zober, and Fein (1985) | 1 | 1 | 149 | × | × | × | × | × | × | | × | |
| Sarata (1974) | 1 | 3 | 222 | × | | × | × | × | | | × | |
| Schiers, Giffort, and Furtcamp (1980) | 1 | 1 | 161 | | | × | | | | | | × |
| Weinburg, Edwards, and Garove (1983) | 1 | 14 | 704 | | | × | × | × | × | | × | |
| Zaharia and Baumeister (1979b) | 1 | 12 | | | × | | × | | | | | × |
| Zaharia and Baumeister (1979a) | 1 | 3 | 357 | × | | × | × | × | | | × | |

| Study | Settings[a] | | | Predictor variables[b] | | | | | Outcome variables[c] | | | |
|---|---|---|---|---|---|---|---|---|---|---|---|---|
| | | | | CV | SL | EEV | ERV | JC | Empl. | Qual. | Sat. | Turn. |
| Hauber and Bruininks (1986) | B | 236 | 852 | X | | X | X | X | | X | | |
| Lakin and Bruininks (1981) | B | 236 | 1,716 | X | X | X | X | X | | X | X | X |
| Silver, Lubin, and Silverman (1984) | B | 14 | 128 | X | X | X | | X | X | X | X | X |
| State of Minnesota (1989) | B | 235 | | X | | X | X | X | | X | | X |
| Bersani and Heifetz (1985) | C | 22 | 39 | X | X | X | X | X | X | X | X | |
| George and Baumeister (1981) | C | 47 | 58 | X | X | X | X | X | | X | | X |
| Jacobson and Ackerman (1989a) | C | 38 | 114 | X | X | X | X | X | X | X | X | X |
| Jacobson and Ackerman (1989b) | C | 38 | 269 | X | X | X | X | X | X | X | X | |
| Ursprung (1986) | C | 113 | | X | X | X | X | X | X | X | X | |

[a] Settings: I, institution; B, both community and institution; C, community.

[b] Predictor variables: CV, client variables; SL, setting or locational descriptors; EEV, employee variables; ERV, employer variables; JC, job characteristics.

[c] Outcome variables: Empl., employee outcomes; Qual., quality of life for residents; Sat., satisfaction; Turn., turnover or withdrawal.

Certainly the relationship between job satisfaction and quality of care re-mains largely an assumed one. But the utility of the job satisfaction literature and the entire construct for that matter remain unclear. Although the re-search base reviewed here was relatively small (13), it was comprehensive enough to challenge future investigators to justify more clearly the impor-tance of studying job satisfaction and to identify specific characteristics of job satisfaction which are most important. A primary issue is whether staff satisfaction should be treated as an independent variable predicting some more relevant outcome (e.g., residents' quality of life), as a potential medi-ating variable influencing the relationship between relevant independent and dependent variables, or as a dependent variable. If the reason for studying satisfaction is to better predict desired outcomes, such as community partici-pation of residents, relevant measures of these must be included in designs. If job satisfaction is being studied as a dependent variable, designs that ma-nipulate conditions to test their utility in producing changes in satisfaction are needed. It is especially important to conduct intervention studies that in-volve manipulation of employer and job characteristics variables. Inter-ventions aimed at increasing the quality of life of residents (i.e., organiza-tional job performance) may be the most useful context for studying staff satisfaction.

## REVIEW OF THE TURNOVER LITERATURE

Four studies in community settings and four studies in institutional set-tings examined 73 different variables to identify correlates of staff turnover (job quitting) or tenure (length of job staying). Of the 63 variables found to be related to turnover only the 14 examined in more than one study are con-sidered here. In some cases studies reported findings for more than one type of facility. This summary lists each report as a separate finding. Variables showing statistically significant findings in a single direction in two or more reports included staff salary (five reports, four found higher turnover for staff with lower starting salaries); resident adaptive behavior (five reports, three found higher turnover for lower adaptive behavior); staff to resident ratio (five reports, three found less favorable staff to resident ratios associ-ated with higher turnover); size of the surrounding community (five reports, two found lower turnover in smaller communities); years agency has been open (five reports, two found higher turnover in agencies open for a shorter time); unemployment rate in the local area (five reports, two found that higher unemployment was associated with lower turnover); age of staff member (four reports, all found lower turnover among older staff); staff length of service (three reports, all found higher turnover among staff with shorter length of service); resident IQ (four reports, two found more turn-over for higher IQ); and finally number of residents (three reports, two found more turnover in smaller facilities). Two variables examined in more than one study had a single significant finding, one had significant findings in two directions, and no significant findings were reported for one.

Many promising variables have been included in only one study. For example, a study of staff retention in institutions (Schiers, Giffort, and Furt-kamp 1980) found a relationship between recruitment source and staff reten-tion; staff who were rehired or who were recruited by current employees were most likely to have longer tenure. Such a study suggests a potentially important variable that ought to be examined and verified in other personnel studies. Unfortunately, only 14 of 63 variables reported to be associated with turnover in one study were included in another. Clearly, further re-search must strive to replicate findings and to integrate consistent findings into future research designs.

Suggested strategies to address turnover problems include consideration of hiring practices; orientation, training, and inservice strategies; and man-agement and compensation strategies. In terms of hiring practices it has been suggested that management should maximize their use of people who promise stability such as older, less formally educated people who are long-term area residents (Lakin 1988). In the area of orientation, training, and inservice strategies it has been suggested that management should provide improved training and support strategies during the initial employment pe-riod; a graduated entry process whereby a new staff are initially exposed to less demanding residents; and personnel preparation and orientation pro-grams at the direct service level (Baumeister and Zaharia 1987; Ganju 1979; George and Baumeister 1981; Lakin 1988; Lakin et al. 1982; Zaharia and Baumeister 1978b). Finally, changes put forward in management practices and compensation strategies include suggestions to communicate that staff are valuable and valued; ensure that positions are well designed and ade-quately supported; conduct exit interviews to determine problems; maximize direct financial compensation; use supplementary means of compensation such as travel to workshops; improve career advancement opportunities; in-stitute promotion, recognition, and other practices that help maintain staff within their current work groups; and target improved supervision and sup-port to less tenured staff (Baumeister and Zaharia 1987; Ganju 1979; George and Baumeister 1981; Jacobson and Ackerman 1989a; Lakin 1988; Lakin and Bruininks 1981).

Turnover is frequently mentioned as one of the most serious problems for residential providers. To use research findings to reduce turnover and its negative consequences on individuals and organizations it will be necessary to improve the isolation of variables associated with turnover and to develop demonstration efforts that assess the ability to integrate their findings into personnel practices and to test their effects on employee outcomes.

### THE LITERATURE ON JOB SATISFACTION AND TURNOVER

This review of the relationship between job satisfaction and employee stability is based on four community-based and three institution-based studies. One examined the relationship between turnover and job satisfaction, and the others looked at the relationship between tenure and job satisfaction. Within those studies, 23 of 35 associations were found to be statistically insignificant. Of the 11 types of satisfaction studied 8 were found to be unrelated to turnover at least half of the time. Mixed associations with staff stability (i.e., low turnover or high tenure) were noted for three aspects of job satisfaction (overall satisfaction, extrinsic satisfaction, and work-related satisfaction). Of the seven reports of association between overall job satisfaction and staff stability three found no relationship, two found a negative relationship, and two found a positive relationship. Of the five reports of association between extrinsic satisfaction and staff stability two found no relationship, two found a positive association, and one found a negative association. Of the four reports of association between work-related satisfaction and staff stability two found no relationship, one reported a positive relationship, and one reported a negative relationship. These findings, although summarized very briefly here, demonstrate the inconclusive nature of the information about the relationship between job satisfaction and staff stability. The most consistent finding was that there is no relationship between aspects of job satisfaction and staff stability.

### METHODOLOGIC CHARACTERISTICS OF THE LITERATURE

The sheer number of variables identified in one or more studies as being associated with aspects of job satisfaction or job stability make application of research findings difficult. Clearly, multivariate statistical designs are needed to reduce information and to identify shared variance in the factors associated with satisfaction and stability. This review also raised questions of whether job satisfaction and turnover are the most important dependent variables in personnel research. Consumer quality of life as measured by community participation, relationships, and satisfaction; quality of the residential environment as measured by autonomy, privacy of space, choice making, opportunity for personal development; and staff job performance may profitably be selected as key outcome variables in future research on personnel issues. Quality of life outcomes have rarely been examined with staff satisfaction or staff turnover. Yet the broader personnel literature is beginning to suggest that the purpose and productivity of organizations and the extent to which individual workers are committed and integrated into them are important features in their morale (Mobley et al. 1979). The exploration of such possibilities requires approaches that integrate data on resident quality of life, organizational effectiveness, and personnel productivity. These approaches must also begin to move away from the current near total reliance on correlational and descriptive studies to increased use of prospective designs. Studies that manipulate variables identified as associated with desired outcomes to determine if successful interventions can be designed and implemented and at what cost must also be a growing aspect of personnel research.

## Implications of the Literature

Recommendations based on this review fall into three categories: recommendations for service providers, for future research, and for policymakers. Service providers should seek an appreciation of how, where, and if aspects of staff satisfaction or staff turnover are associated with resident quality of life, the quality of work life for staff, and effectiveness in their organizations. They should attend particularly to factors that appear to affect staff morale, staff stability, and staff effectiveness. Increasing staff compensation and opportunities for advancement are examples of such factors. Concerted efforts of many providers may be the most effective approaches for effecting administrative and political action. In the critical area of staff recognition there is much that can be done. Organizational assessment of staff satisfaction and turnover should be used to assess the need for intervention, to identify organizational intervention strategies and goals, and to monitor the results of interventions. Finally, organizations should be particularly attentive to the growing perception in the human resources field that membership in effective, productive, high-quality organizations, with which one shares a sense of mission and accomplishment, is satisfying, morale boosting, and promotes stability. This growing perception directs attention to an improved quality of life for residents and to increased staff appreciation of those improvements.

Researchers need to increase conceptual clarity regarding why job satisfaction is being studied, including consolidating and categorizing independent variables. One of the more promising areas for future research is job characteristics, including job content, job context, managerial behavior, organizational culture, and organizational climate. The vast majority of variables which were found to be significantly associated with job satisfaction fell into these manipulable categories. There is also a great need for experimental research in this area. One particular need is the assessment of benefits from targeted recruitment of personnel. The effects of job orientation, training, and ongoing supports also need study. No personnel study is complete without considering the impact of personnel actions on the quality of life for persons receiving services; that is, personnel research should be sensitive to the outcomes that these employees are hired to produce.

Policy and decision makers must attend to the need to increase compensation to staff in community-based settings. Compensation is one of the few areas in which studies consistently find relationships with turnover. Policymakers should seek ways to enhance opportunities for career advancement of community personnel. Policymakers should also support the expanded research agenda recommended above. Sorting through the myriad of variables identified in previous research will require large sample sizes sufficient for the use of multivariate approaches. People in the position to do so should ensure that publicly funded research on community-based services remains sensitive to benefits for the service recipients by stressing the use of dependent variables that include effects upon these individuals. Policymakers must recognize this topic of research as critically important. Personnel expenditures make up the bulk the costs of community services, and personnel performance ultimately determines the benefits derived from those expenditures. The type and amount of research funded should reflect the importance of personnel performance.

## Acknowledgments

Preparation of this manuscript was supported through a subcontract from the Center on Human Policy, Research and Training Center on Community Integration, Syracuse University. The Research and Training Center on Community Integration is funded through Cooperative Agreement H133B00003-90 awarded by the National Institute on Disability and Rehabilitation Research (NIDRR), Division of Special Education and Rehabilitative Services, U.S. Department of Education to the Center on Human Policy, Syracuse University. The opinions expressed herein do not necessarily represent those of the U.S. Department of Education, and no endorsement should be inferred.

# 18

# Human Resource, Program, and Client Correlates of Mental Health Outcomes

David L. Shern, Ph.D., Mary E. Evans, Ph.D., and Bonita M. Veysey, M.S.

According to the National Association of State Mental Health Program Directors personnel expenditures represent the largest single component of public mental health budgets, accounting for more than 75% of total expenditures in 1985 (NASMHPD 1987a). In addition, caregivers are the primary point of contact between consumers and the service system. Changes in service approaches will be principally brought about by them. To the degree to which caregiver characteristics affect their behavior and, ultimately, the outcomes experienced by consumers, managers can develop strategies to impact work force composition and indirectly consumer and system outcomes. Information on the characteristics and behaviors of employees would therefore seem central to the management of public mental health systems.

A recent report by Sherman and David (1989), however, indicated that 28% of states do not routinely collect significant portions of the minimum work force data elements recommended by the National Institute of Mental Health (NIMH) (Leginski et al. 1989). Only 32% of state mental health authorities routinely collect these human resource data on all members of the public mental health work force, including both hospital and community providers. Our experience indicates that states may not collect or use HR data because of the lack of demonstrated relationships between caregiver characteristics and system or client outcomes (See, for example, Luborsky et al. 1986). Additionally, the complexity of the arena in which mental health policy is formed and executed makes it unlikely that simple descriptions of the work force will be valued if they are not integrated with other variables that also may affect system functioning. A challenge of mental health services research is to embed human resource data within this complex context. Thereby, the relationships between the characteristics of caregivers and the outcomes experienced by consumers can be understood in light of other relevant system characteristics such as consumer mix, reimbursement strategies, and services organization.

Part of the problem of integrating human resource data into services research relates to the lack of a general model for how these data may be included. In this chapter we will present a heuristic model that integrates human resource data with other important mental health services domains. After introducing the model, we will provide some examples of research on each of the content domain. Finally, we will use survey data on clients served in New York's residential program to operationalize the model and investigate the relationships between human resource variables and client outcomes in the context of other important influences.

## A Heuristic Model for Integrating Human Resource Data

The heuristic model presented in Figure 18.1 displays the major domains that we believe should be included in mental health services research to promote a comprehensive understanding of consumer outcomes. The model is intended to provide a framework for describing the relationships among variables which are required to understand the interactions of consumers and caregivers. The model may also serve as an aid to management by suggesting points at which interventions may be implemented profitably

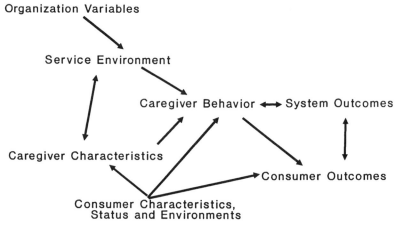

Figure 18.1. A heuristic model for research in mental health services.

to influence outcomes. The arrows portray a set of testable hypotheses for research although other relationships are conceivable.

AN OVERVIEW OF THE MODEL

Consumer outcomes are displayed as the most endogenous variables in the model, influenced either directly or indirectly by variables from all of the other domains. In contrast, work force characteristics are shown as one of the most exogenous variables. No direct relationship between the characteristics of caregivers and consumer outcomes is hypothesized. Instead, caregiver characteristics are hypothesized to influence caregiver behaviors in the service environment directly. These behaviors, in turn, are hypothesized to influence the outcomes experienced by consumers directly.

Caregiver characteristics may be conceived as those factors that are relatively fixed (e.g., gender, ethnicity, and age) and those that are more variable and subject to environmental influence (e.g., motivation, attitudes toward consumers, knowledge, skills and abilities). These latter factors are influenced by the qualities and characteristics of the people being served and the environment in which the services are delivered. The service environment, in turn, is influenced by organizational variables such as reimbursement mechanisms. Characteristics of caregivers, the service environment, and consumers are depicted as influencing caregiver behavior which, in its turn, affects both system and consumer outcomes. System outcomes are focused on the efficiency with which the system operates, as in the number of persons served or the costs per unit of service. Consumer outcomes are focused on the effectiveness of system interventions, for example, improved quality of life and increased community tenure. The remainder of this section examines each domain in the model and cites illustrative research that has examined these variables.

Caregiver Characteristics

Caregiver characteristics include relatively enduring factors such as demographic characteristics and professional training as well as characteristics that may be more amenable to change (e.g., attitudes, values, and beliefs regarding consumers, the services they need, and the likely outcomes of providing services to them). They also include caregiver beliefs about their role in the treatment or rehabilitative process, and their perceived efficacy in bringing about changes in the service environment or in the organization. These attitudes, opinions, and beliefs may be amenable to change as a result of inservice training, preceptorship experiences, and other interventions.

Other caregiver characteristics, such as commitment to the work environment, burnout, time and attendance performance, and supervisory ratings of effectiveness, may also be relevant.

Of these caregiver variables, burnout has been studied intensively in mental health services settings. It has been defined as a syndrome of emotional exhaustion, depersonalization, and a reduced sense of personal accomplishment (Maslach and Jackson 1984). Research evidence has indicated that environmental factors, particularly characteristics of the work (service) setting, are more strongly related to burnout than are personal factors (Leiter and Maslach 1986). Examples of these environmental factors have included the percentage of time spent in direct care duties (Maslach and Jackson 1982), a low degree of peer support (Jackson, Schwab, and Schuler 1986), and interactions with co-workers (Leiter and Maslach 1988).

The Melick, Johnson, and Duffee (1981) study of psychiatric aides employed in inpatient settings sought to predict successful performance (tenure and supervisory ratings of performance) using a variety of measures of job satisfaction, attitudes toward consumers and the organization, and demographic characteristics. Successful performance was associated with gender and age (with older females being rated as more effective), hopeful and optimistic attitudes toward consumers, a satisfactory relationship with supervisors, and the caregiver's sense of self-efficacy. In addition to service environment characteristics, caregiver characteristics are influenced by consumer characteristics (Cutler 1986; Meadow 1981; Pines and Maslach 1978).

Consumer Characteristics

Consumer characteristics include variables such as demographics and clinical and functional status as well as salient characteristics of the consumers' environment. Clinical status refers to symptomatology, treatment history, and behavioral manifestations of the disorder. *Functioning* encompasses the person's ability to adapt to the environment, specifically the possession and expression of skills. In addition, the person's service, support, and residential needs are included in this domain, as is information about personal service preferences and vocational and personal goals. These variables have been the most extensively studied of those represented in the model.

Classifying consumers on the basis of their characteristics and functioning has been used for needs assessment purposes (Gudeman and Shore 1984); to identify inpatients appropriate for community placement (Becker and Banks 1986); to develop staffing standards, particularly for inpatient settings (Surles 1989); and to identify facilities, programs, or services required by various consumer groups (Cutler 1986). Finally, consumer characteristics, often in conjunction with individual outcome data, have been used to validate and evaluate program models (Wherley and Bisgaard 1987).

Organizational Variables

These variables include factors related to the structure and management of the service system as well as to the characteristics of the organization itself. This domain thus includes the profit/nonprofit status, statutory base, the reimbursement system under which the system operates, and the related performance incentives governing the organization's behavior. The roles of the organization in the human service system, including cooperative agreements, referral patterns, affiliation agreements, and the degree of specialization in the service environment (Morrissey, Hall, and Lindsey 1981), are also organizational characteristics. Organizational variables are hypothesized to impact directly on the service environment and indirectly on caregiver behavior.

Recent attempts at system reform embodied in the Robert Wood Johnson nine-cities projects (Aiken, Somers, and Shore 1986) reflect the belief that establishing a single administrative authority for mental health services and enhanced coordination of benefits will improve consumer outcomes. Changes in the reimbursement systems such as diagnosis-related groups (DRGs) are considered organizational variables that have been shown to shorten the length of stay in both medical and psychiatric settings.

Service Environment

The service environment includes both objective and subjective phenomena. Generally it relates to the program model that is being employed in a treatment setting as well as the management strategies used to implement the model. For purposes of system change strategies the variables of particular interest are those that can be influenced by management decisions, such as performance management systems, differing approaches to work scheduling, and specific training interventions. In a residential treatment environment a complete assessment of the service environment would include an evaluation of the unit or residence atmosphere (see Moos 1972; Moos and Otto 1972) from the perspective of the setting's major participants. The service environment is the cultural setting in which service is provided. For consumers residing in residential treatment settings the service environment becomes their most proximal living environment and, therefore, may become synonymous with the living environment included in the consumer characteristics domain (see also Paul 1986). Cournos (1987) suggested that in most studies environmental factors were better predictors of consumer outcomes than were consumer variables, especially low levels of expressed emotion and the presence of supportive and satisfying relationships in conjunction with moderate expectations for personal functioning.

Focusing on an inpatient environment, Ellsworth and co-workers (1979) conducted an exceptionally large study ($N = 21,667$) of the characteristics of Veterans Administration psychiatric treatment programs associated with positive consumer outcomes (community adjustment). They examined both treatment characteristics (those under the control of the mental health team, e.g., ward environment) and setting characteristics (those not under the team's control, e.g., consumer characteristics and assignment to ward). They found that the setting characteristics related to positive individual outcomes were the lack of a separate television room, having a higher percentage of never-married consumers, and having a mixture of persons with acute and chronic disorders on the ward. In further analyses of these data (Collins et al. 1984) the treatment characteristics most predictive of positive consumer outcomes were staff who perceived less order and organization on the ward, fewer shift rotations, a lower percentage of socially passive consumers, a higher percentage of persons with neurotic disorders but who were on no antipsychotic medication at discharge, and lower dosages of minor tranquilizers.

Much less is known about the relationship between the nature of congregate care settings and positive individual outcomes. Kruzich and Kruzich (1985), for example, found that moderate levels of skills programming and intermediate measures of social distance were both associated with improved individual integration into residential facilities. Additionally, Bond and co-workers (1989) compared outcomes for two groups of demographically matched consumers: one group assigned to lodging in an eight-bed crisis house, and the other to shelter purchased in hotels and boarding houses. Equal proportions in both groups, two thirds, avoided rehospitalization during the four-month follow-up period, but more persons in the purchased shelter condition showed substance abuse problems.

### Caregiver Behavior

These variables are related to specific work behaviors of caregivers including the content of service contacts, the frequency and duration of contacts, and whether the service is provided directly to the consumer (e.g., counseling) or is an indirect activity (e.g., advocacy, support to collaterals, linkages). In the national standard data set proposed by NIMH (Leginski et al. 1989) caregiver behaviors are captured in the "event" recording data that characterize the service contact. In these data "Who receives what from whom at what cost" (p. 50) is recorded as a chronicle of consumer/caregiver interactions. Caregiver behavior is hypothesized to be the most proximal variable affecting individual outcomes.

A study by Luborsky and colleagues (1986) of the factors associated with therapist success indicated that differences among therapists in relationship and technique factors (e.g., the purity of the technique) were partly responsible for differences in effectiveness. Relatively little seems to be known about the caregiver behavior associated with superior consumer outcomes in community residential settings (for exceptions, see Cournos 1987).

### System Outcomes

The most endogenous variables in this model are system and consumer outcomes, the foci of treatment outcome studies. System outcomes are changes in the care delivery system or the impact on the system resulting directly from caregiver behavior and indirectly from other system inputs. These outcomes, including numbers of persons receiving services, cost per unit of service, and waiting time before services are given, represent the efficiency with which the system operates. Caregiver behavior has direct effects on these outcomes whereas system and consumer outcomes are highly interrelated and affect each other. Perhaps the most commonly documented system outcomes involve the reduced use of inpatient environments attendant upon receipt of case management services (Bond et al. 1985; Setze and Bond 1985). Similarly, reduced lengths of stay have been associated with the use of prospective payment systems both in medical and psychiatric care (Pincus, West, and Goldman 1985; Taube et al. 1988).

Many treatment programs are designed primarily to result in particular system outcomes, for example, serving a larger number of persons, decreasing the costs of care, lowering the census in inpatient settings, and increasing the number of consumers linked to services. Other interventions have been designed to decrease the average length of inpatient stay, thus creating bed capacity in the system. On occasion, these system outcomes have been viewed as ends in themselves without regard to their impact on consumers. For example, deinstitutionalization was once considered a desirable outcome without regard for ensuring that resources were available to support the quality of the consumer's life in the community.

### Consumer Outcomes

Consumer outcomes are the changes experienced by individuals which can be attributed, at least in part, to purposeful interventions. Such outcomes include quality of life, symptomatology, functioning, community tenure, satisfaction with services, self-esteem, and the degree to which needs are met. Consumer outcomes are hypothesized to be influenced directly by caregiver behavior and by consumers' characteristics, statuses, and environment. They are related reciprocally to system outcomes (see Braun et al. 1981). Positive consumer outcomes, we believe, are the primary purpose of mental health system interventions and represent the effectiveness of interventions. As such, they ought to be measured as part of summative program evaluation efforts.

In the following section we will illustrate the use of the heuristic model to examine outcomes experienced by consumers served in New York State's community residential program.

## New York State's Community Residence Program

As in many other states, New York is currently in the process of reconceptualizing its provision of residential services (Shern, Surles, and Waizer 1989). The change involves moving from a system of relatively rigid residential alternatives in which consumers are "placed" in residences to one in which the modes of service provision and residential support emphasize consumer preferences in selecting residential settings and provision of variable levels of supportive and rehabilitative services consistent with consumers' needs and goals (see Carling and Ridgway 1989).

As in other states, New York's traditional residential programs involve an array of residential alternatives that were intended to be transitional. Three major types of residences comprise the system, with each felt to be appropriate for persons with specific characteristics and related needs. These program types, persons appropriate for each, and service models incorporated within each residential program are summarized below.

The *supervised community residence* program is designed to receive persons directly from institutional care as well as from the community and to assist them in receiving necessary community support services. Caregivers provide supervision 24 hours a day in congregate settings typically ranging from 6 to 24 persons. Individuals entering this level should possess basic skills, and caregivers provide close supervision. Instruction and assistance are generally necessary to accomplish tasks of daily living. The primary goal at this level is to improve competence in basic skills and behavioral self-control.

The *intensive supportive community residence* program provides daily visits but does not require overnight supervision. Generally, these are apartment programs with one or two persons living together in each unit. Instruction and assistance are necessary only occasionally to accomplish tasks. Individuals entering this level of residential services should be able to function effectively in the majority of daily living activities. Most caregiver activities are directed toward reinforcing skills and community-appropriate behavior.

The *supportive community residence* is the least restrictive program level. People living in these apartments receive one to three visits per week. At this level the individual is able to function independently in most situations. Caregiver activities are oriented primarily toward support and reviewing a person's need for assistance. There were 6,453 certified community residence beds in 1989; 2,766 in supervised, 2,169 in intensive supportive, and 1,518 supportive community residences (Bureau of Residential Services 1989).

Client Characteristics and Needs Survey (CCNS)

The data analyzed in this paper are derived from the Client Characteristics and Needs Survey, which has been administered annually since 1981 in all New York State Office of Mental Health certified or operated community residences, crisis residences, and residential care centers for adults. Each agency is requested to select a seven-day period during a particular month to complete surveys on all people living in their residential programs who have at least a seven-day length of stay, including consumers on temporary leave. Surveys are completed by on-site residential staff who are familiar with the consumer and have seen the consumer within the three days prior to survey administration.

The survey summarizes consumers' demographic characteristics, clinical history, and psychosocial functioning as well as their service and residential needs. The clinical history includes psychiatric diagnosis, other disabilities, psychiatric hospitalization history, and community residence information, including referral source, length of stay, and sources of income. Psychosocial status encompasses three domains: symptomatology exhibited in the 30 days prior to the survey, maladaptive behavior displayed in the last 30 days, and typical functional abilities. The severity of symptomatology is assessed using the 16-item Brief Psychiatric Rating Scale (Overall and Gorham 1962). Fifteen items are assessed under *maladaptive behaviors* including dangerous behavior toward self and others, substance abuse, and behaviors considered inappropriate within community contexts such as *exhibits bizarre behavior in public settings*. Seven additional items document whether the resident has a history of dangerous or life-threatening behavior. Generally, residential staff report the severity of the problem using a four-point scale ranging from *no problem* through *severe problem*. Forty-three items measuring the consumers' personal care, home care, interpersonal skills, and other skills necessary to maintain oneself independently in the community are assessed. These items comprise the functioning measure. For the behaviorally descriptive items, raters judge the degree to which the consumer can complete each activity independently. In the section on program and residential needs respondents judge the need for outpatient services, whether those services were received, environmental or consumer barriers to receiving the required services, appropriateness of the current residential setting, and social supports in the community.

The most recent CCNS, administered in February 1989, surveyed 410 community residences, representing 115 agencies statewide. Data were collected on 5,481 persons: 2,685 in 210 supervised community residences, 1,838 in 115 intensive supportive community residences, and 1,318 in 85 supportive community residences (representing 101.7% of the estimated occupied beds based on an average occupancy rate of 88.5%; Bureau of Residential Services 1989). The response rate of greater than 100% is a result of the collection of information on persons who were hospitalized at the time of the survey but not discharged from the program and new admissions during the survey period.

The Human Resources Survey (HRS) was administered concurrently with the CCNS. Agencies participating in the CCNS were requested to complete the HRS on all staff members working on-site in residential programs during February 1989. Personnel offices completed questions on job title, professional discipline, years of education, job status (full-time, part-time), and years of experience. Demographics were provided by affirmative action officers within each agency after all other items were completed. To ensure confidentiality, no identifying information was gathered. Items in this survey are based on the NIMH minimum data set (Leginski et al. 1989). HRS data were collected on 234 programs in 95 agencies. Information was gathered on 3,153 clinical, direct care, and administrative staff working in community residence programs. Fifty-seven percent of the programs returned the survey.

Operationalizing the Heuristic Model

The HRS and the CCNS provide in-depth, case-specific information on caregivers and consumers, and to some degree, program and agency characteristics. Much information critical to the exposition of the full model is not currently available. Four domains of the model may be operationalized with existing information: service environment, caregiver characteristics, consumer characteristics, and consumer outcomes.

The service environment is operationalized as the residential setting with three levels: supervised, intensive supportive and supportive. Caregiver characteristics are summarized as demographics (sex, age, race, and education level) and status (years of inpatient experience, outpatient experience, and degree level). Consumer characteristics are subdivided into two subcomponents including the set of demographic variables employed for caregivers as well as diagnosis and numbers of hospitalizations, services needed, and social supports.

Three outcome measures are employed in the analysis: functioning, symptomatology, and behavior problems. Current symptomatology and behavior problems were measured by computing the mean of all items in the respective subsections. Symptomatology summarizes the 16 items from the Brief Psychiatric Rating Scale, and behavior problems summarizes the 15 maladaptive behavior items. Functioning level was measured by calculating the mean of 10 factor analytically estimated scores derived from the 44 functioning items.

Two sets of scores in each outcome domain were calculated, one each from the 1987 and the 1989 surveys. The scores were then standardized: the higher the score, the greater the attribute, that is, higher scores in symptomatology and behavior problems indicate a greater pathology whereas higher scores in functioning indicate a greater ability to perform community activities. The final outcome measures are expressed as residual gain scores in which the consumers' 1989 score was regressed on their 1987 value. The resulting standardized residuals represent the change in each outcome area controlling for the 1987 score.

Whereas the service environment variable is measured at the program level all other variables were aggregated to the program unit level for analysis. All data are averages of the individual human resources or consumer data for each program. Scattered site apartment programs were combined within the program that operates them. The final data set includes 209 program settings.

Representativeness of Sample

Because of the moderate HRS return rate selected characteristics of persons living in programs that responded to the HRS were contrasted with those not represented to determine the representativeness of the sample. Minor but statistically significant differences were obtained between the people living in programs represented in the HRS sample and those in programs not represented. There was a greater proportion of non-Caucasian residents in programs without human resources data, and these residents were also older and required fewer services than the sample with human re-sources data. Although there are minor differences between the HRS sample and the remaining programs, we do not feel that generalizability is severely compromised.

Consumer outcomes at the program level are based on the residualized change in functioning, behavior, and symptomatology between two admin-istrations of the CCNS (1987–89). Since this outcome measure requires that persons be present in both the 1987 and 1989 surveys, individuals whose length of stay was less than 16 months were excluded from the analysis. A comparison of people admitted in 1987 and represented in the 1989 survey, with people admitted in 1987 and discharged before 1989 indicates that those discharged were more symptomatic, exhibited more behavior prob-lems, were younger, and were less likely to be diagnosed as having a schizo-phrenic disorder. Results must be interpreted carefully as the persons who remained in the residential programs differ significantly in a number of areas from all admissions.

RESULTS

The model proposes that consumer outcomes are most influenced by consumer characteristics, status, and environment, and by caregiver behav-ior. Caregiver demographics and statuses are hypothesized to have indirect effects on consumer outcomes through the intervening effects of caregiver behavior. Since we have no data on caregiver behaviors in this study, care-giver characteristics will be used as proxy.

Multiple-regression analysis was conducted using service environment, caregiver demographics and statuses, and consumer characteristics and status variables to predict outcomes. Separate equations were run for each of the three outcome variables and are reported in both stepwise and direct entry fashion in Table 18.1. Columns 1–3 under each outcome measure present the model using a stepwise procedure whereas columns 4 and 5 de-scribe the full model when all variables are entered simultaneously. Dis-played under the stepwise procedures are the $R^2$ statistics after each set of variables is added (column 1), the change $R^2$ between the baseline and each subsequent model (column 2), and the significance of the difference in $R^2$ (column 3). Standardized regression coefficients were computed for the model components (column 4) and the significance of each beta (column 5) for the direct entry procedure.

The program type was dummy-coded (supportive community residence was the omitted category) and entered first as the most exogenous variable in the stepwise procedure, followed by caregiver demographics, care-

**Table 18.1.  Multiple-regression Analysis of Three Outcome Measures**

| | Outcome | | | | | | | | | | | | | | |
|---|---|---|---|---|---|---|---|---|---|---|---|---|---|---|---|
| | Symptomatology | | | | | Functioning | | | | | Behavior Problem | | | | |
| | Stepwise | | | Direct Entry | | Stepwise | | | Direct Entry | | Stepwise | | | Direct Entry | |
| Model Component | R² Diff. | R²[a] | Sig. | Beta[b] | Sig. | R² Diff. | R² | Sig. | Beta | Sig. | R² Diff. | R² | Sig. | Beta | Sig. |
| Program characteristics | .047 | | .01 | .129 | N.S.[c] | .148 | | .001 | .123 | N.S. | .043 | | .05 | .102 | N.S. |
| Caregiver demographics | .063 | .016 | N.S. | .112 | N.S. | .201 | .053 | .01 | .214 | N.S. | .048 | .005 | N.S. | .080 | N.S. |
| Caregiver status | .072 | .009 | N.S. | .129 | N.S. | .215 | .014 | N.S. | .125 | N.S. | .055 | .007 | N.S. | .120 | N.S. |
| Consumer demographics | .078 | .006 | N.S. | .152 | N.S. | .233 | .018 | N.S. | .092 | N.S. | .069 | .012 | N.S. | .206 | N.S. |
| Consumer status | .201 | .123 | N.S. | .452 | .000 | .314 | .081 | .001 | .382 | .000 | .154 | .085 | .001 | .410 | .001 |

[a] F-test of difference (Diff.) in R² was used to test the significance (Sig.) of each model component entered sequentially.

[b] Sheaf coefficients were computed for sets of variables representing the standardized regression coefficient for each model component.

[c] N.S., not significant.

giver statuses, consumer demographics, consumer statuses. The results reveal that residential level is significantly related to all outcome measures. Further, after controlling for program characteristics, caregiver demographics are predictive of the functioning but not the symptomatology of behavior problems. Consumer status is the strongest predictor of all outcomes, accounting for 8–12% of the variance in the measures.

Comparison of the stepwise procedure and the direct entry model reveals that much of the variance accounted for by program characteristics is shared with consumer status. Upon closer inspection, two variables (number of services needed and number of social supports) are the strongest predictors across all outcome measures (a complete regression model is available on request). These two variables are inversely related and indicate that as the number of needed services increases and the number of social supports decreases, psychosocial status declines. Keeping in mind that the unit of analysis is the program, it would appear that programs with the lowest average consumer need for services and the highest average number of social supports per consumer experience greater average gains across consumer outcome measures. Other single variables are significantly related to outcomes. Higher functioning is related to greater proportions of non-Caucasian caregivers and higher percentages of professional staff. Fewer behavior problems than expected are associated with programs having older consumers.

The New York State community residence program is based on a linear model, in which consumers with the most deficits and the fewest resources live within the most structured environments. As skills improve, consumers are expected to move to less restrictive settings. Significant differences in caregiver characteristics, consumer characteristics, and consumer outcomes might exist within the three types of programs. Table 18.2 shows that of the seven caregiver characteristics only two significant differences were noted. Education varied across program type, with caregivers in supported programs having the highest educational levels whereas those in supervised programs had the lowest. This seems reasonable given the need for 24-hour a day coverage in the latter. The percentage of professional staff showed the same distribution, with a higher proportion of professional staff in supported programs and the lowest proportion in supervised programs.

Differences in consumer characteristics and statuses across program levels should occur as a result of the transitional nature of the programs, with individuals who are demonstrating improvement in functional skills being encouraged to move to less restrictive settings. The analysis supported this hypothesis, with 9 of 12 program level comparisons reaching conventional levels of statistical significance (see Table 18.2). Specifically, people living in supported programs were more highly educated, more likely to be female, and demonstrated a lower level of symptomatology, higher functioning, and fewer behavior problems than consumers in more restrictive settings. A lower proportion of supportive program consumers had a diagnosis of a schizophrenic disorder. They experienced fewer hospitalizations, had a larger number of social supports, and required fewer outpatient services than people living in other program types. All three consumer outcome variables differed significantly across program types, with people living in supported programs showing the greatest improvement over time in symptomatology, level of functioning, and behavior.

Our descriptive analysis also includes an examination of the correlations among consumer and caregiver characteristics (a full correlation matrix is available on request). Selected sets of variables are of theoretical interest. A comparison of caregiver demographics and consumer demographics reveals a strong positive correlation among age ($r = .23$), years of education ($r = .31$), percent male ($r = .32$), and percent Caucasian ($r = .77$).

We have noted significant relationships among program types and consumer outcomes. The correlational analysis of consumer outcomes with consumer demographics and status as well as caregiver demographics and status lends some support to this, particularly to the salience of the relationships between consumer status and consumer outcomes. The strongest relationships with outcome in symptomatology were number of services needed ($r = .37$) and number of hospitalizations ($r = .12$). Outcome in functioning is significantly related to caregiver characteristics, including education ($r = .16$), percent male ($r = .15$), and percent professional staff ($r = .21$). Changes in level of functioning are also related to consumer characteristics including age ($r = -.19$), education ($r = .27$), percent diagnosed with schizophrenia ($r = -.17$), number of hospitalizations ($r = -.19$), number of social supports ($r = .37$), and number of outpatient services needed ($r = -.32$). The maladaptive behavior outcome is correlated with consumer education ($r = -.17$), number of social supports ($r = -.19$), and number of services needed ($r = .28$).

### DISCUSSION

Before discussing the implications of these results, it is important to reiterate some of the limitations of the study. First, as a result of the centrality of consumer outcomes in assessing the importance of staff, program, and consumer characteristics, it was necessary to restrict these analyses to individuals who have resided in the programs for more than one year. Longer-stay persons differ from shorter-stay persons in that they are older, more

Table 18.2. Program Level Caregiver and Consumer Characteristics within Residential Categories[a]

| | Residential Categories | | | | |
| | Supervised (N = 113) | Intensive Support (N = 60) | Supportive (N = 45) | Total (N = 218) | Signifi-cance |
|---|---|---|---|---|---|
| | Caregiver Characteristics | | | | |
| Years of education | | | | | |
| Mean | 14.58 | 14.99 | 15.06 | 14.79 | .006 |
| S.D. | 0.87 | 1.06 | 1.21 | 1.02 | |
| Percent with professional job titles | | | | | |
| Mean | 4.90 | 8.58 | 11.03 | 7.18 | .032 |
| S.D. | 10.23 | 14.48 | 20.25 | 14.00 | |
| | Consumer Characteristics | | | | |
| Years of education | | | | | |
| Mean | 11.29 | 11.88 | 12.26 | 11.66 | .001 |
| S.D. | 1.13 | 1.05 | 1.04 | 1.15 | |
| Percent male | | | | | |
| Mean | 57.22 | 55.84 | 48.86 | 55.12 | .016 |
| S.D. | 15.64 | 15.96 | 19.29 | 16.78 | |
| Symptomatology | | | | | |
| Mean | 0.211 | 0.062 | −0.406 | 0.401 | .001 |
| S.D. | 0.739 | 0.616 | 0.477 | 0.698 | |
| Functioning | | | | | |
| Mean | −0.389 | 0.159 | 0.677 | −0.015 | .001 |
| S.D. | 0.563 | 0.539 | 0.384 | 0.673 | |
| Behavior problems | | | | | |
| Mean | 0.238 | −0.052 | −0.361 | 0.033 | .001 |
| S.D. | 0.691 | 0.472 | 0.348 | 0.622 | |
| Percent schizophrenia | | | | | |
| Mean | 56.62 | 51.77 | 43.17 | 52.51 | .001 |
| S.D. | 19.10 | 20.14 | 20.91 | 19.77 | |
| No. of hospitalizations | | | | | |
| Mean | 5.07 | 4.33 | 3.87 | 4.62 | .001 |
| S.D. | 1.43 | 1.13 | 1.06 | 1.37 | |
| No. of social supports | | | | | |
| Mean | 7.05 | 8.38 | 8.86 | 7.79 | .001 |
| S.D. | 1.65 | 1.43 | 1.58 | 1.75 | |
| No. of services needed | | | | | |
| Mean | 8.66 | 7.61 | 6.56 | 7.94 | .001 |
| S.D. | 1.51 | 1.64 | 2.03 | 1.85 | |

**Table 18.2.** *Continued*

| | *Residential Categories* | | | | |
|---|---|---|---|---|---|
| | *Supervised* (N = 113) | *Intensive Support* (N = 60) | *Supportive* (N = 45) | *Total* (N = 218) | *Signifi-cance* |
| | *Consumer Outcome Measures (Improvement)* | | | | |
| *Symptomatology* | | | | | |
| Mean | 0.197 | 0.134 | −0.246 | 0.085 | .007 |
| S.D. | 0.919 | 0.680 | 0.502 | 0.783 | |
| *Functioning* | | | | | |
| Mean | −0.333 | 0.014 | 0.380 | −0.084 | .001 |
| S.D. | 0.815 | 0.722 | 0.478 | 0.779 | |
| *Behavior problems* | | | | | |
| Mean | 0.222 | 0.076 | −0.199 | 0.091 | .009 |
| S.D. | 0.922 | 0.585 | 0.420 | 0.765 | |

[a] Other nonsignificant staff variables in the analysis were age (mean = 33.17), percent male (mean = 34.47), percent Caucasian (mean = 74.53), years of inpatient experience (mean = 0.99), and years of outpatient experience (mean = 3.52). Other nonsignificant consumer variables were age (mean = 35.61) and percent Caucasian (mean = 78.53).

likely to have a diagnosis of schizophrenia, and have fewer symptoms and behavior problems. Although differences between short- and long-stay clients are small, they may indicate that longer-stay consumers are slightly less troublesome than shorter-stay consumers who are not represented in the sample. Some selection bias may be present, and generalization to the total residential population may be compromised.

A second limitation involves the source of the CCNS data. These data reflect only the judgments of the residential staff and not those of consumers or their collaterals. To the degree to which caregivers' perceptions of consumers are biased and their expectations regarding the consumers' psychiatric status, needs, and opportunities are limited by this bias these results may be misleading. Collection of primary data from consumers may have produced substantially different results.

Finally, although we proposed the heuristic model as a helpful device to organize the content domains in services research and identify points for policy intervention, it is not fully implemented here. Clearly, our description of the residential environments is limited to very general characteristics and lacks measures of the more proximal residential environment that Cournos

(1987) and others have shown to affect consumer outcomes. We lack data on caregiver behavior; therefore, our ability to assess the effects of caregiver characteristics on outcome may be limited. Nonetheless, the model seems useful in organizing the field and in suggesting some interesting relationships among the model domains.

Within these constraints, the results suggest that the residential continuum model in New York has been effective in guiding consumers who differ in their psychiatric status into differing residential settings. From the caregiver perspective, consumers who are served in more restrictive and supervised settings are more impaired than individuals served in less restrictive environments. Since a transitional, continuum model has historically been used in New York and elsewhere (Shern et al. 1986) these data indicate that it has been implemented effectively.

Few differences are obtained among the caregivers who work in these differing environments, however. Probably because of the differences in staffing requirements associated with the 24-hour coverage in supervised settings and the use of more paraprofessionals to accomplish this coverage, better educated and more professionally degreed caregivers are employed in supportive programs than in programs serving more impaired individuals. Differences in training may be important since this is the only caregiver characteristic that appears to influence consumer outcome in these analyses.

The outcome analyses are complex primarily because of the nature of these survey data and the relationships among variables in the heuristic model. With the exception of the gain score outcome measures, all data in the model are cross-sectional. This substantially limits our ability to assess other causal relationships. The shared variance among domains in the model makes it impossible to attribute the common variance shared by predictors and outcomes to any of the predictors. So, although program type is clearly associated with differential outcomes in the stepwise regression solution, no significant unique component of the variance is attributable to it after all of the variables have been entered into the equation. This does not mean that program type is unimportant but simply that its shared variance with consumer and caregiver characteristics mitigates its unique influence. Selection characteristics of consumers and, to a lesser degree, caregivers confound the relationship of the program type with outcomes. It is important therefore to view each of the domains of the model individually to appreciate its association, albeit confounded, with outcomes.

Differential outcomes are associated with participation in differing levels of residential programming. In terms of the residual gain scores, consumers in the supportive settings experience more positive change in each of the three outcome areas than individuals served in the other two settings. Consumers who reside in intensive supportive environments experience outcomes that are intermediate to those of consumers in supervised or supportive settings whereas consumers in the supervised programs show the worst outcomes. Importantly, this last group of consumers showed an increase in symptomatology and maladaptive behavior and a decrease in their functional levels relative to what would be expected from their 1987 scores. Since these residual gain scores correct for the consumers' initial clinical status in 1987, these gains are independent of the selection biases operating in consumer assignment with regard to changes in symptoms, functioning, or maladaptive behavior.

If, for the moment, we neglect the confounding effects of other consumer variables that are not corrected by the residual gain score, consumers served in the supportive program experience the most positive outcomes. This program involves consumers who reside in apartments with a minimum of weekly visits from caregivers. Given the policy direction in New York State and elsewhere to develop supportive housing as an alternative to transitional housing models (Shern et al. 1989; Carling and Ridgway 1989) and given the similarity between the supportive setting and the supportive housing philosophy, these results may be quite heartening. Individuals in these inherently more normalizing environments may improve more rapidly than individuals who reside in relatively more "institutional" settings such as congregate community residences. These preliminary data, therefore, may suggest the efficacy of the supportive housing philosophy.

Although program type is associated with outcome in every area and in a quite consistent fashion, caregiver variables are generally not associated with differential outcomes. Only caregiver demographics explain a significant portion of the variance in consumer functioning. The proportion of professional staff and, relatedly, average education are positively associated with gains in consumer functioning. Years of inpatient experience are negatively correlated with gains in functioning at a modest level. Since training is significantly associated with program type, the results for these caregiver variables parallel those discussed earlier for programs. The weak effect of inpatient experience may reflect the expectations that these residential staff have regarding consumers' potential for improved functioning. The generally weak correlations, however, do not suggest that caregiver variables in these residential environments are importantly associated with consumer outcomes. This may be caused, in part, by the restricted range of caregiver characteristics in these settings and also to the types of variables available in this data set. Perhaps variables such as those discussed earlier involving burnout and work attitudes would be associated more strongly. Further research that includes a richer set of measures will be needed to identify those characteristics that may be important potentially.

Although residential environments differ consistently from one another in terms of consumer characteristics, they do not differ in caregiver characteristics. In these residential programs and within the constraints of this measurement approach, these data suggest that regardless of the severity of the consumers' problems they may expect to encounter roughly the same types of caregivers. It is conceivable that with greater variation among the staffing, outcome results would have been more substantial.

Clearly, the most powerful correlates of outcome are the characteristics of the consumers, which account for a significant additional component of the variance after covarying the program and caregiver characteristics. Gains in symptomatology, behavior, and functioning are all associated with consumer characteristics. Two variables are prominent: social support and number of services needed. The relationship between social support and mental health status is well established (Brown, Bhrolchain, and Harris 1975; Miller and Ingham 1976). Services needed may be a proxy measure for severity of disorder and is, therefore, negatively related to gains. On the other hand, it may be a measure of the consumers' dependence on formal support systems which may intensify the individual's sense of disability and contribute to poorer outcomes. Both of these variables suggest that individuals who rely more completely on the formal treatment and support system and, subsequently, less on informal sources of social support experience poorer outcomes. Since social support and needed services are both strongly related to program type, these findings may also suggest why individuals in congregate settings evidence relatively poorer outcomes than individuals in more "normal" living environments. These data are not adequate to disentangle or elucidate further the processes underlying the outcome results.

In the full model, only consumer characteristics uniquely contribute to differences in consumer outcome whereas the overall predictive models for each type of outcome account for 15–31% of the variance in outcome. Since it is arbitrary to assign components of the common variance among predictors, we must conclude that with the exception of social supports and services needed, it is the combination of consumer, caregiver, and program characteristics which accounts for differences in outcome. More research is needed to disentangle the ways in which these variables influence consumer outcomes. However, it appears that, holding initial consumer status constant, consumers will experience better outcomes when served in decentralized apartment programs by relatively more professional staff who decrease consumer reliance on formal supports and foster the development of social support networks. These tenets underlie the supported housing approach described by Carling and Ridgway (1989).

It is only by combining these constructs within one model that we can appreciate the complexity of the causal relationships. This demonstration of the model, albeit incomplete, suggests its usefulness for displaying central features of the services research problem. Perhaps embedding human resource data within this more comprehensive context will enhance their usefulness for policy development.

Finally, regarding the usefulness of human resource data with which we introduced this chapter, these findings are generally unsatisfying. At least in these residential programs, our standard set of descriptors is not related strongly to consumer outcomes. This may suggest a need to expand the coverage of human resources data to include constructs more directly related to caregiver/consumer interactions and to collect, whenever feasible, data on these interactions in terms of caregiver behavior. Perhaps with this richer data set the indirect effects of caregiver characteristics could be shown to influence consumer outcomes. Documenting these effects should suggest options for policy regarding caregiver selection and training.

# 19

# The Dynamics of Change
# in Residential Services for
# People with Developmental Disabilities

Valerie J. Bradley, M.A., and Mary Ann Allard, Ph.D.

As recently as 10 years ago most persons with developmental disabilities who required a residential placement were admitted to a publicly managed and funded facility. Although approximately 100,000 persons with mental retardation and other developmental disabilities still reside in public facilities (White et al. 1986), the number of people living in privately run community residences is well over 115,000 (Hill et al. 1985). Many of the individuals placed in private community residences over the past several years are certainly as disabled as their counterparts in public facilities (Efthimiou and Conroy 1980).

The purpose of the study described in this chapter was to respond to a significant and somewhat unfocused concern for the stability and permanence of the privately operated community residential system for persons with developmental disabilities. Clearly one of the aims of a normalized service system is to make it possible for persons with developmental disabilities to enjoy the richness of experiences available to all citizens, which may include an occasional change in residence. However, the potential stress and dislocation that the recurrent termination of a residence may create for persons with developmental disabilities—especially those with more severe disabilities—are important concerns. Anxiety about the permanence of community living arrangements among family members (Conroy and Bradley 1985) contributed an additional impetus for this study.

Another stimulus was the financial threat to residential stability. In 1985, when this study began, many agencies were suffering from inadequate public support and the effects of prolonged inflation—factors that were particularly challenging to small residential providers. Further, although there are agencies that provide substandard services and should go out of business, some providers may be in jeopardy of closing because of factors unrelated to their capacity to provide quality care.

Although the public provision of services to persons with developmental disabilities is declining nationally, there remains a public responsibility to ensure that people with disabilities experience a minimum of dislocation and insecurity in residences in the community. There is also a need to guarantee that public funds are used in the most efficient and effective manner.

## Aims of the Study

With this vision of public responsibility in mind, the focus of the study was on privately operated community residences for people with developmental disabilities. The specific objectives of the study were: (1) to document the extent of the problem of instability; (2) to identify those factors that influence the stability and instability; (3) to explore the issue in two states; and (4) to identify policies at the state and federal level likely to enhance long-term viability.

## Literature Review

In the developmental disabilities literature, several authors have pinpointed "warning" signs concerning the stability and continuity of residences for persons with disabilities. For example, Bradley (1981) cited the problems of public accountability in a private proprietary system of residential services, and Bruininks et al. (1980) stressed that only those organizations with the necessary management, programmatic, and capital resources will survive in the long term. In most analyses of the private residential system, small providers are seen as the most vulnerable to destabilizing factors such as staff turnover and inadequate reimbursement rates.

Specific data on stability generally have been lacking, and the only recent attempt to quantify this issue was done by the University of Minnesota, Center for Residential and Community Services (Hill et al. 1985). Of the 6,340 residential programs (including state institutions) originally surveyed in 1977 by center staff, 38.4% (mostly private residences) were no longer providing services to persons with developmental disabilities at the same address when the follow-up survey was conducted in 1982. Small, semiindependent residences (for one to three persons) were the least stable, and small residences generally were less stable than large residences (Hill et al. 1985).

The Minnesota study raised two other points that should be highlighted. First, even when broken down by size of residence, the rate of movement for persons with mental retardation in 1982 as a result of either formal discharges of facility closure or relocation was somewhat less than the rate of household movement for the general population for a comparable five-year period. For example, between 1977 and 1982 42.1% of all 1- to 15-person residences closed or moved whereas between 1975 and 1980 only 51.1% of U.S. households relocated. Second, even though the movement rate for persons with mental retardation reflects "normal" community standards, the researchers (Hill et al. 1985) suggested that moves that are not providing "habilitative or social opportunities" for the residents should be examined more closely.

These initial national findings on the stability of residential programs were bolstered by findings in the Pennhurst longitudinal study. Conroy and Bradley (1985) noted that approximately 40% of the residences established in 1980–81 as a result of the Pennhurst court order were no longer at the same address in 1984. The reason for residences moving or closing and the nature of the planning process that occurs during the relocation of residents and services are not addressed in either the Minnesota study or the Pennhurst longitudinal study.

The effects of relocation on persons with mental retardation have been studied, albeit in a limited fashion. Most studies have examined "transition shock" experienced by people undergoing intrainstitutional movement (Carsrud et al. 1978; Cohen et al. 1977). Only a few studies have examined this phenomenon within the community (Heller 1982). In general, the results are mixed; some individuals may experience a decline in health status or some loss of skills, but the effects do not appear to be long term. Indeed, it may be the fragile social relationships, friendships, and supports for persons with mental retardation which suffer the most when movement occurs within either an institutional or community setting (Berkson and Romer 1980). Finally, some researchers have concentrated on the transition process itself and have attempted to identify those factors, including careful planning and preparation, which diminish the possible adverse relocation effects (Heller 1982). One topic that has been addressed in the literature is the family perception of the stability of community living arrangements. Turnbull and Turnbull (1985) observed that many family members who support community living also seek assurances that the systems will be secure.

Likewise, Conroy and Bradley (1985) noted that despite the personal gains made by former Pennhurst residents who returned to the community, families remained very concerned about the permanence and security of the community living arrangements. On the other hand, Eastwood (1985) found that the families of persons deinstitutionalized from a Western Massachusetts state facility and subsequently living in the community believed that community services providers were capable and that funding was secure and permanent for living arrangements. Families of persons who had not been institutionalized, however, indicated concerns about program continuity and stable staffing. In states that have experienced some instability within their community residential systems parents blame the system for not addressing the disruption that occurs for both the individual and his or her family and for discounting an individual's personal need for stability and security (Moise 1984; Dikkers 1986). One researcher calls the movement of persons with developmental disabilities within the community system the "residential shuffle" (Evans 1983).

Finally, some of the organizational and economic reasons that directly affect the permanence of organizations serving persons with developmental disabilities have only recently been addressed in the literature (Castellani 1987). Castellani emphasized that the dramatic change in developmental disabilities organizations from small, parent advocacy groups to large, million-dollar enterprises has obvious implications for the continued viability and effectiveness of such service entities. Castellani identified several factors that are detrimental to the stability and viability of community organizations: (1) lack of clarity regarding their primary role, especially between advocacy and service delivery; (2) boards of directors which are not capable of addressing complex financial and management challenges; (3) management problems presented by the sheer number and complexity of programs that private agencies now handle; (4) unwillingness to see developmental disabilities services as an "industry;" (5) lack of training in skills necessary to manage a business (e.g., marketing, capital acquisition, fiscal management); and (6) the pressures of rapid growth and organizational development (Castellani 1987, 66–67).

The formal literature on organizational development also sheds light on the issue of stability. Schein (1980), for instance, suggests that stability within an organization results when the organization transcends its original goals (e.g., providing a needed service) and takes on larger functions such as playing a role in the community and providing an identity for employees. An agency, however, must first accomplish its primary goals (Schein 1980). The degree to which an organization can meet its own goals is a function of the degree to which it can control the environment in which it operates

(Thompson and McEwen 1958). Unclear or conflicting agency roles and uncertainty are two key constraints that face developmental disabilities providers and may affect their stability.

Given the potential link between program stability and the continuity of staff, the literature on personnel recruitment and retention also has bearing. Studies have addressed the phenomenon of staff turnover and its differential impact on facilities of various sizes (Lakin et al. 1982); the influence of career ladders and salary levels on retention (Bruininks et al. 1980); the lack of parity between the salaries of public versus private employees (Massachusetts Council of Human Services Providers 1982); and the relationship of size to turnover (Fritz 1987; Rucker, L. C., pers. com. 14 January 1987). These studies, taken together, strongly suggest the importance of competitive salary support for staff and the possible advantage that smaller residences may have in maintaining staff.

High vacancy and turnover rates in residences affect the economic stability of private providers and, if left unchecked, could lead to serious dislocations. As Castellani (1987) highlights, some state rate-setting formulas and budget-based contracts allow for the absorption of the increased labor costs associated with turnover and recruitment (e.g., retraining efforts, marketing, and advertising for positions). In general, however, Castellani portends greater threats to the financial stability of community residences as it becomes harder to pass along increased labor costs because of an overall decrease in public funding and increased use of caps and block grant mechanisms.

Finally, there is a large body of literature which addresses funding issues in residential services, specifically, recent moves in some states to retreat from "full cost of care" (Harding 1984); the importance of surplus revenues as a cushion against cash flow problems (Young 1982); the problem of capitalization among residential providers (Castellani 1987); and the complexities of state rate setting endeavors (Richardson 1981). These assessments suggest that the private residential provider in many states is walking an increasingly thin line between economic viability and fiscal precariousness.

Although the literature provides a qualitative examination of the administrative and management issues that affect residential providers, there are few systematic attempts to assess the phenomenon of stability. The study reported below provides initial qualitative and quantitative information that highlights the complexities of the problem and points to some areas for policy development and further research.

## The Study

METHODS

Before the design of the specific methodology, a number of hypotheses likely to explain or predict the phenomenon of stability were advanced. Two major areas were explored: (1) factors likely to contribute to instability (e.g., lack of adequate management expertise, inadequate rate structure) and (2) factors likely to facilitate or enhance stability (e.g., comprehensive training and technical assistance, comprehensive quality assurance mechanisms). These preliminary assumptions were used to design the survey instruments and interview guides.

Initial Survey of Residential Providers

To develop an overview of the phenomenon of residential stability around the country, we used the University of Minnesota Community Residential Services Data Base. These are the only recent data on community residences for persons with mental retardation and other developmental disabilities. Individual residence information was available for both 1977 and 1982—the two points in time at which that the university collected information from residential programs.

A sample of the 1982 residential respondents in 20 states (10 states with high rates of movement or closure and 10 states with relatively low rates) was chosen for resurvey. *Closure* or *movement* was defined as no longer providing services to persons with developmental disabilities, moved or closed. High/low rates were based on the closure or movement data from 1977 to 1982 and on information about specific state systems (e.g., the rate of deinstitutionalization, level of funding for community programs, and regional variation).

Residences within the 20 states were divided into three sizes: 1 to 6 beds, 7 to 15 beds, and 16 to 63 beds. Facilities over 63 beds, foster homes, and nursing facilities were removed because these settings were affected by influences that were significantly different from those affecting environments of small to medium-sized staffed residential facilities.

Some states were not consistently high or low across all size categories. As a result, additional criteria were used to make the final selection. The specific criteria were: (1) high or low rates across all size categories; (2) a significant or dramatic change across one size category (e.g., Massachusetts had a high close/move rate for 1- to 6-bed residences but moderately high on the other two categories); (3) geographic distribution; and (4) characteristics that may influence stability of community residences (e.g., proportion of community funding versus institutional support). The 10 states with relatively high close/move rates were: Colorado, Georgia, Illinois, Indiana, Maryland, Massachusetts, Nebraska, New Mexico, Pennsylvania, and Tennessee: the 10 low states were California, Connecticut, Louisiana, Michigan, Minnesota, New York, North Carolina, Ohio, Oregon, and Texas. Within these 20 states 600 residences were surveyed. The expectation was, as in the original study (Hill et al. 1985), that a follow-up of this sample would find roughly two thirds of the facilities unchanged and one third changed since 1982.

A total random sample of 592 residences across the three size categories was identified. The survey, which was limited to a postcard, asked several questions: (1) Was the residence currently serving persons with mental retardation or developmental disabilities? (2) Was it still providing this service at the current address (as specified on the address label)? and (3) Had there been a change in ownership or proprietorship since 1981? After three successive mailings, 572 residences were located by April 1986, and the remaining 20 were contacted by early June 1986.

### 50-State Survey

A survey was sent to all 50 state directors of mental retardation or developmental disabilities services. They were asked to provide two types of information: (1) a quantitative analysis of community residential systems, including the types of providers in the system, the number of residences that had experienced changes, the number of residences whose licenses had been suspended or revoked, the number of persons moving within the community and the reasons for such movement, salaries for direct care staff, and quality assurance and monitoring activities; (2) a qualitative description of residential services, including perceptions of stability or instability within the system, factors that contributed either to stability or instability of community residences, strategies that might enhance stability of residential programs, criteria used to evaluate the capabilities of residential providers, areas in which providers needed assistance, and issues regarding recruitment of both staff and providers.

### Case Studies

Two states were chosen for more detailed case studies: Massachusetts and California. They were chosen because (1) both state systems had been in operation for several years; (2) both states responded to the state survey by indicating an increase in residential instability; (3) the postcard survey results from the two states indicated a fair amount of change among residential respondents; and (4) project staff had some knowledge of the organizational structures in the two states.

### In-depth Provider Survey

Two in-depth surveys were designed. One was sent to providers whose residences had experienced no change since 1982 (the "unchanged" survey). The other was sent to providers whose residences had closed, moved, changed in size, changed ownership, changed the type of residents it served, or experienced any other major change since 1982 (the "changed" survey). Based on the results of the postcard survey, 592 surveys were mailed out, 440 "unchanged" and 152 "changed."

### RESULTS

### Postcard Survey

The postcard survey distinguished between providers that had changed and those that had not. Of the initial 572 residences that responded (an additional 20 were identified subsequently), 143 (25%) had changed, and 429 (75%) had not changed since the 1982 University of Minnesota survey. Table 19.1 provides an overview of the 572 residences by status and size. The table shows that residences of one to six beds experienced the most change (34.9%). This percent change among one- to six-bed residences is slightly lower than the 41.4% close/move rate found by the University of Minnesota (Hill et al. 1985) for the same size group. The residential category that experienced the least amount of change was residences in the 7- to 15-bed range (82.9% remained stable). Finally, only 22.8% of residences

Table 19.1. Relationship of Stability of a Community Residence by Size[a]

| Stability of Residence | Size | | | Total |
|---|---|---|---|---|
| | 1–6 Beds | 7–15 Beds | 16–63 Beds | |
| Change | 67 | 32 | 44 | 143 (25.0%) |
| | (34.9%) | (17.1%) | (22.8%) | |
| No change | 125 | 155 | 149 | 429 (75.0%) |
| | (65.1%) | (82.9%) | (77.2%) | |
| Total | 192 | 187 | 193 | 572 |

[a]$\chi^2(572) = 16.71; p < .001$.

Table 19.2. Organizational Changes in Community by Size of Residence

| | Size | | | |
|---|---|---|---|---|
| Type of Change | 1–6 Beds | 7–15 Beds | 16–63 Beds | Total |
| Moved | 40 | 14 | 11 | 65 (39.9%) |
| | (50.0%) | (40.0%) | (22.9%) | |
| Change in ownership | 24 | 14 | 34 | 72 (44.2%) |
| | (30.0%) | (40.0%) | (70.8%) | |
| Merged | 6 | 1 | 0 | 7 (4.3%) |
| Out of business | 10 | 6 | 3 | 19 (11.7%) |
| | (12.5%) | (17.1%) | (6.3%) | |
| Total | 80 | 35 | 48 | 163 |

with 16 to 63 beds had experienced a change since 1982. In summary, there appears to be a strong association between the size of a residence and the likelihood that it will undergo alteration.

Table 19.2 shows the type of change experienced by residences in the three size categories. Significantly, not many residences had gone out of business since 1982 (11.71%), but a substantial number either moved (39.9%) or experienced a change in ownership (44.2%)—the latter occurring most frequently among large, 16- to 63-bed residences. At the same time, at least half of the one- to six-bed residences moved during the past four years. Some residences may have been counted twice because they had moved and also experienced a change in ownership.

Initial impressions concerning changes in residences were obtained from telephone interviews. For those residences that went out of business, at least six were family care homes (residences with six or fewer people and a paid caretaker), another six were small group homes, four were 7- to 15-bed group homes, and one was an intermediate care facility for the mentally retarded (ICF/MR). Several of these providers indicated that they were leaving the field because of their age or ill health or, as one provider noted, he "did not want anything more to do with community care." Several others went bankrupt. Among those residences that moved approximately 13 residences in the 7- to 15-bed category were group homes whereas in the one- to six-bed category it was difficult to distinguish apartment programs from group homes. Several of the residences that moved were intermediate care facilities for the developmentally disabled (ICF/DDs)—the small ICF/MR program in California. Finally, in most cases changes in ownership involved the sub-

Table 19.3. Types of Service Providers ($N$ = 15,363)

| Provider Type | N | % |
|---|---|---|
| Nonprofit corporations | 7,389 | 48 |
| Individuals and families | 5,330 | 35 |
| Government: state and county programs | 1,290 | 8 |
| For-profit corporations | 1,090 | 7 |
| Religious organizations | 276 | 2 |

stitution of a new provider for an old provider. In other instances the change involved a shift from nonprofit to for-profit status and vice versa.

Survey of State Developmental Disabilities Agencies

The findings from the national survey of state developmental disabilities agencies provides a snapshot of existing community residential systems in more than two thirds of the states. Thirty-nine (78%) responded to the survey, but only 37 completed all relevant sections of the questionnaire. Among the respondents, 37 states identified a total of 18,116 operational community residences. These residences ranged from 1 to more than 100 beds. Thirty-five states provided information on the auspices of 15,363 residences. Table 19.3 shows, of this total, almost half (48%) are operated by nonprofit organizations, only 7% by for-profit corporations, and at least 35% are operated by individual partners or families.

Another variable that may be related to stability is the size of the provider agency. Twenty-seven states noted that only 207 providers operated more than ten residences whereas 4,982 providers operated only one residence. California, however, accounted for the majority of providers operating only one residence ($N$ = 3,058 or 61.4%). Finally, approximately 789 providers operated two to four residences, and another 711 operated from 5 to 10 residences. Although there are clearly many small providers around the country, there are several factors that may diminish their number in the future. First, in states such as Massachusetts, the trend is to purchase services from very large organizations. Second, even though larger providers may not be totally financially secure, smaller agencies appear to have more financial difficulties. Finally, many small agencies are also being absorbed by larger agencies (S. Smith, pers. com. July 1986).

*Closure of Residences.* Thirty-one states provided information on residential stability. Ten states reported no program closures within the last five years whereas 18 states reported a total of 530 closures. The bulk of these closures ($N$ = 450 or 84.9%) occurred in California. Similarly, nine states did not indicate any movement of residences in the community. Although 15 states estimated that a total of 223 residences moved, another 216 residences were identified as no longer serving residents with developmental disabilities. Given the estimated total number of community residences covered in the survey ($N^*$ = 18, 116), the number of residences either closing, moving, or no longer serving persons with developmental disabilities seems relatively small. Again, these data are highly speculative because most states provided only estimates, and time periods may not be comparable.

*Individual Movement.* With respect to individual resident movement or change only 16 states provided estimates. In these states 4,755 persons were released, transferred, or moved within the community system in 1985–86, including estimates from five states that could not break out the reasons for such movement. As shown in Figure 19.1, 13.6% of persons moved because either their health or behavior deteriorated; 33.5% of persons moved because they either improved behaviorally or gained new skills and therefore required a new residence; 14.1% moved as a result of organizational instability; and 13.1% moved for other reasons.

In 1987 the California Department of Developmental Services began to monitor more closely the movement of persons who were placed from state

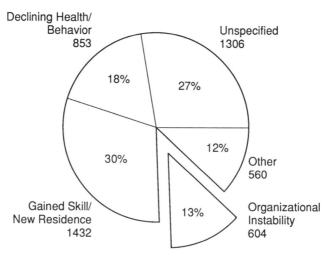

Figure 19.1. **Reasons for client movement given in a 50-state survey** ($N$ = 4,755).

developmental centers into the community. People who changed their "vendor" in the community were called *movers* and were matched with certain individual characteristics information to determine if these were correlated with movement from one residence to another. Interestingly, for 1985–86, persons in the age group 18–49 moved the most frequently—76.9% of the 2,348 persons tracked for one year moved at least once. However, there was no significant individual variable (e.g., maladaptive behaviors, developmental level, assessed rate for care) that appeared to be related to movement. The author of that study concluded that the other factors might have been responsible for individual movement, and therefore, a more rigorous study of factors related to stability of placement was merited (White 1987).

An analysis of a longitudinal data base on persons with developmental disabilities who were living in the Philadelphia area indicated that movers were slightly different from nonmovers on certain individual characteristics. Specifically, those individuals who moved more than twice in a given year were more likely to show increases in maladaptive behaviors. This finding is consistent with the 1987 California Department of Developmental Services data that also show that people who moved more than once had increased maladaptive behavior scores (White 1987). Although these changes were not great, they do raise questions about the practice of moving people to new settings to stabilize and ameliorate behavioral problems.

*Licensing and Quality Assurance.* Twenty-nine states noted that residences are reviewed annually by the licensing or regulatory agency with primary responsibility for mental retardation or developmental disabilities services. All of the respondents noted that most of the traditional licensing areas are covered in their reviews (e.g., physical plant, health and safety, food and sanitation). Very few states indicated that they had revoked or suspended any residential program licenses in fiscal year 1985 or 1986; 32 states had no suspensions, and 24 states had no revocations. Ten states noted that they had revoked fewer than 10 residential licenses whereas two states had revoked 20 and 45, respectively.

Only 23 states monitored individual outcomes, and 21 states obtained information on individual satisfaction and the quality of life. Only five states noted that they included individual rights issues in their reviews. Although 24 states said that they had a formal quality assurance process other than licensing, only 17 indicated that it was linked to a fiscal review or reimbursement process. Finally, 24 states responded that they used one or more "alternative" monitoring or quality assurance mechanisms in the community. Of this number 16 used a formal accreditation process such as the Commission on Accreditation of Rehabilitation Facilities or the Accreditation Council on Services for People with Developmental Disabilities, 12 used parents, 12 used community groups, and 12 included consumers in their quality assurance process.

*Staffing Issues.* Among the 23 states with information on direct care staff salaries in the community, 17 noted that starting pay was less than $10,500 annually, and six states indicated that staff started at more than $10,500. Salaries for direct care positions across the 23 states that responded ranged from approximately $7,000 to $14,000, a range that is not that wide given the differences in the economies of these states. Not surprisingly, 35 states indicated that community residential programs have trouble finding trained and qualified staff to fill program vacancies. Twenty-three states suggested that noncompetitive salaries, wages that were not commensurate with job responsibilities, competition with better paying industries, and other funding issues were major contributors to staffing problems. Other issues cited by the respondents may also be related to funding: 11 states could not attract qualified or skilled staff, especially specialists such as physical and other therapists; and six states suggested that it was difficult to recruit staff to work with consumers who had more intensive needs.

*Fiscal and Administrative Capabilities.* An important element in developing and maintaining qualified residential programs is evaluating the qualifications of providers. Twenty-four (62%) states noted that they have criteria by which they evaluate the fiscal and management capabilities of residential providers. Several states indicated that such criteria were more often developed at the local or regional level in which the recruitment of providers occurs. The techniques employed included fiscal audits, certification, reviews of past organizational history, accreditation, and certificate of need. Finally, 33 respondents (85%) indicated that providers could benefit from additional training in such areas as personnel management, budgeting, development, access to community resources, and quality assurance.

*State Perspectives Concerning Stability.* Ten state respondents indicated that the stability of their community residential systems was a problem. Several other states believed that their residential systems were basically stable but that certain components were in trouble or that their knowledge of stability was limited. Indicators of instability included facilities operating at a deficit, changes in ownership, facility closures, facility movement, staff turnover, staff burnout, inadequate rates and cost of living adjustments, general budget cutbacks, low salaries, inexperienced providers, lack of capacity to work with consumers with special needs, inadequate community support, rapid growth caused by deinstitutionalization plans, inappropriate person-environment fit, and too much red tape and paperwork.

The remaining 29 states cited the following factors as contributing to stable community systems: adequate and stable funding, strong state commitment and involvement or partnership with the service provider systems, a history of stable and mature providers, good case management and monitoring systems, local economic factors, involvement of legislatures, advocacy groups for developing strong community systems, commitment of area/ local/regional systems of management, training and technical assistance, and a focus on movement to small (family size) living arrangements.

*In-depth Provider Survey.* Out of 592 surveys mailed (440 unchanged and 152 changed), the total number of completed surveys received was 180, 57 changed and 123 unchanged. Among those facilities that changed the most striking finding concerned the reasons for change. Of the 49 respondents who provided reasons, 49% indicated a positive reason for facility change, including the opportunity to obtain a new home, home maintenance, and changing needs of the consumers (see Tables 19.4 and 19.5). Further, only 30% of those that changed were closed.

In 37% ($N = 20$) of the changed cases consumers stayed together in the new residence; in 35% ($N = 21$) the consumers remained in the same facility. In only 16% ($N = 9$) of the cases were consumers split up and relocated

**Table 19.4. Reasons for Change among Changed Facilities**

|                                        | N  | %  |
| -------------------------------------- | -- | -- |
| *Neutral reasons*                      | 5  | 11 |
| Family or personal problem of          |    |    |
| previous operator                      | 4  | 8  |
| Illness of operator                    | 1  | 2  |
| *Desirable reasons*                    | 24 | 48 |
| Opportunity to obtain new home         | 15 | 31 |
| Home maintenance                       | 5  | 10 |
| Changing needs of consumer             | 4  | 8  |
| *Undesirable reasons*                  | 20 | 41 |
| Inadequate funding                     | 12 | 24 |
| Licensing problem                      | 5  | 10 |
| Poor management                        | 2  | 4  |
| Problem with neighbor                  | 1  | 2  |

Table 19.5. Type of Change among Changed Facilities
($N = 57$)

| Type of Change | N | %[a] |
|---|---|---|
| Residence relocated | 23 | 40 |
| Agency ownership changed | 20 | 35 |
| Residence closed | 17 | 30 |
| Provider legal/tax status changed | 2 | 5 |
| Other types of change | 17 | 30 |

[a] The percent column indicates the percentage of respondents who indicated each type of change. Since respondents could identify more than one type of change, the column totals to more than 100%.

to another residence, or other changes occurred in the consumer living arrangements. In 74% ($N = 42$) of the cases, staff remained with the consumers; and in only 28% ($N = 16$) were staff dispersed or laid off. In 58% ($N = 33$) of the cases respondents indicated that sufficient time was available for the change whereas for 12% of the respondents ($N = 7$) the change took longer than was planned, and for 10% ($N = 6$) of respondents there was insufficient time for the change. In 53% ($N = 30$) of the cases respondents felt that the change had either no impact or a positive impact on consumers whereas 21% ($N = 12$) felt that the change caused some emotional stress for consumers.

Although it is evident that a substantial portion of the change in residences can be considered to have a positive character, some portion of the respondents indicated change of a negative character. Forty-one percent ($N = 20$) of facilities experienced change for the following reasons: inadequate funding ($N = 12$), licensing problems ($N = 5$), poor management ($N = 2$), and problems with neighbors ($N = 1$). None of the negative changes appeared to be related to the level of disability of the consumers.

Among facilities that had not undergone change but had considered one, a primary concern was inadequate funding. Many of these residential agencies had been forced to conduct their own fund raising or to draw upon agency savings to remain open. A large portion of both changed and unchanged facilities indicated that they were operating at a deficit. The data suggest that more assistance in financial planning and management is necessary for community service providers along with adequate reimbursement levels. The data also suggest that facilities undergoing serious financial turmoil receive only sporadic assistance from the relevant state authority.

It is noteworthy that both changed and unchanged facilities limited staff salaries and facility repairs in order to meet their budget. In light of this it is interesting to note that the most frequent notices of deficiencies received for both types of facilities were directed at the physical plant. Although some of these deficiencies could be a function of emphasis in the regulations, ignoring the physical plant repairs must certainly have consequences. Clearly, higher reimbursement rates for capital maintenance are needed to provide consumers with safe and wholesome living environments. According to the responses another substantial portion of change in community facilities is a result of the illness, retirement, or other change of family care providers. Although family-operated facilities may be a desirable model for community integration, it is evident that this model is subject to higher rates of instability than are facilities operated by an agency in which key persons can be more readily replaced.

Additionally, unchanged facilities, when compared with changed facilities, show a much higher percentage of agency ownership. This suggests that ownership of the property is conducive to stability and lends support to the importance of allowing some form of capitalization for providers. Some of the data on staffing point out differences between the two survey samples. A greater percentage of unchanged facilities did not consider turnover to be a serious problem and they showed an average length of employment which was 12 months longer than that found in changed facilities. Interestingly, although both samples attributed turnover to inadequate salaries, the changed facilities also listed burnout as a substantial reason for turnover. Taken together these data suggest that there was something in the working conditions of the changed facility, such as financial strain or poor management, which led to higher turnover and burnout.

CAVEATS AND CONSTRAINTS

The issues addressed in this study are complex and confounding and have not been covered in depth in previous policy analyses in the field. The findings therefore should be considered a formative rather than summative evaluation of residential stability and continuity. The resources available to conduct the study allowed for only an initial exploration of a range of important concerns. The findings should be viewed as preliminary and the recommendations as suggestive rather than conclusive; this is a policy area that clearly requires additional attention.

The data from the survey of state directors should be interpreted cautiously. In some cases respondents simply could not provide the information requested either because such information was not collected at the state level or could not be disaggregated or retrieved from a management information system. These issues reflect concerns about the utility of state management information systems during the period 1985–86 (Jacobson 1989b). With respect to the in-depth provider survey, the relatively low rate of response for changed facilities begs the question of the nature of the change among those facilities that did not respond. Had the data on these facilities been obtained it is possible that the percentage of changes which occurred for negative reasons might have been increased.

These preliminary findings suggest that the residential system for persons with developmental disabilities is a dynamic one that is continuing to change and evolve from larger, more institutional facilities to smaller, more homelike settings. This is borne out by the positive character of much of the change uncovered and its relationship to reduction in residence size. However, the study also suggests that there are some residences that have experienced serious problems, and some agencies have gone out of business or have contemplated phasing out their operations. To assist states and providers to develop mechanisms that will maximize the future coherence and stability of residences for people with developmental disabilities the following recommendations are made.

### State Planning

States need to develop a coherent vision of the residential system that will best meet their needs. This vision must be supported by a system of technical assistance to ensure that the vision is accomplished and maintained. An overall programmatic statement will eliminate uncertainty in the provider community regarding the nature of the market over time. States must also consider the needs of smaller providers, including families, to ensure that they receive the supports necessary to perform. Finally, state planning should be a collaborative activity between the state, consumers, advocates, and providers to solidify the relationship and to build trust.

### Fiscal Policy

State developmental disabilities authorities should build indicators of financial health into their routine financial audit and reporting procedures, and assistance should be provided as necessary to counteract financial weaknesses. Further, residential program funding schemes should allow providers to accumulate or borrow enough cash to cover their ongoing costs of operation. States should also consider the use of multiyear contracting practices for those agencies that meet an acceptable level of performance on a year-to-year basis. In this way agencies can gauge their level of income over time and will be in a better position to secure credit when necessary.

In devising changes to existing funding schemes which will increase provider stability, care should be taken that the schemes enhance other objectives. For instance, if the continuation of smaller, community-centered providers is a high state priority, then it may be that the reimbursement plans should be redesigned to assist these providers rather than to encourage larger corporate enterprises. This is especially important given the preliminary indications in this survey that smaller providers are less able to meet the sophisticated financial demands of many centralized state reimbursement systems. Similarly, if a state is interested in increasing nonfacility-based service alternatives, underwriting residential provider investments in facilities and equipment may not be a programmatically desirable approach to improving stability. Finally, to maximize residential stability states should explore a range of mechanisms to assist persons with developmental disabilities and their families to finance or to own their own residences.

### Organization and Management

States should develop a technical assistance and training program to assist with the implementation of long-range plans for residential development. Such assistance should include programmatic consultation as well as training in key management and leadership areas. States should also assist providers to develop their board of directors and to attract individuals with professional skills in program and financial management.

### Staffing

States should adopt sound human resource policies including providing competitive compensation for residential staff which reflects local market conditions, creative strategies to retain and promote career workers, and the inclusion of compensation in rate setting for the costs of high staff turnover (e.g., for recruitment and retraining). States should also explore nonfacility alternatives that do not rely on on-site staffing but rather use staff as supports to the person with a disability or his or her caretaker to ensure that least restrictive and appropriate alternatives are available to supervised care.

### Quality Assurance

Case managers should be the front line program monitors and should also be placed in a position that is maximally independent of service provision. Further, quality assurance mechanisms should include ongoing assessment of individual progress and well-being. Such systems should also ensure that placement and movement decisions take into account individual choices and preferences and that they maximize the stability of the individual's social network.

Quality assurance systems should be coupled with program enhancement mechanisms to assist agencies to rectify deficiencies. Finally, quality assurance systems should include multiple mechanisms including family monitoring, self-advocate monitoring, outcome assessments, and state level oversight.

### Federal Policy

Federal policy, especially within the Medicaid program, should ensure ongoing, stable, and flexible sources of funding to support individuals with developmental disabilities in a range of living environments. Federal funding should be made available to support research on the impact of individual residential movement on functioning as well as on the maintenance of social supports.

## Acknowledgments

This chapter was prepared under the Office of Human Development Services Grant 90DD0105/01, U.S. Department of Health and Human Services, Administration on Developmental Disabilities. The views expressed herein are solely those of the grantee and should not be construed as representing the opinions or policy of the Administration on Developmental Disabilities, Office of Human Development Services, Department of Health and Human Services.

# Summary

## Community Living and Community Engagement

This book is being written at a time of rapid and pervasive change in the field of mental health, as far as its focus on people with psychiatric disabilities is concerned. The individual chapters in the book, in their diversity and perspectives, bear testimony to both the exciting level of innovation in the field as well as the extent to which we are still working with programs, services, and assumptions that are rapidly becoming things of the past. In just over a decade the field has moved from a model that relied principally upon hospitals and hospitallike settings for treatment to the acceptance and proliferation of a community support system and rehabilitation approach. The field is beginning to embrace the vision of full community membership and participation for all citizens, in housing, employment, and social networks that are fully integrated. The pace of this change has accelerated, in large part, because of the growing advocacy movement of people with psychiatric disabilities themselves and their families.

As we write, the field is simultaneously evolving a new set of assumptions about people with a label of psychiatric disability and is reconsidering the kinds of services which will most effectively, and acceptably, meet their needs. As the broad level of disagreement between professionals and consumer advocates about these needs and how to meet them becomes clearer the field is attempting to identify its own role in promoting the process of successful community integration through as yet largely undefined "consumer-driven" service systems.

As this systematic rethinking occurs no one is exempt from the process, whether they are planners in public mental health departments who must

303

prepare a vision of the service system of the future, university faculty members who must prepare students with skills relevant to the future, professionals who must redesign their services so that consumers will find them relevant to their own goals, or advocates who increasingly must press for more far-reaching changes, often in society as a whole, rather than incremental change within mental health systems.

The new mandate for community integration challenges us as both a field and as individuals to move beyond assumptions that people with a psychiatric disability are hopeless or helpless (the image that brought us mental institutions as well as similar institutional facilities in the community) and even beyond seeing people as service recipients (the image that brought us community support systems, which surround people with professional services). Instead, we are coming to see people with psychiatric disabilities and their families as partners in a process of rediscovering the nature of community in America as a place in which:

—people, empowered to control and operate their own services, can come to rely first and foremost on themselves for necessary services, and then on their friends and family, and then on generic agencies that all citizens use, and only then on the formal mental health systems

—all citizens share the right to decent housing, meaningful work, and a network of social relationships.

The growing advocacy of people with these disabilities and of their families along with the increasing acceptance of this image of community integration by professionals may well be the most significant hope for the future.

Although changes in mental health policy and service delivery appear to be undergoing fairly dramatic transformation, developmental services continue to undergo more gradual evolution. However, both systems appear to share increasingly similar ideologic perspectives and to possess technologies and approaches that could be usefully transferred between the two fields. The modalities of intervention and support which are embodied in the psychiatric rehabilitation perspective stand in stark contrast, for example, with the practices of establishing specialized community residences and day service settings for persons with dual diagnoses of mental retardation and psychiatric conditions or severe behavior disorders. At the same time, certain elements of more institutional models of care which characterize some developmental services systems, such as the provision of various forms of long-term community residential services, assurance of access to comprehensive interdisciplinary professional resources, and the close coordination these resources, appear to have utility if implemented more consistently within mental health services systems.

Although, as in mental health services, policymakers in developmental services are increasingly turning to consumers as a major source of direction-setting guidance, many consumers are not able to communicate their personal priorities and preferences effectively, and behavioral indications of preference are often ambiguous. Consequently, in many instances parents and other family members represent the interests of these latter individuals in providing guidance and advisement. One important consequence of this guidance has been the legitimation of family members as direct consumers of developmental services resources through formalized family services and supports such as subsidies and voucher programs.

However, it is also apparent that when consumers of developmental services and their families are able to express clearly their priorities for social, residential, and vocational aspects of life-style, their viewpoints often differ. In sum, it seems that consumers place more emphasis on expression of autonomy than do their families, who may adopt a more protective perspective and may be more skeptical about the adequacy of the consumers' social and community living skills. Parents have come to expect, from their experience within the special education system, that services to promote skill development will be required well into adulthood, if not on a lifelong basis, as will a living situation that has some protective features. Similarly, professionals, trained to provide services, often share the assumptions that: (1) many persons, even those with comparatively mild forms of disability, will require extended or lifelong skill enhancement services; (2) considerable skills are needed for supported, assisted, or fully independent living; and (3) the goal of service provision is the closest possible emulation of a middle-class (or better) life-style. It is obvious that more able persons with developmental disabilities face considerable challenges both within their own support systems (from family members) and the formal service systems, in advocating for their own autonomy. Family members engaging in advocacy on behalf of their relatives inevitably face the realities that the demand for services exceeds supply and that aspirations for service and support can seldom be fulfilled in their entirety.

Both mental health and developmental services systems have engaged in extensive efforts to decongregate services. Because the mental health systems typically did not establish the comprehensive presence of community residences in local communities, the emerging shift from congregate institutional services to a more individualistic residential assistance model is especially dramatic. In developmental services decongregation has been exemplified by an interim stage, the community residence (which may provide extensive clinical services) although there are clear indications of desires by many consumers, advocates, and families that even more individualistic accommodations to residential support should be regarded as the only acceptable alternatives. Further decongregation of developmental services community residences to these more personal arrangements is hindered by competition for community residential resources by persons leaving institutions and by persons living with family who are seeking new residential situations.

It is evident that changes that have already taken place in mental health and developmental services systems over the past 40 years have established the presence of persons with severe chronic disabilities in communities. It is not as evident that social integration has been achieved. These are the same communities, it must be remembered, that banished many individuals with disabilities to distant institutions, that often persist in providing unnecessarily segregated educational services to persons with severe (and not so severe) disabilities, and that are organized in terms of social structures that reflect racial, cultural, and economic differences. These are communities in which the status of the typical individual tends to be appraised on the basis of personal achievement primarily and contribution to community secondarily.

These realities mean that many of the types of supports which persons with severe disabilities require to be socially integrated generally do not already exist. Structures to enhance social support systems and expertise in and understanding of chronic disability are not inherent in local communities but must be developed and then preserved. These realities point to the important roles for professionals and paraprofessionals in stimulating not only acceptance of persons with disabilities through community, consumer, and advocate education but also in defining involvement in activities that engage consumers with other members of the community as a valid therapeutic endeavor. The goal of social integration will not be achieved easily or result from advocacy at the level of administration or political activity. Rather, social integration will be achieved one person at a time, at the point of service, at the point at which supports become available, and with the gradual withdrawal of professional and specialized service involvement as together, consumers, families, and professionals collaborate to foster a supportive communal culture for consumers and those who participate with them in society.

# References

Aiken, L. H., Somers, S. A., and Shore, M. F. 1986. Private foundations in health affairs: A case study of the development of a national initiative for the chronically mentally ill. *American Psychologist* 41:1290–95.

Alford, B. A. 1986. Behavioral treatment of schizophrenic delusions: A single-case experimental analysis. *Behavior Therapy* 17:637–44.

Allness, D. J., Knoedler, W. H., and Test, M. A. 1985. The dissemination and impact of a model program in process, 1972–84. In L. I. Stein and M. A. Test (eds.), *The Training in Community Living Model: A Decade of Experience* (New Directions for Mental Health Services, No. 26). San Francisco: Jossey-Bass.

Altmeyer, B. K., Locke, B. J., Griffin, J. C., Ricketts, R. W., Williams, D. E., Mason, M., and Stark, M. T. 1987. Treatment strategies for self-injurious behavior in a large service-delivery system. *American Journal of Mental Deficiency* 91:333–40.

Anderson, L. M., and Weiss, D. J. 1971. *Stability of Measured Work Adjustment.* Minneapolis: University of Minnesota, Department of Psychology, Work Adjustment Project.

Anthony, W. A. 1977. Psychological rehabilitation: A concept in need of a method. *American Psychologist* 32:658–67.

Anthony, W. A., and Blanch, A. 1989. Research on community support services: What have we learned? *Psychosocial Rehabilitation Journal* 12:55–81.

Anthony, W. A., Cohen, M. R., and Danley, K. S. 1988. The psychiatric rehabilitation model as applied to vocational rehabilitation. In J. A. Ciardiello and M. D. Bell (eds.), *Vocational Rehabilitation of Persons with Prolonged Psychiatric Disorders,* 59–80. Baltimore: Johns Hopkins University Press.

Anthony, W. A., Cohen, M. R., and Farkas, M. 1986. Training and technical assistance in psychiatric rehabilitation. In A. Meherson and T. Fine (eds.), *Psychiatric Disability: Clinical, Legal and Administrative Dimensions,* 251–69. Washington, D.C.: American Psychiatric Association.

Anthony, W. A., and Farkas, M. D. 1989. The future of psychiatric rehabilitation. In M. D. Farkas and W. A. Anthony (eds.), *Psychiatric Rehabilitation Programs: Putting Theory into Practice,* 226–40. Baltimore: Johns Hopkins University Press.

Anthony, W. A., and Jansen, M. A. 1984. Predicting the vocational capacity of the chronically mentally ill: Research and policy implications. *American Psychologist* 39:537–48.

Anthony, W. A., and Liberman, R. P. 1986. The practice of psychiatric rehabilitation: Historical, conceptual, and research base. *Schizophrenia Bulletin* 12: 542–59.

Anthony, W. A., and Margules, A. 1974. Towards improving the efficacy of psychiatric rehabilitation: A skills training approach. *Rehabilitation Psychology* 21:101–5.

Auerbach, S. M. 1989. Stress management and coping research in the health care setting: An overview and methodological commentary. *Journal of Consulting and Clinical Psychology* 57:388–95.

Aveno, A. 1987. A survey of leisure activities engaged in by adults who are severely retarded living in different residence and community types. *Education and Training in Mental Retardation* 22:121–27.

Aviram, U., and Segal, S. P. 1973. Exclusion of the mentally ill: Reflection on an old problem in a new context. *Archives of General Psychiatry* 29:126–31.

Axelrod, S. 1987. Functional and structural analyses of behavior: Approaches leading to reduced use of punishment procedures? *Research in Developmental Disabilities* 7:165–78.

Bachrach, L. L. 1980. Model programs for chronic mental patients. *American Journal of Psychiatry* 137:1023–31.

Bachrach, L. L. 1984. The homeless mentally ill and mental health services: An analytical review of the literature. In H. R. Lamb (ed.), *The Homeless Mentally Ill,* 11–54. Washington, D.C.: American Psychiatric Association.

Baker, B. L., Seltzer, G. B., and Seltzer, M. M. 1974. *As Close as Possible: Community Residences for Retarded Adults.* Boston: Little, Brown & Co.

Banks, J. K., and Gannon, L. R. 1988. The influence of hardiness on the relationship between stressors and psychosomatic symptomatology. *American Journal of Community Psychology* 16:25–37.

Barrera, M. 1981. Social support's role in the adjustment of pregnant adolescents: Assessment issues and findings. In B. H. Gottleib (ed.), *Social Networks and Social Support in Community Mental Health,* 69–96. Beverly Hills, Calif.: Sage.

Baumeister, A. A. 1988. The new morbidity: Implications for prevention. In J. A. Stark, F. J. Menolascino, M. H. Albarelli, and V. C. Gray (eds.), *Mental Retardation and Mental Health,* 71–80. New York: Springer-Verlag.

Baumeister, A. A., and Zaharia, E. S. 1987. Withdrawal and commitment of basic-care staff in residential programs. In S. Landesman and P. Vietze (eds.), *Living Environments and Mental Retardation,* 229–67. Washington, D.C.: American Association on Mental Retardation.

Baxter, E., and Hopper, K. 1984. Troubled in the streets: The mentally disabled homeless poor. In J. A. Talbott (ed.), *The Chronic Mental Patient: Five Years Later,* 49–62. New York: Grune & Stratton.

Becker, R., and Banks, S. M. 1986. Identifying inpatients appropriate for community placement: Linking statistical and clinical approaches. *Hospital and Community Psychiatry* 37:261–64.

Bell, N. J., Schoenrock, C., and Bensberg, G. 1981. Change over time in the community: Findings of a longitudinal study. In R. H. Bruininks, C. E. Myers, B. B. Sigford, and K. C. Lakin (eds.), *Deinstitutionalization and Community*

*Adjustment of Mentally Retarded People,* 195–206. Washington, D.C.: American Association of Mental Deficiency.

Bellamy, G. T., Rhodes, L. E., and Albin, J. M. 1986. Supported employment. In W. E. Kiernan and J. A. Stark (eds.), *Pathways to Employment for Adults with Developmental Disabilities,* 129–38. Baltimore: Brookes.

Berkson, G., and Romer, D. 1980. Social ecology of supervised communal activities for mentally disabled adults. *American Journal of Mental Deficiency* 85: 219–28.

Bersani, H. A., Jr., and Heifetz, L. J. 1985. Perceived stress and satisfaction of direct-care staff members in community residences for mentally retarded adults. *American Journal of Mental Deficiency* 90: 289–95.

Beyer, H. 1983. Litigation with the mentally retarded. In J. Matson and J. Mulick (eds.), *Handbook of Mental Retardation,* 79–83. New York: Pergamon.

Biklen, D., and Knoll, J. 1987. The disabled minority. In S. Taylor, D. Biklen, and J. Knoll (eds.), *Community Integration for People with Severe Disabilities,* 3–24. New York: Teachers College Press.

Black, B. J. 1987. Reflections on the social in psychosocial. *Psychosocial Rehabilitation Journal* 10: 3–9.

Blanch, A. K., Carling, P. J., and Ridgway, P. 1988. Normal housing with specialized support: A psychiatric rehabilitation approach to living in the community. *Rehabilitation Psychology* 4: 47–55.

Bock, W. 1979. *Minnesota Developmental Programming System Behavioral Scales, Alternate Form C.* St. Paul: University of Minnesota.

Bond, G. R., Witheridge, T. F., Setze, P. J., and Dincin, J. 1985. Preventing rehospitalization of clients in a psychosocial rehabilitation program. *Hospital and Community Psychiatry* 36: 993–95.

Bond, G. R., Witheridge, T. F., Wasmer, D., Dincin, J., McRae, S. A., Mayes, J., and Ward, R. S. 1989. A comparison of two crisis housing alternatives to psychiatric hospitalization. *Hospital and Community Psychiatry* 40: 177–83.

Borkovec, T. D., Mathews, A. M., Chambers, A., Ebrahimi, E., Lytle, R., and Nelson, R. 1987. The effects of relaxation training with cognitive or nondirective therapy and the role of relaxation-induced anxiety in the treatment of generalized anxiety. *Journal of Consulting and Clinical Psychology* 55: 883–88.

Borthwick-Duffy, S. A. 1989. Quality of life: The residential environment. In W. E. Kiernan and R. L. Schalock (eds.), *Economics, Industry, and Disability: A Look Ahead,* 351–63. Baltimore: Brookes.

Boyer, C. A. 1987. Obstacles in urban housing policy for the chronically mentally ill. In D. Mechanic (ed.), *Improving Mental Health Services: What the Social Sciences Tell Us* (New Directions for Mental Health Services, No. 36), 71–79. San Francisco: Jossey-Bass.

Braddock, D. 1986a. Federal assistance for mental retardation and developmental disabilities. II. The modern era. *Mental Retardation* 24: 209–18.

Braddock, D. 1986b. From Roosevelt to Reagan: Federal spending analysis for mental retardation and developmental disabilities. *American Journal of Mental Deficiency* 90: 479–89.

Braddock, D., Hemp, R., Fujira, G., Bachelder, L., and Mitchell, D. 1989. *Public Expenditures for Mental Retardation and Developmental Disabilities in the*

*United States*, 3d ed., FY 1977–88. Chicago: University of Illinois at Chicago, Institute for the Study of Developmental Disabilities.

Bradley, V. 1981. Developmental disability services in the 80s: Maintenance of public accountability in a privately operated system. In T. C. Muzzio, J. J. Koshel, and V. J. Bradley (eds.), *Alternative Community Living Arrangements and Nonvocational Services for Developmentally Disabled Persons*, 251–57. Washington, D.C.: Urban Institute.

Braun, P., Kochansky, G., Shapiro, R., Greenberg, S., Gudeman, J., Johnson, S., and Shore, M. F. 1981. Overview: Deinstitutionalization of psychiatric patients—A critical review of outcome studies. *American Journal of Psychiatry* 138:736–49.

Brennan, P. L., Moos, R. L., and Lemke, S. 1989. Preferences of older adults and experts for policies and services in group living facilities. *Psychology and Aging* 4:48–56.

Brown, G. W., Bhrolchain, M., and Harris, T. 1975. Social class and psychiatric disturbance among women in an urban population. *Sociology* 9:225–54.

Brown, J. D., and Siegel, J. M. 1988. Attributions for negative life events and depression: The role of perceived control. *Journal of Personality and Social Psychology* 54:316–22.

Brown, S. D. 1980. Coping skills training: An evaluation of a psychoeducational program in a community mental health setting. *Journal of Community Psychology* 27:340–45.

Browner, C., Ellis, K., Ford, T., Silsby, J., Tampoya, J., and Yee, C. 1987. Stress, social support, and health of psychiatric technicians in a state facility. *Mental Retardation* 25:31–38.

Bruininks, R., Kudla, M., Wieck, C., and Hauber, F. 1980. Management problems in community residential facilities. *Mental Retardation* 18:125–30.

Bruininks, R., Meyers, C., Sigford, B., and Lakin, K. (eds.) 1981. *Deinstitutionalization and Community Adjustment of Mentally Retarded People* (Monograph 4). Washington, D.C.: American Association on Mental Deficiency.

Bruininks, R. H., Hill, B. K., Weatherman, R. F., and Woodcock, R. W. 1986. *Examiner's Manual: Inventory for Client and Agency Planning*. Allen, Tex.: Developmental Learning Materials Teaching Resources.

Bruininks, R. H., Rotegard, L. L., Lakin, K. C., and Hill, B. K. 1987. Epidemiology of mental retardation and trends in residential services in the United States. In S. Landesman and P. Vietze (eds.), *Living Environments in Mental Retardation*, 17–42. Washington, D.C.: American Association of Mental Retardation.

Bruininks, R. H., Woodcock, R. W., Weatherman, R. F., and Hill, B. K. 1984. *Scales of Independent Behavior*. Richmond, Tex.: Developmental Learning Materials Teaching Resources.

Budde, J. F., and Bachelder, J. L. 1986. Independent living: The concept, model, and methodology. *Journal of the Association for Persons with Severe Handicaps* 11:240–45.

Budson, R. D. 1978. *The Psychiatric Halfway House: A Handbook of Theory and Practice*. Pittsburgh, Penn.: University of Pittsburgh Press.

Budson, R. D. (ed.) 1981. *New Directions for Mental Health Services: Issues in Community Residential Care.* San Francisco: Jossey-Bass.

Burchard, S. N., Hasazi, J. E., Gordon, L. R., and Yoe, J. T., in press. A comparison of lifestyle and adjustment in three community residential alternatives. *Research in Developmental Disabilities.*

Burchard, S. N., Pine, J., and Gordon, L. R. 1990. Manager competence, program normalization and client satisfaction in group homes. *Education and Training in Mental Retardation* 25:277–85.

Burchard, S. N., Pine, J., Gordon, L. R., Joffe, J. M., Widrick, G. C., and Goy, E. 1987. The relationship of manager competence to program quality in small community residences. In J. A. Mulick and R. F. Antonak (eds.), *Transitions in Mental Retardation* (Northeast Region X American Association of Mental Deficiency Monograph), 2:47–69. Norwood, N.J.: Ablex.

Burchard, S. N., and Thousand, J. 1988. Staff and manager competencies. In M. P. Janicki, M. W. Krauss, and M. M. Seltzer (eds.), *Community Residences for Persons with Developmental Disabilities,* 251–66. Baltimore: Brookes.

Bureau of Residential Services. 1989. *Monthly Statistical Report: February 1989.* Albany: New York State Office of Mental Health.

Bureau of Staff Development and Training. 1987. *Direct Care Staff Competencies.* Albany: New York State Office of Mental Retardation and Developmental Disabilities.

Butler, E., and Bjaanes, A. 1977. A typology of community care facilities and differential normalization outcomes. In P. Mittler (ed.), *Research to Practice in Mental Retardation,* 1:337–47. Baltimore: University Park Press.

Campbell, D. 1969. Reforms as experiments. *American Psychologist* 24:409–29.

Campbell, M. 1981. The three-quarterway house: A step beyond the halfway house toward independent living. *Hospital and Community Psychiatry* 32:500–1.

Campbell, V. A., and Bailey, C. J. 1984. Comparison of methods for classifying community residential settings for mentally retarded individuals. *American Journal of Mental Deficiency* 89:44–49.

Caplan, G. 1974. Support systems. In G. Caplan (ed.), *Systems in Community Mental Health,* 1–40. New York: Basic Books.

Carling, P. J. 1978. Residential services in a psychosocial rehabilitation context: The Horizon House model. In P. J. Carling (ed.), *New Directions in Mental Health Care: Cooperative Apartments,* 52–64. Adelphi, Md.: National Institute of Mental Health.

Carling, P. J. 1981. Nursing homes and chronic mental patients: A second opinion. *Schizophrenia Bulletin* 7:574–79.

Carling, P. J. 1984. *Developing Family Foster Care Programs in Mental Health: A Resource Guide.* Rockville, Md.: National Institute of Mental Health.

Carling, P. J. 1987. *The Community Support Movement: Transforming Our Future* Keynote presentation at the Eighth National CSP Learning Community Conference, Burlington, Vt.

Carling, P. J. 1988. *Coming Home: Meeting the Housing Needs of People with Long-term Mental Illnesses.* Testimony presented to the Housing and Urban Affairs Sub-Committee of the Banking Committee, United States Senate, Washington, D.C.

Carling, P. J. 1989. Access to housing: Cornerstone of the American dream. *Journal of Rehabilitation* 55:6–8.

Carling, P. J. 1990. Supported housing: An evaluation agenda. *Psychosocial Rehabilitation Journal* 13:95–104.

Carling, P. J., Daniels, L., and Ridgway, P. 1985. *Meeting the Housing Needs of Persons with Psychiatric Disabilities: Comments on the State-of-the-art.* Boston, Mass.: Boston University, Center for Psychiatric Rehabilitation.

Carling, P. J., Randolph, F. L., Blanch, A. K., and Ridgway, P. 1987. *Rehabilitation Research Review: Housing and Community Integration for People with Psychiatric Disabilities* (National Rehabilitation Information Center Review). Washington, D.C.: D:ATA Institute.

Carling, P. J., and Ridgway, P. 1989. A psychiatric rehabilitation approach to housing. In M. D. Farkas and W. A. Anthony (eds.), *Psychiatric Rehabilitation Programs: Putting Theory into Practice,* 28–80. Baltimore: Johns Hopkins University Press.

Carling, P. J., and Wilson, S. F. 1988a. *Implementing a Supported Housing Approach: Final Report of a Meeting of State Mental Health Directors.* Burlington, Vt.: University of Vermont Center for Community Change Through Housing and Support.

Carling, P. J., and Wilson, S. F. 1988b. *Strategies for State Mental Health Directors in Implementing Supported Housing* (Report of the Denver Meeting on Implementation of Supported Housing). Burlington, Vt.: University of Vermont Center for Community Change Through Housing and Support.

Carpenter, M. D. 1978. Residential placement for the chronic psychiatric patient: A review and evaluation of the literature. *Schizophrenia Bulletin* 4:384–98.

Carsrud, A. L., Carsrud, K. B., Henderson, D. P., Alish, C. J., and Fowler, A. V. 1978. Effects of social and environmental change on institutionalized mentally retarded persons: The relocation syndrome reconsidered. *American Journal of Mental Deficiency* 84:266–76.

Caruso, D. R., and Hodapp, R. M. 1988. Perceptions of mental retardation and mental illness. *American Journal on Mental Retardation* 93:118–24.

Castellani, P. 1987. *The Political Economy of Developmental Disabilities.* Baltimore: Brookes.

Castellani, P. J. 1986. Symposium overview. Policy perspectives on the economics of mental retardation. The new environment of developmental services. *Mental Retardation* 24:58.

Cataldo, M. F. 1989. *The Effects of Punishment and Other Behavior-reducing Procedures on the Destructive Behaviors of Persons with Developmental Disabilities* (Background paper prepared for the National Institutes of Health Consensus Development Panel on the Treatment of Destructive Behavior). Bethesda, Md.: National Institutes of Health.

Chamberlin, J. 1978. *On Our Own: Patient-controlled Alternatives to the Mental Health System.* New York: Hawthorne Books.

Chaney, E. F., O'Leary, M. R., and Marlatt, G. A. 1978. Skill training with alcoholics. *Journal of Consulting and Clinical Psychology* 46:1092–1104.

Chaney, R., Eyman, R., and Miller, C. 1979. Comparison of respiratory mortality in the profoundly mentally retarded and in the less retarded. *Journal of Mental Deficiency Research* 23:1–7.

Chatetz, L., and Goldfinger, S. M. 1984. Residential instability in a psychiatric emergency setting. *Psychiatric Quarterly* 56:20–34.

Cherniss, C. 1981. Organizational design and the social environment in group homes for mentally retarded persons. In H. C. Haywood and J. R. Newbrough (eds.), *Living Environments for Developmentally Retarded Persons*, 103–23. Baltimore: University Park Press.

Cherniss, C., and Egnatios, E. 1978. Participation in decision-making by staff in community mental health programs. *American Journal of Community Psychology* 6:171–90.

Close, D. W., and Halpern, A. S. 1988. Transitions to supported living. In M. P. Janicki, M. W. Krauss, and M. M. Seltzer (eds.), *Community Residences for Persons with Developmental Disabilities*, 159–72. Baltimore: Brookes.

Code of Maryland Regulations 10.21.01.04, 1979.

Cohen, C. I., and Berk, L. A. 1985. Personal coping styles of schizophrenic outpatients. *Hospital and Community Psychiatry* 36:407–10.

Cohen, H., Conroy, J., Frazer, D., Snelbecker, G., and Spreat, S. 1977. Behavioral effects of interinstitutional relocation of mentally retarded persons. *American Journal of Mental Deficiency* 82:12–18.

Cohen, S., Kamarck, T., and Mermelstein, R. 1983. A global measure of perceived stress. *Journal of Health and Social Behavior* 24:385–96.

Collins, J. F., Ellsworth, R. B., Casey, N. A., Hickey, R. B., and Hyer, L. 1984. Treatment characteristics of effective psychiatric programs. *Hospital and Community Psychiatry* 35:601–5.

Cometa, M. S., Morrison, J. K., and Ziskoven, M. 1979. Halfway to where? A critique of research on psychiatric halfway houses. *Journal of Community Psychology* 7:23–27.

Compas, B. E. 1987a. Stress and life events during childhood and adolescence. *Clinical Psychology Review* 7:275–302.

Compas, B. E. 1987b. Coping with stress during childhood and adolescence. *Psychological Bulletin* 101:393–403.

Compas, B. E., Wagner, B. M., Slavin, L., and Vannatta, K. 1986. A prospective study of life events, social support, and psychological symptomatology during the transition from high school to college. *American Journal of Community Psychology* 14:241–57.

Condeluci, A., and Gretz-Lasky, S. 1987. Social role valorization: A model for community re-entry. *Journal of Head Trauma Rehabilitation* 2:49–56.

Conroy, J., and Bradley, V. 1985. *The Pennhurst Longitudinal Study: Combined Report of Five Years of Research and Analysis*. Philadelphia: Temple University Developmental Disabilities Center and Human Services Research Institute.

Conroy, J., Efthimiou, J., and Lemanowicz, J. 1982. A matched comparison of the developmental growth of institutionalized and deinstitutionalized mentally retarded clients. *American Journal of Mental Deficiency* 86:581–87.

Conte, H. R., Plutchik, R., Buckley, P., Spence, D. W., and Karasu, T. B. 1989. Outpatients view their psychiatric treatment. *Hospital and Community Psychiatry* 40:641–43.

Cope, J. G., Grossnickle, W. F., Covington, K. B., Durham, T. W., and Zaharia, E. S. 1987. Staff turnover as a function of performance in a public residential facility. *American Journal of Mental Deficiency* 92:151–54.

Coulton, C. L., Fitch, V., and Holland, T. P. 1985. A typology of social environments in community care homes. *Hospital and Community Psychiatry* 36:373–77.

Coulton, C. L., Holland, T. P., and Fitch, V. 1984. Person-environment congruence and psychiatric patient outcome in community care homes. *Administration in Mental Health* 12:71–88.

Cournos, F. 1987. The impact of environmental factors on outcome in residential programs. *Hospital and Community Psychiatry* 38:848–52.

Craig, E., and McCarver, R. 1984. Community placement and adjustment of deinstitutionalized clients: Issues and findings. In N. Ellis and N. Bray (eds.), *International Review of Research in Mental Retardation,* 12:95–122. Orlando, Fla.: Academic Press.

Craighead, W. E., Kazdin, A. E., and Mahoney, M. J. 1976. *Behavior modification: Principles, Issues, and Applications.* Boston: Houghton Mifflin.

Crnic, K. A., Friedrich, W. N., and Greenberg, M. T. 1983. Adaptation of families with mentally retarded children: A model of stress, coping, and family ecology. *American Journal of Mental Deficiency* 88:125–38.

Crnic, K. A., and Greenberg, M. T. 1985. *Parenting Daily Hassles: Relationships among Minor Stresses, Family Functioning and Child Development.* Paper presented at the biennial meeting of the Society for Research in Child Development, Toronto, Ontario, Canada.

Cronbach, L. J. 1951. Coefficient alpha and the internal structure of tests. *Psychometrika* 52:857–65.

Cutler, D. L. 1986. Community residential options for the chronically mentally ill. *Community Mental Health Journal* 22:61–73.

Cytryn, T., and Lourie, R. S. 1967. Mental retardation. In A. Freedman and H. Kaplan (eds.), *Comprehensive Textbook of Psychiatry.* Baltimore: Williams and Wilkins.

Daniels, L. V., and Carling, P. J. 1986. *Community Residential Rehabilitation Services for Psychiatrically Disabled Persons in Kitsap County.* Boston: Boston University Center for Psychiatric Rehabilitation.

Danley, K. S., and Anthony, W. A. 1987. The choose-get-keep model: Serving the severely psychiatrically disabled. *American Rehabilitation* 13:6–9, 27–29.

Davidson, P. W., and Adams, E. 1989. Indicators of impact of services on persons with developmental disabilities: Issues concerning data collection mandates in P.L. 100-146. *Mental Retardation* 27:297–304.

Davidson, P. W., Calkins, C. F., Griggs, P. A., Sulkes, S. B., Burns, C. M., Chandler, C. L., and Bennett, F. 1987. The implementation of postgraduate training programs through state and local resources. *Research in Developmental Disabilities* 8:487–98.

Deiner, E. 1984. Subjective well-being. *Psychological Bulletin* 95:542–75.

Dellario, D., and Anthony, W. 1981. On the relative effectiveness of institutional and alternative placements of the psychiatrically disabled. *Journal of Social Issues* 37:21–33.

Department of Health and Human Services. 1983. *Report to Congress on Shelter and Basic Living Needs of Chronically Mentally Ill Individuals.* Washington, D.C.: Author.

Department of Health and Human Services Steering Committee. 1980. *Toward a National Plan for the "Chronically Mentally Ill."* (Report to the Secretary by the DHHS Steering Committee on the Chronically Mentally Ill). Rockville, Md.: Public Health Service.

Dhooper, S. S., Royse, D. D., and Rihm, S. J. 1989. Adults with mental retardation in community residential settings: An exploratory study. *Adult Residential Care Journal* 3:33–51.

Dikkers, N. 1986. Letter to Lotte E. Moise, 24 September.

Dion, G., and Anthony, W. A. 1987. Research in psychiatric rehabilitation: A review of experimental and quasi-experimental studies. *Rehabilitation Counseling Bulletin* 30:177–203.

Division 33, American Psychological Association. 1989. Guidelines on effective behavioral treatment for persons with developmental disabilities. *Psychology in Mental Retardation and Developmental Disabilities* 14:3–4.

Dohrenwend, B. S., Dohrenwend, B. P., Dodson, M., and Shrout, P. E. 1984. Symptoms, hassles, social supports and life events: Problem of confounded measures. *Journal of Abnormal Psychology* 93:222–30.

Dumars, K. W., Gawron, T. W., Perce, C. L., and Foster, C. A. 1987. Prevention of developmental disabilities: A model for organizing clinical activities. *Research in Developmental Disabilities* 8:507–20.

D'Zurilla, T. J., and Goldfried, M. R. 1971. Problem solving and behavior modification. *Journal of Abnormal Psychology* 78:107–26.

Eastwood, E., and Fisher G. 1988. Skills acquisition among matched samples of institutionalized and community-based persons with mental retardation. *American Journal on Mental Retardation* 93:75–83.

Eastwood, E. A. 1985. *Community Living Study: Three Reports of Client Development, Family Impact and Cost of Services for Community-based and Institutionalized Persons with Mental Retardation.* Belchertown, Mass.: Belchertown State School.

Edgerton, R. B. 1984. *Lives in Process: Mildly Retarded Adults in a Large City* (Monograph 6). Washington, D.C.: American Association of Mental Deficiency.

Edgerton, R. B. 1988. Aging in the community: A matter of choice. *American Journal on Mental Retardation* 92:331–35.

Efthimiou, J., and Conroy, J. 1980. *Trends in Residential Service Patterns in Southeastern Pennsylvania* (Brief Report DR-4). Philadelphia: Temple University Developmental Disabilities Center.

Ellsworth, R. B., Casey, N. A., Hickey, R. H., Twemlow, S. W., Collins, J. F., Schoonover, R. A., Hyer, L., and Nesselrode, J. R. 1979. Some characteristics of effective psychiatric treatment programs. *Journal of Consulting and Clinical Psychology* 47:799–817.

Emerson, E. B. 1985. Evaluating the impact of deinstitutionalization on the lives of mentally retarded people. *American Journal of Mental Deficiency* 90:277–88.

Erickson, M., and Upshur, C. C. 1989. Caretaking burden and social support: Comparisons of mothers of infants with and without disabilities. *American Journal on Mental Retardation* 94:250–58.

Evans, D. 1983. *The Lives of Mentally Retarded People*. Boulder, Colo.: Westview Press.

Eyman, R., Chaney, R., Givens, C., Lopez, E., and Lee, C. 1986. Medical conditions underlying increasing mortality of institutionalized persons with mental retardation. *Mental Retardation* 24:301–6.

Eyman, R., Grossman, H., Tarjan, G., and Miller, C. 1987. *Life Expectancy and Mental Retardation: A Longitudinal Study in a State Residential Facility* (Monograph 7). Washington, D.C.: American Association on Mental Deficiency.

Eyman, R. K., Demaine, G. C., and Lei, T. 1979. Relationship between community environments and resident changes in adaptive behavior: A path model. *American Journal of Mental Deficiency* 83:330–38.

Eyman, R. K., Silverstein, A. B., and McLain, R. 1975. Effects of treatment programs on the acquisition of basic skills. *American Journal of Mental Deficiency* 79:573–82.

Fairweather, G. W. (ed.) 1964. *Social Psychology in Treating Mental Illness: An Experimental Approach*. New York: John Wiley & Sons.

Fairweather, G. W. 1980. The Fairweather Lodge: A twenty-five year retrospective. In G. Fairweather (ed.), *New Directions for Mental Health Services*, 13–32. San Francisco: Jossey-Bass.

Farkas, M., and Anthony, W. A. 1987. Outcome analysis in psychiatric rehabilitation. In M. J. Fuhrer (ed.), *Rehabilitation Outcomes: Analysis and Measurement*, 43–56. Baltimore: Brookes.

Farkas, M. D., Anthony, W. A., and Cohen, M. R. 1989. Psychiatric rehabilitation: The approach and its programs. In M. D. Farkas and W. A. Anthony (eds.), *Psychiatric Rehabilitation Programs: Putting Theory into Practice*, 1–27. Baltimore: Johns Hopkins University Press.

Farran, D. C., Metzger, J., and Sparling, J. 1986. Immediate and continuing adaptations in parents of handicapped children: A model and an illustration. In J. J. Gallagher and P. M. Vietze (eds.), *Families of Handicapped Persons*, 143–66. Baltimore: Brookes.

Felce, D. 1988. Behavioral and social climate in community group residences. In M. Janicki, M. Krauss, and M. Seltzer (eds.), *Community Residences for Persons with Developmental Disabilities*, 133–47. Baltimore: Brookes.

Felce, D., deKock, U., Thomas, M., and Saxby, H. 1986. Change in adaptive behaviour of severely and profoundly mentally handicapped adults in different residential settings. *British Journal of Psychology* 77:489–501.

Field, G., Allness, D., and Knoedler, W. H. 1980. Application of the training in community living program to rural areas. *Journal of Community Psychology* 8:9–15.

Fimian, M. J. 1984. Organizational variables related to stress and burnout in community-based group homes. *Education and Training of the Mentally Retarded* 19:201–9.

Fischer, C. S. 1982. *To Dwell among Friends: Personal Networks in Town and City*. Chicago: University of Chicago Press.

Flanagan, J. C. 1978. A research approach to improving our quality of life. *American Psychologist* 33:138–54.

Foa, E. B., and Kozak, M. J. 1985. Treatment of anxiety disorders: Implications for psychopathology. In A. H. Tuma and J. Maser (eds.), *Anxiety and the Anxiety Disorders*, 421–52. Hillsdale, N.J.: Erlbaum.

Foley, F. W., Bedell, J. R., LaRocca, N. G., Scheinberg, L. C., and Resnikoff, M. 1987. Efficacy of stress-inoculation training in coping with multiple sclerosis. *Journal of Consulting and Clinical Psychology* 55:919–22.

Folkman, S., Lazarus, R. S., Dunkel-Schetter, C., DeLongis, A., and Gruen, R. J. 1986a. Dynamics of a stressful encounter: Cognitive appraisal, coping and encounter outcomes. *Journal of Personality and Social Psychology* 50: 992–1003.

Folkman, S., Lazarus, R. S., Gruen, R. J., and DeLongis, A. 1986b. Appraisal, coping, health status and psychological symptoms. *Journal of Personality and Social Psychology* 50:571–79.

Frank, R. G., Gluck, J. P., and Buckelew, S. P. 1990. Rehabilitation: Psychology's greatest opportunity? *American Psychologist* 45:757–61.

Friedrich, W. N., Greenberg, M. T., and Crnic, K. A. 1983. A short form of the questionnaire on resources and stress. *American Journal of Mental Deficiency* 88:41–48.

Fritz, J. 1987. NAPRFMR identifies barriers to community placement. *LINKS* 17:1–7.

Fuhrer, M. J. (ed.). 1987. *Rehabilitation Outcomes: Analysis and Measurement.* Baltimore: Brookes.

Galligan, B., McArdle, J., and Zazycki, F. 1989. *From Institution to Small Residential Units: A Program Evaluation* (Technical Report). Perrysburg, N.Y.: J. N. Adam Developmental Disabilities Service Office.

Ganju, V. 1979. *Turnover Trends among MHMR Series Employees in Texas State Schools.* Austin: Texas Department of Mental Health and Mental Retardation, Office of Program Analysis and Statistical Research.

Gardner, W. I. 1989. But in the meantime: A client perspective of the debate over the use of aversive/intrusive therapy procedures. *The Behavior Therapist* 12: 179–82.

Gardner, W. I., and Cole, C. L. 1987. Behavior treatment, behavior management, and behavior control: Needed distinctions. *Behavioral Residential Treatment* 2:37–53.

Garmezy, N., and Rutter, R. 1983. *Stress, Coping, and Development in Children.* New York: McGraw-Hill.

Geller, M. P. 1982. The "revolving door": A trap or a life style? *Hospital and Community Psychiatry* 33:388–89.

General Accounting Office. 1988. *Estimating the Size and Location of Homeless Persons with Mental Illness.* Washington, D.C.: Author.

George, M. J., and Baumeister, A. A. 1981. Employee withdrawal and job satisfaction in community residential facilities for mentally retarded persons. *American Journal of Mental Deficiency* 85:639–47.

Ghaziuddin, M. 1988. Behavioural disorder in the mentally handicapped: The role of life events. *British Journal of Psychiatry* 152:683–86.

Goldman, H. H., Gatozzi, A. A., and Taube, C. A. 1981. Defining and counting the chronically mentally ill. *Hospital and Community Psychiatry* 32:21–27.

Goldmeier, J., Shore, M. F., and Mannino, F. V. 1977. Cooperative apartments: New programs in community mental health. *Health and Social Work* 2: 119–40.

Gollay, E., Freedman, R., Wyngaarden, M., and Kurtz, N. 1978. *Coming Back: The Community Experiences of Deinstitutionalized Mentally Retarded People.* Cambridge, Mass.: Abt Books.

Gothelf, C. R. 1985. Variations in resource provision for community residences serving persons with developmental disabilities. *Education and Training of the Mentally Retarded* 20:130–38.

Governor's Planning Council on Developmental Disabilities. 1983. *Developmental Disabilities and Public Policy: A Review for Policymakers.* St. Paul: Author.

Governor's Planning Council on Developmental Disabilities. 1984. *Toward a Developmental Disabilities Policy Agenda: Assuring Futures of Quality.* St. Paul: Author.

Gray, C., and Conley, R. 1988. Expanding horizons in services to people with developmental disabilities. *Mental Retardation* 26:59–62.

Griffin, J. C., Keyes, J. B., Emerson, J. H., Paisey, T. J., Stark, M. T., Williams, D. E., Dayan, M., Ricketts, R. W., and Zukotynski, G. 1989. *Survey on the Use of Aversive Therapy: National Association of Superintendents of Public Residential Facilities.* Paper presented at the Annual Conference of the American Association on Mental Retardation, Chicago.

Gudeman, J., and Shore, M. 1984. Beyond deinstitutionalization: A new class of facilities for the mentally ill. *New England Journal of Medicine* 311:832–36.

Guess, D., Benson, H. A., and Siegel-Causey, E. 1985. Concepts and issues related to choice-making and autonomy among persons with severe disabilities. *Journal of the Association for Persons with Severe Handicaps* 10:79–86.

Gumrukru, P. 1968. The efficacy of a halfway house: Three-year study of a therapeutic residence. *The Sociological Quarterly* 9:374–86.

Hackman, J. R., and Oldham, G. R. 1980. *Work Redesign.* Reading, Mass.: Addison-Wesley.

Hall, G. B., Nelson, G., and Fowler, H. S. 1987. Housing for the clinically mentally disabled. Part I. Conceptual framework and social context. *Canadian Journal of Mental Health* 2:65–78.

Halpern, A. S., Close, D. W., and Nelson, D. J. 1986. *On My Own: The Impact of Semi-independent Living Programs for Adults with Mental Retardation.* Baltimore: Brookes.

Halpin, A. W., and Winer, B. J. 1957. A factorial study of the leader behavior descriptions. In R. M. Stodgill and A. E. Coons (eds.), *Leader Behavior: Its Description and Measurement.* Columbus, Ohio: Ohio State University Bureau of Business Research.

Haney, J. I. 1988. Toward successful community residential placements for individuals with mental retardation. In L. W. Heal, J. I. Haney, and A. R. Novak-Amado (eds.), *Integration of Developmentally Disabled Individuals into the Community,* 125–68. Baltimore: Brookes.

Jacobson, J. W., and Ackerman, L. J. 1989a. *Factors Associated with Staff Tenure in Group Homes*. Albany, N.Y.: New York State Office of Mental Retardation and Developmental Disabilities.

Jacobson, J. W., and Ackerman, L. J. 1989b. *Staff Attitudes and the Group Home as a Work Place*. Albany, N.Y.: New York State Office of Mental Retardation and Developmental Disabilities.

Jacobson, J. W., and Janicki, M. P. 1983. Observed prevalence of multiple developmental disabilities. *Mental Retardation* 21:87–94.

Jacobson, J. W., and Janicki, M. P. 1987. Needs for professional and generic services within a developmental disabilities service system. In J. A. Mulick and R. F. Antonak (eds.), *Transitions in Mental Retardation* 2:23–46. Norwood, N.J.: Ablex.

Jacobson, J. W., and Mulick, J. A. 1989a. Behavior modification standards for practice. *Psychology in Mental Retardation* 14:3–7.

Jacobson, J. W., and Mulick, J. A. 1989b. Some contingencies affecting restrictive behavioral procedures. *Psychology in Mental Retardation and Developmental Disabilities* 14:9–13.

Jacobson, J. W., and Schwartz, A. A. 1983. The evaluation of community living alternatives for developmentally disabled persons. In J. L. Matson and J. A. Mulick (eds.), *Handbook of Mental Retardation*, 39–66. New York: Pergamon Press.

Jacobson, J. W., and Schwartz, A. A., in press. Evaluating the living situations of persons with developmental disabilities. In J. L. Matson and J. A. Mulick (eds.), *Handbook of Mental Retardation*, 2d ed. New York: Pergamon Press.

Jacobson, J. W., Schwartz, A. A., and Janicki, M. P. 1984. Rehabilitative models and residential program services. In R. I. Brown (ed.), *Rehabilitative Education: Integrated Programs for Handicapped Children and Adolescents*, 107–43. London: Croom/Helm.

Jacobson, L. D., and Schwartz, G. E. 1986. Self-deception predicts a self-report and endurance of pain. *Psychosomatic Medicine* 48:211–23.

Janicki, M. P., and Jacobson, J. W. 1982. The character of developmental disabilities in New York State: Preliminary observations. *International Journal of Rehabilitation Research* 5:191–202.

Janicki, M. P., Jacobson, J. W., Zigman, W. B., and Lubin, R. A. 1987. Group homes as alternative care settings: System issues and implications. In S. Landesman, P. M. Vietze, and M. J. Begab (eds.), *Living Environments and Mental Retardation*, 173–95. Washington, D.C.: American Association on Mental Deficiency.

Janicki, M. P., Krauss, M. W., and Seltzer, M. M. 1988a. Context, models, and community residences. In M. P. Janicki, M. W. Krauss, and M. M. Seltzer (eds.), *Community Residences for Persons with Developmental Disabilities*, 1–14. Baltimore: Brookes.

Janicki, M. P., Krauss, M. W., and Seltzer, M. M. 1988b. Agenda for service, policy, and research. In M. P. Janicki, M. W. Krauss, and M. M. Seltzer (eds.), *Community Residences for Persons with Developmental Disabilities*, 365–72. Baltimore: Brookes.

Harding, N. 1984. Who cares for the uncared? *Public Administration Review* 44:530–33.

Harris, V. S., and McHale, S. M. 1989. Family life problems, daily caretaking activities, and psychological well-being of mothers of mentally retarded children. *American Journal on Mental Retardation* 94:231–39.

Hasazi, J. E., Burchard, S. N., Gordon, L. R., Vecchione, E., and Yoe, J. 1990. "Life Event Stress and Behavioral Adjustment in Adults with Mental Retardation" (unpublished manuscript). Burlington, Vt: University of Vermont, Department of Psychology.

Hasazi, S. B., Gordon, L. R., and Roe, C. A. 1985. Factors associated with the employment status of handicapped youths exiting high school from 1979 to 1983. *Exceptional Children* 51:455–69.

Hatfield, A. B., Fierstein, R., and Johnson, D. 1982. Meeting the needs of families of the psychiatrically disabled. *Psychosocial Rehabilitation Journal* 6:27–40.

Hauber, F. A., and Bruininks, R. H. 1986. Intrinsic and extrinsic job satisfaction among direct care staff in residential facilities for mentally retarded people. *Education and Psychological Measurement* 46:95–105.

Hauber, F. A., Bruininks, R. H., Wieck, C. A., Sigford, B. B., and Hill, B. K. 1981. *1978–79 In-depth National Interview Survey of Public and Community Residential Facilities for Mentally Retarded Persons: Methods and Procedures*. Minneapolis: University of Minnesota Center for Residential and Community Services.

Haveman, M., and Maaskant, M. 1989. Defining fragility of the elderly severely mentally handicapped according to mortality risk, morbidity, motor handicaps and social functioning. *Journal of Mental Deficiency Research* 33:389–97.

Hawkins, R. P., Fremouw, W. J., and Reitz, A. L. 1981. A model for use in designing or describing evaluations of mental health or educational intervention programs. *Behavioral Assessment* 3:307–24.

Heal, L. W. 1985. Methodology for community integration research. In R. H. Bruininks and K. C. Lakin (eds.), *Living and Learning in the Least Restrictive Environment*, 199–224. Baltimore: Brookes.

Heal, L. W. 1988. Evaluating residential alternatives. In L. W. Heal, J. I. Haney, and A. R. Novak-Amado (eds.), *Integration of Developmentally Disabled Individuals into the Community*, 2d ed., 211–26. Baltimore: Brookes.

Heal, L. W., and Chadsey-Rusch, J. 1985. The lifestyle satisfaction scale (LSS): Assessing individual's satisfaction with residence, community setting, and associated services. *Applied Research in Mental Retardation* 6:475–90.

Heal, L. W., and Daniels, S. 1986. A cost-effectiveness analysis of residential alternatives for selected developmentally disabled citizens of three northern Wisconsin counties. *Mental Retardation Systems* 3:35–49.

Heal, L. W., Haney, J. I., and Novak-Amado, A. R. (eds.). 1988. *Integration of Developmentally Disabled Individuals into the Community*. Baltimore: Brookes.

Health Care Financing Administration. 1988. 42 CFR Parts 431, 435, 440, 442, and 483 Medicaid program: Conditions for intermediate care facilities for the mentally retarded, final rule. *Federal Register:* 53:20492–505.

Heller, T. 1982. Social disruption and residential relocation of mentally retarded children. *American Journal of Mental Deficiency* 87:48–55.

Heller, T. 1984. Issues in the adjustment of mentally retarded individuals to residential relocation. In N. Ellis and N. Bray (eds.), *International Review of Research in Mental Retardation*, 12:123–47. Orlando, Fla.: Academic Press.

Heller, T. 1988. Transitions: Coming in and going out of community residences. In M. P. Janicki, M. W. Strauss, and M. M. Setzer (eds.), *Community Residences for Persons with Developmental Disabilities*, 149–58. Baltimore: Brookes.

Hemming, H. 1986. Follow-up of adults with mental retardation transferred from institutions to new small units. *Mental Retardation* 24:229–35.

Hemming, H., Lavender, T., and Pill, R. 1981. Quality of life of mentally retarded adults transferred from large institutions to new small units. *American Journal of Mental Deficiency* 86:157–69.

Herr, S. 1988. Clients in limbo: Asserting the rights of persons with dual disabilities. In J. Stark, F. Menolascino, and M. Albarelli (eds.), *Mental Retardation and Mental Health: Classification, Diagnosis, Treatment, Services*, 338–53. New York: Springer-Verlag.

Hill, B. K., and Bruininks, R. H. 1981a. *Physical and Behavioral and Maladaptive Behavior Characteristics of Mentally Retarded People in Residential Facilities* (Project Report 12). Minneapolis: University of Minnesota, Department of Psychoeducational Studies.

Hill, B., and Bruininks, R. H. 1981b. *Family Leisure and Social Activities of Mentally Retarded People in Residential Facilities* (Project Report 13). Minneapolis: University of Minnesota, Department of Psychoeducational Studies.

Hill, B. K., and Bruininks, R. H. 1984. Maladaptive behavior of mentally retarded individuals in residential facilities. *American Journal of Mental Deficiency* 88:380–87.

Hill, B. K., Bruininks, R. H., Lakin, K. C., Hauber, F. A., and McGuire, S. P. 1985. Stability of residential facilities for people who are mentally retarded: 1977–82. *Mental Retardation* 23:108–44.

Hill, B. K., Lakin, K. C., Bruininks, R. H., Amado, A. N., Anderson, D. J., and Copher, J. I. 1989. *Living in the Community: A Comparative Study of Foster Homes and Small Group Homes for Persons with Mental Retardation* (Report 28). Minneapolis: University of Minnesota Center for Residential and Community Services.

Hobfoll, S. 1989. Conservation of resources: A new attempt at conceptualizing stress. *American Psychologist* 44:513–24.

Hogan, R. 1985a. "Gaining Community Support for Group Homes" (unpublished manuscript). Lafayette, Ind.: Purdue University.

Hogan, R. 1985b. "Not in My Town: Local Government Opposition to Group Homes" (unpublished manuscript). Lafayette, Ind.: Purdue University.

Holburn, C. S., and Forrester, J. 1984. Alterable correlates of extrinsic and intrinsic job satisfaction at a state residential facility. *American Journal of Mental Deficiency* 89:50–59.

Holland, T. 1973. Organizational structure and institutional care. *Journal of Health and Social Behavior* 14:241–51.

Holmes, T. H., and Rahe, R. H. 1967. The social readjustment rating scale. *Jour of Psychosomatic Research* 11:213–18.

Holroyd, J. 1974. The questionnaire on resources and stress: An instrument to sure family response to a handicapped member. *Journal of Community P ogy* 2:92–94.

Howell, D. C. 1987. *Statistical Methods for Psychology*, 2d ed. Boston: Press.

Hull, J. T., and Thompson, J. C. 1981a. Factors contributing to normali identical facilities for mentally retarded persons. *Mental Retardatio*

Hull, J. T., and Thompson, J. C. 1981b. Factors which contribute to in residential facilities for the mentally ill. *Community Mental* 17:107–13.

Iaffaldano, M. T., and Muchinsky, P. M. 1985. Job satisfactio mance: A meta-analysis. *Psychological Bulletin* 97:251–7

Ibister, F., and Donaldson, G. 1987. Supported employment are mentally ill: Program development. *Psychosocial F* 11:45–54.

Intagliata, J., Rinck, C., and Calkins, C. 1986. Staff respon ior in public and community residential facilities. 93–98.

Intagliata, J., and Willer, B. 1982. Reinstitutionalizatic sons successfully placed into family care and gro of Mental Deficiency 87:34–39.

Jackson, S. E., Schwab, R. L., and Schuler, R. S. 1 phenomenon. *Journal of Applied Psychology*

Jacob, R. G., and Chesney, M. A. 1986. Psycho reduce cardiovascular reactivity. In K. A. M Falkner, S. B. Manuck, and R. B. William *activity, and Cardiovascular Disease*, 41

Jacobson, J. W. 1982. Problem behavior an mentally disabled population. II. Beha *Retardation* 3:369–81.

Jacobson, J. W. 1988a. *"Impact of Staff 7 Developmental Disabilities"* (unp Vt.: University of Vermont, Dep

Jacobson, J. W. 1988b. Problem beh mentally disabled population. I *opmental Disabilities* 9:23–3

Jacobson, J. W. 1989a. Doing the *Developmental Disabilities*

Jacobson, J. W. 1989b. Microcc J. A. Mulick and R. F. 4:128–54. Norwood, N

Jacobson, J. W. 1990. Asse mentally disabled po of Behavior Problem nity, 19–70. Rock

Janis, I. L. 1983. Stress inoculation in health care: Theory and research. In D. Meichenbaum and M. E. Jarenko (eds.), *Stress Reduction and Prevention*, 67–99. New York: Plenum.

Jansen, E. 1970. The role of the halfway house in community mental health programs in the United Kingdom and America. *American Journal of Psychiatry* 10:1498–1504.

Johnson, J. H. 1986. *Life Events as Stressors in Childhood and Adolescence*. Beverly Hills, Calif.: Sage.

Kahn, R. L. 1974. The work module: A proposal for the humanization of work. In J. O'Toole (ed.), *Work and the Quality of Life*, 199–206. Cambridge, Mass.: MIT Press.

Kanner, A. D., Coyne, J. C. Schaefer, C., and Lazarus, R. S. 1981. Comparison of two modes of stress measurement: Daily hassles and uplifts versus major life events. *Journal of Behavioral Medicine* 4:1–39.

Kaswan, J. 1981. Manifest and latent functions of psychological services. *American Psychologist* 36:290–301.

Kazak, A. E., and Marvin, R. S. 1984. Differences, difficulties, and adaptation: Stress and social networks in families with a handicapped child. *Family Relations* 33:67–77.

Keck, J. 1990. Responding to consumer housing preferences: The Toledo experience. *Psychosocial Rehabilitation Journal* 13:51–58.

Kennedy, C. H., Horner, H. H., and Newton, J. S. 1989. Social contacts of adults with severe disabilities living in the community: A descriptive analysis of relationship patterns. *Journal of the Association for Persons with Severe Handicaps* 14:190–96.

Kiechel, W. 1989. How important is morale, really? *Fortune* 121–22.

Kiesler, C. A. 1982a. Mental hospitals and alternative care: Noninstitutionalization as potential public policy for mental patients. *American Psychologist* 37:349–67.

Kiesler, C. A. 1982b. Public and professional myths about mental hospitalization: An empirical assessment of policy-related beliefs. *American Psychologist* 37:1323–30.

King, R., Raynes, S., and Tizard, J. 1971. *Patterns of Residential Care: Sociological Studies in Institutions for Handicapped Children*. London: Routledge and Kegan Paul.

Kishi, G., Teelucksingh, B., Zollers, N., ParkLee, S., and Meyer, L. 1988. Daily decision-making in community residences: A social comparison of adults with and without mental retardation. *American Journal on Mental Retardation* 93:430–35.

Kleinberg, J., and Galligan, B. 1983. Effects of deinstitutionalization on adaptive behavior of mentally retarded adults. *American Journal of Mental Deficiency* 88:21–27.

Knight, C. B., Karan, O. C., Timmerman, M., Griffith, S. C., and Dufresne, D. 1986. Training community developmental disabilities associates: A collaborative model. *Applied Research in Mental Retardation* 7:229–40.

Knoedler, W. H. 1988. The treatment of substance abuse in the training in community living (TCL) model. Principles. In Oklahoma Mental Health Research Institute (ed.), *Proceedings: Oklahoma Mental Health Research Institute 1988 Professional Symposium,* 2:35–44. Oklahoma City, Okla.: Author.

*Knott v. Hughes,* Civil Action Y-80-2832 (Federal District Court of Maryland, 17 October 1980).

Knowles, M., and Landesman, S. 1986. National survey of state-sponsored training for residential direct-care staff. *Mental Retardation* 24:293–300.

Kohen, W., and Paul, G. L. 1976. Current trends and recommended changes in extended care placement of mental patients: The Illinois system as a case in point. *Schizophrenia Bulletin* 2:575–94.

Krantz, D. S., Contrada, R. J., Hill, D. R., and Friedler, E. (1988) Environmental stress and biobehavioral antecedents of coronary heart disease. *Journal of Consulting and Clinical Psychology* 56:333–41.

Krantz, G., Bruininks, R., and Clumpner, J. 1982. *Mentally Retarded People in State-operated Residential Facilities: Year Ending June 30, 1980.* Minneapolis: University of Minnesota, Department of Psychoeducational Studies.

Kratchowill, T. R. 1985. Selection of target behaviors: Issues and directions. *Behavioral Assessment* 7:3–6.

Krauss, M. W. 1986. Patterns and trends in public services to families with a mentally retarded member. In J. J. Gallagher and P. M. Vietze (eds.), *Families of Handicapped Persons,* 237–48. Baltimore: Brookes.

Kruzich, J. M., and Kruzich, S. J. 1985. Milieu factors influencing patients' integration into community residential facilities. *Hospital and Community Psychiatry* 36:379–82.

Lakin, K. C. 1987. *A Rationale and Projected Need for University Affiliated Facility Involvement in the Training of Paraprofessionals for Direct-care Roles for Persons with Developmental Disabilities.* Paper presented for the American Association of University Affiliated Programs for presentation to the Consortium for Citizens with Disabilities to support a recommendation for a Direct-care Training Initiative in the 1987 DD Act.

Lakin, K. C. 1988. Strategies for promoting the stability of direct care staff. In M. P. Janicki, M. W. Krauss, and M. M. Seltzer (eds.), *Community Residences for Persons with Developmental Disabilities,* 231–38. Baltimore: Brookes.

Lakin, K., and Bruininks, R. 1981. *Occupational Stability of Direct Care Staff of Residential Facilities for Mentally Retarded People* (Project Report 14). Minneapolis: University of Minnesota, Department of Psychoeducational Studies.

Lakin, K. C., and Bruininks, R. H. (eds.). 1985. *Strategies for Achieving Community Integration of Developmentally Disabled Citizens.* Baltimore: Brookes.

Lakin, K. C., Bruininks, R. H., and Hill, B. K. 1982. *Factors Related to Job Stability of Direct-care Staff of Residential Facilities for Mentally Retarded People.* Minneapolis: University of Minnesota, Department of Psychoeducational Studies.

Lakin, K. C., Bruininks, R. H., Hill, B. K., and Hauber, F. A. 1982. Turnover of direct-care staff in a national sample of residential facilities for mentally retarded people. *American Journal of Mental Deficiency* 87:64–72.

Lakin, K. C., Hill, B., Bruininks, R., Hauber, F., and Krantz, G. 1983. Factors re-

lated to job stability of direct-care staff of residential facilities for mentally retarded people. *Journal of Community Psychology* 11:228–35.

Lakin, K. C., Hill, B. K., Hauber, F. A., Bruininks, R. H., and Heal, L. W. 1983.
New admissions and readmissions to a national sample of public residential facilities. *American Journal of Mental Deficiency* 88:13–20.

Lakin, K. C., Jaskulski, T. M., Hill, B. K., Bruininks, R. H., Menke, J. M., White,
C. C., and Wright, E. A. 1989. *Medicaid Services for Persons with Mental Retardation and Related Conditions.* Minneapolis: University of Minnesota Center
for Residential and Community Services.

Lakin, K. C., Krantz, G. C., Bruininks, R. H., Clumpner, J. L., and Hill, B. K.
1982. One hundred years of data on public residential facilities for mentally retarded people. *American Journal of Mental Deficiency* 87:1–8.

Landesman, S. 1986. Quality of life and personal life satisfaction: Definition and
measurement issues. *Mental Retardation* 24:141–43.

Landesman, S. 1988. Preventing "institutionalization" in the community. In M. P.
Janicki, M. W. Krauss and M. M. Seltzer (eds.), *Community Residences for
Persons with Developmental Disabilities,* 45–56. Baltimore: Brookes.

Landesman, S., and Butterfield, E. C. 1987. Normalization and deinstitutionalization of mentally retarded individuals: Controversy and facts. *American Psychologist* 42:809–15.

Landesman-Dwyer, S. 1981. Living in the community. *American Journal of Mental
Deficiency* 86:223–34.

Landesman-Dwyer, S. 1985. Describing and evaluating residential environments. In
R. H. Bruininks and K. C. Lakin (eds.), *Living and Learning in the Least Restrictive Environment,* 185–96. Baltimore: Brookes.

Landesman-Dwyer, S., and Berkson, G. 1984. Friendships and social behavior. In
J. Wortis (ed.), *Mental Retardation and Developmental Disabilities: An Annual
Review,* 13:129–54. New York: Plenum.

Lazarus, R. S. 1984. Puzzles in the study of daily hassles. *Journal of Behavioral
Medicine* 7:375–89.

Lazarus, R. S., and Folkman, S. 1985. *Stress, Appraisal, and Coping.* New York:
Springer-Verlag.

Leete, E. 1989. How I perceive and manage my illness. *Schizophrenia Bulletin*
15:197–200.

Leff, J., and Vaughn, C. 1985. *Expressed Emotion in Families.* New York: Guilford
Press.

Leginski, W. A., Croze, C., Driggers, J., Dumpman, S., Geersten, D., Kamis-
Gould, E., Namerow, M. J., Patton, R. E., Wilson, N. Z., and Wurster, C. R.
1989. *Data Standards for Mental Health Decision Support Systems* (ADM
89-1589). Rockville, Md.: National Institute of Mental Health.

Leiter, M. P., and Maslach, C. 1986. *Job Stress and Social Involvement among
Nurses.* Paper presented at the Annual Conference of the International Network
for Social Network Analysis. Santa Barbara, Calif.

Leiter, M. P., and Maslach, C. 1988. The impact of interpersonal environment on
burnout and organizational commitment. *Journal of Organizational Behavior*
9:297–308.

Levine, H. G. 1985. Situational anxiety and everyday life experiences of mildly mentally retarded adults. *American Journal of Mental Deficiency* 90:27–33.

Liberman, R. P., DeRisi, W. J., and Mueser, K. T. 1989. *Social Skills Training for Psychiatric Patients*. Elmsford, N.Y.: Pergamon Press.

Linn, M. W., Caffey, E. M., Klett, J., and Hogarty, G. 1977. Hospital vs. community (foster) care for psychiatric patients. *Archives of General Psychiatry* 34:78–83.

Living Alternatives Research Project. 1981. *Community Residence Employee Opinion Scale*. Staten Island, N.Y.: New York State Institute for Basic Research in Developmental Disabilities.

Long, C. G., and Bluteau, P. 1988. Group coping skills training for anxiety and depression: Its application with chronic patients. *Journal of Advanced Nursing* 13:358–64.

Lord, J., Schnarr, A., and Hutchinson, P. 1987. The voice of the people: Qualitative research and the needs of consumers. *Canadian Journal of Community Mental Health* 6:25–35.

Low-income Housing Information Service. 1988. *Low Income Housing Bulletin* 1, Washington, D.C.: Author.

Lubin, R., Jacobson, J. W., and Kiely, M. 1982. Projected impact of the federal functional definition of developmental disabilities: The categorically disabled population and service eligibility. *American Journal of Mental Deficiency* 87:73–79.

Luborsky, L., Crits-Cristoph, P., McLellan, A. T., Woody, G., Piper, W., Liberman, B., Imber, S., and Pilkonis, P. 1986. Do therapists vary much in their success? Findings from four outcome studies. *American Journal of Orthopsychiatry* 56:501–12.

Lukoff, D., Snyder, K., Ventura, J., and Nuechterlein, K. H. 1984. Life events, familial stress, and coping in the developmental course of schizophrenia. *Schizophrenia Bulletin* 10:258–92.

Lukoff, D., Wallace, C. J., Liberman, R. P., and Burke, K. 1986. A holistic program for chronic schizophrenic patients. *Schizophrenia Bulletin* 12:276–82.

Maccoby, E. E., Kahn, A. J., and Everett, B. A. 1983. The role of psychological research in the formation of policies affecting children. *American Psychologist* 38:80–84.

MacEachron, A. 1983. Institutional reform and adaptive functioning of mentally retarded persons: A field experiment. *American Journal of Mental Deficiency* 88:2–12.

MacEachron, A. E., Zober, M. A., and Fein, J. 1985. Institutional reform, adaptive functioning of mentally retarded persons, and staff quality of work life. *American Journal of Mental Deficiency* 89:379–88.

Maryland Humane Practices Commission. 1975. *Second Report to the Governor and General Assembly of Maryland*. Baltimore: Author.

*Maryland Laws*. 1972. Chapter 345.

Maslach, C., and Jackson, S. E. 1981. *The Maslach Burnout Inventory*. Palo Alto, Calif.: Consulting Psychologists Press.

Maslach, C., and Jackson, S. E. 1982. Burnout in health professions: A social psychological analysis. In G. S. Sanders and J. Suls (eds.), *Social Psychology of Health and Illness*, 227–54. Hillsdale, N.J.: Erlbaum.

Maslach, C., and Jackson, S. E. 1984. Burnout in organizational settings. *Applied Social Psychology Annual* 5:133–53.

Massachusetts Council of Human Service Providers. 1982. *Colleagues in Service, Variants in Pay: A Study of Massachusetts Human Service Workers' Compensation Trends*. Boston: Author.

Matson, J. L. 1985. Biosocial theory of psychopathology: A three-by-four factor model. *Applied Research in Mental Retardation* 6:199–227.

Matson, J. L., and Frame, C. L. 1986. *Psychopathology among Mentally Retarded Children and Adolescents*. Beverly Hills, Calif.: Sage.

Matson, J. L., and Gorman-Smith, D. 1986. A review of treatment research for aggressive and disruptive behavior in the mentally retarded. *Applied Research in Mental Retardation* 7:95–103.

McAfee, J. K., and Sheeler, M. C. 1987. Accommodation of adults who are mentally retarded in community colleges: A national study. *Education and Training in Mental Retardation* 22:262–67.

McCubbin, H. I., and Patterson, J. M. 1983. Family transitions: Adaptation to stress. In H. I. McCubbin and C. R. Figley (eds.), *Stress and the Family*. New York: Brunner/Mazel.

McDonnell, J. J., and Horner, R. H. 1985. Effects of in vivo versus simulation plus in vivo training on the acquisition and generalization of grocery item selection by high school students with severe handicaps. *Analysis and Intervention in Developmental Disabilities* 5:323–44.

McMahon, R. J., Tiedemann, G. L., Forehand, R., and Griest, D. 1984. A review of treatment research for aggressive and disruptive behavior in the mentally retarded. *Applied Research in Mental Retardation* 7:295–303.

Meadow, K. Y. 1981. Burnout in professionals working with deaf children. *American Annals of the Deaf* 126:12–22.

Mechanic, D. 1987. Evolution of mental health services and areas for change. In D. Mechanic (ed.), *Improving Mental Health Services: What the Social Sciences Tell Us* (New Directions for Mental Health Services, No. 36), 3–13. San Francisco: Jossey-Bass.

Meichenbaum, D. 1985. *Stress Inoculation Training*. New York: Pergamon Press.

Meichenbaum, D., and Cameron, R. 1983. Stress inoculation training: Toward a general paradigm for training coping skills. In D. Meichenbaum and M. E. Jarenko (eds.), *Stress Reduction and Prevention*, 115–54. New York: Plenum.

Melick, M. E., Johnson, E. M., and Duffee, B. W. 1981. Factors related to the successful performance of psychiatric aides. *Hospital and Community Psychiatry* 32:401–4.

Menolascino, F. 1977. *Challenges in Mental Retardation*. New York: Human Sciences Press.

Menolascino, F. J. 1983. Overview. In F. J. Menolascino and B. M. McCann (eds.), *Mental Health and Mental Retardation: Bridging the Gap*, 3–64. Baltimore: University Park Press.

Mikulincer, M. 1988. Reactance and helplessness following exposure to unsolvable problems: The effects of attributional style. *Journal of Personality and Social Psychology* 54:679–86.

Miller, C., and Eyman, R. 1978. Hospital and community mortality rates among the retarded. *Journal of Mental Deficiency Research* 22:137–45.

Miller, P., and Ingham, J. G. 1976. Friends, confidants, and symptoms. *Social Psychiatry* 11:51–58.

Miller, S. 1988. *GET WISE*. Bronx, N.Y.: Albert Einstein College of Medicine.

Miller, S. M., Brody, D. S., and Summerton, J. 1988. Styles of coping with threat: Implications for health. *Journal of Personality and Social Psychology* 54:142–48.

Miller, S. M., Leinbach, A., and Brody, D. S. 1989. Coping style in hypertensive patients: Nature and consequences. *Journal of Consulting and Clinical Psychology* 57:333–37.

Miller, S., and Miller, R., in press. An exploration of daily hassles for persons with severe psychiatric disabilities. *Psychosocial Rehabilitation Journal*.

Minkoff, K. 1987. Beyond deinstitutionalization: A new ideology for the postinstitutional era. *Hospital and Community Psychiatry* 38:945–50.

Minks, D. A, and Graham, R. S. 1989. Starting a new psychiatric rehabilitation residential program. In P. J. Carling and P. Ridgway. A psychiatric rehabilitation approach to housing. In M. D. Farkas and W. A. Anthony (eds.), *Psychiatric Rehabilitation Programs: Putting Theory into Practice,* 28–80. Baltimore, Md.: Johns Hopkins University Press.

Mobley, W. H., Griffeth, R. W., Hand, H. H., and Meglino, B. M. 1979. Review and conceptual analysis of the employee turnover process. *Psychological Bulletin* 86:493–522.

Moise, L. 1984. "The Betrayal of Barbara" (unpublished correspondence. Available from Lotte Moise, Ft. Bragg, Calif.).

Molaison, V. A., Black, M. M., Smull, M. W., and Sachs, M. L., under submission. *Families Caring for an Adult with Mental Retardation: Perceptions of Service Accessibility and Satisfaction*.

Monroe, S. M. 1983. Major and minor life events as predictors of psychological distress: Further issues and findings. *Journal of Behavioral Medicine* 6:189–205.

Moos, R. H. 1972. Assessment of the psychosocial environments of community-oriented psychiatric treatment programs. *Journal of Abnormal Psychology* 79:9–18.

Moos, R. H., and Otto, J. 1972. The community-oriented programs environment scale: A methodology for the facilitation and evaluation of social change. *Community Mental Health Journal* 8:28–37.

Moroney, R. M. 1983. Families, care of the handicapped, and public policy. In R. Perlman (ed.), *Family Home Care: Critical Issues for Services and Policies,* 188–212. New York: Haworth Press.

Morrissey, J. P., Hall, R. H., and Lindsey, M. L. 1981. *Interorganizational Relations: A Sourcebook of Measures for Mental Health Programs*. Albany: New York State Office of Mental Health Special Projects Research Unit.

Mueser, K. T., and Liberman, R. P. 1988. Skills training in vocational rehabilitation. In J. A. Ciardiello and M. D. Bell (eds.), *Vocational Rehabilitation of Per-*

*sons with Prolonged Psychiatric Disorders,* 81–103. Baltimore: Johns Hopkins University Press.

National Association of State Mental Health Program Directors. 1986. *Position Statement on Community Systems for People with Severe and Persistent Mental Illnesses.* Alexandria, Va.: Author.

National Association of State Mental Health Program Directors. 1987a. *Funding Sources and Expenditures of State Mental Health Agencies: Revenue/Expenditures Study Results, Fiscal Year 1985.* Alexandria, Va.: Author.

National Association of State Mental Health Program Directors. 1987b. *Position Statement on Housing and Support for People with Long-term Mental Illness.* Alexandria, Va.: Author.

National Housing Institute. 1988. *A Status Report on The American Dream.* Princeton, N.J.: RL Associates.

National Institute of Mental Health. 1987. *Guidelines for Meeting the Housing Needs of People with Psychiatric Disabilities.* Rockville, Md.: Author.

Nihira, K., Foster, R., Shellhaus, M., and Leland, H. 1974. *AAMD Adaptive Behavior Scale for Children and Adults: 1974 Revision.* Washington, D.C.: American Association on Mental Deficiency.

Novaco, R. W., and Vaux, A. 1985. Human stress. A theoretical model for the community-oriented investigator. In E. C. Susskind and D. C. Klein (eds.), *Community Research,* 360–420. New York: Praeger.

Neuchterlein, K., and Dawson, M. 1984. A heuristic vulnerability/stress model of schizophrenic episodes. *Schizophrenia Bulletin* 10:300–312.

O'Connor, G. 1983. Presidential address: Social support of mentally retarded persons. *Mental Retardation* 21:187–96.

Ohio Mental Health Housing Task Force. 1986. *Final Report.* Columbus, Ohio: Ohio Department of Mental Health.

Overall, J. E., and Gorham, D. R. 1962. The brief psychiatric rating scale. *Psychological Reports* 10:799–812.

Panel on the Future of the Work Force. 1987. *Future of the Work Force.* Albany: New York State Office of Mental Retardation and Developmental Disabilities.

Parsons, J. A., May, J. G., and Menolascino, F. J. 1984. The nature and incidence of mental illness in mentally retarded individuals. In F. J. Menolascino and J. A. Stark (eds.), *Mental Illness in the Mentally Retarded,* 3–43. New York: Plenum.

Paul, G. L. 1986. *Assessment in Residential Treatment Settings.* Champaign, Ill.: Research Press.

Pearlin, L., and Schooler, C. 1978. The structure of coping. *Journal of Health and Social Behavior* 19:2–21.

Perrucci, R., and Targ, D. B. 1982. *Mental Patients and Social Networks.* Boston: Auburn House.

Peterson, C., Seligman, M. E., and Vaillant, G. E. 1988. Pessimistic explanatory style is a risk factor for physical illness: A thirty-five year longitudinal study. *Journal of Personality and Social Psychology* 55:23–27.

Phillips, I. 1971. Psychopathology and mental retardation. In F. Menolascino (ed.), *Psychiatric Aspects of the Diagnosis and Treatment of Mental Retardation,* 39–68. Seattle: Special Child Publications.

Phillips, J. F., Reid, D. H., Korabek, C. A., and Hursh, D. E. 1988. Community-based instruction with profoundly mentally retarded persons: Client and public responsiveness. *Research in Developmental Disabilities* 9:3–21.

Pincus, H. A., West, J., and Goldman, H. 1985. Diagnosis-related groups and clinical research in psychiatry. *Archives of General Psychiatry* 42:627–29.

Pine, J. 1983. "Activity as a Measure of Quality of Life in Group Homes" (unpublished doctoral dissertation). Burlington, Vt.: University of Vermont.

Pines, A., and Maslach, C. 1978. Characteristics of staff burnout in mental health settings. *Hospital and Community Psychiatry* 29:233–37.

Prager, E. 1980. Evaluation in mental health: Enter the consumer. *Social Work Research and Abstracts* 4:5–10.

Pratt, M. W., Luszcz, M. A., and Brown, M. E. 1980. Measuring dimensions of quality of care in small community residences. *American Journal of Mental Deficiency* 85:188–94.

Price, J. L. 1972. *Handbook of Organizational Measurement.* Lexington, Mass.: D. C. Heath.

Price, J. L. 1977. *The Study of Turnover.* Ames, Iowa: Iowa State University Press.

Rabkin, J. G., and Struening, E. L. 1976. Life events, stress and illness. *Science* 194:1013–20.

Randolph, F. L., Sanford, C., Simoneau, D., Ridgway, P., and Carling, P. J. 1988. *The State of Practice in Community Residential Programs: A National Survey* (Monograph Series on Housing and Rehabilitation in Mental Health). Boston: Boston University Center for Psychiatric Rehabilitation.

Raynes, N., Pratt, M., and Roses, S. 1977. Aides' involvement in decision-making and the quality of care in institutional settings. *American Journal of Mental Deficiency* 81:570–77.

Rehm, L. P., Kaslow, N. J., and Rabin, A. S. 1987. Cognitive and behavioral targets in a self-control therapy program for depression. *Journal of Consulting and Clinical Psychology* 55:60–67.

Reiss, S., and Benson, B. A. 1985. Psychosocial correlates of depression in mentally retarded adults. I. Minimal social support and stigmatization. *American Journal of Mental Deficiency* 89:331–37.

Reiss, S., and Szyszko, J. 1983. Diagnostic overshadowing and professional experience with mentally retarded persons. *American Journal of Mental Deficiency* 87:396–402.

Repp, A. C., Felce, D., and deKock, U. 1987. Observational studies of staff working with mentally retarded persons: A review. *Research in Developmental Disabilities* 8:331–50.

Reynolds, W. M., and Coats, K. I. 1986. A comparison of cognitive-behavioral therapy and relaxation training for treatment of depression in adolescents. *Journal of Consulting and Clinical Psychology* 54:653–60.

Richards, B. 1976. Health and longevity. In J. Wortis (ed.), *Mental Retardation and Developmental Disabilities: An Annual Review,* 8:168–87. New York: Brunner/Mazel.

Richardson, D. 1981. *Rate Setting in the Human Services: A Guide for Administrators.* Washington, D.C.: Department of Health and Human Services Project Share.

Richardson, S., Koller, H., and Katz, M. 1985. Relationship of upbringing to later behavior disturbance of mildly retarded young people. *American Journal of Mental Deficiency* 90:1–18.

Ridgway, P. 1986. *Meeting the Supported Housing and Residential Services Needs of Americans with Psychiatric Disabilities: A State by State Review* (Full Report). Boston: Boston University Center for Psychiatric Rehabilitation, Community Residential Rehabilitation Project.

Ridgway, P. 1987. *Avoiding Zoning Battles*. Washington, D.C.: Intergovernmental Health Policy Project.

Ridgway, P. (ed.). 1988a. Coming home: Ex-patients view housing options and needs. *Proceedings of a National Housing Forum*, 1–33. Burlington, Vt.: University of Vermont Center for Community Change Through Housing and Support.

Ridgway, P. 1988b. *The Voice of Consumers in Mental Health Systems: A Call for Change* (Literature Review). Burlington, Vt.: University of Vermont Center for Community Change Through Housing and Support.

Ridgway, P., and Carling, P. J. 1988. *A Users' Guide to Needs Assessment in Community Rehabilitation* (Monograph Series on Housing and Rehabilitation in Mental Health). Boston: Boston University Center for Psychiatric Rehabilitation.

Robinson, N. M. 1987. Directions for person-environment research in mental retardation. In S. Landesman and P. M. Vietze (eds.), *Living Environments and Mental Retardation*, 477–86. Washington, D.C.: American Association on Mental Retardation.

Romer, D., and Berkson, G. 1980a. Social ecology of supervised communal facilities for mentally disabled adults. II. Predictors of affiliation. *American Journal of Mental Deficiency* 85:229–42.

Romer, D., and Berkson, G. 1980b. Social ecology of supervised communal facilities for mentally disabled adults. III. Predictors of social choice. *American Journal of Mental Deficiency* 85:243–52.

Rosen, J. W. 1988. "Community Adjustment and Integration of Mentally Retarded Adults: Relationships among Residential Setting, Community-based Activity, Social Support, Residential Satisfaction, and Psychological Well-being" (unpublished doctoral dissertation). Burlington, Vt.: University of Vermont.

Rosen, J. W., and Burchard, S. N. 1990. Community activities and social support networks: A social comparison of adults with and without mental retardation. *Education and Training in Mental Retardation* 25:193–204.

Roskies, E. 1983. Stress management for Type A individuals. In D. Meichenbaum and M. E. Jarenko (eds.), *Stress Reduction and Prevention*, 471–557). New York: Plenum.

Rotegard, L. L., Hill, B. K., and Bruininks, R. H. 1983. Environmental characteristics of residential facilities for mentally retarded persons in the United States. *American Journal of Mental Deficiency* 88:49–56.

Rowitz, L. 1989. Trends in mental retardation in the 1990s. *Mental Retardation* 27:iii–vi.

Ruback, R. B., and Innes, C. A. 1988. The relevance and irrelevance of psychological research: The example of prison crowding. *American Psychologist* 43:683.

Rudrud, E. H., and Vaudt, T. M. 1986. Prerequisite skills for semiindependent living services (SILS) placement. *Journal of the Association for Persons with Severe Handicaps* 11:182–87.

St. Claire, L. 1989. A multi-dimensional model of mental retardation: Impairment, subnormal behavior, role failures, and socially constructed retardation. *American Journal on Mental Retardation* 94:88–96.

Sachs, S. 1979. "Letter to Mrs. Max VanSickle" (Sachs Report; unpublished) Baltimore: Office of the Attorney General of the State of Maryland.

Salisbury, C. 1986. Adaptation of the questionnaire for resources and stress: Short form. *American Journal of Mental Deficiency* 90:456–59.

Sandall, H., Hawley, T. T., and Gordon, G. 1975. The St. Louis community homes program: Graduated support for long-term care. *American Journal of Psychiatry* 132:617–22.

Sarata, P. B. V. 1974. Employee satisfactions in agencies serving retarded persons. *American Journal of Mental Deficiency* 79:434–42.

Schalock, R. 1976. *Community Living Skills Screening Test.* Hastings, Neb.: Mid-Nebraska Mental Retardation Services.

Schalock, R., and Lilley, M. 1986. Placement from community-based mental retardation programs: How well do clients do after 8 to 10 years? *American Journal of Mental Deficiency* 90:669–76.

Schalock, R. L., Foley, J. W. Toulouse, A., and Stark, J. A. 1985. Medication and programming in controlling the behavior of mentally retarded individuals in community settings. *Applied Research in Mental Retardation* 5:425–38.

Schalock, R. L., and Harper, R. S. 1981. A systems approach to community living skills training. In R. H. Bruininks, C. E. Meyers, B. B. Sigford, and K. C. Lakin (eds.), *Deinstitutionalization and Community Adjustment of Mentally Retarded People,* 316–36). Washington, D.C.: American Association on Mental Deficiency.

Schalock, R., Harper, R., and Carver, G. 1981. Independent living placement: Five years later. *American Journal of Mental Deficiency* 86:170–77.

Schalock, R. L., Harper, R. C., and Genung, T. 1981. Community integration of mentally retarded adults: Community placement and program success. *American Journal of Mental Deficiency* 85:478–88.

Schalock, R. L., Keith, K. D., Hoffman, K., and Karan, O. C. 1989. Quality of life: Its measurement and use. *Mental Retardation* 27:25–31.

Scheerenberger, R. 1981. Deinstitutionalization: Trends and difficulties. In R. H. Bruininks, C. E. Meyers, B. B. Sigford, and K. C. Lakin (eds.), *Deinstitutionalization and Community Adjustment of Mentally Retarded People* (Monograph 4), 3–13. Washington, D.C.: American Association on Mental Deficiency.

Scheier, M. F., and Carver, C. S. 1985. Optimism, coping, and health: Assessment and implications of generalized outcome expectancies. *Health Psychology* 4:219–47.

Schein, E. H. 1980. *Organizational Psychology,* 3d ed. Englewood Cliffs, N.J.: Prentice-Hall.

Schiers, W., Giffort, D., and Furtkamp, E. 1980. Recruitment source and job survival for direct-care staff. *Mental Retardation* 18:285–87.

Schotte, D. E., and Clum, G. A. 1987. Problem-solving skills in suicidal psychiatric patients. *Journal of Consulting and Clinical Psychology* 55:49–54.

Schroeder, S. R., Rojahn, J., and Oldenquist, A. 1989. *Treatment of Destructive Behaviors among People with Developmental Disabilities*. Background paper prepared for the National Institutes of Health Consensus Development Panel on the Treatment of Destructive Behavior. Bethesda, Md.: National Institutes of Health.

Segal, S. P., and Aviram, U. 1978. *The Mentally Ill in Community-based Sheltered Care: A Study of Community Care and Social Integration*. New York: John Wiley & Sons.

Segal, S. P., Baumohl, J., and Moyles, E. W. 1980. Neighborhood types and community reaction to the mentally ill: A paradox of intensity. *Journal of Health and Social Behavior* 21:345–59.

Selman, R.L. 1980. *The Growth of Interpersonal Understanding*. New York: Academic Press.

Seltzer, G. 1981. Community residential adjustment: The relationship among environment, performance, and satisfaction. *American Journal of Mental Deficiency* 85:624–30.

Seltzer, G. B. 1980. *Residential Satisfaction and Community Adjustment*. Paper presented at the meeting of the American Association of Mental Deficiency, San Francisco.

Seltzer, G. B., and Seltzer, M. M. 1976. *The Community Adjustment Scale*. Cambridge, Mass.: Educational Projects.

Seltzer, M. M. 1984a. Nonexperimental field research methods. In J. L. Matson and J. A. Mulick (eds.), *Handbook of Mental Retardation*, 557–70. New York: Pergamon Press.

Seltzer, M. M. 1984b. Patterns of job satisfaction among mentally retarded adults. *Applied Research in Mental Retardation* 5:147–60.

Seltzer, M. M., and Krauss, M. W. 1989. Aging parents with adult mentally retarded children: Family risk factors and sources of support. *American Journal on Mental Retardation* 94:303–12.

Setze, P. J., and Bond, G. R. 1985. Psychiatric recidivism in a psychosocial rehabilitation setting: A survival analysis. *Hospital and Community Psychiatry* 36:521–24.

Seys, D., and Duker, P. 1988. Effects of staff management on the quality of residential care for mentally retarded individuals. *American Journal on Mental Retardation* 93:290–99.

Shadish, W. R., Jr. 1984. Policy research: Lessons learned from the implementation of deinstitutionalization. *American Psychologist* 39:725–38.

Sherman, B. R. 1988. Predictors of the decision to place developmentally disabled family members in residential care. *American Journal on Mental Retardation* 92:344–51.

Sherman, B. R., and Cocozza, J. J. 1984. Stress in families of the developmentally disabled: A literature review of factors affecting the decision to seek out-of-home placements. *Family Relations* 33:95–103.

Sherman, P. S., and David, M. 1989. *Mental Health Workforce Data Collection and Utilization: Status, Issues and Recommendations*. Rockville, Md.: National Institute of Mental Health.

Shern, D. L., Surles, R. C., and Waizer, J. 1989. Designing community treatment systems for the most seriously mentally ill: A state administrative perspective. *Journal of Social Issues* 45:105–17.

Shern, D. L., Wilson, N. Z., Ellis, R. H., Bartsch, D. B., and Coen, A. S. 1986. Planning a continuum of residential/service settings for the chronically mentally ill: The Colorado experience. *Community Mental Health Journal* 22:190–202.

Shevin, M., and Klein, N. 1984. The importance of choice-making skills for students with severe disabilities. *Journal of the Association for Persons with Severe Handicaps* 9:159–66.

Sigelman, C., Schoenrock, C., Budd, E., Winer, J., Spanhel, C., Martin, P., Hromas, S., and Bensberg, G. 1981b. *Communicating with Mentally Retarded Persons: Asking Questions and Getting Answers.* Lubbock, Tex.: Texas Tech University Research and Training Center in Mental Retardation.

Sigelman, C. K., Budd, E. C., Spanhel, C. L., and Schoenrock, C. J. 1981a. When in doubt, say yes: Acquiescence in interviews with mentally retarded persons. *Mental Retardation* 19:53–58.

Silver, E. J., Lubin, R. A., and Silverman, W. P. 1984. Serving profoundly mentally retarded persons: Staff attitudes and job satisfaction. *American Journal of Mental Deficiency* 89:297–301.

Silverman, W., Silver, E., Lubin, R., and Zigman, W. 1983. *Health Status of Profoundly Retarded Persons in a Specialty Hospital and in Small Community Programs* (Technical Report 83-1). New York: New York State Office of Mental Retardation and Developmental Disabilities, Institute for Basic Research in Developmental Disabilities.

Silverman, W., Silver, E., Lubin, R., Zigman, W., Janicki, M., and Jacobson, J. 1987. Health status and community placement of people who are profoundly retarded and multiply handicapped. In R. Antonak and J. Mulick (eds.), *Transitions in Mental Retardation. 3: The Community Imperative Revisited*, 3:108–24. Norwood, N. J.: Ablex.

Silverman, W., Silver, E., Sersen, E., Lubin, R., and Schwartz, A. 1986. Factors related to adaptive behavior changes among profoundly retarded, physically disabled persons. *American Journal of Mental Deficiency* 90:651–58.

Sinyor, D., Schwartz, S. G., Perronet, F., Brisson, G., and Seraganian, P. 1983. Aerobic fitness level and reactivity to psychosocial stress: Physiological, biochemical and subjective measures. *Psychosomatic Medicine* 45:205–17.

Sluyter, G., and Mukherjee, A. 1986. Validation of a job satisfaction instrument for residential-care employees. *Mental Retardation* 4:223–27.

Smircich, L. 1983. Concepts of culture and organizational analysis. *Administrative Science Quarterly* 28:339–58.

Smith, P. C., Kendall, L. M., and Hulin, C. L. 1969. *The Measurement of Satisfaction in Work and Retirement.* Chicago: Rand McNally.

Smith, T. W. 1986. Cognitive distortion and psychological distress in chronic low back pain. *Journal of Consulting and Clinical Psychology* 54:573–75.

Smull, M. W. 1989. *Crisis in the Community.* Alexandria, Va.: National Association of State Mental Retardation Program Directors.

Smull, M. W., and Bellamy, G. G. 1991. Community services for adults with disabilities: Policy challenges in the emerging support paradigm. In L. M. Meyer,

C. Peck, and L. Brown (eds.), *Critical Issues in the Lives of People with Severe Disabilities*, 527–36. Baltimore: Brookes.

Smull, M. W., and Sachs, M. L. 1983. "Issues Regarding Operationalizing the Federal Definition of Developmental Disability" (unpublished manuscript). Baltimore: University of Maryland, Applied Research and Evaluation Unit, Department of Pediatrics.

Spector, P. 1985. Measurement of human service staff satisfaction: Development of the job satisfaction survey. *American Journal of Community Psychology* 13: 693–713.

Spreat, S., and Lipinski, D. 1986. A survey of state policies regarding the use of restrictive/aversive behavior modification procedures. *Behavioral Residential Treatment* 1:137–52.

Spring, B. 1981. Stress and schizophrenia: Some definitional issues. *Schizophrenia Bulletin* 7:24–33.

State of Minnesota Department of Employee Relations for the Department of Human Service. 1989. *Study of Employee Wages, Benefits and Turnover in Minnesota Direct Care Facilities Serving Persons with Developmental Disabilities.* St. Paul: Author.

Stein, F., and Nikolic, S. 1989. Teaching stress management techniques to a schizophrenic patient. *American Journal of Occupational Therapy* 43:162–69.

Stein, L. I., and Ganser, L. J. 1983. The dollars follow the patient: Wisconsin's system for funding mental health services. In *New Directions for Mental Health Services*, 18:25–32. San Francisco: Jossey-Bass.

Stein, L. I., and Test, M. A. 1980. Alternative to mental hospital treatment. I. Conceptual model, treatment program, and clinical evaluation. *Archives of General Psychiatry* 37:392–97.

Stein, L. I., and Test, M. A. 1985. The evolution of the training in community living model. In L. I. Stein and M. A. Test (eds.), *The Training in Community Living Model: A Decade of Experience* (New Directions for Mental Health Services, No. 26), 7–16. San Francisco: Jossey-Bass.

Stein, L. I., Test, M. A., and Marx, A. J. 1975. Alternative to the hospital: A controlled study. *American Journal of Psychiatry* 132:517–21.

Strauss, J. 1989. Subjective experiences of schizophrenia: Toward a new dynamic psychiatry. *Schizophrenia Bulletin* 15:179–188.

Strauss, J. S., and Carpenter, W. T. 1983. What is schizophrenia? *Schizophrenia Bulletin* 9:7–10.

Strauss, J. S., Harding, C. M., Silverman, M., Eichler, A., and Lieberman, M. 1988. Work as treatment for psychiatric disorder: A puzzle in pieces. In J. A. Ciardiello and M. D. Bell (eds.), *Vocational Rehabilitation of Persons with Prolonged Psychiatric Disorders*, 47–58. Baltimore: Johns Hopkins University Press.

Stroul, B. 1989. Community support systems for people with long-term mental illness: A conceptual framework. *Psychosocial Rehabilitation Journal* 12:9–26.

Suls, J., and Fletcher, B. 1985. The relative efficacy of avoidant and nonavoidant coping strategies: A meta-analysis. *Health Psychology* 4:249–88.

Surles, R. C. 1989. *New York State Office of Mental Health Requirements for Staffing Adult Inpatient Wards.* Albany: New York State Office of Mental Health.

Sutter, P., Mayeda, T., Call, T., Yanagi, G., and Yee, S. 1980. Comparison of successful and unsuccessful community-placed mentally retarded persons. *American Journal of Mental Deficiency* 85:262–67.

Tabor, M. A. 1980. *The Social Context of Helping: A review of the Literature on Alternative Care for the Physically and Mentally Handicapped.* Rockville, Md.: National Institute of Mental Health.

Tannenbaum, A. 1968. *Control in Organizations.* New York: McGraw-Hill.

Tannenbaum, A., Kavcic, B., Rosner, M., Vianellow, M., and Wieser, G. 1974. *Hierarchy in Organizations.* San Francisco: Jossey-Bass.

Taube, C. A., Lave, J. R., Rupp, A., Goldman, H. H., and Frank, R. G. 1988. Psychiatry under prospective payment: Experience in the first year. *American Journal of Psychiatry* 145:210–13.

Taylor, S. J., Racino, J., Knoll, J., and Lutfiyya, Z. 1987. *The Nonrestrictive Environment: A Resource Manual on Community Integration for People with the Most Severe Disabilities.* New York: Human Policy Press.

Test, M. 1981. Effective community treatment of the chronically mentally ill: What is necessary? *Journal of Social Issues* 37:71–86.

Test, M. A., in press. The training in community living model: Delivering treatment and rehabilitation services through a continuous treatment team. In R. P. Liberman (ed.), *Rehabilitation of the Seriously Mentally Ill.* New York: Plenum.

Test, M. A., Knoedler, W. A., and Allness, A. J. 1985. The long-term treatment of young schizophrenics in a community support program. In L. I. Stein and M. A. Test (eds.), *The Training in Community Living Model: A Decade of Experience* (New Directions for Mental Health Services, No. 26), 17–27. San Francisco: Jossey-Bass.

Test, M. A., Knoedler, W. H., Allness, A. J., and Burke, S. S. 1985. Characteristics of young adults with schizophrenic disorders treated in the community. *Hospital and Community Psychiatry* 36:853–58.

Test, M. A., Knoedler, W. H., Allness, D. J., Burke, S. S., Brown, R. L., and Wallisch, L. S. 1989. *Community Care of Schizophrenia: Two Year Findings.* Presented at the 142nd Annual Meeting of the American Psychiatric Association, San Francisco.

Test, M. A., and Stein, L. 1978. Community treatment of the chronic patient: Research overview. *Schizophrenia Bulletin* 4:350–64.

Test, M. A., and Stein, L. I. 1980. Alternative to mental hospital treatment. III. Social cost. *Archives of General Psychiatry* 37:409–12.

Test, M. A., Wallisch, L. S., Allness, D. S., and Ripp, K. 1989. Substance use in young adults with schizophrenic disorders. *Schizophrenia Bulletin* 15:465–76.

Thaw, J., and Wolfe, S. 1986. The direct-care worker: A socio-cultural analysis. In J. Thaw (ed.), *Developing Responsive Human Services,* 83–145. Hillsdale, N.J.: Erlbaum.

Thoits, P. A. 1983. Dimensions of life events that influence psychological distress: An evaluation. In H. B. Kaplan (ed.), *Psychosocial Stress: Trends in Theory and Research,* 33–103. New York: Academic Press.

Thoits, P. A. 1986. Social support as coping assistance. *Journal of Consulting and Clinical Psychology* 54:416–23.

Thompson, J. 1980. "Burnout" in group home houseparents. *American Journal of Psychiatry* 137:710–14.

Thompson, J. D., and McEwen, W. J. 1958. Organizational goals and environment. *American Sociological Review* 23:23–30.

Thompson, T., Gardner, W. I., and Baumeister, A. A. 1988. Ethical issues in intervention with retardation, autism, and related developmental disorders. In J. A. Stark, F. J. Menolascino, M. H. Albarelli, and V. C. Gray (eds.), *Mental Retardation and Mental Health,* 211–17. New York: Springer-Verlag.

Thompson, T., Hackenberg, T., and Schaal, D. 1989. *Pharmacological Treatments for Behavior Problems in Developmental Disabilities.* Background paper prepared for the National Institutes of Health Consensus Development Panel on the Treatment of Destructive Behavior. Bethesda, Md.: National Institutes of Health.

Thousand, J. S., Burchard, S. N., and Hasazi, J. E. 1986. Field-based generation and validation of manager and staff competencies for small community residences. *Applied Research in Mental Retardation* 7:263–83.

Torrey, E. F., and Wolfe, S. M. 1986. *Care of the Seriously Mentally Ill: A Rating of State Programs.* Washington, D.C.: Public Citizen Health Research Group.

Trent, J. W. 1989. Associations for retarded citizens and residential care: Is there only one effective role? *Adult Residential Care Journal* 3:79–92.

Turnbull, A. P., Summers, J. A., and Brotherson, M. J. 1986. Family life cycle: Theoretical and empirical implications and future directions for families with mentally retarded members. In J. J. Gallagher and P. M. Vietze (eds.), *Families of Handicapped Persons,* 45–66. Baltimore: Brookes.

Turnbull, H. R. 1988. Ideological, political, and legal principles in the community living movement. In M. P. Janicki, M. W. Krauss, and M. M. Seltzer (eds.), *Community Residences for Persons with Developmental Disabilities,* 15–24. Baltimore: Brookes.

Turnbull, H. R., Ellis, J. W., Boggs, E. M., Brooks, P. O., and Biklen, D. P. 1981. *The Least Restrictive Alternative: Principles and Practices.* Washington, D.C.: American Association on Mental Deficiency.

Turnbull, H. R., and Turnbull, A. 1985. Family perspective. *TASH Newsletter* 2:7–11.

Turner, J., and TenHoor, W. 1979. The NIMH community support program: Pilot approach to a needed social reform. *Schizophrenia Bulletin* 4:319–44.

United States Senate Special Committee on Aging, Subcommittee on Long-term Care. 1976. *Supporting Paper No. 7: The Role of Nursing Homes in Caring for Discharged Mental Patients (and the Birth of a For-profit Boarding Home Industry).* Washington, D.C.: U.S. Government Printing Office.

Ursprung, A. W. 1986. Incidence and correlates of burnout in residential service settings. *Rehabilitation Counseling Bulletin* 29:225–39.

Van Houten, R., Axelrod, S., Bailey, J. S., Favell, J. E., Foxx, R. M., Iwata, B., and Lovaas, O. I. 1988. The right to effective behavioral treatment. *The Behavior Analyst* 11:111–14.

Vorspan, R. 1988. Activities of daily living in a clubhouse: You can't vacuum in a vacuum. *Psychosocial Rehabilitation Journal* 12:15–21.

Wallace, C. J., Nelson, C. J., Liberman, R. P., Aitchison, R. A., Lukoff, D., Elder,

J. P., and Ferris, C. 1980. A review and critique of social skills training with schizophrenic patients. *Schizophrenia Bulletin* 6:42–63.

Wasow, M. 1982. *Coping with Schizophrenia: A Survival Manual for Parents, Relatives, and Friends.* Palo Alto, Calif.: Science and Behavior Books.

Wasow, M. 1986. The need for asylum for the chronically mentally ill. *Schizophrenia Bulletin* 12:162–67.

Wehman, P., Hill, M., Hill, J., Brooke, V., Pendleton, P., and Britt, C. 1985. Competitive employment for persons with mental retardation: A follow-up six years later. *Mental Retardation* 23:274–81.

Wehman, P., Moon, M. S., and McCarthy, P. 1986. Transition from school to adulthood for youth with severe handicaps. *Focus on Exceptional Children* 18:1–12.

Weinberg, R. B. 1984. *Development of Self-report for Reliably Measuring the Social Support System.* Paper presented at the Annual Convention of the American Psychological Association, Toronto, Ontario, Canada.

Weisbrod, B. A., Test, M. A., and Stein, L. I. 1980. Alternative to mental hospital treatment. II. Economic benefit-cost analysis. *Archives of General Psychiatry* 37:400–405.

Weiss, D., Davis, R., England, G., and Lofquist, L. 1967. *Manual for the Minnesota Satisfaction Questionnaire. Minnesota Studies in Vocational Rehabilitation* (Report 22). Minneapolis: University of Minnesota.

Weiss, D. J., Davis, R. V., England, G. W., and Lofquist, L. H. 1966. *Minnesota Satisfaction Questionnaire—Short Form.* Minneapolis: University of Minnesota Industrial Relations Center.

Weiss, J. A., and Weiss, C. H. 1981. Social scientists and decision makers look at the usefulness of mental health research. *American Psychologist* 36:837–47.

Wherley, M., and Bisgaard, S. 1987. Beyond model programs: Evaluation of a county-wide system of residential treatment programs. *Hospital and Community Psychiatry* 38:852–57.

White, C. C., Lakin, K. C., Hill, B., Wright, E., and Bruininks, R. 1986. *Persons with Mental Retardation in State-operated Residential Facilities: Year Ending June 30, 1986 with Longitudinal Trends from 1950 to 1986* (Report 24). Minneapolis: University of Minnesota, Department of Educational Psychology.

White, J. F. 1987. *Stability of Placements in Community Care.* Sacramento, Calif.: California Department of Developmental Services.

Wicker, A. W., Kirmeyer, S. L., and Alexander, D. 1976. Effects of manning levels on subjective experiences, performance, and verbal interaction in groups. *Organizational Behavior and Human Performance* 17:251–74.

Wilcox, B. L. 1987. Pornography, social science, and politics: When research and ideology collide. *American Psychologist* 42:941–52.

Wilder, J., Miller, S., Gewirtz, N., and Stewart, D. 1989. *The ABC's of Handling Hassles.* Bronx, N.Y.: Albert Einstein College of Medicine.

Wilkins, A. L., and Ouchi, W. B. 1983. Efficient cultures: Exploring the relationships between culture and organizational performance. *Administrative Science Quarterly* 28:468–81.

Willer, B., and Guastaffero, J. R. 1989. Community living assessment for persons with severe and persistent mental illness. *Journal of Community Psychology* 17:267–76.

Willer, B., and Intagliata, J. 1982. Comparison of family-care and group homes as alternatives to institutions. *American Journal of Mental Deficiency* 86:588–95.

Wilson, P. G., Cuvo, A. J., and Davis, P. K. 1986. Training a functional skill cluster: Nutritious meal planning within a budget, grocery list writing, and shopping. *Analysis and Intervention in Developmental Disabilities* 6:179–202.

Wilson, S. F., in press. Community support and integration: New directions for outcome research. In S. Rose (ed.), *Case Management: An Overview and Assessment*. White Plains, N.Y.: Longman.

Wilson, S. F., Mahler, J., and Tanzman, B. 1991. *Consumer and Ex-patient Roles in Supported Housing*. Burlington, Vt.: University of Vermont Center for Community Change through Housing and Support.

Witheridge, T. F., and Dincin, J. 1985. The bridge: An assertive outreach program in an urban setting. In L. I. Stein and M. A. Test (eds.), *The Training in Community Living Model: A Decade of Experience* (New Directions for Mental Health Services, No. 26), 65–76. San Francisco: Jossey-Bass.

Wolfensberger, W. 1983. Social role valorization: A proposed new term for the principle of normalization. *Mental Retardation* 21:234–39.

Wolfensberger, W., and Glenn, L. 1975. *Program Analysis of Service Systems (PASS): A Method for the Quantitative Evaluation of Human Services*. Toronto, Ont.: National Institute on Mental Retardation.

Wolfensberger, W., Nirje, B., Olshansky, S., Perske, R., and Roos, P. (eds.). 1972. *The Principle of Normalization in Human Services*. Toronto, Ont.: National Institute on Mental Retardation.

Wood, W. S. 1975. What is "applied" in the applied analysis of behavior? In W. S. Wood (ed.), *Issues in Evaluating Behavior Modification*, 23–38. Champaign, Ill.: Research Press.

Woodhead, M. 1988. When psychology informs public policy: The case of early childhood intervention. *American Psychologist* 43:443–58.

World Health Organization. 1980. *International Classification of Impairments, Disabilities, and Handicaps*. Geneva, Switzerland: Author.

Wortman, C. B., and Silver, R. C. 1989. The myths of coping with loss. *Journal of Consulting and Clinical Psychology* 57:349–57.

Yoe, J., Gordon, L. R., Burchard, S. N., and Hazasi, J. E. 1986. *Job Satisfaction and Burnout among Staff Employed in Residential Settings for Retarded Adults*. Paper presented at the Annual Conference of the American Association on Mental Deficiency, Denver, Colo.

Young, D. 1982. Nonprofits need surplus too. *Harvard Business Review* 60:124–131.

Zaharia, E. S., and Baumeister, A. A. 1978a. Estimated position replacement costs for technical personnel in a state's public facilities. *Mental Retardation* 16:131–34.

Zaharia, E. S., and Baumeister, A. A. 1978b. Technician turnover and absenteeism in public residential facilities. *American Journal of Mental Deficiency* 82:580–93.

Zaharia, E. S., and Baumeister, A. A. 1979a. Cross-organizational job satisfactions of technician-level staff members. *American Journal of Mental Deficiency* 84: 30–35.

Zaharia, E. S., and Baumeister, A. A. 1979b. Technician losses in public residential facilities. *American Journal of Mental Deficiency* 84:36–39.

Zautra, A., Eblen, C., and Reynolds, K. 1986. Job stress and task interest: Two factors in work life quality. *American Journal of Community Psychology* 14: 377–93.

Zigler, E., and Muenchow, S. 1979. Mainstreaming: The proof is in the implementation. *American Psychologist* 34:993–99.

Zigman, W. B., Schwartz, A. A., and Janicki, M. P. 1982. *Group Home Employee Job Attitudes and Satisfactions* (Technical Report 82-8). Staten Island, N.Y.: New York State Institute for Basic Research in Developmental Disabilities.

Zipple, A., Carling, P., and McDonald, J. 1988. A rehabilitation response to the call for asylum. *Schizophrenia Bulletin* 13:539–46.

# Subject Index

# Author Index

345